Inclusive Growth in Africa

Inclusive Growth in Africa analyzes the concept of inclusion within the challenges facing Africa's rapidly growing economies, where rising affluence for some has been accompanied almost everywhere with rising inequality.

Using a combination of political economy analyses, sector studies, and econometric models, the contributors delve into a range of areas associated with the new realities on the continent. Topics covered include issues of disability, corruption, capital flight and their implications for economic sustainability. There is also a discussion of the impact on development of dependence on externally determined prices for Africa's natural resources. Other sector analyses look at agriculture and wind power, and the innovations required to make a difference for the poorer majority.

The book comprises a rich array of essays on socio-economic inclusion in Africa by authors drawn from academia, African think tanks and international organizations. It would be of interest to scholars and students of many disciplines, including Economics, Sociology, Development Studies, and African Studies.

Steve Kayizzi-Mugerwa is Acting Chief Economist and Vice-President at the African Development Bank.

Abebe Shimeles is currently Acting Director and Manager of Development Research Division at the African Development Bank.

Angela Lusigi is a Policy Advisor on Macroeconomics for UNDP's Regional Bureau for Africa.

Ahmed Moummi is Senior Research Economist at the Development Research Department of the African Development Bank.

Routledge African Studies

12 **Securing Africa**
Local Crises and Foreign Interventions
Edited by Toyin Falola and Charles Thomas

13 **African Youth in Contemporary Literature and Popular Culture**
Identity Quest
Edited by Vivian Yenika-Agbaw and Lindah Mhando

14 **Indigenous Discourses on Knowledge and Development in Africa**
Edited by Edward Shizha and Ali A. Abdi

15 **African Culture and Global Politics**
Language, Philosophies, and Expressive Culture in Africa and the Diaspora
Edited by Toyin Falola and Danielle Porter Sanchez

16 **Urbanization and Socio-Economic Development in Africa**
Challenges and Opportunities
Edited by Steve Kayizzi-Mugerwa, Abebe Shimeles and Nadège Désirée Yaméogo

17 **Continuity and Change in Sub-Saharan African Demography**
Edited by Clifford O. Odimegwu and John Kekovole

18 **Sexual Violence in Conflict and Post-Conflict Societies**
International Agendas and African Contexts
Edited by Doris Buss, Joanne Lebert, Blair Rutherford, Donna Sharkey and Obijiofor Aginam

19 **Land Reforms and Natural Resource Conflicts in Africa**
New Development Paradigms in the Era of Global Liberalization
Edited by Tukumbi Lumumba-Kasongo

20 **Cultural Entrepreneurship in Africa**
Edited by Ute Röschenthaler and Dorothea Schulz

21 **The New African Diaspora in the United States**
Edited by Toyin Falola and Adebayo Oyebade

22 **Human Rights, Race, and Resistance in Africa and the African Diaspora**
Edited by Toyin Falola and Cacee Hoyer

23 **Inclusive Growth in Africa**
Policies, Practice, and Lessons Learnt
Edited by Steve Kayizzi-Mugerwa, Abebe Shimeles, Angela Lusigi and Ahmed Moummi

Inclusive Growth in Africa

Policies, Practice, and Lessons Learnt

Edited by
Steve Kayizzi-Mugerwa,
Abebe Shimeles,
Angela Lusigi and
Ahmed Moummi

Routledge
Taylor & Francis Group
LONDON AND NEW YORK

First published 2017
by Routledge

2 Park Square, Milton Park, Abingdon, Oxfordshire OX14 4RN
711 Third Avenue, New York, NY 10017

Routledge is an imprint of the Taylor & Francis Group, an informa business

First issued in paperback 2017

Library of Congress Cataloging in Publication Data
Names: Kayizzi-Mugerwa, Steve, editor. | Abebe Shimeles, editor. | Lusigi, Angela, editor. | Moummi, Ahmed, editor.
Title: Inclusive growth in Africa : policies, practice, and lessons learnt / by Steve Kayizzi-Mugerwa, Abebe Shimeles, Angela Lusigi and Ahmed Moummi.
Other titles: Routledge African studies ; 23.
Description: New York : Routledge, 2016. | Series: Routledge African studies ; 23 | Includes bibliographical references and index.
Identifiers: LCCN 2016018319| ISBN 9781138673052 (hardback) | ISBN 9781315562179 (ebook)
Subjects: LCSH: Economic development–Social aspects–Africa, Sub-Saharan. | Poverty–Africa, Sub-Saharan. | Africa, Sub-Saharan–Economic conditions–21st century.
Classification: LCC HC800 I525 2016 | DDC 338.967–dc23
LC record available at https://lccn.loc.gov/2016018319

ISBN: 978-1-138-67305-2 (hbk)
ISBN: 978-0-8153-5811-4 (pbk)

Typeset in Times New Roman
by Wearset Ltd, Boldon, Tyne and Wear

Contents

Figures

Tables

Contributors

Steve Kayizzi-Mugerwa, PhD, is Acting Chief Economist and Vice-President at the African Development Bank (AfDB). He has a long and extensive experience in economic and development research garnered at the University of Gothenburg, where he received his PhD in 1988 and later became Associate Professor. He was a Senior Economist at the IMF and a Fellow and Project Director at the World Institute of Development Economics Research of the UN University, based in Helsinki. At the AfDB he has been Director of Research, Regional Director of East Africa, Director of Policy, Lead Economist and Head of the Extended Mission to Zimbabwe.

Angela Lusigi is a policy advisor on Macroeconomics for UNDP's Regional Bureau for Africa. She has over 15 years' experience in the field of socio-economic analysis, pro-poor policy development, resource mobilization, program management and UN Coordination. She leads in UNDP's contribution to the annual African Economic Outlook working closely with the AfDB, OECD, and the UNECA. She has broad experience in development, gained from working for several UN agencies including UNDP, UNEP, the International Fund for Agricultural Development (IFAD), and the UN Food and Agriculture Organization (FAO). She has worked in Botswana, Italy, Kenya, Nigeria, South Africa, Tanzania, and Zambia. She holds a Master's and a Doctoral degree in agricultural economics from the University of Reading, UK, and a Bachelor's degree (honors) in economics and computer science from the University of Waterloo in Canada.

Ahmed Moummi is Senior Research Economist at the Development Research Department of the AfDB since October 2007. Before joining the Bank in October 2007, he was Assistant Professor for ten years at the University of Mascara, Algeria, where he taught quantitative techniques, operational research, and development economics. Ahmed Moummi holds a PhD in Economics from the University of Tlemcen, Algeria and CERDI-Clermont-Ferrand, France, a Master's in Economics and Engineering Statistics from the Statistics Institute of Algiers.

Abebe Shimeles is currently Acting Director and Manager of the Development Research Division at the AfDB. Previously he worked for the World Bank,

UNECA, ACTIONAID, and Addis Ababa University in different capacities. His recent research interest includes labor market integration, migration issues in Africa, and impact evaluation of policy interventions. He holds a PhD in economics from the University of Goteborg, an MSc from Delhi School of Economics, and an undergraduate degree in economics from Addis Ababa University.

Yannis Arvanitis is Principal Country Economist for Guinea-Bissau. He joined the AfDB's West Africa Department in 2013 as a principal country economist. Prior to that, he worked within the AfDB's Chief Economist's office as a research/project economist. In a pre-AfDB life, Yannis also spent time at the European Bank for Reconstruction and Development Office of the Chief Economist amongst others. He holds a BA in Economics and East European studies from University College London, and Master's degrees in Development Studies and Political Economy from Sciences-Po Paris and the London School of Economics respectively.

Bola Amoke Awotide obtained a PhD in Agricultural Economics from the Department of Agricultural Economics, University of Ibadan, Nigeria. She is presently a consultant at the International Institute of Tropical Agriculture (IITA), Ibadan, Nigeria. Her research interests include impact evaluation, poverty and welfare assessment, value chain analysis, gender and development.

Taiwo Timothy Awoyemi is an Associate Professor of Agricultural Economics at the Department of Agricultural Economics, University of Ibadan, Nigeria. His areas of specialization are agricultural finance, health, and development economics.

Aliou Diagne (PhD) was formerly the leader of the Impact Assessment and Policy Unit of the Africa Rice Centre Cotonou, Benin Republic. He is currently a Director of Research at the Faculty of Economic Sciences and Management, Gaston Berger University, Saint-Louis, Senegal.

Arlette Simo Fotso is a PhD student in Applied Economics at the University Cheikh Anta Diop and at the French Institute for Demographic Studies (Ined). Her main areas of interest are health economics, labor economics, economics of education, and development economics.

Daniel Gbetnkom holds a PhD in Economics and is a Senior Economist at the UNDP Country Office in Burundi. He has been a visiting scholar at the Research Departments of the IMF and at the World Bank in Washington DC. He has a record of publications in development economics, regional and monetary integration, and international trade and international finance in several leading scientific journals.

Friederike Greb is Economist at the FAO's Market and Trade Division in Rome.

Nelissa Jamora is Research Fellow at the Global Crop Diversity Trust in Bonn.

Stephen Karingi is currently the Director, Regional Integration and Trade Division of the Economic Commission for Africa. He joined the UN in April 2004 after having been appointed in 1999 as a Senior Analyst and later the Head of Macroeconomics Division in the Kenya Institute for Public Policy Research and Analysis (KIPPRA) in Nairobi, a Public Policy Think-Tank. Before KIPPRA, he served as a Lecturer of Economics at Egerton University.

Carolin Kouyaté (née Mengel) is a political scientist and agricultural economist.

Albert Makochekanwa has a PhD in economics from the University of Pretoria, South Africa, and has over 12 years' experience in economics and social science issues. He has worked extensively in Africa, specifically, Zimbabwe, South Africa, Botswana, and Ethiopia. He has published several journal and working papers, and contributed to several studies on economic issues in Eastern and Southern Africa.

Simon Mevel is currently an Economic Affairs Officer at the United Nations Economic Commission for Africa. He joined the UN in August 2011. Prior to joining the UN, from 2008 he was a Research Analyst at the World Bank, in Washington DC. Before the World Bank he had been working for the International Food Policy Research Institute (IFPRI), in Washington DC, and for the Centre d'Études Prospectives et d'Informations Internationales (CEPII), in Paris.

Alli D. Mukasa is a Senior Investment Officer in the Infrastructure Finance and PPP Division of the Private Sector Department of the AfDB. He has also worked as a researcher at the Development Research Department of the AfDB mainly focusing on infrastructure and private sector development in Africa. He holds an MSc in Environmental and Resource Engineering, a BSc in Civil Engineering, and is currently pursuing an MBA at the Warwick Business School.

Emelly Mutambatsere is a Chief Research Economist in the Development Research Department at the AfDB. She has also worked as a Principal Regional Economist at the Bank's Southern Africa Resource Center, and as an Economist in the Infrastructure and Evaluation Departments. She holds a PhD in Applied Economics and Management from Cornell University.

Ameth Saloum Ndiaye is Assistant Professor at the Department of Economics of the University Cheikh Anta Diop, Dakar, Senegal. He is also Research Fellow at the Centre de Recherches Economiques Appliquées (CREA) at the University of Dakar.

Janvier D. Nkurunziza is the Chief of Research and Analysis Section in the Special Unit on Commodities, UNCTAD, and a resource person in the AERC. He also worked at UNECA, UNDP, IMF, World Bank, Harvard University, University of Yaoundé, and University of Burundi. He holds a doctorate in Economics from the University of Oxford.

Siope Vakataki 'Ofa holds a PhD from the Crawford School of Economics and Government at the Australian National University. He has worked for the government of Tonga, the Permanent Delegation of the Pacific Islands Forum to the WTO, the World Trade Organization, and the United Nations Economic Commission for Africa. He is currently working in the United Nations Economic and Social Commission for Asia and the Pacific.

B.T. Omonona is a senior lecturer at the Department of Agricultural Economics, University of Ibadan, Nigeria. His areas of specialization are production and development economics.

Malcolm Spence is a development economist with a particular interest in regional integration in Africa and the relationship between trade and poverty alleviation. He has worked with the United National Economic Commission for Africa, the World Bank, and the Government of Uganda, and currently manages British charity Comic Relief's trade, enterprise, and employment program.

Alun Thomas is a senior economist in the Africa Department of the IMF. He has previously worked on the biannual Regional Economic Outlook that the Department produces and is currently scheduled to take up a new position as the IMF representative in Rwanda. He has written extensively on labor market, growth, income distribution, and oil related issues.

Thouraya Triki is Chief Country Economist at the North Africa Department of the AfDB. She is primarily responsible for oversight of the bank's engagement and operations in Tunisia and Libya with a particular focus on private and financial sector operations and entrepreneurship. She holds a PhD in Finance from HEC Montreal.

Roger Tsafack Nanfosso is Professor of Economics at the University of Yaoundé II-Soa (Cameroon). He specializes in microeconomics and has contributed in recent years to such topics as child labor, labor unions, and labor market earnings.

Stephan von Cramon-Taubadel is Agricultural Policy Professor at Georg-August-University of Göttingen.

Nadine Würriehausen is an agricultural economist working at Georg-August-University of Göttingen.

Christian Marie Zamo Akono is an Associate Professor in the Department of Economics of the University of Yaoundé II-Soa (Cameroon). He specializes in microeconomics with a strong preference for labor, health, and education economics. He is a member of the African Economic Research (AERC) network, both as a CPP Graduate and Researcher of the thematic group.

Foreword

Africa's Challenges: Inclusive Economic Development in the Age of Uncertainty

In November 2012, the African Economic Conference (AEC) was organized under the theme "Inclusive and Sustainable Development in Africa in an Age of Economic Uncertainty". The main objective of the conference was to help policy makers understand key economic trends in order to enable them to formulate appropriate and flexible policies to deal with different challenges confronting their countries in an age of increasing uncertainty. Four years later, the global economic environment is not markedly different from conditions 2012. Although the performance of the United States' economy has markedly improved, it remains fundamentally weak and the slowdown in China is weighing down on other emerging markets. Furthermore, the threat of secular stagnation has held back Europe's economic recovery and lower commodity prices are significantly hampering growth in natural resource dependent African economies.

Amidst persistent global headwinds and regional shocks, how can Africa's economic growth be accelerated and made more inclusive? The chapters in this volume attempt to answer this fundamental question, drawing from country experiences. Inclusive economic growth, defined by the African Development Bank (AfDB) as "economic growth that results in a wider access to sustainable socio-economic opportunities for a broader number of people, regions or countries, while protecting the vulnerable, all being done in an environment of fairness, equal justice, and political plurality" is now widely accepted as central to Africa's future prosperity. The inclusiveness of Africa's recent high-growth episode is therefore analyzed with a special focus on political economy factors, the spatial dimension, and sectoral implications of this growth.

The chapters in this volume have been carefully selected from conference presentations by eminent scholars from within and outside Africa. The chapters emphasize the following issues: corruption, entrepreneurship, trade, energy, labor force participation, etc., and how these relate to the achievement or hindrance of inclusive growth in Africa.

The first part of the book analyzes the political economy of inclusive growth in Africa. It starts by quantifying the growth–poverty nexus in six African countries, namely Cameroon, Ghana, Mozambique, Tanzania, Uganda, and Zambia. These countries have been among some of Africa's fastest growing economies over the past decade. The authors use annual per capita consumption of the poorest quartile relative to the richest quartile in analyzing the impact of recent growth performance on poverty in these countries. The main message from these analyses confirms the age-old dictum that growth is critical for poverty reduction but not sufficient.

Widespread corruption affects many aspects of the economy in African countries. In particular, it impedes the establishment and growth of small- and medium-sized enterprises (SMEs). This has implications for overall economic growth and its inclusiveness given the potential of the SMEs in employment and wealth creation as well as entrepreneurship. In Africa, entrepreneurship has had minimal impact on poverty reduction, due to a number of constraints. Studies in this volume find that the relationship between entrepreneurship and income level is U-shaped, suggesting that at low levels of income, entrepreneurship is lower and picks up after a given income threshold. This finding is relevant for policy making in developing countries in general and in Africa particularly.

The second part of the book analyzes inclusive growth in Africa from the context of regional integration and international trade. The chapters in this second part of the book examine avenues for African countries to diversify their exports and move away from reliance on non-processed primary commodities. The importance of intra-Africa trade is also highlighted, but boosting intra-regional trade requires deepening of regional trade agreements. The impact of regional trade agreements on intra-African trade is tested using traditional gravity models.

The book concludes with an analysis of the sectoral requirements for inclusive growth in Africa. The role of energy in general, and electricity in particular, on stimulating economic development is well established. For Africa to meet its energy demand, all sources of energy, including renewables, need to be explored and exploited. The factors affecting the development of wind energy projects in Africa provide some useful insights on the importance of clean energy for inclusive growth in Africa. Furthermore, agriculture remains the mainstay of many African economies. Thus, improvements in agricultural productivity have potential to change the landscape of the sector in addressing poverty and improving food security on the continent. The last chapter of the book analyzes the impact of adopting improved rice varieties on productivity and the welfare of rice farmers.

Steve Kayizzi-Mugerwa, Abebe Shimeles, Angela Lusigi
and Ahmed Moummi Abidjan, April 2016

Part I

Political Economy of Inclusion

1 The Inclusiveness of Africa's Recent High-Growth Episode

Evidence from Several Countries

Alun Thomas

Introduction

Since the mid-1990s, many Sub-Saharan African (SSA) countries have experienced a marked acceleration in economic growth. Whereas region-wide real GDP growth averaged some 2.25 percent annually between 1980 and 1995, since 1995 growth has averaged more than 5 percent and even higher at 5.5 percent from 2000 to 2010.

Progress on poverty reduction, however, looks to have been much more limited. Region-wide estimates show that the proportion of people living below the poverty line (US$1.25 a day purchasing power parity adjusted) declined only modestly from 59 percent in 1996 to 47 percent in 2008. And when one looks at the link between per capita growth and poverty reduction in a sample of SSA countries that includes more recent data points, the relationship is weak.

The weak relationship between per capita growth and poverty reduction has prompted concern that the region's recent high growth has not been sufficiently inclusive. But the cross-country analysis on which this conclusion is based has significant limitations. For one, when the sample size is limited to those SSA countries that have actually sustained high growth for a longer period, the elasticity of poverty reduction with respect to growth is higher. But beyond this, the elasticity depends greatly on the interaction between the distribution of income and the position of the poverty line in individual countries. A robust assessment of the inclusiveness of the region's growth requires more of a case study approach through closer examination of household data. We set out to do this in this chapter.

The following section focuses on well-being indicators measured by access to basic services, ownership of durable goods, and household consumption using household survey data from Cameroon, Ghana, Mozambique, Rwanda, Tanzania, Uganda, and Zambia.[1] The section looks at the distribution of changes over time in real consumption per capita among the population through the estimation of growth incidence curves (GIC) and also analyzes the determinants of household consumption using Mincer-type regressions, and the impact of growth on employment opportunities through the estimation of standard measures of labor market performance. The basic conclusions of the chapter are:

- Close examination of household survey data suggests that high per capita economic growth does have a strong bearing on the inclusiveness of growth measured in terms of consumer durables, access to services, and aggregate consumption growth. Ownership of consumer durables has increased extremely rapidly over the sample period in all countries while access to services has also expanded almost universally.

- In terms of consumption growth, we consider two measures of inclusiveness. Our first (absolute measure) is whether the poorest quartile of the consumption distribution registered positive real per capita consumption growth. The second measure, which is more of a relative concept of inclusiveness, compares the ratio of consumption growth between the lowest quartile and the average value of the consumption distribution. Under the absolute measure, the poorest quartile experienced substantial annual household per capita consumption growth in four of the seven countries (Ghana, Tanzania, Uganda, and Zambia). By contrast, the poorest quartile of the consumption distribution in low-growth Cameroon and high-growth Rwanda saw small increases in real consumption per capita. The results for Mozambique depend on whether one uses the consumer price index (CPI) or the regional price indices to deflate nominal household consumption per capita, with the former showing relatively high growth and the latter showing negative growth for the poorest quartile.
- We also find evidence of the importance of employment opportunities in rural areas, in particular in agriculture, for higher consumption growth among the poorer households. The stronger per capita consumption growth observed in Cameroon and Uganda at the poorest levels seems related to high agricultural employment growth. By contrast, rural agricultural employment between the surveys considered fell in both Mozambique and Rwanda where the poorest experienced weaker per capita consumption growth. The importance of rural employment outcomes is intuitive given the fact that about 70 percent of the population in the seven countries resided in rural areas in the early 2000s.
- There is also evidence of significant employment growth in the case study countries. Surveys include questionnaires about the level of formal employment as well as involvement in other income-generating activities (which would also capture subsistence agriculture). Considering the two numbers together, with the exception of Ghana and Rwanda, the employment-to-population ratio in the other five countries increased between surveys.

Measures of Welfare

The issue of whether GDP is an appropriate measure of economic performance and welfare has been debated ever since the introduction of the system of national accounts (SNA) in the late 1940s, and remains a hotly contested issue (see Sen *et al.* 2010). While there is general agreement that well-being is multidimensional and covers material living standards, health, education, political voice, social connections, environment, and security (see Sen *et al.* 2010), this chapter limits its analysis to material living standards and employment opportunities. We first consider welfare measured through ownership of assets and access to public services and then turn to household consumption and employment opportunities.

Welfare Measured through Asset Holdings and Access to Services

A number of analysts have used indices based on ownership of consumer durable goods and assets and access to public services as an alternative measure of economic well-being to household consumption.[2] Items such as a radio, television, refrigerator, bicycle, motorcycle, and car are normally chosen as the consumer durables, while dwelling characteristics such as building materials, the quality of flooring and roofing, main source of drinking water, type of toilet facilities, etc. are used to measure access to services. The methodology of principal components is a common method for providing the weights used to aggregate these indicators into a single asset index.

The rank correlation between per capita expenditures and these types of asset indices is typically greater than 0.5, with the correlation higher for countries outside SSA. For example, Filmer and Scott (2008) find that the correlation for Brazil is 0.64, while the correlation for Ghana and Zambia is about 0.4. The lower correlation among SSA countries is likely related to the fact that a large subset of low-income households do not own the consumer durables used in the index while access to piped water and sanitation is very low, especially in rural areas. Booysen *et al.* (2008) emphasize that the limited discrimination ability at the lower end of the income scale makes asset indices a poor tool for analyzing the extremely poor.

This section aims to enrich our understanding on the inclusiveness of growth in the region using seven case studies – from Cameroon, Ghana, Mozambique, Rwanda, Tanzania, Uganda, and Zambia. The sample choice is driven by data availability and is not fully representative of SSA countries in general – there are no post-conflict or fragile states, no large oil exporters (Cameroon is a marginal net exporter), and only one francophone country is included. With the exception of Cameroon and Zambia, the other four countries all enjoyed average per capita income growth of more than 2.25 percent during 1995–2010 (among the region's faster growing economies).

For the sample of countries, data on access to consumer durables and access to publicly provided services is provided through the Afrobarometer surveys supplemented by the household budget surveys.[3] Both types of surveys indicate that ownership of consumer durables has increased extremely rapidly over the past decade in all countries. If we weight ownership of radios, televisions, and cars equally, the annual change in consumer durables varies between no change in Zambia to an increase of 2.2 percent per annum in Ghana. Except for Ghana, the changes are broadly inversely related to initial ownership shares. Cameroon has the highest television and motor vehicle ownership share with a 0.4 percent annual increase in ownership shares while Mozambique had the lowest share in 2002 and the highest annual increase (1.5 percent).

Access to publicly provided services has also become much more widespread over time across counties (Figures 1.1 and 1.2).[4] Ghana and Cameroon have the highest levels of access to the electricity grid, piped water and sewage system, consistent with their higher levels of GDP per capita. Moreover, Ghana has also demonstrated the fastest increase in coverage over this period with Mozambique

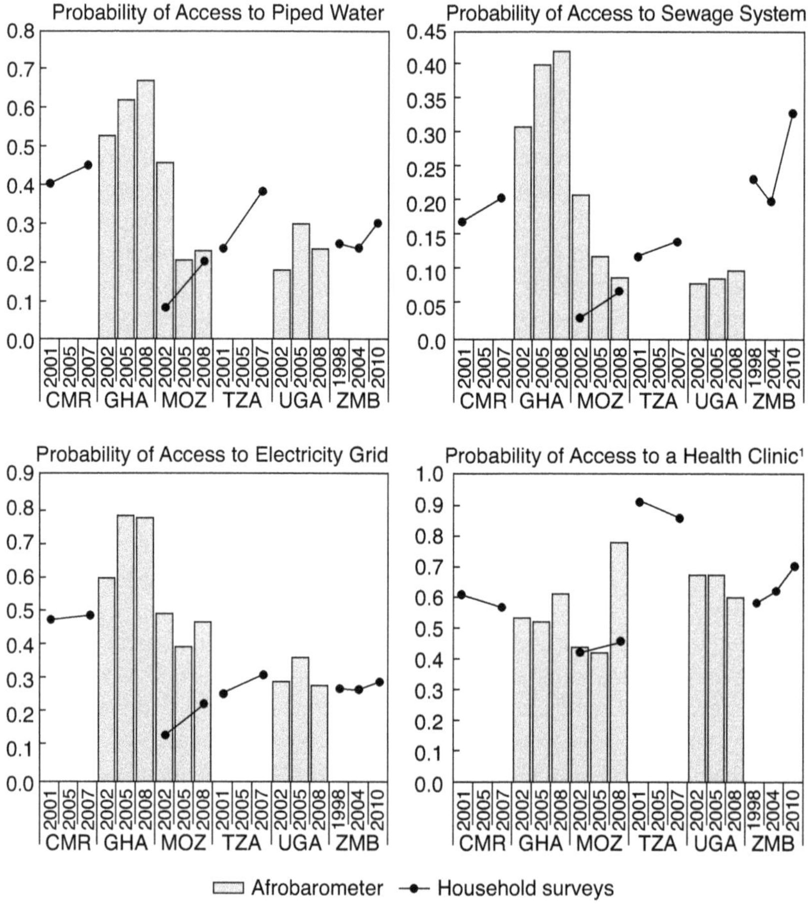

Figure 1.1 Access to Resources

Source: Afrobarometer; and household surveys.

Notes

Probability of 0 signifies no access and 1 signifies full access.

1 Data for Cameroon in 2007 includes hospitals and health clinics. For Mozambique and Zambia, the data reflects the probability of reaching a health unit within 30 minutes.

a close second. Zambia has shown a sharp improvement in access to services between 2004 and 2010. The increase in access to publicly-provided goods is buttressed by the proportion of respondents who indicate that they seldom go without food, water, medical care, and cooking fuel. Except for access to cooking fuel in Uganda, all countries show a rising share over time of households that report seldom going without these basis needs, with Ghana remaining above the other countries in terms of levels.

Based on the demand for durables, various housing characteristics, children's health status, and family conditions, Young (2010) has argued that the growth

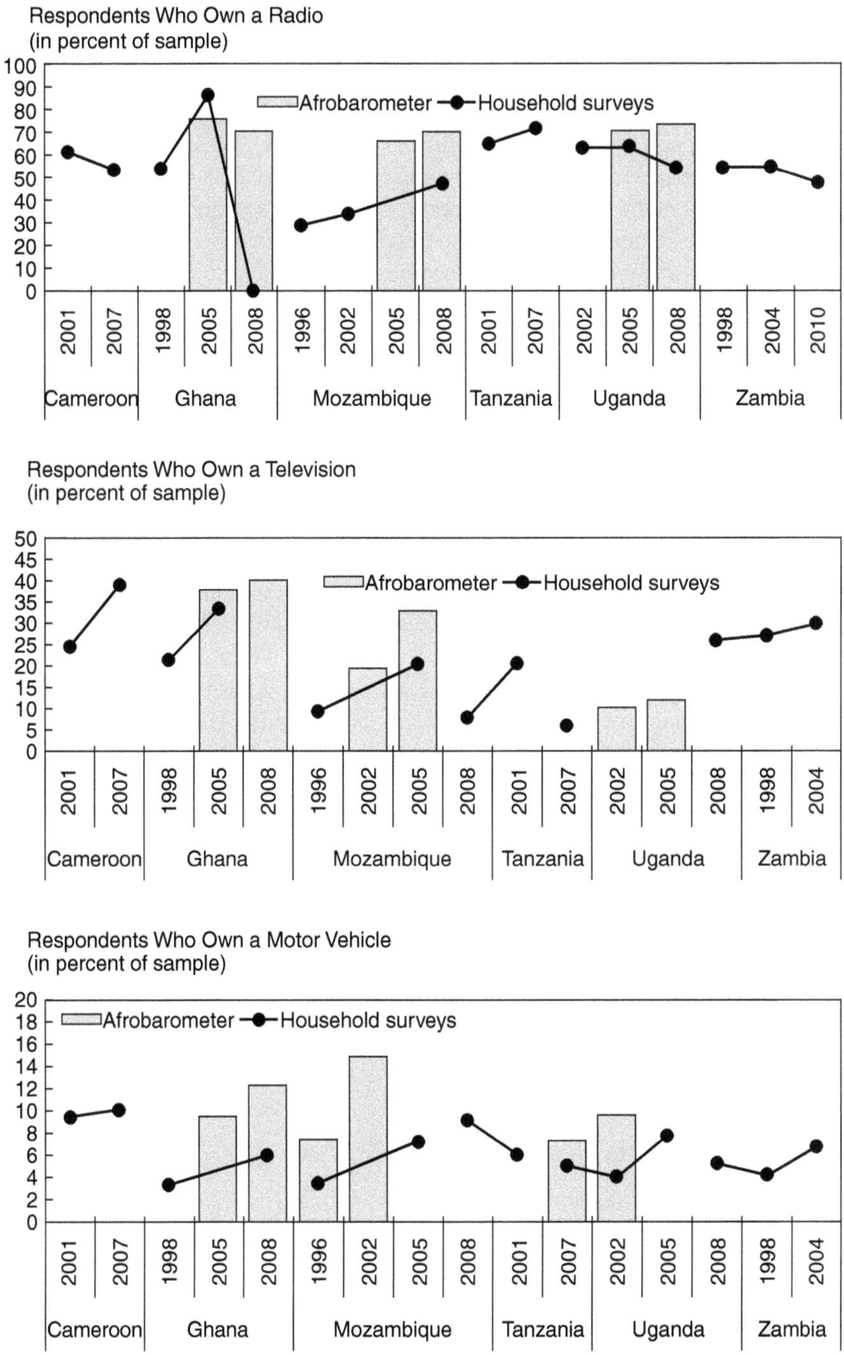

Figure 1.2 Consumer Durables

Sources: Afrobarometer; and household budget surveys.

rate of per capita consumption among SSA countries was about 3.5 percent per annum over the 15 year period through 2005/06, which is three times the average estimate from national income product accounts (NIPA) data. His analysis is based on the relationship between these factors and educational attainment, under the assumption that educational attainment is a good proxy for family income (as supported by the Mincer regressions, below). He shows that the elasticity of education with respect to owning a car is positive and significant, and is much higher than the elasticity with respect to owning a radio.

Using these relationships between educational attainment and the identified characteristics, combined with an assumption about the rate of return to education, he derives consumption growth estimates.[5] As a counter to Young's argument, Harttgen *et al.* (2011) argue that the relationship between asset growth and per capita income growth is very weak especially among non-African countries where concerns about NIPA statistics are less serious. They conclude that inferring income growth from changes in asset indices is not very robust.

Welfare Measured through Household Consumption

An alternative benchmark of household welfare is aggregate consumption using household survey data on home production for self-consumption, consumption of purchased goods (i.e., expenditure), and consumption of imputed housing services. Consumption is preferred over income as the measure of welfare or living standards for a variety of reasons. First, since surveys can only hope to measure financial flows over a short period, consumption is a better measure of living standards since it is less volatile than income. Indeed, many people in low-income countries (LIC) do not receive any income during their lifetime, because they are paid in kind or are unremunerated employees in unincorporated family enterprises. Therefore, measuring inequality based on data on the previous month's income will overstate inequality. Second, the concept of consumption is clearer to survey participants than the concept of income, especially in countries where income from self-employment is the norm and salaried employment is the exception. Third, respondents are generally more reluctant to share information about their income than about their consumption. Since income is usually taxable, it may be hard for respondents to be persuaded that their income information will not be passed to the tax authorities.

Evidence on the Incidence of Growth in SSA

One common concern among policy makers and citizens alike in the SSA region is whether the recent growth average has been evenly distributed among the population. Estimating the GIC proposed by Ravallion and Chen (2003) can identify the incidence of growth in real consumption per capita. The GIC depict the annual growth rate of real consumption per capita between two periods (vertical axis) with comparable surveys for each group of households ordered according to their position in the distribution of consumption per capita (horizontal axis). If the GIC lies above zero all along the whole distribution of real consumption per capita, then all households experienced positive growth and growth is said to be pro-poor according to the absolute definition of pro-poor growth. If, in addition to lying above the zero growth line, the GIC has a negative slope throughout (i.e., it decreases monotonically), then growth is said to be pro-poor according to the relative definition of pro-poor growth. In practice, GIC tend to have more complex forms, often crossing the horizontal axis (negative growth) at one or more points, so one cannot categorically say that growth was pro-poor or nonpro-poor for the whole distribution.

Figure 1.3 shows the GIC of real household consumption per capita for the total populations of our case study countries. The solid black line surrounded by the shaded area is the actual GIC, the black dotted line is the average consumption level for all deciles, and the gray dotted line corresponds to the growth rate for households in the middle of the consumption per capita distribution (the representative household). Our main findings are:

In absolute terms, the poorest quartile fare best where economic growth is higher. In particular, in the case studies, the pattern of household consumption growth for the poorest quartile is closely linked to the evolution of overall per capita GDP growth, although less so for Mozambique and Rwanda. Indeed, the correlation between the two variables is 0.7. In four countries (Mozambique, Tanzania, Uganda, and Zambia), per capita GDP expanded by 4 percent annually between the relevant surveys, and mirroring this annual household consumption grew at a comparable rate for the poorest quartile of the consumption distribution.[6] In two countries (Cameroon and Rwanda), the poorest quartile fared worse. In Cameroon, annual household consumption per capita growth was 1 percent for the poorest quartile, and in Rwanda this group experienced an increase of 2.5 percent.

In relative terms, however, the extent to which growth is inclusive is not related to the level of economic growth. The poorest quartile did better in relative terms than richer households in low-growth Cameroon and high-growth Uganda and Zambia. In the other high-growth countries (Ghana, Mozambique, Rwanda, and Tanzania), the poorest quartile experienced lower growth in consumption relative to the highest quartile.

In terms of national poverty estimates, both the relative and absolute measures of the inclusiveness of consumption seem to matter. Thus, in five of the countries in which overall consumption growth was positive (Ghana, Mozambique, Tanzania, and Uganda) or relatively inclusive (Cameroon, where the poorest quartile fared much better than the richest quartile even though overall growth was low), estimates show a sizeable decline in the poverty headcount. Surprisingly, it was in the high-growth countries of Rwanda and Zambia where the annual poverty decline was small. The reason for this is the large disparity in outcomes between the rural and urban areas. While the urban poor in both countries experienced fairly strong real consumption growth, little increase in real consumption expenditures was recorded in rural areas.

The diverse pattern of inclusive growth observed in SSA is broadly similar to the experience of a number of comparable Asian countries. In Bangladesh (between 1991 and 2000) and Vietnam (1993–2002), overall consumption growth was positive (5.5 percent per annum in Vietnam and 2 percent in

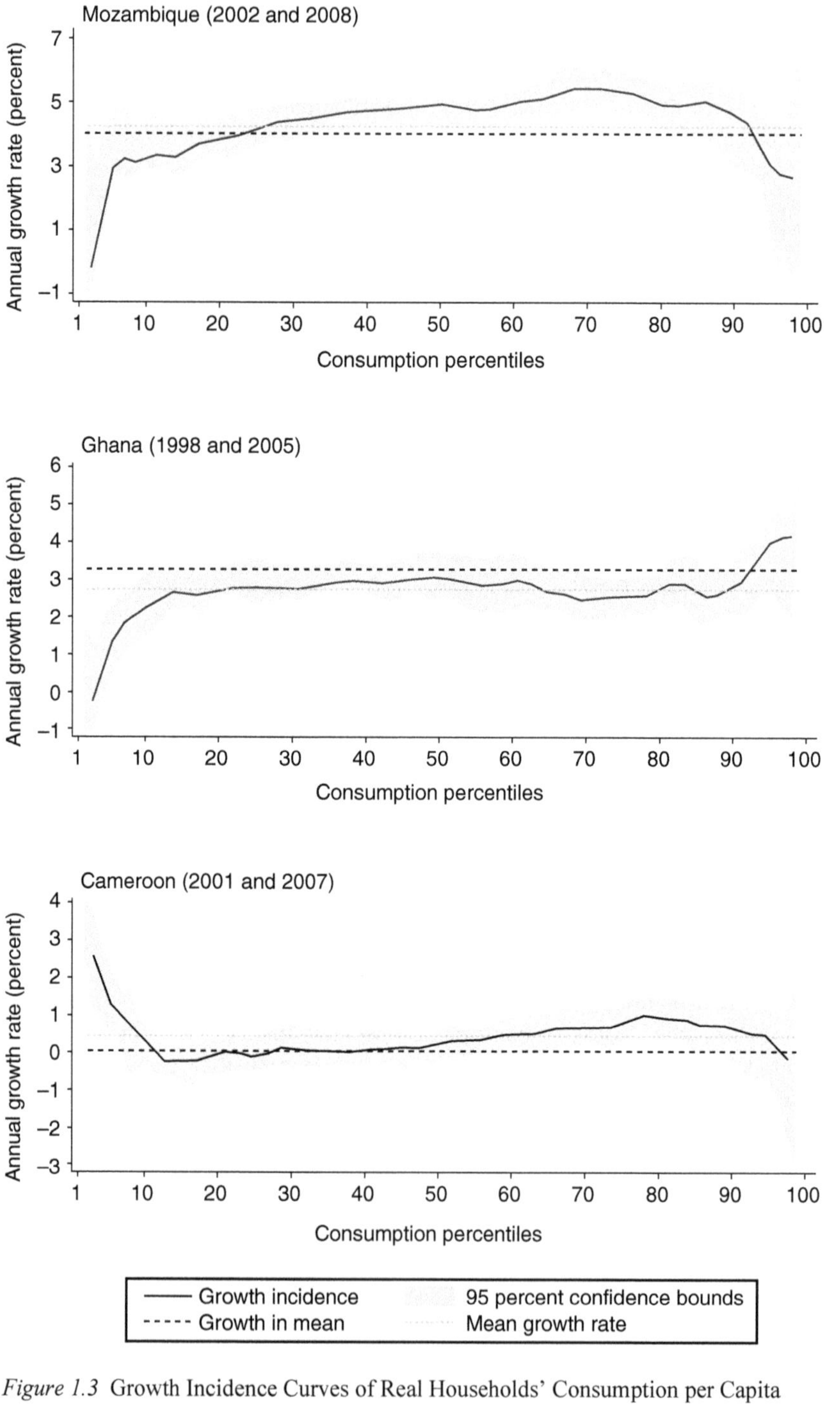

Figure 1.3 Growth Incidence Curves of Real Households' Consumption per Capita

Source: IMF staff estimates based on data from various household surveys (see Appendix).

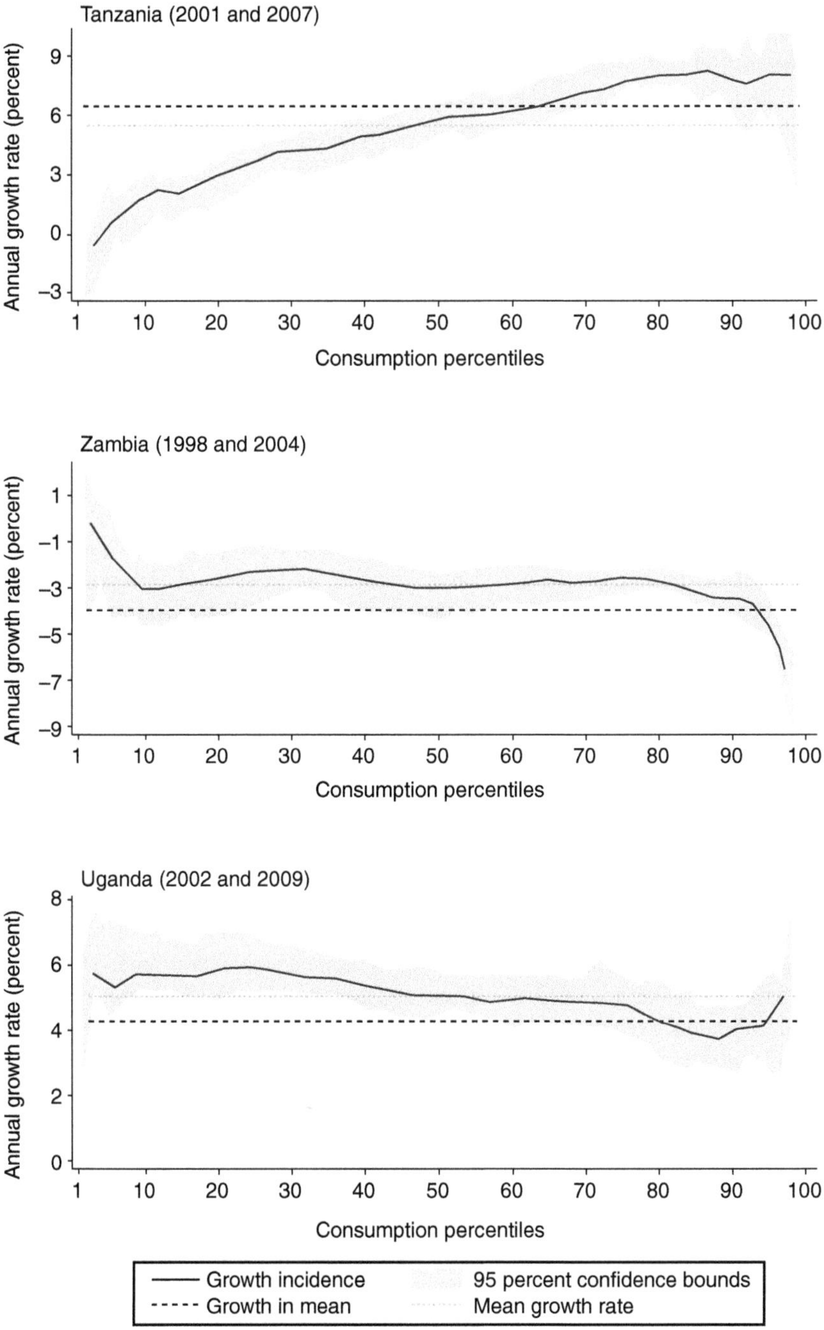

Figure 1.3 Continued

Bangladesh). The highest consumption quartiles also saw significantly higher consumption increases than the poorest quartiles (Table 1.1). In Cambodia (between 1994–99), the consumption growth rate was high among the urban population (3.5 percent per annum) but not in rural areas, similar to Rwanda and Zambia. Consistent with higher growth at the upper end of the income distribution in all three Asian countries, their Gini coefficients rose during the 1990s.

Determinants of Household Consumption

Having identified large differences in the incidence of growth across countries, this section considers the factors that might help explain these differences, with particular focus on the households in the lowest quartile of the consumption distribution.

The coefficients associated with the determinants of consumption are similar among the sample of countries and can explain a large fraction of the variation in household consumption. As can be seen in Table 1.1, on average, between 60 and 70 percent of the variation in household consumption can be explained by household size, age, sex, employment status, sector of employment, and education level of the household head, and whether the household is located in an urban or rural area. Household size has the highest explanatory power in all six countries, with each additional household member raising household consumption but at a declining rate. This may reflect more children that consume less than household heads and/or more family members with less earnings potential than the household head. The log of the age of the household head is also positive and reflects a rising consumption/income profile for more experienced adults, whereas a consistent positive education–consumption profile is evident across countries. Specifically,

- Large urban–rural consumption differentials are evident in the country cases, varying between 12 percent (Mozambique) and 24 percent (Ghana and Zambia), and these have generally remained stable over time. These differentials have provided the incentives for workers to move from rural to urban areas over the past decade, consistent with the Harris–Todaro model of migration. Between 2001 and 2009 the share of the population in rural areas fell more than six percentage points (median) in the sample of countries to 62 percent. Moreover, Nsowah-Nuamah *et al.* (2010) show for Ghana that the likelihood of being employed in urban areas rises in line with the level of education so it is likely that the more educated have made the rural-to-urban move.
- Regional consumption differentials have hardly changed in any country over recent surveys, remaining stable in Ghana and Mozambique and actually diverging in Cameroon (not shown). The differential between Cameroon's richest regions (Yaounde and Douala) and other regions doubled between 2001 and 2007 to 30 percent while, in Mozambique, central Maputo has maintained a 50 percent positive consumption differential over other regions, and in Ghana, Accra has maintained a 40 percent consumption

Table 1.1 Log Household Consumption Determinants for a Variety of Countries

	Ghana 2005	*Cameroon 2007*	*Rwanda 2011*	*Uganda 2009*	*Mozambique 2008/09*	*Tanzania 2007*	*Zambia 2010*[2]
Household size (log)	0.37***	0.29***	1.04***	0.24***	0.26***	0.31***	0.30***
Age (log)	0.13***	0.18***	0.00	0.20***	0.16***	0.02	0.10***
Male head of household	0.03***	0.01	–0.002	0.08***	0.04***	0.06**	0.03***
Employment dummy	0.16***	0.04**		0.02	0.07***	0.21***	0.11***
Agriculture sector dummy	–0.23***	–0.15***	–0.16***	–0.09***	–0.12***	–0.26***	–0.03**
Manufacturing sector dummy[1]	–0.08***	–0.03**	–0.20***	–0.10*	–0.11***		0.12***
Government sector dummy	–0.12***	0.19***	0.18***	0.16***	0.02	0.15***	0.06***
Primary schooling	0.07**	0.08***	0.16***	–0.14***	0.12***	0.13***	–0.15***
Lower secondary schooling	0.16***	0.16***	0.46***	–0.04	0.22***	0.44***	–0.04*
Upper secondary schooling	0.38***	0.29***	0.68***	0.01	0.56***	0.71***	0.18***
College/nursing/teacher training	0.69***	0.59***	1.22***	0.87***	1.00***	1.23***	0.63***
Urban dummy	0.24***	0.21***	0.29***	0.20***	0.12***	0.23***	0.22***
Coefficients of lowest quartile							
Employment dummy	0.05	–0.01		0.06	0.29***	0.00	0.05
Agriculture sector dummy	0.13***	0.04		0.02	0.07*	0.16	0.03
Manufacturing sector dummy	–0.03	–0.01		0.03	0.06		–0.04
Government sector dummy	0.38***	–0.21***		0.00	–0.15	–0.07	0.00
Primary schooling	0.06	0.08***		0.21***	0.03	0.10	0.21***
Lower secondary schooling	0.04	0.11***		0.13**	–0.04	–0.19	0.16***
Upper secondary schooling	–0.39***	0.02		0.18**	–0.29**	–0.64	–0.06
College/nursing/teacher training	–0.76***	–0.16**			–1.01***	–1.50	–0.42***
Urban dummy	–0.13***	–0.13***		–0.21***	–0.13***	–0.17	–0.10***
Diagnostic statistics							
Number of observations	7280	10,416	35,364	6117	9836	9332	17,679
R-squared	0.68	0.69	0.59	0.63	0.66	0.66	0.69

Sources: IMF staff estimates based on data from various household surveys.

Notes

***, **, * indicate statistical significance at the 99, 95, and 90 percent levels, respectively.

1 For Zambia, the manufacturing dummy refers to nonagriculture, nongovernment salaried employment.

2 The 2010 data excludes education, health, and recreation expenses because they showed large declines compared to 2006.

differential over its poorest region (Upper East and West). These nominal consumption differentials are likely to be partially compensated by differences in regional price indices. Indeed, deflating nominal consumption in Ghana by the regional price indices reduces the differential between the richest and poorest regions by ten percentage points to 30 percent and the ranking of the richer regions is changed, with Accra losing the top spot.

- Household heads with primary school education earn up to 13 percent (Tanzania) more than those without education, whereas college-educated household heads earn between 60 percent (Cameroon) and more than 100 percent (Mozambique, Tanzania, Zambia) more than uneducated household heads. Moreover, in contrast to the stability of education differentials at lower levels of education, the college premium has increased substantially over time (not shown), consistent with the findings of Fox and Gaal (2008).[7]
- Large consumption differentials also exist for household heads employed in government relative to the primary sector. In most countries, government workers are among the highest paid (for example, Cameroon, Tanzania, and Uganda), whereas agricultural workers earn the least and manufacturing workers are only slightly higher up the consumption scale than agriculture workers in half of the countries in the sample (the reference group omitted from the sectoral coefficients in nongovernment services). Over the past decade, the consumption differential between agricultural workers and those in other sectors has declined over time.

Very limited differences exist between characteristics for the poorest quartile of the consumption distribution.

- Across time within a single country and across countries, the distribution of consumption between those living in urban and rural areas is very similar, suggesting limited incentives to migrate to urban areas for those at the bottom end of the consumption distribution. Controlling for other characteristics (work experience, household size, and employment sector), an urban premium for the poor is only identified in Cameroon and Ghana. This is supported by Kakwani *et al.* (2005), who find that a cash transfer system that targets the poor in rural areas is able to reduce the poverty gap considerably more in Cameroon and Ghana than in the other countries.
- Controlling for other factors, the regression estimates reveal a positive consumption differential for primary and lower secondary education for the poorest individuals, suggesting that education incentives exist for the poorest in these countries.

Employment Developments

Against the backdrop of strong growth in SSA in recent years, the perception exists that this growth experience was not accompanied by increased employment opportunities, especially in countries concentrated on the extraction of natural resources. This is an important issue because household consumption is clearly dependent on employment income as shown in the coefficient estimates from the regressions in the previous section. One difficulty in making this assessment is the general absence of employment data among SSA countries (only Botswana, Mauritius, and South Africa provide annual data).

Household income and expenditure surveys can be used to overcome this problem because almost all surveys have a labor market component and can provide periodic snapshots of employment developments. However, the frequency of data is limited to two or three data points and changes in questionnaires between surveys make comparisons difficult (see Appendix for a discussion of the methodology used to generate the labor force data for the chapter and Fox and Thomas (2013) for an update of the analysis). Moreover, the meaning of employment for SSA households differs considerably from that used in developing countries because subsistence living represents a large share of household activity and formal employment represents a low share of total employment. For these reasons we prefer to view employment as all income-generating activities rather than just formal employment.

The increase in the number of people engaged in income-earning activities (a proxy for employment) has been strong over the past decade among the sample of countries analyzed, with a median estimate of 3.5 percent per annum (Table 1.2). This outcome compares favorably with Cambodia and Vietnam, two other fast-growing LICs. The high employment growth rates have helped raise the ratio of employment to the working-age population in all sample countries except Ghana (with a sharp increase in the number of people out of the labor force attributable to youth remaining in school for a longer period) and Rwanda (which has an extremely high employment to population ratio). Economic growth in these countries has been characterized by a higher employment intensity than in Asia, with the median employment–output growth elasticity at 0.6 compared with 0.4 for Cambodia and Vietnam.

Agricultural employment growth has been particularly strong in countries that have demonstrated pro-poor growth over the past decade. Agricultural employment has grown at 6 percent per year in both Cameroon and Uganda, whereas the growth rate has been much weaker in the other countries, except for Zambia. The correlation between consumption growth of the poorest quartile and agricultural employment growth is even stronger for the rural population at 0.62, slightly below the correlation between growth of real GDP per capita and consumption growth of the poor.

The growth in urban employment has been extremely rapid with a median estimate of almost 6 percent per year, twice the employment growth rate among the whole population. However, given the migration from rural to urban areas, the increase in the ratio of employment to the working-age population has been more modest, at almost one percentage point. The increase in the ratio of employment to the working-age population among SSA countries is comparable to the experience in Cambodia and Vietnam in recent years.

Formal sector employment is often used as a measure of the development process among LICs because formal jobs generally provide social security benefits and more stable incomes. Formal employment is proxied by salaried

Table 1.2 Employment Indicators

(Annual percentage change, except where stated)

	Period	*Total Employment*	*Employment Output Elasticity*	*Urban Employment*	*Agricultural Employment*	*Rural Agricultural Employment*	*Formal Sector Employment*[1]
Cameroon	2001–07	2.7	0.8	5.6	5.9	4.2	9.5
Ghana	1999–2005	3.4	0.7	6.1	3.5	1.4	13.3
Mozambique	2003–09	4.4	0.6	7.4	3.4	–0.4	16.7
Tanzania	2000–09	3.3	0.5	8.8	2.3	2.1	9.5
Uganda	2002–09	7.5	1.0	9.8	6.0	6.4	13.9
Zambia	1998–2004	1.9	0.6	5.1	–0.2	–1.6	13.8
Memo items:							
Cambodia	2004–07	4.2	0.4	4.5	3.9	4.7	25.0
Vietnam[2]	2000–07	2.9	0.4	6.1	–0.3	n.a.	44.0
SSA (sample median)		3.3	0.6	6.8	3.5	1.8	13.6

Sources: household surveys; Vietnam Ministry of Planning and Investment and UNDP (2010); World Bank (2008).

Notes
1 Latest estimate in percent of working-age population.
2 Agricultural employment is for 2000–08.

employment (government and other salaried workers) in this chapter given the unavailability of information on social benefits from most surveys. Based on this definition, formal employment in relation to the working-age population for the whole economy has risen in all sample countries except for Cameroon, and in regard to urban areas, it has risen in all sample countries except for Cameroon and Tanzania. However, at 13.6 percent of the working-age population (median estimate), it remains considerably below the levels registered in Cambodia (25 percent in 2007) and Vietnam (28 percent in 2007).

On the other hand, the fact that salaried employment has grown less rapidly than total employment among SSA countries is not necessarily synonymous with adverse welfare developments. First, formal employment may not reflect jobs with health and social security benefits because of lack of data. Second, Fox and Gaal (2008) show that informal sector earnings grew more rapidly than formal sector earnings during the 1990s in Cameroon and Mozambique. Third, Perry (2008) argues that many labor force participants in Latin America prefer the flexibility afforded by working for themselves in a nonfarm business rather than being an employee. This is because of low economy-wide productivity levels and the fact that informal sector workers may have access to mechanisms that substitute for formal social protection programs financed by payroll taxes.

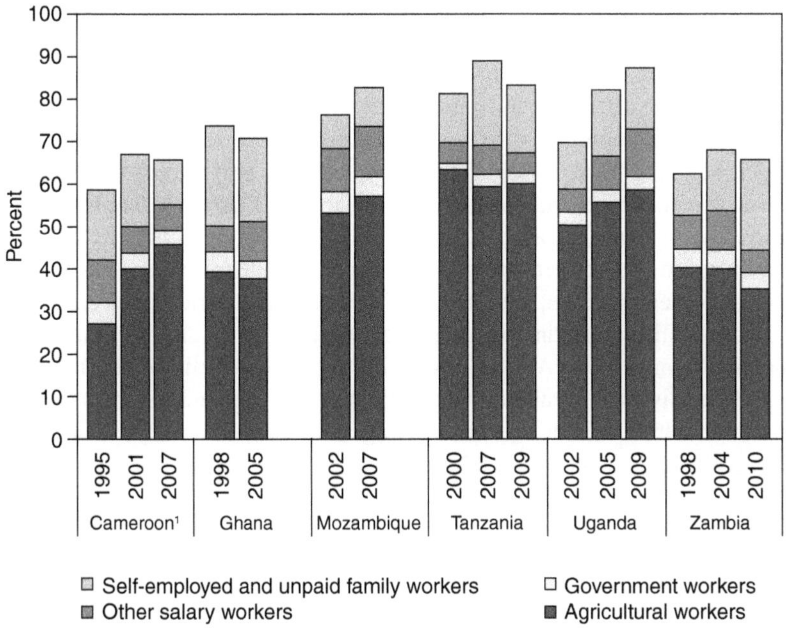

Figure 1.4 Total Employment: Working Age Population Ratio

Source: household surveys.

Note

1 Cameroon's employment–population ratio in 2007 refers to those who work at least 25 hours per week.

Conclusions

Broadly, then, our main findings are as follows.

- There is evidence of growth having been fairly inclusive in the region's high-growth countries. We find, for example, that the lowest quartile in four of the high-growth case studies (Mozambique, Tanzania, Uganda, and Zambia) enjoyed fairly high increases in consumption. But there are signs that in many of these countries higher income households enjoyed still higher growth in consumption. This implies some increase in inequality, broadly in line with patterns observed in a number of high-growing Asian countries.

Some of the policy implications that we can infer from our findings are as follows:

- The focus of many Sub-Saharan policy makers on policies that promote broad and sustainable growth are likely the means by which the poor can be helped the most.
- Still, this does not imply that high average growth is a sufficient condition to ensure inclusiveness. Once it has been established that growth has not indeed been inclusive, temporary and well-targeted transfer programs could be considered to help those being left out by the growth process. In terms of targeting, as shown above, even a few observable household characteristics – such as education levels, region of residence, sector of employment, employment status, and so on – go a long way toward explaining, in a statistical sense, the difference in consumption levels across households.
- Perhaps more importantly, except for Zambia, those countries that experienced higher growth in agricultural employment also experienced higher poverty reduction. Some public policies could, if properly implemented, lead to short-term increases in agricultural output and productivity, including diffusion of fertilizers and improved seeds, while others, such as investments in electrification, irrigation, rural roads, and agricultural extension services, will require time to be implemented properly and will thus have medium-term effects. At any rate, with about two-thirds of the region's population living in rural areas and with most of them deriving their income from agricultural activities, increasing agricultural productivity is necessary for accelerating poverty reduction.

Appendix: Methodology for Calculating Labor Force Components

The labor force definition used in this chapter comprises individuals between 16 and 65 years old who are employed or are actively seeking work, and this definition is comparable to the UN definition used for most countries. In all countries employment status corresponds with the main job so that students working part-time are not counted in the labor force because they are not working as their primary activity.

For Ghana and Cameroon, the employed are defined as those who have worked during the past 12 months and this amount is divided by the total working-age population to derive the employment ratio. This figure is compared with the number of people who indicate their sector of employment and the minimum of these two figures is used. For Zambia, the employed are defined as those that had an active economic status in terms of working for wages, running a business, working in agriculture, and unpaid family workers while for Tanzania those that indicate an industry affiliation are assumed employed. For Mozambique and Uganda, only their status during the last seven days is used for employment with the employment total defined as the sum of those who worked during the past seven days and those who did not work during this period but normally have a job.

In Ghana and Cameroon, the split between the unemployed and those out of the labor force is obtained by using the question: did you search for work during the past seven days? Those that searched for work are defined as the unemployed and the unemployment rate is derived using this figure divided by the working-age population. Those out of the labor force are defined as working-age population minus employed minus unemployed. If the number of unemployed derived in this way looks as if it is miscoded, the figure for those out of the labor force is used based on the question "why have you not worked or looked for work?" with the unemployment rate derived as a residual. If there is disparity between the employment totals based on questions about activities during the past 12 months and the unemployment and out-of-the-labor force totals based on questions about activities during the past week, the ratios of the latter two variables are applied to the difference between the working-age population and the employment total.[8]

To identify salaried employees, government workers are first separated out in all countries based on the assumption that all of these workers receive wage income. Nongovernment salaried workers are defined as follows: in Ghana, a worker potentially receiving payment is asked "How are you paid in your main job?" All categories except "payment in kind" and "not remunerated" are summed. In Mozambique, salaried workers are identified in response to the question "Are you a salaried worker?" In Cameroon, salaried workers are defined as senior executives, middle management, and qualified and semi-qualified workers. In Tanzania, nongovernment salaried workers are defined as NGOs, religious workers, parastatal employees, and other employees, while in Zambia, nongovernment salaried workers are defined as parastatal, private sector, and NGO employees. In Uganda, salaried workers are derived from the question on employment status. The Rwanda data is based on government reports with the working-age population classified as 16 years of age and above.

Notes

1 The choice of countries analyzed in this chapter was driven by data availability and, in particular, by the need to have at least two household surveys collected using the same methodology, so that changes in measured total household consumption and changes in household characteristics are not the result of changes in sampling scheme, questionnaires, definitions, data collection procedures, etc.

2 See, for example, Booysen *et al.* (2009), Filmer and Scott (2008), Sahn and Younger (2000), and Young (2010).
3 Afrobarometer is an independent, non-partisan research group funded by UK DFID and USAID that surveys nationally representative, random, stratified probability samples for 20 SSA countries every three years.
4 Although access to health clinics in Cameroon and Uganda seems to have stalled, the question asked in Cameroon is not comparable across surveys because in 2007 access to hospitals was included together with access to health clinics.
5 Luminosity data from satellites and anthropometric measures such as height for age and weight for age provide additional measures of welfare, but these give a mixed picture of living standards in SSA. See Deaton (2010) and Henderson *et al.* (2010) for a discussion.
6 For Mozambique, if one uses the regional CPIs to deflate nominal household consumption per capita, one obtains a growth incidence curve that is shifted downwards, with the lowest three deciles in fact experiencing negative consumption growth. While regional price indices are generally preferable to the use of the CPI to deflate nominal consumption because of price differences across regions, this chapter uses the CPI for uniformity since regional price deflators are not available for the other countries.
7 The stability of the coefficients over time provides support for the estimation of GIC based on repeated cross-sectional household survey data because it requires the assumption that the same groups of households occupy the same position in the distribution of consumption over time.
8 This is the case for Ghana.

References

Booysen, Frikkie, Servaas van der Berg, Ronelle Burger, Michael von Maltitz, and Gideon du Rand, 2008, "Using an Asset Index to Assess Trends in Poverty in Seven Sub-Saharan African Countries", *World Development,* Vol. 36, No. 6, pp. 1113–1130.

Deaton, Angus, 2010, "Price Indexes, Inequality, and the Measurement of World Poverty," *American Economic Review*, Vol. 100, No. 1, pp. 5–34.

Filmer, D. and K. Scott, 2008, "Assessing Asset Indices", World Bank Policy Research Paper No. 4605.

Fox, Louise and M. Gaal, 2008, *Working out of Poverty: Job Creation and the Quality of Growth in Africa* (Washington, DC: World Bank).

Fox, Louise and A. Thomas, 2013, "Sub-Saharan Africa Has Work to Do: Employment Prospects in the New Century", IMF Working Paper 13/213.

Harttgen, K., S. Klasen, and S. Vollmer, 2011, "An African Growth Miracle? Or What do Asset Indices Tell Us about Trends in Economic Performance?" Mimeo, University of Gottingen.

Henderson, V., A. Storeygard, and D. Weil, "A Bright Idea for Measuring Economic Growth", Brown University mimeo, December.

Kakwani, N., F. Soares, and H. Son, 2005, "Conditional Cash Transfers in African Countries," International Poverty Centre, United Nations Development Programme, Working Paper 9, New York.

Nsowah-Nuamah, N., F. Teal, and M. Awoonor-Williams, 2010, "Jobs, Skills and Incomes in Ghana: How Was Poverty Halved?" Center for Study of African Economies, Oxford, WPS/2010-01.

Perry, Guillermo, 2008, *Informality: Exit and Exclusion* (Washington, DC: World Bank).

Ravallion, M. and S. Chen, 2003, "Measuring Pro-poor Growth", *Economic Letters*, Vol. 78, No. 1, pp. 93–99.

Sahn, D. and S. Younger, 2000, "Expenditure Incidence in Africa: Microeconomic Evidence", *Fiscal Studies*, Vol. 21, No. 3, pp. 329–347.

Sen, A., J. Stiglitz, and J.-P. Fitoussi, 2010, *Report by the Commission on the Measurement of Economic Performance and Social Progress*. Available at: www.insee.fr/fr/publications-et-services/dossiers_web/stiglitz/doc-commission/RAPPORT_anglais.pdf.
Vietnam Ministry of Planning and Investment and UNDP, 2010, "Getting to Work: Labor Market, Employment and Urbanization in Vietnam to 2020", Hanoi, Vietnam: UNDP.
World Bank, 2008, "Cambodia's Labor Market and Employment", Cambodia Country Economic Memorandum, Washington, DC: World Bank.
Young, Alwyn, 2010, "The African Growth Miracle," unpublished, London School of Economics.

2 Disability and Labour Force Participation in Cameroon

Arlette Simo Fotso, Christian Marie Zamo Akono and Roger Tsafack Nanfosso

Introduction

Disability is increasingly regarded as a major development issue for international organizations and national governments, especially in view of the growing numbers of people with disabilities. In 2007, the International Labour Organization (ILO) estimated the disabled population at approximately 650 million people. That represents about 10 per cent of the world population. Of these, 80 per cent live in developing countries. This population has been estimated at 15 per cent of the world's population. Also, much evidence exists that disability can lead to poverty, because of its negative effect on earnings and labour force participation (Dumont, 2000).

Disabled people face many difficulties entering the labour market both in developed and developing countries. The ILO report says that most of the 470 million disabled people of working age in the world are excluded from the labour market. For those who are in work, average earnings are substantially lower than for the non-disabled (ILO, 2007). As far as Cameroon is concerned, the National Institute of Statistics reports that only 69 per cent of people with disabilities (PWDs) have a job while the employment rate of the non-disabled is more than 75 per cent. This situation prevails despite the fact that Cameroon has had laws promoting PWD employment over several decades. In 1983, the Cameroonian Government passed the first PWDs act. This law was followed by a 1990 executive order and in 2010 by the Act on the Protection and Promotion of the Disabled.[1] According to this law, disability is a limitation of opportunities for full participation of a person with impairment in an activity in a given environment. However, this Act has no provisions on the non-discrimination in the built environment. It also removed the quota imposed by the 1990 decree making it difficult to demonstrate any deviations from the legislation by employers. The failure of these legal measures to cancel the differences between disabled and non-disabled emphasizes the need to question *ex ante* on the real determinants of differences between these two groups in the labour market. The question is as to whether PWDs have lower labour market participation than persons without disabilities due to lower productivity or due to labour market discrimination.

Some economists argue that inequalities in access to employment between non-disabled and disabled would be explained mainly by differences in productive capacity between the two groups. This is the result obtained by Madden (2004), which found that in the UK the gap in participation in the labour market between non-disabled and disabled people at 70 per cent is explained by differences in productivity. Others designate discrimination as the main explanatory factor of this gap. Mitra and Sambamoorthi (2008) found that the differential of employment between men with disabilities and without disabilities in India is not explained by observable characteristics. Between these two extremes, other authors like Kidd *et al.* (2000) and Blackaby *et al.* (1999) estimated that each component explains approximately 50 per cent of the differences in employment.

These contradictory explanations show the interest of this work which attempts to explain employment differences between people with and without disability in Cameroon. To our knowledge, this is the first paper to investigate the labour market participation differentials across disability status in Cameroon. It therefore takes into account the specifications of this labour market and, for the first time in this type of study, makes the distinction between public, private formal and informal institutional sectors. The analysis is made both for men and women for comparison on whether disabled women are similarly disadvantaged relative to disabled men. Here unique household survey data is used, the Third Cameroonian household survey (ECAM3) conducted by the National Institute of Statistics (INS) in 2007.

The structure of the chapter is as follows: after introducing the literature review in the next section, the third section gives details on the data used. Next, the determinants of inequalities in employment are identified in the fourth section, which is followed by the conclusion.

Literature Review

Theoretical Framework and Previous Research

Substantial evidence exists that a lower proportion of disabled people is employed than non-disabled people (DeLeire, 2001; Jones *et al.*, 2003; Hum and Simpson, 1996), but there are different potential reasons why this may be the case. The interaction between disability and labour participation can be rationalized along the lines of disability affecting both the supply of labour and the demand for labour (Madden, 2004; Mitra and Sambamoorthi, 2008). All these thoughts take place in the standard labour leisure choice model which assumes that workers and employers are rational.

On the supply side, this model assumes that each worker has limited hours to allocate to labour and leisure to maximize his utility under constraints of income. Given this, people decide to work if the offered salary is above the reservation wage which depends on each worker's non-labour incomes and his utility function (Cahuc and Zylberberg, 1996).[2] Disability can affect participation via the raising of the reservation wage due, first, to unearned income coming from disabled-related transfers. This is easy to understand as, in general, individuals with disabilities have a greater propensity to receive transfers from charitable organizations, their relatives or from the state as a disability pension. These transfers would be the cause of differences in labour market participation (Jones *et al.*, 2003; Madden, 2004; Mitra, 2009). Second, PWDs will experience a higher cost of working given that greater efforts may be needed compared to persons without disabilities to get to the workplace and do the work (Mittra and Sambamoorthi, 2008). This will decrease the opportunity cost of leisure and thus indirectly increase the reservation wage (Jones *et al.*, 2003) which may be greater than the prevailing wage. Finally, some disabled individuals will prefer leisure to work. The reservation wage is also a function of some personal characteristics, like education or experience, which can be negatively affected by the disability, given the fact that the disability can be a long term health problem. However it is also possible that impairment affects the job search process and explains the unemployment duration differential between the two groups. Given that in the job search model the search effort increases with the health state (Zamo, 2007), disability – or ill health in general – will reduce the intensity of search and thus increase unemployment duration for PWDs. This length of time will be further prolonged, given that disabled people cannot do every kind of work on offer.

The supply side explanations of the employment gap have been confirmed by Hum and Simpson (1996) who found that in Canada the wage gap between disabled and non-disabled men is entirely explained by differences in observable characteristics. Concerning the gap between women, they found that it is explained 92 per cent of the time by observable characteristics. In the same vein, DeLeire (2001) shows that the characteristics of labour supply explained 92 per cent of the wage gap between people with and without disabilities in the US. Madden (2004) and Johnson and Lambrinos (1985), for their part, estimate respectively that this component explains 70 per cent of the employment gap and 70 per cent of the pay gap in the UK. As for Longhi *et al.* (2010), they found that differences in productive capacities explain almost the entire pay differential between disabled and non-disabled people in the UK, but not the difference for the disabled by virtue of a mental health condition.

It is also possible that disability may affect labour market outcomes via the demand for labour. Two aspects can be quoted here. First, PWDs may be offered a lower wage due to lower productivity, and these lower wages offered may also contribute to lower employment rates. A person's human capital is affected by poor health; especially, disabled people can experience lower productivity if the workplace environment is not accommodating. Thus, if they are reattributed at their marginal product of labour, the PWDs may be offered a lower market wage, leading some to prefer leisure (wage offered became less than the reservation wage). However, all disabilities are not always a source of lower productivity, depending on the type of disability, type of employment and development of the work environment (see Winance, 2008) and discrimination can also take place.

The second factor on the demand side is discrimination. Economists define discrimination as a situation where two groups of workers with equal average productivity have different average wages or opportunities for employment

(Baldwin and Johnson, 2001). Discrimination can occur when an employer is prejudiced against certain groups of workers – taste or pure discrimination (Becker, 1971) – or because of differential information about the average productivity of persons with and without disabilities – statistical discrimination (Mitra and Sambamoorthi, 2008; Arrow, 1971; Phelps, 1972; Aigner and Cain, 1977). Many authors have attempted to measure this. Like Mitra and Sambamoorthi (2008) who found that the total differential of employment between men with disabilities and without disabilities in India is explained by discrimination. Kidd *et al.* (2000) in the UK and Baldwin and Johnson (2005) in the US found that discrimination has between 30 and 60 per cent in earnings differences. Nevertheless, one core difficulty of all these works resides in the measurement of disability itself.

Disability Measurement

The definition of disability in the Cameroonian Act of 2010 has the advantage of operating reconciliation between the medical model which considers disability as caused by a disease, an injury or other health conditions, and the social model which considers disability as created by social conceptions and living and work place environment (Mitra and Sambamoorthi, 2008). However, any study investigating the labour market participation differentials across disability status has to deal with the challenges of measuring disability because of the lack of a standard definition.

Determining the existence of a disability can be done in two ways: disability can either be self-assessed looking for its capacity to affect work undertaken (subjective measure) or self-reported information on specific health conditions (objective measure) (Jones, 2005).

In the case where the disability is self-assessed relating to the work, each individual assesses his or her own health condition, stressing often on the effects it has on the capacity to undertake work, without any reference to outside standards. The exact wording of the survey question can vary but it takes often this typical form: *Do you have a health condition that limits the kind or amount of work you can perform?* (Jones, 2005). Asked like this, the question gives direct information on work capacities, that is why the self-assessed method is appreciated for empirical labour market analysis (Kidd *et al.*, 2000; DeLeire, 2001; Madden, 2004). However, put together, disability and ability to work can lead to the misreporting of disability status. First, because the answer may depend on a person's preference for work. People with a greater aversion to work will justify themselves by reporting disability. Thus there could exist a "justification bias". Given that the report of disability depends on employment status, disability becomes endogenous in regression analysis (Jones, 2005). Second, the propensity to declare any disability may depend on the possibility of claiming disability benefits. Conversely, stigmatization may also be an incentive to underestimate disability.

Another way to evaluate disability is to ask individuals to report information on specific health conditions. This survey question takes the form of collecting information on a specific impairment (deaf, blind, mental illness, etc.), functional activity (capacity to see, hear, speak, walk, etc.) or medical diagnoses, mortality rate, body mass index, etc. If the information on disability can suffer from measurement error, due to the fact that the information on disability tends not to be as closely related to limitations on work, which will underestimate the true effect of disability on labour market outcomes, it is less likely to suffer from justification bias. The objectivity of this procedure justified its use by some studies (Johnson and Lambrinos, 1985; Mitra and Sambamoorthi, 2008). For this reason and because of the available data, we use this disability measurement in this work. In this study, a person is considered to have a disability if he has at least one of these impairments: visual impairment (blind, partly sighted), auditory impairment (deaf, hard of hearing), speech impairment (dumb, stammerer), mental disability (mad, alienated, autistic), mobility impairment (lame, paralysed or atrophied limb, amputation) and other (specified by the individual). The disability variable (D) is constructed as follows:

$$\text{Disability} = \begin{cases} 1 \; \textit{if person is disabled} \\ \qquad 0 \; \textit{if not} \end{cases}$$

In order to identify within-group differences, dummies are generated for each impairment.

Data

This study uses secondary data coming from the Third Cameroonian Household Survey conducted by the INS in 2007, a survey of 652 households which represented 51,232 people distributed throughout Cameroon. Its main objective was to update the poverty profile in Cameroon and to evaluate the impact of major policies and programmes implemented to fight against poverty (INS, 2008). It is the most recent survey containing information on disability in the Cameroonian context, even if its main drawback is the lack of information on disability severity. Only people of working age (15–64 year old) are considered.[3] Of 28,047 people, 4.09 per cent have a disability and 75.52 per cent are in employment.

Table 2.1 displays the prevalence of each impairment (visual, speech, auditory, mental and mobility). The sample of 28,047 people is made up of 13,593 men and 14,454 women. The prevalence of disability is higher in the male population (4.56 per cent) than in the female one (3.65 per cent). The most current impairment is visual, follow by mobility and mental impairments.

The summary statistics for some variables of the estimation sample are shown separately for disabled and non-disabled men and women in Table 2.2.

Overall, non-disabled people have an employment rate of 75.79 per cent, while disabled people have an employment rate of 69.08 per cent, a 6.71 per cent point gap. The employment gap is more severe between male (8.98 per cent) than between female (5.214 per cent) (but, even so, the employment rate of disabled men is greater than of non-disabled women). For both men and women, disabled persons are on average older, reflecting the fact that many disabilities

Table 2.1 Profile of Disability

	Men		*Women*		*Total*	
	Frequency	*%*	*Frequency*	*%*	*Frequency*	*%*
Impairment						
Visual	198	31.94	227	42.99	425	37.02
Speech	52	8.39	26	4.92	78	6.79
Auditory	48	7.74	49	9.28	97	8.45
Mental	84	13.55	44	8.33	128	11.15
Mobility	214	34.52	152	28.60	365	31.79
Any impairment	24	3.87	31	5.87	55	4.79
Total	620	100	528	100	1148	100

Source: authors.

can be age-related (Jones *et al.*, 2003). They are less educated, which could result from unequal access to education. The disabled are also more likely to be sick, to live in urban areas and have higher non-labour income.

Employment and Disability

This section examines the determinants of the employment gap across disability status. This is made using two steps. In the first step, logistic regressions are run in order to identify the determinants of labour force participation for the disabled, non-disabled and for the whole sample; which permits, in the second step, running a non-linear version of the Oaxaca–Blinder technique, which was developed by Fairlie (2006).

Logistic Regressions on Employment

In this work, labour force participation is modelled via a binary variable indicating whether the person is employed or not.[4] In order to take into account the segmentation of the Cameroonian labour market, the dependent variable is also modelled as follows in the multinomial regression: employment is equal to 1 if the individual is employed in the public sector, 2 if he or she is employed in the private formal sector, 3 if he or she is in the informal sector and 0 if he or she is not employed. The control for worker productivity is made through education dummies and work experience as measured by age. In addition, a health dummy variable indicating whether the person has been sick over the past two weeks measures the potential productivity limitation that may result from the disability (see Mitra and Sambamoorthi, 2008). We also introduced a non-labour income variable and demographic variables as control variables.

The first column of Table 2.3, presenting the logit of employment for the whole sample, shows that the dummy indicating that a person has a disability does have a negative and statistically significant coefficient. It means that having a disability is associated with a lower probability of employment. This result is

Table 2.2 Descriptive Statistics on People With and Without Disabilities

Variables	Entire Sample				Men				Women			
	Non-Disabled		Disabled		Non-Disabled		Disabled		Non-Disabled		Disabled	
	Mean	SD	Mean	SD	Mean	SD	Mean	SD	Mean	SD	Mean	SD
Employed	0.75	0.43	0.69	0.46	0.81	0.39	0.72	0.45	0.71	0.45	0.66	0.47
Public sector	0.07	0.25	0.09	0.28	0.09	0.29	0.10	0.30	0.04	0.20	0.07	0.25
Private formal sector	0.06	0.24	0.06	0.23	0.10	0.29	0.08	0.28	0.03	0.18	0.03	0.16
Private informal sector	0.87	0.34	0.85	0.35	0.81	0.39	0.81	0.39	0.93	0.26	0.90	0.29
Age	30.46	12.49	37.04	14.66	30.45	12.52	36.78	14.69	30.47	12.46	37.34	14.62
Age^2	1083.81	894.86	1586.53	1140.75	1083.831	894.68	1568.21	1147.35	1083.79	895.06	1608.05	1133.65
Health problem	0.24	0.43	0.38	0.48	0.21	0.41	0.34	0.47	0.27	0.44	0.43	0.49
Annual non-labour income	867,093.8	9,195,425	1,391,200	1.15e+07	904,864.3	9,303,438	1,111,927	1.01e+07	831,908.1	9,093,842	1,719,134	1.30e+07
Education												
Illiterate	0.18	0.39	0.26	0.44	0.12	0.33	0.23	0.42	0.24	0.43	0.32	0.47
Primary school	0.30	0.46	0.32	0.47	0.30	0.46	0.35	0.48	0.31	0.46	0.30	0.45
Secondary school	0.28	0.45	0.22	0.42	0.29	0.45	0.23	0.42	0.27	0.45	0.22	0.42
Higher secondary school	0.16	0.37	0.12	0.33	0.20	0.40	0.13	0.34	0.13	0.34	0.11	0.31
Diploma, graduate or postgraduate level	0.05	0.23	0.05	0.23	0.08	0.27	0.06	0.24	0.04	0.19	0.05	0.21
Married	0.44	0.50	0.37	0.48	0.39	0.49	0.40	0.49	0.48	0.50	0.33	0.47
Urban	0.59	0.49	0.55	0.497	0.60	0.48	0.54	0.498	0.58	0.49	0.56	0.49
Region												
Adamaoua	0.06	0.23	0.046	0.21	0.058	0.23	0.039	0.19	0.057	0.23	0.055	0.22
Centre	0.16	0.37	0.16	0.369	0.17	0.37	0.17	0.37	0.159	0.36	0.15	0.36
East	0.055	0.23	0.04	0.20	0.055	0.23	0.04	0.20	0.055	0.22	0.04	0.20
Extreme north	0.14	0.34	0.14	0.34	0.13	0.34	0.14	0.34	0.14	0.35	0.13	0.34
Littoral	0.15	0.35	0.19	0.39	0.15	0.36	0.19	0.396	0.14	0.35	0.19	0.39
North	0.077	0.27	0.059	0.24	0.079	0.27	0.06	0.24	0.076	0.26	0.054	0.22
North-west	0.12	0.32	0.12	0.33	0.11	0.31	0.12	0.32	0.12	0.33	0.13	0.33
West	0.11	0.31	0.10	0.30	0.098	0.297	0.09	0.29	0.11	0.31	0.11	0.32
South	0.05	0.21	0.05	0.22	0.051	0.22	0.047	0.21	0.045	0.20	0.055	0.23
South-west	0.09	0.29	0.08	0.27	0.09	0.29	0.087	0.28	0.088	0.28	0.074	0.26
Female	0.52	0.49	0.46	0.498	–	–	–	–	–	–	–	–
Observations	26,899	1148	12,973	620	13,926	528						

Source: authors.

Note
SD: Standard deviation.

Table 2.3 Labour Force Participation Logit Estimates

Variables	*All*		*Non-Disabled*		*Disabled*	
	Coefficients	*t-student*	*Coefficients*	*t-student*	*coefficients*	*t-student*
Disabled	–0.89***	–11.41	–	–	–	–
Log non-labour income	–0.011**	–2.19	–0.01**	–1.97	–0.026	–1.44
Age	0.37***	43.63	0.38***	42.91	0.19***	6.39
Age^2	–0.004***	–37.85	–0.004***	–37.07	–0.002***	–5.83
Health problem	–0.02	–0.63	–0.022	–0.54	–0.059	–0.40
Education						
Primary school	0.61***	10.10	0.58***	9.22	0.607***	2.96
Secondary school	–0.16***	–2.74	–0.227***	–3.59	0.352	1.58
Higher secondary school	–0.69***	–10.62	–0.78***	–11.39	0.242	0.93
Diploma, graduate or postgraduate level	–0.869***	–10.53	–0.98***	–11.47	0.44	1.30
Married	–0.03	–0.68	–0.09**	–2.14	0.806***	4.62
Urban	–1.25***	–31.96	–1.276***	–31.47	–1.02***	–6.37
Region						
Adamaoua	–0.18**	–2.33	–0.22***	–2.73	0.47	1.23
East	0.28***	3.52	0.277***	3.32	0.307	0.79
Extreme north	0.27***	4.10	0.26***	3.76	0.256	0.96
Littoral	0.07	1.31	0.058	1.06	0.196	0.87
North	0.19***	2.65	0.177**	2.31	0.384	1.08
North-west	0.39***	6.14	0.40***	6.12	0.257	0.94
West	1.13***	15.98	1.17***	15.92	0.615**	2.08
South	–0.134*	–1.70	–0.152*	–1.88	0.21	0.59
South-west	0.013	0.20	0.001	0.02	0.19	0.66
Female	–0.79***	–23.30	–0.825***	–23.40	–0.23	–1.59
Constant	–3.99***	–28.15	–4.097***	–27.66	–2.762***	–4.96
–log likelihood	11,874.83		11,211.22		612.72	
LR $Chi^2(21)$ [(20). (20)]=	7471.92		7353.57		194.60	
Prob.>Chi^2=	0.0000		0.0000		0.0000	
Observations	28,047		26,899		1148	

Source: authors.

Notes
***, ** and * denote significance at the 1, 5 and 10 per cent levels respectively. The *illiterate* and *Centre* variables are residual respectively for education and region.

confirmed in the public, private formal and informal sectors with, however, a greater prejudice of disability on employment in these two last sectors (see Table 2.6, in the Appendix).

The summary of separate employment equations among individuals with and without disability is presented in the second and third columns of Table 2.3. There are strong age effects, with positive and negative signs on the linear and quadratic terms respectively observed in all cases, meaning the younger are less likely to have a job but there is a threshold beyond which seniors have difficulty integrating into the labour market. In accordance to neo-classical theory, non-labour income measured in logarithmic terms has a negative effect on employment; however, this effect is significant only for non-disabled people, it may be due to the smaller sample size for the disabled (Mitra and Sambamoorthi, 2008). The results observed seem to show that, overall, individuals with higher educational qualifications are significantly less likely to be in employment than those without any qualifications. This surprising result demonstrates the domination of the informal sector in the Cameroonian labour market. In fact, when we look at employment access to different institutional sectors, the negative effect of education on employment appears mostly in the informal sector. The result in this sector could be due to the effect of education on the reservation wage, so that in developing countries unemployment among educated people may indicate they are waiting to enter the formal job sector (see Dumont, 2000). In addition, people living in urban zones (disabled or not) are less likely to be employed than those living in rural areas. Overall, the results presented in the second and third columns of Table 2.3 suggest that there is a lot of heterogeneity in the determinants of employment across disability status, so it necessary to conduct decomposition to identify the determinants of the employment gap existing between these groups.

Decomposition of Differences in Labour Force Participation

The method usually used to evaluate the effect of disability on employment is the employment logit model with a disabled dummy. The significance of the disabled variable is thus interpreted like discrimination. However, this interpretation is made under the strong hypothesis that the coefficients of the characteristics are the same across disability status (Mitra and Sambamoorthi, 2008). This assumption now no longer holds, as shown in the second and third columns of Table 2.3. To relax this hypothesis, a decomposition of the employment rate gap is run. Given that the dependent variable (labour force participation) is binary, we adopt non-linear decomposition techniques proposed by Fairlie (2006). It is inspired from the Oaxaca-Blinder decomposition (Oaxaca, 1973; Blinder, 1973) traditionally used to run decompositions using coefficient estimates from linear regressions for the outcome of interest.

For the non-linear equation $Y=F(X\hat{\beta})$, where F is the cumulative distribution function from the logistic distribution (the cumulative distribution function from the standard normal distribution can be also used), the Fairlie decomposition can be presented as follows:

$$\bar{Y}^{ND} - \bar{Y}^{D} = \left[\sum_{i=1}^{N^{ND}} \frac{F(X_i^{ND}\hat{\beta}^{ND})}{N^{ND}} - \sum_{i=1}^{N^{D}} \frac{F(X_i^{D}\hat{\beta}^{ND})}{N^{D}}\right] + \left[\sum_{i=1}^{N^{D}} \frac{F(X_i^{D}\hat{\beta}^{ND})}{N^{D}} - \sum_{i=1}^{N^{D}} \frac{F(X_i^{D}\hat{\beta}^{D})}{N^{D}}\right] \quad (1)$$

Here, $\bar{Y}^j$ is the average probability to be employed for the group j [j=non-disabled (ND), disabled (D)], N^j is the sample size of the population j, $\hat{\beta}^{ND}$ and $\hat{\beta}^{D}$ are, respectively, the estimated coefficients from the binary regressions among ND and D and X_i^{ND} and X_i^{D} represent observed characteristics in each group, respectively. The first component represents the employment gap that is due to the differences in endowments of human capital and other observable characteristics. The second component may be viewed as the discrimination; it represents the part due to differences in the group processes determining employment. The following expression for the decomposition is also valid even if the results may vary from those obtained in equation (1):

$$\bar{Y}^{ND} - \bar{Y}^{D} = \left[\sum_{i=1}^{N^{ND}} \frac{F(X_i^{ND}\hat{\beta}^{D})}{N^{ND}} - \sum_{i=1}^{N^{D}} \frac{F(X_i^{D}\hat{\beta}^{D})}{N^{D}}\right] + \left[\sum_{i=1}^{N^{D}} \frac{F(X_i^{ND}\hat{\beta}^{ND})}{N^{ND}} - \sum_{i=1}^{N^{D}} \frac{F(X_i^{ND}\hat{\beta}^{D})}{N^{ND}}\right] \quad (2)$$

In equation (2) the disabled coefficient estimate is used as weight for the first term and distributions of the non-disabled as weight in the second term. But, for this work, we adopt the specification suggested by Oaxaca and Ransom (1994), using coefficient estimates from a pooled sample of the two groups to weight the first term of the decomposition.

We made here two types of employment decomposition. The first compares the disabled with the non-disabled overall (Table 2.4). The second compares disabled women with disabled men (Table 2.5) to consider whether disabled women are more discriminated against than men.

The first column of Table 2.4 shows that there exists a significant employment gap of 6.7 percentage points between disabled and non-disabled. Results based on the use of coefficient estimates from a pooled sample as weights suggest that the portion explained by individual endowments is negative (–78 per cent), meaning that if the disabled had the characteristics of the non-disabled, the employment rate of the disabled would be lower and the employment gap would be larger. Thus discrimination could explain the whole employment gap. A similar result has been obtained by Mitra and Sambamoorthi (2008) in India. Given the surprising effect of education obtained above, the decomposition is also made by taking in account different sectors.[5] These decompositions show that the existing gap between people without and with disability is about 1.2 per

Table 2.4 Decomposition of Labour Force Participation Gap among People With and Without Disability

	All	*Public*	*Private Formal*	*Informal*
Non-disabled	0.75790922	0.17444219	0.16715693	0.73108688
Disabled	0.69076655	0.16273585	0.11691542	0.65600775
Difference	0.06714267	0.01170634	0.0502415	0.07507913
Explained by				
Log non-labour income	0.0008194 (1.22%)	0.0008225 (7.03%)	0.0004039 (0.80%)	0.0011896 (1.58%)
Age	–0.0418803 (–62.37%)	–0.0947887 (–809%)	–0.0473593 (–94.26%)	–0.0374825 (–49.92%)
Health problem	0.0007853 (1.16%)	0.0035029 (29.92%)	0.0024989 (4.97%)	0.0004675 (0.62%)
Education	–0.008292 (–12.34%)	0.0350589 (299.49%)	0.0152989 (30.45%)	–0.0151413 (–20.16%)
Married	3.20e–06 (0.00%)	0.0015915 (13.59%)	0.0017184 (3.42%)	–0.0002616 (–0.34%)
Urban	–0.0012766 (–1.90%)	–0.0038584 (–32.95%)	–0.0009276 (–1.84%)	–0.0027067 (–3.60%)
Region	0.0010673 (1.58%)	0.0014431 (12.33%)	–0.0002891 (–0.57%)	0.0019984 (2.66%)
Female	–0.0038049 (–5.66%)	–0.0107892 (–92.16%)	–0.0257899 (–51.33%)	–0.0047542 (–6.33%)
Total explained	–0.05272264 (–78%)	–0.06488007 (–554%)	–0.05458985 (–108%)	–0.05668944 (–75%)
Discrimination	0.11986531 (178%)	0.07658641 (654%)	0.10483135 (208%)	0.13176857 (175%)

Source: authors.

Table 2.5 Decomposition of Labour Force Participation Gap among Disabled Men and Disabled Women

Difference	*Explained by Characteristics*	*Discrimination*
0.0551	0.0097 18%	0.0454 82%

Source: authors.

cent in the public sector, 5 per cent in the private formal sector and 7.5 per cent in the informal sector. While in the public and private formal sector, differences in education tend to increase the employment gap, they reduce this gap in the informal sector. This confirms the fact that in this later sector, education reduces the likelihood to be employed.

In addition, the comparison of disabled women with disabled men (Table 2.5) tells us that disabled women are the most disadvantaged in entering the labour market. The employment difference between these is 5.5 percentage points and is explained both by the differential in endowment (28.84 per cent) and discrimination (81.16 per cent).

Conclusion

In this work, the determinants of the employment gap between disabled and non-disabled people have been examined. To our knowledge, this is the first paper to conduct this kind of study in the Cameroonian labour market and to include the segmentation of the labour market observed in the developing countries in its analysis.

A substantial difference appears in the likelihood of employment, even after several decades of various legislation promoting the employment of the disabled in Cameroon. Only 69.07 per cent of people with disabilities are in employment compared to 75.79 per cent for people without disabilities, a gap of 6.71 per cent. This gap is about 8.98 per cent between men and 5.21 per cent between women even if the employment rate of men (disabled or not) is greater than that for women (disabled or not). The gap is also observed whatever the institutional sector. Significant heterogeneity within the disabled group is also identified with greater prejudice against those suffering from mental forms of disability. The Fairlie decomposition reveals that, overall, the employment gap is not explained by differentials in human capital, demographic and other observed characteristics between disabled and non-disabled. This may result from discrimination by employers.

All these results call for the following policy implications. Anti-discriminatory legislation must be reinforced with legislation combining a policy of reservation and punishment measures to discourage employers from discrimination. Second, employers' access to information concerning the various types of disability and their implications for work must be improved to rectify the popular conception of disability and to lower prejudice. It may also be helpful in order to reduce discrimination at the entrance to the labour market, to emphasize the adjustments that can help disabled people to create their own jobs. It may equally be worthwhile to concentrate efforts upon disabled women who are more vulnerable and upon the private sector where disability creates more prejudice. To conclude, it would be necessary to improve the quality of disability data in developing countries in general and in Cameroon in particular for more rigorous future analyses on the implication of disability.

Appendix

Table 2.6 Disabled Labour Force Participation Multinomial Logit

Variables	*Public*		*Private Formal*		*Informal*	
	Coefficients	*t-student*	*Coefficients*	*t-student*	*Coefficients*	*t-student*
Disabled	−0.70***	−4.42	−0.92***	−5.41	−0.92***	−11.49
Log non-labour income	−0.01*	−1.74	−0.01	−1.32	−0.014***	−2.67
Age	0.72***	30.46	0.62***	30.10	0.34***	40.03
Age^2	−0.008***	−26.83	−0.0075***	−26.85	−0.004***	−35.09
Health problem	0.007	0.10	−0.02	−0.25	−0.014	−0.35
Education						
Primary school	2.33***	9.92	1.74***	9.02	0.52***	8.71
Secondary school	2.79***	11.96	1.41***	7.22	−0.31***	−5.19
Higher secondary school	3.74***	16.00	1.52***	7.73	−1.03***	−15.28
Diploma, graduate or postgraduate level	4.31***	17.81	1.64***	7.89	−1.84***	−19.38
Married	0.14*	1.74	−0.10	−1.32	−0.10**	−2.36
Urban	−0.72***	−8.56	−0.34***	−3.95	−1.29***	−33.14
Region						
Adamaoua	0.008	0.05	0.25	1.61	−0.24***	−3.06
East	0.43***	2.58	0.22	1.32	0.25***	3.08
Extreme north	0.88***	5.97	−0.37**	−2.11	0.24***	3.59
Littoral	−0.72***	−6.31	0.47***	4.97	0.07	1.36
North	0.91***	5.67	−0.23	−1.23	0.17**	2.24
North-west	0.32**	2.46	0.25*	1.94	0.39***	5.97
West	0.81***	6.04	0.71***	5.12	1.18***	16.36
South	0.14	0.94	0.43***	2.97	−0.21***	−2.59
South-west	0.41***	3.36	0.15	1.18	−0.038	−0.57
Female	−1.13***	−15.34	−1.69***	−23.27	−0.68***	−19.63
Constant	−17.81***	−35.47	−12.99***	−32.36	−3.48***	−24.11
−log likelihood	18,969.571					
LR $Chi^2(63)$=	13,699.56					
Prob.>Chi^2=	0.0000					
Observations	28,047					

Source: authors.

Notes
***, ** and * denote significance at the 1, 5 and 10 per cent levels respectively. Baseline: not employed. The *illiterate* and *Centre* variables are residual respectively for education and region.

Notes

1 The 2010 Act on the Protection and Promotion of the Disabled, ARTICLE 45:

> Are punished of imprisonment of three (3) to six (6) months and a fine of 100,000 (one hundred thousand) to 1,000,000 (one million) CFA francs or one of two penalties only those responsible for schools, professionals and academics, employers or business leaders who are discriminated against in admission, hiring or remuneration of persons with disabilities.

2 Reservation wage is defined as the lowest wage at which a person is willing to work (Mitra and Sambamoorthi, 2008).

3 Indeed, below 15 years old, the ILO considers individuals as school age and above 64 year old, they are supposed to be retirees; these individuals should not be on the labour market.

4 An individual is considered as employed is he is occupied in the ILO sense.

5 Fairlie decomposition can be run only if the dependant variable is binary. So taking in account the different institutional sectors, three dummies are generated. For example, to estimate the likelihood of being employed in the public sector, the variable generated is equal to 1 if the individual considered is employed in the public sector and 0 if he is not employed. We are aware of omission bias related to the fact that these variables do not consider other positions in the labour market. It is worth noting that this procedure is used simply to give a general idea of differences relying on more usual sign of variables.

References

Aigner, D. and Cain, G. (1977), "Statistical theories of discrimination in labour markets", *Industrial and Labour Relations Review*, 30 (2), 175–187.

Arrow, K. (1971), "Theory of discrimination", Industrial Relations Section, Working Paper, 39A.

Baldwin, M. and Johnson, W. G. (2001), "Dispelling the myths about work disability", Paper prepared for the *1998 IRRA Research Volume*, New Approaches to Disability in the Workplace.

Baldwin, M. and Johnson, W. G. (2005), "A critical review of studies of discrimination against workers with disabilities". In W. M. Rodgers, III (ed.), *Handbook on the economics of discrimination*, Cheltenham, UK: Edward Elgar Publishing, 119–160.

Becker, G. (1971), *Economics of discrimination*, Chicago, IL: University of Chicago Press.

Blackaby, D., Clark, K., Drinkwater, S., Leslie, D., Murphy, P. and O'Leary, N. (1999), "Earnings and employment opportunities of disabled people", Department for Education and Employment, Research Report No. 133, Nottingham, UK.

Blinder, A. (1973), "Wage discrimination: reduced form and structural estimates", *Journal of Human Resources*, 8, 436–455.

Cahuc, P. and Zylberberg, A. (1996), *Economie du travail: la formation des salaires et les déterminants du chômage*, Paris: De Boeck Université, Séries Balises.

DeLeire, T. (2001), "Changes in wage discrimination against people with disabilities: 1948–93", *Journal of Human Resources*, 36 (1), 144–158.

Dumont, J. (2000), "Estimer la relation entre invalidité et emploi dans le cas de Madagascar", *Document de travail*, 05.

Fairlie, R. (2006), "An extension of the Blinder–Oaxaca decomposition technique to logit and probit models", IZA, Discussion Paper, 1917.

Hum, D. and Simpson, W. (1996), "Canadians with disabilities and the labour market", *Canadian Public Policy*, 22 (3), 285–299.

ILO (2007), "Faits et chiffres sur le handicap dans le monde du travail", www.ilo.org/employment/disability.

INS (2008), "Conditions de vie des populations et profil de pauvreté au Cameroun en 2007", Rapport principal de l'ECAM3.

Kidd, M. P., Sloane, P. J. and Ferko, I. (2000), "Disability and the labour market: an analysis of British males", *Journal of Health Economics*, 19, 961–981.

Johnson, W. G. and Lambrinos, J. (1985) "Wage discrimination against handicapped men and women", *Journal of Human Resources*, 20 (2), 264–277.

Jones, M. K. (2005), "Disability and the labour market: a review of the empirical evidence", WELMERC Department of Economics, University of Wales Swansea, Discussion Paper, 04.

Jones, M. K., Latreille, P. L. and Sloane, P. J. (2003), "Disability, gender and the labour market", IZA, Discussion paper, 936.

Loi n°83/013 du 21 juillet 1983 relative à la Protection des Personnes Handicapées, http://digitalcommons.ilr.cornell.edu/gladnetcollect/52.

Loi n°2010/002 du 13 avril 2010 portant Protection et Promotion des Personnes Handicapées.

Longhi, S., Nicoletti, C. and Platt, L. (2010), "Interpreting wage gaps of disabled men: the roles of productivity and of discrimination", ISER, Working paper, 19.

Madden, D. (2004), "Labour market discrimination on the basis of health: an application to UK data", *Applied Economics*, 36 (5), 421–442.

Mitra, S. (2009), "Disability cash transfers in the context of poverty and unemployment: the case of South Africa", Discussion Paper, 08.

Mitra, S. and Sambamoorthi, U. (2008), "Disability and the rural labour market in India: evidence for males in Tamil Nadu", *World Development*, 36 (5), 934–952.

Oaxaca, R. (1973), "Male–female wage differentials in urban labour markets", *International Economic Review*, 14, 693–709.

Oaxaca, R. and Ransom, M. (1994), "On discrimination and the decomposition of wage differentials", *Journal of Econometrics*, 61, 5–21.

Phelps, E. S. (1972), "The statistical theory of racism and sexism", *American Economic Review*, 62 (4), 659–661.

Winance, M. (2008), "La notion de handicap et ses transformations à travers les classifications internationales du handicap de l'OMS, 1980 et 2001", *Dynamis*, 28, 377–406.

Zamo, C. (2007), "Fécondité, santé et offre de travail des femmes au Cameroun", Thèse de doctorat, PhD en Sciences Economiques non publiée, Université de Yaoundé II, Soa.

3 Corruption and Small- and Medium-Sized Enterprise Growth in Cameroon

Daniel Gbetnkom

Introduction

Conventionally, corruption is understood and referred to as the private wealth-seeking behavior of someone who represents the state and the public authority or as the misuse of public goods by public officials for private benefits. This issue has to some extent entered the political and economic sciences from the new interest in the role of the state in the developing world, and in particular from the idea that the state is an indispensable instrument for economic development. There is now much consensus on the relevance of an efficient state in economic development (UNECA, 2011). The World Bank (1997) stated that

> an effective state is vital for the provision of the goods and services and the rules and institutions that allow markets to flourish and people to live healthier, happier lives. Without it, sustainable development, both economic and social is impossible.

Corruption has come up as a thematic constituent of this renewed paradigm, in which development depends on good governance and accountability, and necessitates economic reforms. The decisive role of the state is also reflected in most definitions of corruption. Corruption is a particular state–society relation. On one side is the state, that is the civil servants or bureaucrats who hold a position of authority to allocate rights over scarce public resources in the name of the state or the government. A corrupt act is when these responsible persons accept money or some other form of reward and then proceed to misuse their official powers by returning undue favors. On the other side of a corrupt act is the "corrupters", those who offer the bribes. These suppliers are businessmen, entrepreneurs or the general public.

Corruption is principally a governance issue, perceived as a failure of institutions and a lack of capacity to manage society by means of a framework of social, judicial, political and economic checks and balances. It is an evil, certainly universal, but more widespread in developing countries because conditions favor it. The urge for gain is extremely strong and exacerbated by poverty.

In Cameroon, corruption is constantly manifested in the forms of embezzlement of public funds, bribery, influence peddling and fraud. These abuses are the prime motivation for the series of anticorruption campaigns launched by the Prime Minister of Cameroon since March 1998.

Corrupt officers always seek to bypass legal competition and hamper the rules of normal societal functioning. At the level of public markets (contracts), they influence the choice of suppliers of goods and services to the state and also influence the exact modalities of contracts and their renewal. At the level of state accorded advantages, they favor fiscal fraud, have access to privileged schools, to medical attentions, to housing and lodging or access to shares in enterprises through undergoing privatization.

The abuses enumerated above can lead to reduction in the amount of tax and other levies imputed by the state on individuals. They favor the alteration of the results of juridical regulation by pushing public authorities to avoid reprimanding of illegal activities or to favor unduly one group at the detriment of the other in the framework of court proceedings and other actions in justice. This situation stems from the fact that in Cameroon, the discretionary power of many civil servants is quite extended. Moral laws and principles in the leading of public affairs are less developed and law officers charged with the responsibility of ensuring their implementation and respect are not well prepared for this task. People or organs such as accountants and the press in charge of supplying information on which to detect and apply the law are weak and most of them even partakers of corrupt acts. This has made corruption endemic and systematic such that it is very difficult to punish an individual since many others are also guilty. This situation has made Cameroon the most corrupt country in the years 1998 and 1999.[1]

In the light of economic theory, corruption reduces growth by virtue of its attenuating impact on investment attraction for both local and foreign entrepreneurs. When these entrepreneurs are asked by state authorities to give bribes before creating an enterprise or when some civil servants ask for part of the fruit of investments as such, corruption plays the role of a tax. Corruption also reduces growth by lowering the quality of infrastructure and public services, by reducing fiscal revenues and by fraudulently altering the composition of public expenses. Concerning the alteration of the composition of public expenses, a comparison between countries seems to show that corrupt public authorities particularly allocate a smaller proportion of public expenses to education and health and a greater proportion to public investment especially in non-productive projects, thereby reducing the productivity of the available stock of public capital (Tanzi and Davoodi, 1997). An econometric analysis indicates that countries that advance from six to eight in the corruption perception index (CPI), generally increase their credits to national education by 0.5 of GDP, representing a considerable change (Mauro, 1998). This result is of prime importance, for it has been more and more proved that the level of education has a high correlation with poverty and economic growth (Gbetnkom, 1999). The same country experiences a four percentage points increase in her investment rate (Mauro, 1995).

Beyond the developments highlighted above, theoretical and empirical studies that handle objectively the economic incidence of corruption have generally concluded that:

- Corruption increases the cost of transaction as well as uncertainty.
- Corruption leads to inefficient economic results, brings about a bad talent distribution in favor of rent seeking activities and displacing sectoral priorities as well as technological choices.
- Corruption leads enterprises to underground economies, which reduces public revenue such that a restricted number of taxpayers bear a much greater tax burden. The state thus becomes incapable of supplying essential collective goods, notably those of assuring the implementation and respect of law principles. As such, a vicious circle of growing corruption and clandestine economic activities can develop.
- Corruption imposes a particularly heavy but regressive tax on commercial activities and services of small-scale enterprises. Corruption jeopardizes the legitimacy of the state (Gray and Kaufmann, 1998).

Given these pervasive effects of corruption, its eradication has become a key element in the policy agenda of many governments and international agencies and a fundamental challenge for the long-term development of many African countries.

However, proponents of "efficient corruption" claim that bribery may allow firms to get things done in an economy plagued by bureaucratic holdups.[2] Moreover, it has also been argued that a system built on bribery will lead to an efficient process for allocating licenses and government contracts, since the most efficient firms will be able to afford to pay the highest bribes (Lui, 1985). Leff (1964) argued that corruption is likely to have beneficial effects in developing countries suffering from high levels of state intervention and monopolies. First, corruption corrects the detrimental effects of the indifference and hostility of a government or redirects government priorities toward the business sector to entrepreneurs, thereby offering them a more propitious environment for business. Second, corruption reduces uncertainty and increases the rate of investment by making government behavior more predictable, especially in the presence of an irrational style of decision-making (p. 9). Corruption is also deemed to enable innovators to bypass entrenched economic interests. Finally, corruption introduces an element of competition in market allocation and thereby increases overall efficiency of the economy.

With respect to this controversy, the issue of whether corruption is damaging at all, is primarily an empirical question. In view of this concern, research on the effects of corruption on economic growth has been examined extensively in the macro literature, beginning with Mauro (1995). Generally, these studies have three common features:

- they are based on cross-country analyses;
- they exploit data on corruption derived from perception indices, typically constructed from foreign experts' assessments of overall corruption in a country; and
- they explain corruption as a function of countries' policy-institutional environment (Svenson, 2003).

Though this literature has provided important insights on the aggregate effects and determinants of corruption, it also has its shortcomings. First, the use of perception indices raises concern about perception biases. Second, due to the aggregate nature of the data, it tells us little about the relationship between corruption and individual agents. This relationship is still not fully understood, and is less systematically investigated, particularly in Africa. Most importantly, macro-effects cannot by definition explain the within-country variation in corruption.

Thus, the literature that directly deals with firms under conditions of corruption is somewhat limited in its scope. Meanwhile, small- and medium-sized enterprises (SMEs)[3] play an important role in providing productive employment opportunities for an increasing number of job seekers (Mead, 1994), arguably an important role given recent enterprise restructuring programs that have led to observed high systemic unemployment. Indeed, SMEs have been known to contribute to:

- household income and welfare;
- social change, political stability and democracy;
- distributional or development objectives; as well as,
- self-confidence and empowerment of the individual (Liedholm and Mead, 1999).

Furthermore, a better understanding of a firm's allocation of resources and its economic determinants is crucial for formulating appropriate development policies and projects and for evaluating those already existing.

This chapter examines the impact of bribes on the growth of SMEs in Cameroon based on the primary data on corruption. This approach has a range of features to ensure higher reliability and greater depth in assessing the effects of corruption. Questions are based on the direct experience of firms rather than subjective comparisons across countries. Where possible, numerical cardinal estimates of problems are used (such as share of annual sales spent on bribes) as opposed to subjective assessments of the extent of corruption. Furthermore, data on firm-level performance in terms of sales, investment and employment provide specific estimates of the costs and benefits to firms associated with governance issues. We believe that for a society to engage seriously in the process of identifying the pervasive effects of corruption, both bottom up and top down approaches are necessary. This chapter is a bottom up contribution to this process.

At the conceptual level, the debate on the effects of corruption on economic growth has been going on for several decades (Bardhan, 1997). Despite this, little is known about the incidence and cost of corruption on firm growth and performance. Available literature relies on macroeconomic or cross-country comparisons. Few empirical studies have been conducted at the firm level (Svenson, 2000, 2003). However, this perspective provides a number of advantages. First it allows us to explore the relationship between different characteristics of firms and their effects on the firms' interactions with the state. Second, it provides an opportunity to investigate in depth the types of services for which firms pay bribes and the characteristics of these transactions. Third, it provides a micro-economic perspective on the costs and benefits to firms associated with corruption and different levels of governance. This is why this chapter aims at deepening our understanding of the linkages between bribe payments and firms' growth based on the critical information that firms can provide about the nature and extent of corruption. Our research question is therefore: What are the effects of bribe payments on SMEs' growth? Specifically this chapter investigates the types of services for which firms pay bribes, the characteristics of these transactions and estimates the impact of bribe payments on the SMEs growth.

The remainder of the chapter is structured as follows: the next section presents the literature review, and the third and fourth sections examine the methodological approach and the empirical results respectively.

Literature Review

Theoretical Framework

Various definitions of corruption maintain that the state is always involved, and that corruption is basically a particular state–society relationship. It is furthermore maintained that this relationship is based on a mutual exchange of benefits that is an exchange from which both the state and the society will draw some immediate and private benefit. This state–society relationship is rarely balanced however. In aggregate terms, corrupt practices will generate a flow of resources either from society to state (extractive corruption) or from state to society (redistributive corruption).

This chapter is rooted in the theory of extractive corruption (principal–agent theory) where the state (regulator) is the stronger part in the state–society relationship. According to this theory, the corrupter is more or less a passive player. The public agent who has discretion over disbursements of public goods is tempted corruptly to charge monopoly rents. This creates inefficiencies, as the firm pays too high a price for these goods and services (Klitgaard, 1988). Corruption in this circumstance is considered as an agency problem where an official entrusted with carrying out a task by the state engages in some sort of malfeasance for private enrichment which is difficult to monitor for the principal (Bardhan, 1997). This is an analysis of a regulator who acts as a pure single-product monopolist facing a large number of price-taking buyers. He has full control over his choice of a price function, and can charge different prices to different buyers.

In the theoretical framework presented above, the effect of bribe payments on SMEs can be deleterious on both a sectoral and an individual firm level. Meanwhile, policies that inhibit the development of a small enterprise sector have implications for poverty. In the context of Cameroon, the small enterprise sector is particularly important because extended households and other social insurance mechanisms to deal with unanticipated income shocks, such as sudden unemployment, are not prevalent. In the absence of traditional state-sponsored employment or other social safety nets that have gradually disappeared over the past decades, the income-generating opportunities provided by SMEs play an important role in poverty alleviation and household risk reduction.

Corruption may also cause a loss of efficiency for individual firms because it may force firms to incur a number of unproductive costs, thereby leading to a welfare-reducing allocation of resources. When government officials base their bribe price on what they can observe during a firm inspection, bribe payments act as a tax on certain factors of production. In this sense, corruption changes relative factor prices and may lead to sub-optimal use of inputs. Furthermore, firms may be less inclined to invest in cost-saving or production-enhancing technologies because of the additional regulatory scrutiny that such actions may attract, and because finance, from any source, may be inaccessible.

Review of Empirical Works

Quantitative literature on corruption is not as extensive as the theoretical works. Many papers on corruption are often in theory, at times with a section on empirical examples. Little effort has been deployed to conduct tests systematically on the several hypotheses particularly at the firm level. Despite more than two decades of modern research, beginning with Rose-Ackerman (1975, 1978) on the economics of corruption, however, economic studies on corruption at the firm level are rather scarce. Shleifer and Vishny (1993) analyze a bureaucracy selling a government-produced good (e.g., a permit), noting that if the officials do not coordinate the extraction of bribes, they fail to internalise the effect of their demands for bribes on other officials' income, thereby leading to very high corruption levels. These authors show that the illegality of corruption and the need for secrecy make it more distortionary and costly than its sister activity taxation. Shleifer and Vishny (1993) present a model of bargaining between politicians and managers that explains many stylized facts about the behavior of state firms.

Kaufman and Wei (1999) examine whether bribery offers enterprises the possibility of avoiding excessive bureaucracy, by comparing average time wasted with bureaucratic negotiations and the level of bribery across countries. They conclude that corrupt officials may, instead of speeding up economic activities, actually cause administrative delays in order to attract more bribes. Johnson *et al.* (1998) show that corruption distorts the development of enterprises and favors the emergence of an unofficial or underground economy. Corruption reduces fiscal income especially because it favors the growth of a non-official economy. The practices inherent to rents in the official economy divert enterprises toward parallel economies where they pay fewer taxes. Such reduction in fiscal income return affects the capacity of the state in supplying important public goods such as laws and principles of ethics and this favors the more underground economy to the detriment of public finance.

Bliss and Di Tella (1997) study the relationship between corruption and competition. They show that if bureaucrats have the power to extract money from firms under their control, they will drive the most inefficient firms out of business, thereby enhancing the profitability of remaining firms, which, in turn, makes it possible to demand larger bribes. Choi and Thum (1999) use a similar model to study the effects of repeated extortion. Hellman *et al.* (2000) demonstrate that corruption favors the monopoly of the state by certain groups of privileged population that give bribes to state agents and the police, hence sapping growth of production and private sector investments.

Thomas *et al.* (2000) show that corruption distorts infrastructural investment to the detriment of aid projects to the poor hence compromising the use of small enterprises to fight against poverty. The situation is even worse as corrupt regimes prefer defense contracts to construction of dispensaries and rural schools, a policy that jeopardizes the proper distribution of revenue and diverts rural resources to the metropolis. Based on data collected on bribe payments across firms in Uganda, Svensson (2003) investigated the concern related to who must pay bribes and how much. He came to the following conclusions. First, a firm with extensive dealings with the public sector is more likely to be under bureaucratic control and therefore faces a higher probability of having to pay bribes. Second, there is no evidence that the firm's profitability or alternative return on capital influences the likelihood of having to pay bribes. Thus, even firms with low profits will be forced to pay bribes if officials have control rights over the firm's business. Finally, larger firms also appear to be more likely to have to pay bribes.

Fisman and Svensson (2002) have shown that the effect of corruption on short-run growth rates of Ugandan firms is much larger than the retarding effect of taxation. In the theoretical framework used by these authors, three reasons are put forward to explain differences in amounts of bribe paid across firms. First, firms may be dealing with public officials who differ with respect to the personal (moral) cost of demanding bribes. Second, public officials' perception of the likelihood of getting caught in corrupt practices and the perceived punishment if found guilty may also differ. However, the most important explanation is that officials' opportunity to extract bribes differs across sectors and locations. In brief, the control rights determine the threat point in the negotiation between a public official and a firm. When public officials maintain control over firms through regulation, the firms must either pay the required bribe or exit the market. Thus, if a firm operates in a sector or organizes production in such a way that the need/demand for public services is minimized, then it is also more likely to be able to avoid paying bribes without any major impact on its business. If on the contrary, a firm is under public control, in the sense that it benefits from public services and operates in a sector regulated by public officials, then it is costly to refuse to pay. The authors formalize the control rights hypothesis as follows:

$$P^i = \alpha^0 w_i + \upsilon_i \tag{1}$$

where P^i is the probability that firm i must pay bribes, W_i is a vector measuring dealings with the public sector, α^0 is a coefficient vector and υ_i is an unobserved error term.

To sum up, the micro-level support for firm-based theories on the effects of corruption that have generated much attention in recent years is still in its infancy. Much more work is still required in this area, and this chapter falls in line with this concern.

Methodological Approach

To assess the effect of corruption on firm growth, this chapter utilized the theoretical framework that follows Fisman and Svensson (2002), and Svensson (2003).

Model Specification

The theoretical framework laid out above suggests that the short-run growth rates of firms depend on the bribe amount, the firm age, the initial sales and the type of ownership. Following the basic formulation of Fisman and Svensson (2002) our empirical model is:

$$Y = \alpha_0 + \alpha_1 B_{it} + \alpha_2 A_{it} + \alpha_3 E_{it} + \alpha_4 O_i + \alpha_5 IE_i + \mu_{yt} \qquad (2)$$

where Y is the rate of growth of output, B the ratio of bribe amount over sales, A the firm age, E employment to control for size, O the type of ownership taking 1 if the firm is owned by a Cameroonian and 0 otherwise, IE a dummy variable taking 1 if a firm either exports or imports directly and 0 otherwise, and μ_{yt} the error term.

As our measure of firm growth, we use historical sales data that were collected. Our measure of B is given by (bribe payments)/sales. The most natural approach for bribery would be to look at bribes as a fraction of profits. This, however, would require perhaps excessive confidence in the abilities of firms to produce accounts that adhere to some uniform standard. This is why firm sales are used, since they are much less prone to manipulation and misreporting. A negative relationship is expected.

Firm age has been found to be correlated with growth in many firm-level studies, and may be correlated with bribes if longer established firms have better relationships with banks, suppliers and clients as well as government services. With respect to these advantages, we expect that firm age will positively impact on firm growth. Since firm size may be correlated with bribe payments (as larger organizations are more visible to bureaucrats) and since size may also affect future growth, we include employment to control for size. Foreign ownership (as opposed to local) can affect performance in the sense that such firms may grow more quickly due to greater resources, access to markets and technical expertise, while they may be exempt from bureaucratic harassment as an inducement to locate their operations in Cameroon. A positive relationship is expected. Finally, firms involved in international trade, either exporting or importing, may be more vulnerable to rent extraction and subject to greater bureaucratic scrutiny and regulation than firms with only local sales. Since a correlation between growth and trade has been reported in many studies, this will also be an important control. Hence, we include a dummy variable denoting whether a firm either exports or imports directly (*IE*).

To measure corruption we draw upon questions which ask if firms like yours typically need to make extra, unofficial payments for access to publicly regulated goods. And over the last two years (2003, 2004) what would you estimate as the total amount spent by your firm in unofficial payments or gifts for the following services (connection to electricity, phone, water; acquisition of licenses and permits; dealing with taxes and tax collection; gaining government contracts; dealing with customs/imports)? For each of these areas susceptible to bribery, respondents gave figures that were summed up to get the annual amounts of unofficial payments for each of the firms.

The model takes the form:

$$\begin{cases} LnB = \beta_0 + \beta_1 LnSL_{it} + \beta_2 LnA_{it} + \beta_3 E_{it} + \beta_4 O_i + \beta_5 IE_i + \\ \beta_6 PS_i + \beta_7 LnF_i + \beta_8 Baf + \beta_9 Bam + \beta_{10} Yao + \mu_{Bt} \end{cases} \tag{3}$$

where, *B* is the reported bribe ratio over sales, *E* is firm level employment for 2003 and 2004, *SL* is the gross sales in 2003 and 2004, *F* is a dummy taking 1 if a firm has a bank and/or microfinance loan and 0 otherwise, *IE* is a dummy taking 1 if a firm is involved in import and/or export activities and 0 otherwise, *PS* is an index of public services, including electricity and water that takes 1 if a firm interacts with public services and 0 otherwise, *O* is a dummy for ownership that takes 1 if the owner of the firm is a Cameroonian and 0 if he is a foreigner. The four cities covered are categorized into four dummy variables – Bamenda (Bam), Bafoussam (Baf), Douala (Dou) and Yaoundé (Yao). Each of the categories takes 1 or 0 depending on the location of the firm. The dummy for Douala was dropped to serve as reference location. The combined equation to be estimated is as follows:

$$\begin{cases} LnB = \beta_0 + \beta_1 LnSL_{it} + \beta_2 LnA_{it} + \beta_3 LnE_{it} + \beta_4 O_i + \beta_5 IE_i + \\ \beta_6 PS_i + \beta_7 F_i + \beta_8 Baf + \beta_9 Bam + \beta_{10} Yao + \mu_{Bt} \\ LnY = \alpha_0 + \alpha_1 LnB_{it} + \alpha_2 LnA_{it} + \alpha_3 LnE_{it} + \alpha_4 O_i + \\ \alpha_5 IE_i + \alpha_6 PS_i + \alpha_7 F_i + \alpha_8 Baf + \alpha_9 Bam + \alpha_{10} Dou + \mu_{yt} \end{cases} \tag{4}$$

Data Collection

The first data source was the Department of Statistics and National Accounts where we collected information related to the number of firms and their contribution to the total output in each of the eligible categories, and the volume of employment in each of the firms. This information helped us select the sample of firms that we surveyed.

For the empirical analysis, the main source of data for this study is a firm-level survey that we carried out. The sampling frame was confined to four general industrial categories, namely agro-processing, chemical, light manufacturing and food processing. These four sectors employ a high percentage of the total labor force in the industrial sector. Concerning the geographical regions, our work covers Douala and Yaoundé respectively the economic and the capital cities where most of the firms are based. These cities are large, and each has a population of over one million inhabitants. They are characterized by a high degree of economic diversity. We have also covered other cities namely Bafoussam and Bamenda in the rural area of the country. The choice of procedure in selecting the sample from the eligible categories was governed by three main criteria. First the sample should be representative of the population of firms in the specified industrial categories. Second, the firms surveyed should account for a substantial share of national output in each of the industrial categories. Third, the sample should be sufficiently diverse in terms of firm size to enable empirical analysis on the effects of firm size. To account for these three considerations, employment shares were used as weights.

Given that bribery is illegal, firms were expected to be reluctant to admit that they pay bribes. In implementing the survey, the problems associated with collecting reliable data were kept constantly in mind, and every effort was made to assure respondents that their answers would be treated confidentially. For instance, the empirical strategy to collect information on bribe payments across firms was guided by the following components. First, questions on corruption are phrased indirectly to avoid implicating the respondent of wrongdoing. Second, corruption related questions are asked at the end of the interview, when the enumerators have presumably established credibility and trust. Third, multiple questions on corruption are asked in different sections of the questionnaire. Our effort to collect information was aided by the fact that the issue of corruption is desensitized in Cameroon, due to the Prime Minister's awareness-raising campaigns on the subject.

Estimation Techniques

In assessing the effects of corruption on growth, one main econometric issue is taken into consideration. It is the fact that both growth and corruption are likely to be jointly determined. This problem of endogeneity arises if firms specialize in rent-seeking or efficiency as a means of growth (Fisman and Svensson, 2002). It is possible that firms differently choose to devote resources to obtaining valuable licenses, preferential market access and so forth. Thus some firms choose to compete based on costly preferential bureaucratic access, while others focus on improving productivity and investing in new capital. Both strategies may lead to growth, and in equilibrium, it is not clear that either firm type will grow more rapidly (Fisman and Svensson, 2002). This effect tends to attenuate any measured effect between bribery and growth. In order to account for this problem in estimating the impact of bribe on firm performance, the panel simultaneous equation model in equation (4) is estimated.

Empirical Results

Before presenting the econometric results, the descriptive characteristics of the data are first explored. Table 3.1 presents the breakdown of firms by city, size

Table 3.1 Distribution of Sample Firms by City, Size and Sector (% of Firms in the Category)

	Agro-processing	*Chemical*	*Light Manufacturing*	*Food Processing*	*Total*
Bafoussam					
Small	15.4	30.8	30.8	23	13
Medium	11.2	66.6	22.2	–	9
Subtotal	13.6	45.5	27.3	13.6	22
Bamenda					
Small	20	5	45	30	20
Medium	–	–	100	–	2
Subtotal	18.2	4.5	50	27.3	22
Douala					
Small	12.3	24.5	32.6	30.6	49
Medium	27.8	55.5	11.2	5.5	18
Subtotal	16.5	32.8	26.8	23.9	67
Yaoundé					
Small	5.5	5.5	21	68	19
Medium	–	14	57	29	7
Subtotal	4	8	30	58	26
Total	13.9	25.5	31.4	29.2	*137*

Source: author's calculation based on data from the firm-level survey in Cameroon.

and sector. Both small and medium enterprises were sampled. Small enterprises comprised the clear majority.

The businesses covered were diverse in terms of size and main activities. We interviewed 19 agro-processing firms, 35 chemical enterprises, 43 light manufacturing businesses and 40 food processing firms. With regard to size, the sample covered 101 small- and 36 medium-sized enterprises.

The analyses in this chapter are based on a sample of 137 firms that responded to the core questionnaire.

Firms' Perception of the Environment Climate Constraints

Institutional Capacity for Public Service Delivery

As far as public service delivery is concerned, especially in the domains of public utilities, public transportation, security, education and health, 65 percent of all the firms interviewed think that the government is very inefficient, 19 percent says the public service delivery is inefficient and only 16 percent think that the government is somewhat efficient.

With respect to regulations and government officials' interpretation of such, 85.9 percent of the firms interviewed viewed them as not consistent and unpredictable with respect to their activities. This declaration consolidates the above information on government inefficiency in terms of public service delivery. This inconsistency and unpredictability causes increasing difficulties in the firms–government relationship. A total of 76.6 percent of the firms effectively declared that the difficulties in dealing with government officials have increased in the last five years, 7.4 percent think that these difficulties have remained the same, while only 9 percent thinks that they have decreased.

Corruption Practices in SMEs

SPREAD OF CORRUPTION

According to a number of theoretical views, the spread of corruption is determined by its practical efficiency. The faster and the easier it is to overcome administrative obstacles and restrictions by giving bribes, offering services and/or gifts, the more people will become involved in such activities as this saves time, nerves and resources. Two equally interested parties, therefore, carry out the act of corruption.

The survey data show that a large number of firms interact with various public services. Nearly 90 percent of the respondents declare that they have experienced, when interacting with public services, in one form or another, corruption pressure on the part of public-sector officials, when they tried to facilitate the process or to get things done, 7 percent multiply contacts or make friends and 3 percent of the firms do nothing.

PUBLIC SERVICE DELIVERY

The general observation is that firms always pay more than the official cost for public service delivery. For instance, only 40 percent of firms concerned with telephone connection problems pay 60,000 CFA francs which is the official cost of getting a telephone line. The remaining 60 percent of firms pay between 70,000 and 300,000 CFA francs depending on the urgency of the telephone line and the location of the firm. The same observation applies to other public services such as electricity connection, water connection and obtaining import licenses.

A large proportion of the firms interviewed are required to make extra, unofficial payments or bribes for most of the public services.

Several tentative conclusions may be drawn concerning the spread of corruption practices. After combining the three columns for frequently, mostly and always, paying lower taxes by reduction of the tax base comes first on the list. In nearly 93 percent of cases, firms interviewed reported that they have to give bribes. Payment of customs duties is amongst the services where corruption occurs most frequently. Seven out of every ten respondents (70.5 percent) think that in all cases when it comes to paying customs duties, business people have to make unofficial payments. Obtaining permits and licenses comes third. A total of 56 percent of the respondents reported that in all cases, when interacting with permits and licenses officers, firm's managers have to give bribes in order to get things done. Getting electricity installed and obtaining building permission come fourth and fifth respectively. A total of 47 percent of the firms think that giving bribes is compulsory to get electricity installed.

Table 3.2 Frequency of Bribes for Public Services by Firms

	Never	*Sometimes*	*Frequently*	*Mostly*	*Always*	*N.A.*
Obtaining building permission	–	12%	31%	–	10%	47%
Obtaining permits and licenses	10	–	40	8	8	34
Getting electricity installed	–	51	17	22	8	–
Getting water installed	–	80	20	–	–	–
Acquiring a telephone line	10	46	20	10	–	14
Obtaining credit	20	15	–	–	–	65
Payment of customs duties	–	9.5	13	15	42.5	20
Speeding up juridical process on the court	23	20	7	10	–	40
Registration of a company/enterprise	9	22.5	30	8.5	–	30
Paying lower taxes by reduction of the tax base	–	7	–	10	83	–
Winning public procurement contracts	17	23	–	–	–	60

Source: author's estimation based on data from the firm-level survey in Cameroon.

Table 3.3 Frequency of Exerting Corruption Pressure by Public Officials (%)

	Very Frequently	*Frequently*	*Rarely*	*N.A.*
Customs officers	40.4	17.7	–	41.9
Tax inspectors	78.5	14	–	7.5
The police	47.6	36.9	–	15.5
Lawyers/magistrates	13.6	30.9	7.7	47.8
Officials from ministries and other public bodies	21.5	50.4	13.75	14.35
Hygiene and epidemiological officers	43	32.2	11.8	13
Bank staff	–	4.5	27.3	68.2
Telecommunication officers	–	4.5	54.2	41.3
Electricity officers	22.7	32.8	38.4	6.1
Water officials	–	46.2	34.75	19.05

Source: author's estimation based on data from the firm-level survey in Cameroon.

At the bottom of this classification are public services such as obtaining credit, winning public procurement contracts.

After combining the percentages in the two first columns, tax inspectors, police officers, hygiene and epidemiological officers, officials from ministries and other public bodies, customs officers and electricity officers are reported to have exercised pressure on business people most often. Bank staff officers and telecommunication officers were assessed as being the least corrupt.

Generally the survey showed that after the unofficial payments or bribes are made, 75.6 percent of the promises are kept by government officials vis-à-vis the firms.

The Cost of Corruption

NON-MONETARY COST

The cost of corruption to firms here has been evaluated in terms of time wastage. All the firms interviewed, dealing with imports and exports of goods and raw materials, admitted that they spend one to two weeks in order successfully to send an outgoing container through a port. All of them equally admitted that they spend two to four weeks for the clearance of an incoming container. This time wastage can be shortened to a few days if informal payment is made.

Over the four years taken into account, informal payments have actually hindered the acquisition of new machines for 41.9 percent of the firms interviewed. They have equally hindered the hiring of new employees for 33.7 percent of firms, and other forms of investments for 24.4 percent of the firms interviewed.

MONETARY COST

The ability to cope quickly and easily with administrative and bureaucratic obstacles facing business is an important prerequisite for the efficient functioning of SMEs. Bureaucratic problems are a major factor in generating corruption and account for its spread.

Making unofficial payments leads to profit losses on account of unfulfilled transactions. These payments add to the cost of the deals and are extremely hazardous for small-budget enterprises that have to seek additional funding or restrict their business activity.

The survey provided bribery data for 128 firms out of 137 that reported positive bribe payments. What makes an impression is the relatively high share of respondents in Yaoundé (three out of five) who have assumed a rather passive attitude. They have preferred not to give an answer to the question about the size of the bribes. Two reasons may account for this fact. First, entrepreneurs consider the size of the bribe, regardless of its purpose, to be a company secret or established practice, which should not be made publicly known. On the other hand, second, bribe payments for the various types of activities may vary depending on the specific situation.

The figures in Table 3.4 show that bribe sizes in 2003 and 2004 are very high in Bafoussam and in Douala. For 2003 and 2004, 36.4 percent of the firms interviewed in Bafoussam declared that their annual average bribe sizes were between one and five million CFA francs. In Douala, 33.3 and 23.2 percent respectively of the firms interviewed declared that their annual average bribe sizes were in the same proportion. In Bamenda and Yaoundé, where the annual average of unofficial payments was low, 54.5 and 61.5 percent of firms respectively paid up to 500,000 CFA francs in 2003, while in 2004, 66.6 and 53.8 percent of firms in the respective cities had the same range of annual bribe sizes.

Strategies to Fight Informal Payments

The survey revealed a lack of efficient mechanisms to exercise public control over the activities of public institutions. These mechanisms are a prerequisite to restrict corruption in the public sector and to improve the quality of public services.

Table 3.4 Average Size of Bribes in CFA Franc (%)

2003	*Up to 500,000*	*501,000 to 1,000,000*	*1,000,000 to 5,000,000*
Bafoussam	45.4	18.2	36.4
Bamenda	54.5	13.6	22.7
Douala	33.4	33.3	33.3
Yaoundé	61.5	23	15.5
2004			
Bafoussam	41	22.6	36.4
Bamenda	66.6	4.5	18.2
Douala	33.4	43.4	23.2
Yaoundé	53.8	30.8	15.4

Source: author's estimation based on data from the firm-level survey in Cameroon.

A very small proportion (12.1 percent) of the firms' managers interviewed have made a complaint against low-quality public services, and a high percentage of firms' managers doubt the efficiency of making a complaint.

It comes from the analysis above that a high proportion of bribe victims have abandoned the idea of lodging a claim because they are convinced of being likely to lose more. The share of those who are afraid such a step might have adverse consequences on them is equally high.

In corruption related cases,

- A total of 48.5 percent of the firms think that the bribe demanders should bear the punishment; 16.5 percent think that both the bribe taker and the bribe giver should be punished the same way; 13 percent think that bribe takers should be punished more; 9.8 percent think that punishments should be case specific; while 4.5 percent think that bribe givers should be more punished than bribe demanders.
- A total of 49.5 percent of firms view anti-corruption campaigns as potentially fruitful and that it is possible to improve the quality of public services; 41.1 percent doubt the possibility of success; while 9.4 percent are quite convinced that informal payments cannot be contained in Cameroon.
- A total of 91.8 percent of firms are not confident as to the fruitful nature of the already launched anti-corruption campaign of March 1998; only 8.2 percent of these firms are confident of this.
- A total of 71.8 percent of firms would like to cooperate unconditionally with anti-corruption officials and institutions to denounce corrupt practices.
- A total of 19.9 percent would like to cooperate only if they are guaranteed anonymity of their personalities, whereas 8.3 percent of firms would not like to cooperate at all for other reasons.
- A total of 33 percent of firms think that the act (sanctioning of 70 civil servants involved in corrupt practices) of the new government of Cameroon in January 2005 is a sign of determination to eradicate informal payments or gifts in the Cameroonian society whereas 67 percent think the contrary.

In order to improve the quality of public services and reduce informal payments, 34 percent of firms think that corrupt persons should be punished and 30.8 percent suggest that the punishment process should start from the high ranked government authorities involved in corrupt practices; 17.5 percent think that unjustified assets should be seized; 11.8 percent of firm's managers think that the government should make corrupt cases and punishments public and introduce anti-corruption personnel in every public service; 9 percent of firms believe that emphasis should be put on moral probity in schools and universities; while only 7.25 percent think that the civil servant package of payments should be improved.

Econometric Analysis

This section explores the output of the econometric exercise with model (5). Table 3.5 gives the descriptive statistics of the variables included in the model.

Table 3.5 Descriptive Statistics

	Mean	*Median*	*Maximum*	*Minimum*	*Std Deviation*
Age	13.9333	11	40	1	8.89172
Bribe	1.2754	0.66	52	0	4.669116
E	31.06	17	450	4	52.08167
SL	111.958	54.737	1300	2.35	191.4899
Bribe/sale (%)	7.631	1.081	742.8571	0	64.2758
Taxes/sales (%)	0.2607	0.26	0.5	0	0.097313
Trade	0.437	0.0000	1.0000	0.0000	0.49786
Finance	0.4666	0.0000	1.0000	0.0000	0.500746
Public service	0.9111	1.0000	1.0000	0.0000	0.285643
Ownership	0.9259	1.0000	1.0000	0.0000	0.262867

Source: author's estimation based on data from the firm-level survey in Cameroon.

Table 3.6 reports the results of the two-stage least squares estimation of the model. The explanatory variables are grouped into the following categories: the characteristics of firms, the dynamics of firms and the location. The left hand block of columns shows the coefficients of variables considered in the bribe equation. The right-hand block reports the coefficients of variables in the firms' sale equation.

With 258 observations, a model Chi^2 of 245.55 for the firm performance equation, and 221.40 for the bribe equation suggest that the model has performed reliably. The tests for under-identification and weak instrumentation are both satisfactory. Following this, the impact of bribery on firms' performance is assessed, together with other control variables in the sales equation.

Corruption and Firm Performance

The assessment of the impact of corruption on firm performance reveals some noteworthy results. As expected, bribe payment impacts negatively on the rate of growth of outputs of firms. This variable is significant at 1 percent level. A 1 percent increase in bribe payment leads to 1.179 percent fall in firm performance. This result reflects the daily realities of SMEs. Unofficial payments lead to profit losses on account of unfulfilled transactions such as hiring new employees and acquiring new machines. This causes a loss of efficiency as firms are forced to incur a number of unproductive costs, thereby leading to a welfare-reducing allocation of resources. This situation is extremely costly for small-budget enterprises that have to restrict their business activity.

Firm age has a positive correlation with sales growth and is statistically significant at the 1 percent level. When a firm gets 1 percent older, its sales improve by 0.229 percent. This means that longer established firms master production costs and may also have better relationship with banks, suppliers and clients as well as government services.

Firms with frequent contact with public officials negatively impact on sales growth. This is probably because they are likely to pay more bribes. Being

Table 3.6 Panel Two-Stage Least Square Estimates for Bribe and Firm Performance

Bribe Equation				*Sales Equation*			
lbos	*Coef.*	*Std. Err.*	*z*	*Variable*	*Coef.*	*Std. Err.*	*z*
Constant	5.505	0.789	6.97	Constant	2.747***	0.538	5.10
Ln (SL)	–1.916***	0.146	–13.17	lbos	–1.179***	0.093	–12.72
Ln (E)	0.841***	0.136	6.20	Ln (E)	0.460***	0.098	4.67
Ln (age)	–0.173*	0.101	–1.72	Ln (age)	0.229**	0.116	1.98
Import/export	0.383*	0.196	1.95	Import/export	0.235*	0.140	1.68
Public service	1.147***	0.376	3.05	Public service	–0.625**	0.298	–2.09
Ownership	–0.780**	0.376	–2.08	Ownership	0.154	0.299	0.51
Finance	0.610***	0.213	2.87	Finance	0.198	0.167	1.19
Town dummies (reference town: Douala)							
Bafoussam	–0.207	0.299	–0.69	Bafoussam	–0.385*	0.239	–1.61
Bamenda	–1.840***	0.357	–5.15	Bamenda	–0.757***	0.254	–2.98
Yaoundé	–1.810***	0.342	–5.30	Yaoundé	–0.438***	0.293	–5.93
Obs		258		258			
Model Chi^2		221.40		245.55			
Under-identification (P-val)		0.008		0.001			
Weak instrument test (Wald F-stat)		6.15		5.48			

Source: author's estimation based on data from the firm-level survey in Cameroon.

Notes
***, **, * imply significance at 1, 5 and 10 percent levels respectively.

involved in international trade equally impacts positively on firm growth. This dummy variable is significant at the 10 percent level.

The location dummies are all significant (at the 1 percent level for Yaoundé and Bamenda, and 10 percent level for Bafoussam). Firms located in Bafoussam, Yaoundé and Bamenda experience 0.385, 0.438 and 0.757 less sales growth than those in Douala. This result reflects the reality in Cameroon as external economies of scale beyond the control of firms, such as transportation network, are achieved in large cities. This results in a subsequent decrease of cost for firms and in a boost of production. Furthermore a high percentage of firms owned by foreign investors are located in Douala and Yaoundé, and to some extent Bafoussam. Such firms often grow more quickly due to greater resources, access to markets and technical expertise, while they may be exempt from bureaucratic harassment as an inducement to locate their operations in Cameroon.

Conclusion

This chapter aimed at investigating the types of services in Cameroon for which SMEs pay bribes, the characteristics of these transactions and at estimating the impact of bribe payments on SME growth. In pursuing these objectives, 137 face-to-face interviews were successfully carried out with firm managers in four cities of the country.

The analysis of data from the survey has singled out some characteristics of the Cameroonian private sector and identified public services where informal payments occur very often. These unofficial payments are costly to firms in monetary terms and in terms of unfulfilled transactions. The analysis has come up with some suggestions, which may represent the way to go in the fight against corruption.

A model was also estimated in order to identify the impact of bribe payments on SME growth. The results show that informal payments impact negatively on the rate of growth of outputs of firms. This reflects the detrimental effects of unofficial payments on SMEs in that it leads to unfulfilled transactions such as hiring new employees and acquiring new machines. This causes a loss of efficiency as firms are forced to incur a number of unproductive costs, thereby leading to a welfare-reducing allocation of resources. This situation is extremely costly for small-budget enterprises that have to restrict their business activity. All these concur to loss of profit for the firms. Firm age has a positive correlation with sales growth. This confirms the fact that longer established firms master production costs and may also have better relationship with banks, suppliers and clients as well as government services. Firms located in large cities impact positively the growth of sales of SMEs. This result reflects the reality in Cameroon as external economies of scale such as transportation network are achieved in large cities. This leads to a subsequent decrease of cost for firms and in a boost of production. Furthermore a high percentage of firms owned by foreign investors are located in large cities. Such firms often grow more quickly due to greater resources, access to markets and technical expertise, while they may be exempt from bureaucratic harassment as an inducement to locate their operations in

Cameroon. Being involved in trade equally impacts positively on firm growth but multiplying contacts with public services offers opportunities for bribe extraction from firms and therefore slows down the growth of output.

In general, over the past decades, the development priorities of Cameroon have been centered on private sector development to build a strong market economy that gives a more dynamic role to entrepreneurs and their SMEs. However, institutional failures combined with very poor organization of civil society have made corruption endemic. This has been aggravated by the loss of purchasing power that followed the 1994 devaluation (between 1992 and 1995, the real wage of government workers dropped by 75–80 percent). To compensate, many civil servants top up their wages by taking bribes. This situation is seriously weakening the development of a strong private sector as the main pillar of the economy. However, since 2005, the government has nevertheless adopted a number of clear and dissuasive initiatives to deal with corruption. The National Anti-Corruption Commission (CONAC) was established by presidential decree in March 2006. Over the past five years, a growing number of well-known representatives of the political elite have been arrested on charges of corruption under an anti-corruption campaign called “Operation Sparrow Hawk”. These initiatives are expected to improve the business environment in Cameroon and to allow SMEs to post a sustainable growth.

Notes

1 In fact, four surveys carried out by “Transparency International”, a non-governmental organization (NGO), at the level of the heads of some local enterprises and expatriated businessmen situated Cameroon at 1.4 and 1.5 on the scale of the CPI with a standard deviation of 0.5 for 1998 and 1999 respectively (www.gwdg.de).
2 See Bardhan (1997), Tanzi (1998), and Wei (1997) for reviews of existing literature.
3 Small enterprises are enterprises that have 50 or fewer employees. Medium enterprises have between 51 and 500 employees.

Bibliography

Baltagi, Badi (2008). *Econometric Analysis of Panel Data*, 4th edition, Wiley.

Bardhan, Pranab (1997). “The economics of corruption in developing countries: a review of the issues”. *Journal of Economic Literature, 35 (3)*, 1320–1346.

Bliss, Christopher and R. Rafael Di Tella (1997). “Does competition kill corruption?” *Journal of Political Economy, 105 (5)*, 1001–1023.

Choi, Iay Pil and Marcel Thum (1999). “The economics of repeated extortion”. Columbia University Discussion Paper 9899-03.

Collier, Paul and Jan Willem Gunning (1999). “Why has Africa grown slowly?” *Journal of Economic Perspectives, XIII*, 3–22.

Fisman, Raymond and Jakob Svensson (2002). “Are corruption and taxation really harmful to growth? Firm level evidence”. Working Paper 2485, Development Research Group, World Bank.

Gbetnkom, Daniel (1999). “Libéralisation commerciale et pauvreté en Afrique sub-saharienne: L’examen du cas du Cameroun”. *Revue Africaine des Sciences Economiques et de Gestion, 1 (2)*, 107–135.

Goudie, A.W. and D. Stasavage (1997). "Corruption: the issues". Technical Paper No. 122, OECD Development Centre, January.

Gray, C.W. and Daniel Kaufmann (1998). "Corruption and development". *Finance and Development, 35 (1)*, 7–10.

Hellman, J.S., G. Jones, D. Kaufmann and M. Schankerman (2000). "Measuring governance, corruption and state capture: how forms and bureaucrats shape the business environment in transition". Policy Research Working Paper No. 2313, World Bank, Washington DC.

Johnson, Simon, Daniel Kaufmann and Pablo Zoido-Lobatón (1998). "Regulatory discretion and the unofficial economy". *American Economic Review, 88 (2)*, 387–392.

Kaufmann, D. and S.-J. Wei (1999). "Does 'grease money' speed up the wheels of commerce?" National Bureau of Economic Research Working Paper 7093, Cambridge, MA.

Klitgaard, Robert (1988). *Controlling Corruption*, University of California Press.

Klitgaard, Robert (1998). "International cooperation against corruption". *Finance and Development*, March, 3–6.

Leff, Nathaniel (1964). "Economic development through bureaucratic corruption". *American Behavioral Scientist, 8 (3)*, 8–14.

Liedholm, Carl and Donald C. Mead (1999). *Small Enterprise and Economic Development*, Routledge.

Lui, Francis T. (1985). "An equilibrium queuing model of bribery". *Journal of Political Economy, 93 (4)*, 760–781.

Mauro, Paulo (1995). "Corruption and growth". *Quarterly Journal of Economics, 110 (3)*, 681–712.

Mauro, Paulo (1997). "The effects of corruption on growth, investment, and government expenditure: a cross-country analysis", in *Corruption and the Global Economy*, ed. by Kimberly Ann Elliott, Institute for International Economics.

Mauro, Paulo (1998). "Corruption and the composition of government expenditure". *Journal of Public Economics, 69 (2)*, 263–279.

Mead, D. (1994). "The contribution of small enterprises to employment growth in Southern and Eastern Africa". *World Development, 22 (12)*, 1881–1894.

Murphy, K.M., A. Shleifer and R.W. Vishny (1991). "Why is rent-seeking so costly to growth?" *American Economic Review, 81 (2)*, 409–414.

Myrdal, Gunnar, (1968). *Asian Drama Vol. II*, Random House.

Nelson, F.D. and L. Olson (1978). "Specification and estimation of a simultaneous equation model with limited dependent variables". *International Economic Review, 19*, 695–710.

Persson, T. and G. Tabellini, eds. (1994) "Growth distribution and politics", in *Monetary and Fiscal Policy, Vol. 2 Politics*, MIT Press.

Ravallion, M. (1997). "Can high-inequality developing countries escape absolute poverty? *Economics Letters, 56 (2)*, 51–57.

Ravallion, M. (2001). "Growth, inequality and poverty: looking beyond averages". Development Research Group, World Bank, Washington DC, June.

Ravallion, M. and S. Chen (1997). "What can new survey data tell us about recent changes in distribution and poverty?" *World Bank Economic Review, 11 (2)*, 357–382.

Rose-Ackerman, Susan (1975). "The economics of corruption". *Journal of Public Economics, IV*, 187–203.

Rose-Ackerman, Susan (1978). *Corruption: A Study in Political Economy*. Academic Press.

Schleifer, Andrei and Robert W. Vishny (1993). "Corruption". *Quarterly Journal of Economics, 108 (3)*, 599–617.

Svensson, Jakob (2000). "The cost of doing business: Ugandan firms' experiences with corruption". Africa Region Working Paper Series No. 6, World Bank, October.

Svensson, Jakob (2003). "Who must pay bribes and how much? Evidence from a cross-section of firms". *Quarterly Journal of Economics, 118 (1)*, 207–230.

Tanzi, V. (1995). "Corruption: arm's-length relationships and markets", in *Economics of Organized Crime*, ed. by Gianluca Fiorentini and Sam Peltzman, Cambridge University Press.

Tanzi, V. (1998). "Corruption around the world: causes, consequences, scope, and cures". IMF Working Paper, May, pp. 1–39.

Tanzi, V. and H. Davoodi (1997). "Corruption, public investment, and growth". IMF Working Paper 97/139, Washington DC.

Thomas, Vinod, Mansoor Dailami, Ashok Dhareshwar, Daniel Kaufmann, Nalin Kishor, Ramón López and Yan Wang (2000). *The Quality of Growth.* Washington, DC: World Bank; New York: Oxford University Press.

Tinbergen, J. (1975). *Income Distribution: Analysis and Policies*, North-Holland Publishing Company.

UNECA (2011). "Governing development in Africa: the role of the state in economic transformation". Economic Report on Africa, March.

Wei, S. (1997). "How taxing is corruption on international investors". Working Paper No. 6030, NBER, Cambridge.

World Bank (1997). *World Development Report 1997*, Oxford University Press.

4 Entrepreneurship and Income Level in Developing Countries

Janvier D. Nkurunziza[1]

Introduction

Several studies have analysed different aspects of entrepreneurship, defined as the level of self-employment. They include van Stel *et al.* (2005) who analyse the effect of entrepreneurship on economic growth and find that the former's influence on the latter depends on the level of income. Freytag and Thurik (2007) find that non-economic factors such as culture are important determinants of entrepreneurship. Robson (2007) studies the effect of social protection and political culture on entrepreneurship and finds that political culture has a strong incidence on entrepreneurship: the rate of entrepreneurship tends to be low in countries with a history of communist rule. Ilmakunnas and Kanniainen (2001) highlight the importance of risk and labour insurance on entrepreneurship in OECD countries. Klapper *et al.* (2006) find that entry regulations act as a barrier to entrepreneurship while Klapper and Love (2010) find that the 2008 financial crisis had an important negative impact on entrepreneurship.

This chapter analyses the relationship between income per capita and entrepreneurship, defined here as the number of limited liability firms per 1,000 active persons, registered in a country in one year (Ayyagari *et al.*, 2011).[2] Entrepreneurs in high-income countries are generally considered as people who primarily engage in business as a result of a deliberate personal choice to pursue a perceived business opportunity, be in control of one's life, achieve a feeling of self-esteem or have more independence (Roberts and Robinson, 2010; Hessels *et al.*, 2008). They are called 'opportunity entrepreneurs'. Influential models of occupational choice (e.g. Banerjee and Newman, 1993) consider these individuals as belonging to the high end of the income distribution – given that their activities often require collateral – in opposition to wage earners who are viewed as belonging to the lower end of the income distribution.

This description of entrepreneurship does not fully capture the reality of many low-income countries where two types of entrepreneurship coexist. While people with high incomes may become opportunity entrepreneurs, those with low incomes might be forced to embrace entrepreneurship out of necessity or survival. These 'necessity entrepreneurs' (Acs, 2007; van Stel *et al.*, 2005) are more common in economies where employment opportunities are limited and social safety nets catering for the basic needs of people on very low incomes are weak or lacking. These entrepreneurs are 'reluctant entrepreneurs' (Charman and Petersen, 2009) given that they turn to business as a result of their inability to find paid employment.[3] The implication is that one would expect to find a large number of 'necessity entrepreneurs' in poor countries and more 'opportunity entrepreneurs' in rich countries illustrating the core of Maslow's Hierarchy of Needs Theory.[4] Whereas the main objective of necessity entrepreneurs is to address basic needs at the bottom of Maslow's Pyramid, opportunity entrepreneurs engage in business to satisfy needs at the top of the pyramid. This process suggests a convex relationship between entrepreneurship and income with high levels of entrepreneurship at both low- and high-income levels.

Understanding the relationship between income per capita and entrepreneurship is relevant for industrial policy. In Africa, for example, it is useful to explore how the steady increase in income per capita observed over the last ten years, if it persists, will likely change the dynamic in the private sector with implications for employment creation.[5] Such analysis could help in crafting development policies that seek to transform developing economies into 'entrepreneurial economies'.

So far, the empirical research on the relationship between income level and entrepreneurship has largely been carried out on OECD economies with inconclusive results.[6] Most studies are historical and country based. They explore the evolution of entrepreneurship over a long period of time from as far back as the year 1800. They find some evidence of a U-shape relationship implying a decline followed by a recovery in entrepreneurship, over time. For example, various sources show a long-term decline of entrepreneurship in France, Sweden, USA, Germany, the Netherlands and the UK since the nineteenth century followed by a revival starting from the early 1970s. The analysis of 23 OECD countries covering the period 1972–2007 reveals that the number of business owners increased by 1.38 per cent per year against an increase of 1.15 per cent for the total labour force. This translated in the creation of 18.5 million owner-managed firms over the 35-year period. Other studies find an L-shape relationship suggesting a decline without recovery of entrepreneurship, over time, within the OECD group of countries (Wennekers *et al*., 2010; Carree *et al*., 2002, 2007).

This chapter differs from previous studies on entrepreneurship in several respects. First, it adopts a different approach as it explores the relationship between entrepreneurship and income per capita using a large group of African and other countries at different levels of income over the relatively short period 2004–2009. Second, the chapter uses a different definition of entrepreneurship that allows capturing a large cross-section of countries. The availability of data on the creation of limited liability firms made possible the inclusion in the sample of a number of African countries that are not covered by the Global Entrepreneurship Monitor (GEM) database which has provided the data used in most empirical analyses of the subject. Third, this chapter adopts a quantitative approach that has not been pursued in the existing studies we are aware of.[7] Entrepreneurship is modelled both as a static process using random effects models and as a dynamic phenomenon using the Generalized Method of Moments (GMM) approach. This appears to be a novelty relative to past studies.

This chapter suggests that the results based on OLS estimation could be misleading even though a number of previous studies have relied on this estimation method. Fourth, if a convex relationship is established between income per capita and entrepreneurship, its interpretation differs from the results based on historical analyses.

Empirical results suggest that the relationship between entrepreneurship and income per capita is U-shaped. The analysis identifies an income threshold above which income per capita is associated with increasing entrepreneurship. This result is interpreted in the light of Maslow's Hierarchy of Needs Theory. *Ceteris paribus*, at low levels of income per capita, entrepreneurship may be guided by survival rather than opportunity motives. As income per capita rises up to the threshold the need to engage in necessity entrepreneurship declines. In this income bracket, paid employment is preferred to entrepreneurship as the former offers better risk-adjusted regular income than survival entrepreneurship. Beyond the threshold income, many people who would otherwise be in paid employment choose to become more creative, independent and take more risk by opting for entrepreneurship.

The rest of the chapter is organized as follows. The second section briefly discusses the concept of entrepreneurship in developed and developing country contexts. The third section discusses the relationship between income level and entrepreneurship, as well as other determinants of entrepreneurship such as economic structure and barriers to firm entry. The fourth section establishes a statistical relationship between entrepreneurship and its determinants. The final section concludes with some policy suggestions.

Entrepreneurship in Developed and Developing Countries

This section discusses in some detail the concept of entrepreneurship. The specific case of entrepreneurship in Africa is presented in the second part of the section.

Entrepreneurship in Developed Countries

Most analyses of entrepreneurship, which are dominated by studies on developed countries, have defined entrepreneurship as the rate of self-employment relative to total employment.[8] Using data from GEM, low-income countries are found to have low ratios of entrepreneurship (less than two in Brazil, Uganda, South Africa, Croatia and Poland) while high-income countries have high ratios (ten or more in Sweden, Finland, Denmark, Belgium and Iceland).[9] Risk tolerance is identified as one of the key determinants of the decision to become an entrepreneur in developed economies (Ahn, 2010). It is also suggested that many opportunity entrepreneurs capitalize on ideas and practices they learned through their previous employment to start their own businesses (Braguinsky *et al.*, 2009).

Using self-employment as a measure of entrepreneurship has largely been motivated by the re-emergence of self-employment in developed countries starting from the 1970s, a trend that contradicted previous predictions that small businesses were headed for disappearance in favour of large corporations (Lucas, 1978). The revival of self-employment in the developed world is thought to have resulted from factors including the rapidly growing services sector which has lower entry barriers and requires a smaller scale than agriculture and manufacturing; declining transactions costs; a trend towards more autonomy and self-realization as predicted by Maslow's theory; growth in new technologies that do not require large scale; as well as the information and communication technology (ICT) revolution which has enabled small firms to realize scale economies in the context of loosely organized networks (Wennekers *et al.*, 2005, 2010).

Highlighting the importance they attach to entrepreneurship, many developed countries have established initiatives aimed at nurturing a culture of entrepreneurship. Some countries have integrated entrepreneurship into their education curricula while others have put in place legislation to encourage risk-taking. Since 2004, through its Enterprise Week, the United Kingdom has been holding national campaigns to encourage entrepreneurship. In the same light, Global Entrepreneurship Week is a worldwide celebration and promotion of youth entrepreneurship, which started in 2008. Also, the Aldridge Foundation is a charity that sponsors academies specializing in entrepreneurship with a focus on young people.[10]

Entrepreneurship in Africa

In Africa, the discourse on entrepreneurship is relatively new. For example, it is only in the 1980s that development policy shifted from the 'managed' economy paradigm that was adopted after independences in the 1960s to the 'entrepreneurial' economy (Audretch and Thurik, 2001). As Africa liberalized its economies in the 1980s, the state structures that had constituted a large share of African countries' productive capacity were dismantled (Kiggundu, 1997).[11] Entrepreneurs were expected to seize the opportunity created by the withdrawal of the state in the economy and become key development actors. However, this did not occur mainly because the economic reforms put too much emphasis on macroeconomic stability and economic liberalization with little attention paid to the development of entrepreneurship.

There is no clear evidence that the shrinking of the public sector led to a systematic increase in private sector formal employment as the proponents of economic reforms had expected. On the contrary, some countries experienced a decline in both private and public sector employment during the structural adjustment period. In Kenya, the share of public sector employment declined from 36 per cent of total employment in 1990 to 11.4 per cent in 2000. Over the same period, the share of private sector employment shrank by 50 per cent from 36.5 to 17 per cent of total employment (UNECA, 2005). Indeed, the privatization of loss-making state firms and the retrenchment of the civil service destroyed a substantial number of public jobs in the 1990s (Nkurunziza, 2010). A number of those who lost their jobs in the formal sector might have ended up in the informal sector as 'survival' entrepreneurs. As a result, many countries are still at an early stage of entrepreneurship development so they are unable to use entrepreneurship as an engine of economic development as observed in some previously poor regions of the United States (Stephens and Partridge, 2011).

Entrepreneurs not only create opportunities for themselves but also for society at large (Makura, 2008). Developing countries' entrepreneurs, particularly at the grassroots level, contribute to social development, training and skills development, technology diffusion, gender equity, environmental protection and energy efficiency, among other areas. They can also be a force for positive change by influencing national policy (SEED Initiative, 2010). There is also evidence that entrepreneurship might increase household income while reducing income inequality, particularly in rural areas (Kimhi, 2009). Moreover, entrepreneurs not only create new ideas, products or markets but also jobs for themselves and others. Employment creation is one of the most important externalities of entrepreneurship. A study of the US economy for example found that it is the young firms that create more jobs than old ones (Haltiwanger *et al*., 2009). A more general study of the contribution of firms of different sizes and ages to employment creation in 99 countries also finds that young firms have higher job creation rates than large and old firms and higher productivity growth than small and old firms (Ayyagari *et al*., 2011).

Although the boundaries separating 'survivalists' from opportunity entrepreneurs are sometimes blurred, the former are generally unsophisticated, small and rely on family labour. Outside agriculture, they mostly operate in the informal sector particularly in trading thanks to its low cost of entry. They dominate Africa's business landscape. Necessity entrepreneurs create limited, vulnerable and low-paying jobs even though they can evolve into opportunity entrepreneurs heading conglomerates (Makura, 2008). In contrast, opportunity entrepreneurs create more jobs even within the informal sector. In South Africa's informal economy, for example, a survey found that survivalist entrepreneurs create 0.3 jobs, excluding their own, on average while opportunity entrepreneurs create 2.2 jobs, in addition to their own, on average (Charman and Petersen, 2009). Africa's poor job creation record could be partly due to the failure of the continent to mobilize the right type of entrepreneurship that could create decent jobs in large numbers.

Data from the World Bank (2011b) show that on average, the number of limited liability firms created in Africa is less than one-fifth of the average number in other regions. Even the few firms entering the business sector are smaller than those created elsewhere. Each new firm entering the formal private sector in Africa generates 24.4 permanent jobs on average, which is less than half of the jobs created by firms in other regions. Africa's failure to create more and larger firms as in other regions reduces the chances of using entrepreneurship to expand employment opportunities. Moreover, more unskilled workers are employed in Africa than elsewhere and the continent's firm managers are relatively less experienced than in other regions. This could explain why Africa specializes in the production of low-skill goods as suggested by the lower quality of their exports relative to other regions (Hausmann *et al*., 2007). Moreover, the prevalence of unskilled workers limits entrepreneurship development given that many entrepreneurs use the practical skills they have acquired on the job to launch their own businesses (Robson, 2007).

Income Level, Barriers to Entry and Entrepreneurship

Although some authors have proposed an eclectic theory of entrepreneurship (Verheul *et al.*, 2003) there is no unified model of entrepreneurship and it is impossible to discuss in detail all the potential determinants of entrepreneurship in one study. A review of the literature on entrepreneurship shows that it depends on a large number of economic and non-economic factors linked with demand and supply factors. These include technological development, industrial structure, population dynamics, age structure of the population, women's participation in the labour force, unemployment, social protection, immigration, labour market regulations, the business environment, macroeconomic policy, income level, education, culture and even subjective perceptual variables such as self-confidence (Wennekers, 2006; Wennekers *et al.* 2010; Freytag and Thurik, 2007; Robson, 2007; Verheul *et al.*, 2003; Arenius and Minniti, 2005).

This study explores the relationship between income per capita and entrepreneurship controlling for the effect of barriers to entry and economic structure. Entrepreneurship is understood as 'firm entry'; entrepreneurship in existing firms is not analysed. For example, this study does not look into entrepreneurship and access to credit given that this issue is more relevant for already existing firms.[12] Some of the demographic aspects of entrepreneurship are captured by the definition used in this study as it is weighted by the number of active people. Regional and year dummy variables are also important controls of regional and time variations in entrepreneurship that are not captured by the other variables.

Economic Structure, Income Level and Entrepreneurship

The process of economic development or achieving higher income level is generally correlated with economic transformation from primary-based economies to manufacturing and from manufacturing to the services economy (Chenery and Syrquin, 1989). In turn, the structure of an economy determines how easy it is to start a new business. For example, although there is talent and entrepreneurship in Africa's agricultural sector (SEED Initiative, 2010), it is arguably easier to start a new business in the services sector. Entry costs and the scale required to be successful might not be as high as in the industrial or agricultural sector where large size is an important determinant of efficiency. As a result, the larger is the share of the services sector to GDP in an economy, the higher the level of entrepreneurship. This appears to be one of the reasons why there was a reversal in the trend of entrepreneurship in developed economies since the 1970s. Conversely, the share of the agricultural sector to GDP is expected to have a negative relationship with entrepreneurship.

It is relevant to note that the 'opportunity entrepreneurs' and 'necessity entrepreneurs' start their businesses from two different income levels. Necessity entrepreneurs are expected to have relatively low incomes as they are drawn into business by necessity. Therefore, their firms are small and many operate in the informal sector particularly in countries where the cost associated with starting a business in the formal sector is high.[13] In contrast, even though opportunity entrepreneurs need not be rich, they decide to start a business to pursue an opportunity or become more independent when they have a relatively high level of income to meet the cost of basic needs as well as the cost associated with starting the business (Wennekers *et al.*, 2010). The need to have a high income to start a business in the formal sector is backed by microeconomic empirical evidence which shows that most entrepreneurs start businesses with their own funds, sometimes with the help of family and friends. Start-up conditions in terms of the amount of financial resources available to start a business have a long-term effect on the evolution of enterprises. Firms starting up with a less binding budget constraint, for example the establishment of new branches of existing businesses, usually have larger start-up size and grow faster than budget-constrained start-ups (Nkurunziza, 2010).

We hypothesize that in the low end of the income distribution, the number of entrepreneurs is high as people start small businesses to earn a survival income.[14] This is particularly the case where employment opportunities are limited and social protection weak or inexistent. In this light, the number of people forced to start small businesses declines as income increases and social protection improves, implying that the rate of entrepreneurship declines with income level up to the point where incomes are high enough that people do not need to engage in survival entrepreneurship. Whether or not the rate of entrepreneurship increases in the high end of income distribution is an empirical question. In other words, is the relationship between entrepreneurship and the level of income U-shaped or L-shaped? Figure 4.1 suggests a U-shaped curve but it needs to be confirmed through statistical testing.

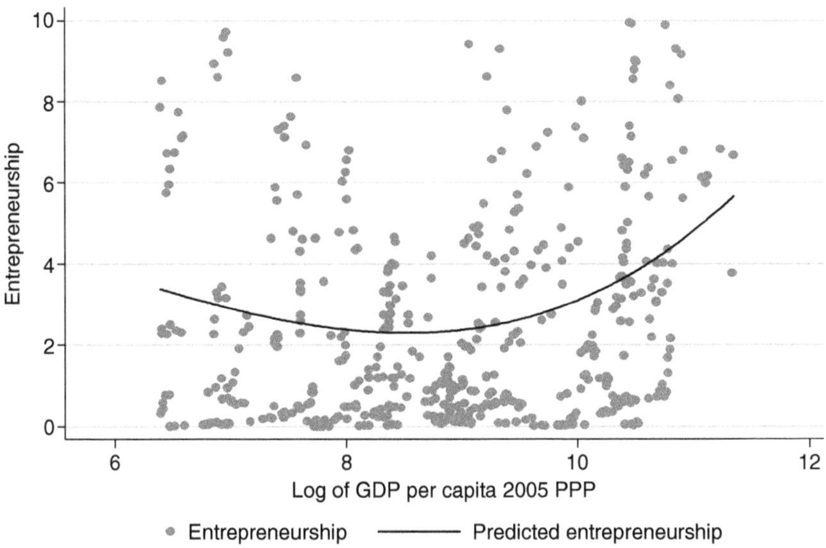

Figure 4.1 Predicted Relationship Between Entrepreneurship and Income Per Capita

We define four income groups which more or less correspond with those used by the World Bank.[15] The first group represents low-income countries which are poor, the second represents lower middle-income countries, the third is the group of upper middle-income countries, while the fourth group captures high-income countries. As hypothesized, entrepreneurship is higher in very poor and in rich economies than in lower and upper middle-income countries, suggesting a U-shaped relationship between entrepreneurship and GDP per capita. The statistical analysis of this relationship is the subject of the fourth section of this chapter, 'Econometric analysis'.

Barriers to Entrepreneurship

Starting a business implies different types of entry costs: financial, time-related and procedural. The cheaper, faster and simpler it is to register a business, the more entrepreneurs would be willing to register their businesses in the formal sector.[16] Many developing countries, particularly in Africa, still maintain important barriers to firm entry which handicap the development of entrepreneurship. Three such barriers are briefly discussed: the number of procedures required to start a new business, the time it takes to comply with the administrative requirements in order to start a new business and the cost of registering a new business.[17]

Procedures Required for Starting a Business

Registering a business is associated with some administrative requirements. When limited in number and necessary, these requirements are important as they help to organize the business sector and to protect consumers and other stakeholders. However, when their number is unnecessarily high, they become bureaucratic hurdles and act as a barrier to entry. Too many procedural requirements to register a business are expected to be negatively related to entrepreneurship.

There is a diversity of situations with countries like Canada and New Zealand where registering a business requires just one procedure, to Afghanistan where the same process requires 28 procedures. *Ceteris paribus*, Canada and New Zealand should experience more business registrations than Afghanistan. In Africa in 2011, Equatorial Guinea and Uganda had the highest number of requirements, 20 and 18, respectively. At the other extreme, Madagascar and Rwanda had only two procedures each, a remarkable improvement from 15 and nine procedures just seven years earlier. These contrasting examples show that it is possible to reduce significantly these entry barriers in a relatively short time period.

Time to Register a Business

Another way of estimating the ease with which businesses are registered in a country is the number of days it takes to comply with registration procedures. This measure is highly correlated with the number of procedures required to register a business with a correlation coefficient of 0.70. More procedures imply longer times and longer times discourage entrepreneurs to comply with registration procedures, prompting many to operate in the informal sector.

The times to register a business also differ across countries. In Africa, the shortest time to register a business in 2011 was three days in Rwanda followed by six days in Mauritius. The longest time was 216 days in Guinea Bissau. Rwanda's performance is the result of years of efforts undertaken to improve the country's business environment. As recently as 2008, the time it took to register a business in Rwanda was 16 days illustrating once more that improvements to the business environment can be made in a short time period.

Cost of Business Registration

In addition to the number of bureaucratic procedures and the time it takes to register a business, there are also financial costs involved. Unlike the first two barriers to entry discussed above which are highly correlated, the financial cost is not as highly correlated with the first two measures. A country could impose a high cost for business registration even when there are few procedures to comply with or even when registration is done relatively fast once the cost has been paid. The coefficient of correlation is 0.54 with respect to the number of procedures and 0.55 with the time to register.

The cost of registering a firm in a country is measured in percentage of per capita income of the country. In 2011, the cost was 2.2 per cent of per capita income in Botswana and 3.8 per cent of per capita income in Mauritius. The highest cost to register a business is in the Democratic Republic of Congo where entrepreneurs are required to pay 735 per cent of per capita income. Similar to the other two measures discussed above, most countries have been reducing the cost to register a business. Across the board, the costs in 2011 are much lower than their level five years ago. Progress has been so impressive in some regions that the International Finance Corporation and the World Bank, the two institutions compiling information on the ease of doing business across the world, declared on 17 August 2011 that East Africa could match Japan in the ease of doing business if each of the five countries forming the East African Community adopted the best of the community's regulations and procedures.[18]

Econometric Analysis

This section first discusses the descriptive statistics of the variables used in the econometric model then presents the modelling strategy and the empirical results.

Descriptive Data

The data are divided into three groups (see Table 4.1). The global sample shows information on all countries included in the dataset. The second and third groups represent the African and non-African sub-samples in order to shed some light on possible differences between entrepreneurship in Africa and non-Africa regions. The data covers the period from 2004 to 2009 but the panel is unbalanced due to missing observations.

Table 4.1 Descriptive Statistics, 2004–2009

Variables	*Full Sample*			*Africa*			*Elsewhere*		
	Mean	*Median*	*Obs.*	*Mean*	*Median*	*Obs.*	*Mean*	*Median*	*Obs.*
Entrepreneurship	3.32	1.73	588	1.11	0.38	89	3.72	2.22	499
Log procedures to register	2.11	2.20	1047	2.29	2.30	272	2.04	2.08	775
Log time to register	3.36	3.43	1047	3.73	3.66	272	3.22	3.29	775
Log cost to register	3.06	3.06	1040	4.51	4.68	272	2.54	2.58	768
Log GDP per capita	8.66	8.75	1074	8.16	8.14	257	8.82	8.89	817
Square log GDP per cap	76.75	76.49	1074	68.15	66.29	257	79.45	79.01	817
Log agriculture value-added to GDP	2.12	2.27	955	2.81	3.15	242	1.89	2.01	713
Log services value-added to GDP	3.97	4.06	965	3.73	3.84	237	4.05	4.10	728

Source: based on World Bank (2011a).

The descriptive statistics in Table 4.1 show that the African sub-sample is limited as it relates to only 16 countries and 89 observations available for the entrepreneurship variable.[19] Despite the relatively limited data, it is possible to gain some interesting insights into the economic determinants of entrepreneurship.

The data in Table 4.1 show that the potential determinants of entrepreneurship in Africa are more constraining than in other regions, on average. Africa's median rate of entrepreneurship is almost one-sixth of its value in other regions. The income variable is the Gross Domestic Product (GDP) per capita in 2005 Purchasing Power Parities (PPP). It is also lower in Africa although the difference is not as large as for entrepreneurship. The data also show that on average it is costlier to register a business in Africa than elsewhere, the relative cost in Africa being almost twice the relative cost in other regions. The size of agriculture in GDP is also about 50 per cent higher in Africa than elsewhere.

It is relevant to note that most of the variables display limited variation. This is the case with the log of the number of procedures required to create a business. With a mean of 2.11 and a standard deviation of 0.44, the coefficient of variation is close to zero. The same obtains for other variables including the following: log time to register, log GDP per capita and log services value-added. Part of this is due to in-country low variation. For example, GDP composition does not change substantially from one year to the next. Similarly, the business climate does not vary substantially across countries over one-year periods. This has implications for econometric modelling.

Modelling Strategy and Empirical Results

Entrepreneurship has traditionally been modelled using an ILS econometric approach (e.g. Carree *et al.*, 2007; Robson, 2007; Parker and Robson, 2004; Noorderhaven *et al.*, 2004; Blanchflower and Oswald, 1998). However, given its econometric limitations, including its failure to account for heterogeneity, the OLS model produces results that could be misleading. Moreover, as some of the variables in the equation have very low within-country variation (e.g. barriers to entry variables) the random effects estimator is used to – at least partially – account for heterogeneity. The interest of the random effects estimator is that it is not based on first-differences but is quasi-time demeaning. It removes a fraction of the time average of each variable rather than the full time average as is the case with fixed effects models (Wooldridge, 2002).

Entrepreneurship is regressed on five variables: a variable indicating the difficulty of registering a business which is expected to have a negative sign, the log of GDP per capita (negative sign), the square of the log of GDP per capita (positive sign) and two variables capturing the structure of the economy, namely the log of the share of agriculture value-added in GDP (negative sign) and the log of the share of the services sector value-added in GDP (positive sign). Regional and year dummy variables are included to control for regional and year effects that are not captured by the other variables. The omitted categories are Europe and 2004 for regional and year dummies, respectively.

In order to establish that random effects estimation is indeed valid, Hausman (1978) test is used to compare the random effects and fixed effects estimators. If the Hausman test validates the use of the random effects estimation, the model is re-estimated with robust standard errors to control for heteroscedasticity. The results are reported in Table 4.2.[20]

There are three models each using a different measure of the difficulty of starting a business. According to the result of the Hausman (1978) test, we cannot reject the null hypothesis that the random effects estimator is more efficient than the fixed effects estimator for models 1 and 2 (but this is not the case with Model 3), implying that the random effects model is more appropriate in the estimation of the determinants of entrepreneurship than the fixed effects model. Given that Model 1 has a better fit than Model 2, the discussion below is based on Model 1 where the difficulty of registering a business is measured by the log of the number of procedures required.

All the variables of interest have the expected signs. The results confirm the hypothesis of a U-shaped relationship between entrepreneurship and GDP per capita. This result lends support to the idea that at low levels of income, countries display high levels of entrepreneurship but not necessarily the preferred type of entrepreneurship. The result could be interpreted as meaning that people start small businesses for lack of better alternatives, particularly limited opportunities in formal sector employment. In developing countries where productive employment is limited and unemployment benefits inexistent, family heads or adult children are forced to start small businesses to earn some income to provide for their families. In countries where real wages and social protection are relatively high, employment is preferred to entrepreneurship as it offers a stable flow of income relative to income from business which is uncertain. Indeed, some studies have found a robust negative relationship between employment benefits and entrepreneurship (Robson, 2007). Over some income threshold, as people's basic needs are satisfied, entrepreneurship becomes more attractive than paid employment. People are more willing to take more risk in order to be more autonomous and achieve self-fulfilment (Wennekers *et al.*, 2010), conforming to Maslow's Hierarchy of Needs Theory.

The results of the econometric analysis point to two conclusions. Overall, increasing GDP per capita by 10 per cent would reduce entrepreneurship by 20 per cent, which suggests that, globally, the negative effect of income per capita on entrepreneurship dominates the positive effect. In other words, increasing income reduces the number of 'survivalist' entrepreneurs while eventually increasing the number of opportunity entrepreneurs.[21] The second conclusion is that the turning point where increases in income start having a positive effect on entrepreneurship seems to be around an income level of $7,293. This falls within the World Bank's upper middle-income group.

Entrepreneurship is also handicapped by unnecessary measures that prevent potential entrepreneurs from registering their businesses. The higher the number of procedures to register a business, the lower the number of firms registered, which limits entrepreneurship and hence its positive effect on employment creation. The estimate in Model 1 shows that reducing by 10 per cent the number of

Table 4.2 Empirical Results of the Random Effects Estimation

	Model 1	*Model 2*	*Model 3*
Log GDP per capita	–3.38*	–3.15	–3.60*
	(1.89)	(2.02)	(1.98)
Square of log GDP per capita	0.19*	0.18	0.20*
	(0.11)	(0.11)	(0.11)
Log agriculture value-added/GDP	–0.67***	–0.69***	–0.58***
	(0.21)	(0.21)	(0.22)
Log services value-added/GDP	0.28	0.24	0.43
	(0.56)	(0.63)	(0.59)
Log number of procedures	–0.82***	–	–
	(0.17)		
Log time to register a business	–	–0.31***	–
		(0.10)	
Log cost to register a business	–	–	–0.28***
			(0.10)
Dummy variables			
Year 2005	0.09*	0.06	0.07
	(0.05)	(0.05)	(0.05)
Year 2006	0.32***	0.27***	0.26***
	(0.09)	(0.09)	(0.09)
Year 2007	0.44***	0.38***	0.38***
	(0.11)	(0.11)	(0.11)
Year 2008	0.24**	0.21**	0.21*
	(0.11)	(0.11)	(0.11)
Year 2009	–0.26*	–0.26*	–0.23*
	(0.15)	(0.15)	(0.13)
Africa	–0.61	–0.59	–0.38
	(0.43)	(0.42)	(0.43)
East Asia	–0.51	–0.45	–0.31
	(0.67)	(0.71)	(0.75)
South Asia	–1.18	–1.12	–1.06
	(0.76)	(0.76)	(0.82)
America	0.18	0.17	0.27
	(0.71)	(0.72)	(0.72)
Middle East	–1.82***	–2.09***	–1.75***
	(0.44)	(0.46)	(0.45)
Constant	19.58***	18.12***	19.49*
	(8.32)	(8.74)	(11.68)
R-squared (overall)	0.41	0.38	0.40
Observations	448	448	442
Hausman test (Prob.>Chi^2)	0.11	0.11	0.00

Notes

Standard errors in parentheses are White (1980) heteroscedasticity-consistent.

***, ** and * correspond to 1, 5 and 10 per cent significance level, respectively. The reference groups are Europe for region and 2004 for year dummies.

procedures needed to register a business would globally increase entrepreneurship by 2.5 to 4.7 per cent.[22] The effect could be even three times stronger if we consider the African sub-sample. Assuming that the elasticity derived from Table 4.2 is stable across regions, reducing the number of registration procedures in Africa by 10 per cent would increase entrepreneurship by 7.4 per cent. For example, if Uganda could reduce its procedures from 18 to 16, which would be about 10 per cent, it would increase the number of firm registrations by 7.4 per cent or 825 additional limited liability firms, using the data for 2009. Considering the average number of permanent employees per firm, these results suggest that between 17,330 and 28,884 additional jobs could be created as a result.[23]

This simple simulation illustrates that by reducing the bureaucratic hurdles to registering a business, some countries can substantially increase their employment. This could be one of the first policies countries adopt in their drive to create more decent jobs. Many of the measures to simplify business registration are administrative by nature so they are relatively easy to implement as they do not require large financial and human resources. This is relatively easy in countries which still have a high number of procedures, including Uganda, Kenya and Malawi. Reducing the number of procedures by 10 per cent would imply an absolute reduction of one to two procedures for those countries.

Rwanda, for example, made remarkable progress in terms of simplifying its business registration procedure – in addition to other measures – in just one year. Between 2009 and 2010, the number of procedures to start a business was reduced from eight to two, the number of days from 14 to three and the cost from 108.9 per cent of GDP per capita to 10.1 per cent of GDP per capita.[24] As a result, the country was hailed as the best reformer in 2010. Largely thanks to these efforts, Rwanda mobilized $414 million in new investments that created about 12,736 jobs (The Whitaker Group, 2011). Data for 2008 and 2009 shows that the number of firms registered in 2009 was almost three times that of 2008 as a result of these reforms.

Table 4.2 also confirms that a country's economic structure has an important impact on its capacity to generate entrepreneurs. As expected, a large share of agriculture in an economy results in smaller rates of entrepreneurship. In the model above, the negative association between agriculture activity and entrepreneurship and its strong statistical significance is the most consistent econometric result across the different models and estimation procedures. A reduction of the share of agriculture value-added to GDP by 10 per cent would increase entrepreneurship by 2 per cent. This does not imply that agriculture should be abandoned. Instead, the result could be interpreted as meaning that more investments should be directed to the rural sector in order to increase non-agriculture activities which complement agriculture in the process of rural economic development (Nkurunziza, 2007). Although the share of the services sector value-added to GDP is positively related to entrepreneurship, the relationship is not statistically significant. This is surprising given the discussions in the literature purporting the existence of a strong relationship.

The time dummy variables show that relative to 2004, entrepreneurship was stronger in 2006 and 2007, just before the world economic and financial crisis, with the strongest result recorded in 2007. Relative to 2004, entrepreneurship declined in 2009, most probably as a result of the crisis affecting developed economies and spreading to other parts of the world. The decline in entrepreneurship after 2007 has been well documented (Klapper and Love, 2010). This finding illustrates that entrepreneurship in a specific environment may be affected by internal as well as external factors.

The regional dummies show that after controlling for other economic factors, entrepreneurship in Africa is not statistically different from entrepreneurship in Europe. However, in the Middle East, entrepreneurship is much lower than in Europe, suggesting that there could be specific regional factors, probably non-economic, explaining this difference.

Modelling Entrepreneurship as a Dynamic Phenomenon

Entrepreneurship could be considered as a dynamic phenomenon. Due to localization economies, entrepreneurs establishing businesses create opportunities that attract other businesses either as suppliers or clients or even competitors. This increases the density of business activity in a specific area which in turn attracts even more firms. These relationships are empirically investigated by modelling entrepreneurship in a dynamic equation and estimating it using the Generalized Method of Moments (GMM) econometric procedure. Note, however, that in the context of slow-changing variables, GMM estimators could be imprecise due to information loss associated with first-differencing. With this caveat in mind, exploring the dynamic behaviour of entrepreneurship could provide interesting insights that the methods used so far cannot provide. The results of the estimation are presented in Table 4.3.

Comparing Tables 4.2 and 4.3, some variables lose their explanatory power when the GMM estimation is used. This is expected given limited variation of several variables. For example, a country does not experience important changes in its GDP composition in a one-year interval. Similarly, in many countries, the three variables used to capture the ease of doing business are usually fixed with one-off changes, if any, every few years.

Despite these data limitations, the positive sign and significance of the lagged dependent variable suggest that past values of entrepreneurship influence current flows implying a cumulative process. According to the results in Table 4.3, past rates of entrepreneurship account for about 40 per cent of the current rate, giving some credence to the hypothesis of network effects. Income per capita and its squared value have the expected signs and both variables are significant. The threshold income per capita where entrepreneurship starts increasing with income is $7,250, which is almost equal to the value of $7,300 determined on the basis of random effect models.

Conclusion and Policy Recommendations

This study has focused on the relationship between entrepreneurship and income per capita. According to the econometric results, the increase of income per

Table 4.3 Empirical Results of the Dynamic Model

	Model 1	*Model 2*	*Model 3*
Entrepreneurship lagged	0.43*	0.44**	0.42
	(0.24)	(0.23)	(0.29)
Log GDP per capita	–19.90***	–17.65*	–17.17**
	(8.43)	(9.49)	(8.43)
Log GDP per capita lagged	16.58**	14.99*	14.09
	(8.69)	(9.25)	(9.18)
Log square of GDP per capita	1.12**	1.00*	0.94**
	(0.49)	(0.53)	(0.48)
Log square of GDP per capita lagged	–0.96**	–0.87*	–0.80
	(0.49)	(0.52)	(0.52)
Log agriculture value-added/GDP	–0.13	–0.01	–0.23
	(0.43)	(0.46)	(0.45)
Log services value-added/GDP	0.03	0.15	0.03
	(0.72)	(0.70)	(0.67)
Log number of procedures	–0.49	–	–
	(0.30)		
Log time to register a business	–	–0.28**	–
		(0.13)	
Log cost to register a business	–	–	–0.17
			(0.15)
Time dummy variables			
Year 2005	0.27	0.31	0.27
	(0.24)	(0.24)	(0.22)
Year 2006	0.53***	0.55***	0.50***
	(0.21)	(0.20)	(0.19)
Year 2007	0.59***	0.59***	0.57***
	(0.18)	(0.17)	(0.15)
Year 2008	0.37***	0.37***	0.36***
	(0.11)	(0.10)	(0.10)
Wald Chi^2 (12)	153.03***	135.87***	149.67***
Observations	281	281	277
Autocorrelation of order 1 (Probability)	0.18	0.18	0.27
Autocorrelation of order 2 (Probability)	0.10	0.12	0.12

Notes

Standard errors in parentheses are White (1980) heteroscedasticity-consistent.

***, ** and * correspond to 1, 5 and 10 per cent significance level, respectively. The reference groups are Europe for region and 2004 for year dummies.

capita could lead to an increase in opportunity entrepreneurship but this effect takes place when income reaches a threshold of $7,300, which falls within the World Bank's upper middle-income group. Economic transformation particularly the modernization of the agriculture sector should also help in the process of fostering entrepreneurship. It is surprising that the econometric results failed to establish a strong relationship between the services sector and entrepreneurship even though the two variables are positively related, as expected. There is evidence that, for example, the development of the mobile telephone industry in Africa has created a large network of enterprises in the services sector. In 1999, by the time the Kenyan telecommunication sector was liberalized, the country had 15,000 mobile telephone subscribers. By the mid-2006, this number had jumped to 5.6 million subscribers. According to the Kenyan government's Economic Survey for 2005, the expanding small business sector created 437,900 new jobs just in 2004, mainly thanks to the spectacular development of the mobile telephone sector.[25] Most African countries are experiencing a mobile telephone revolution that should be harnessed to increase entrepreneurship.

Improving the business climate provides another avenue for fostering entrepreneurship development. For example, conservative estimates show that just removing two of the 18 procedures needed to register a business could result in the creation of close to 1,000 additional limited liability firms in Uganda in just one year. Given how relatively simple it is to take such action, this is a strong message. Even though Uganda cannot be expected to move from 18 procedures to just one as in Canada and New Zealand in a short period of time, the example of neighbouring Rwanda shows that it is possible substantially to reduce this hurdle.

In terms of policy, the convex relationship between income per capita and entrepreneurship suggests that the number of opportunity entrepreneurs would start to increase when income per capita reaches a threshold level estimated at \$7,300. The implication for African countries is that it may take several years of sustained economic growth to reach this average level of income. Hence, African countries where necessity entrepreneurs dominate the business landscape should accept to live with them instead of attempting to transform them into opportunity entrepreneurs. Instead, policymakers should devise specific policies that address the most pressing needs of necessity entrepreneurs such as their access to credit and infrastructure services.

Furthermore, in order to foster entrepreneurship, the education system should be reformed to respond better to the needs of the economy. Encouraging vocational training and apprenticeship is one of the aspects of educational reforms that could have a long-lasting effect on entrepreneurship in Africa. According to empirical research on developed countries, most entrepreneurs use their practical skills previously acquired through apprenticeship rather than their academic training, to establish their own enterprises (Robson, 2007). The generalized practice of apprenticeship in Germany, for example, is credited to be at the basis of the country's economic success; the rate of youth unemployment in the country is half of the rates in the UK, France and USA.[26] African countries should also take advantage of the opportunity created by the information technology revolution taking place throughout the continent. Mobile telephony is revolutionizing communication and business practices in Africa and this new development has the potential to create millions of businesses across the continent. A success story such as Kenya's should be emulated.

Notes

1 This version of the paper has benefitted from insightful comments from Pedro Conceicao, Sebastian Levine, Mathias Kuepie and participants in the workshop on labour markets in West Africa and Central Africa (Dakar, 22–23 September 2011) as well as

the African Economic Conference (Kigali, October 2012). The views expressed are my own and not those of the United Nations Conference on Trade and Development.

2 In Africa as in most developing countries, the inexistence or poor quality of employment data makes it impossible to use self-employment as a reliable indicator of entrepreneurship.

3 Several other terms have been used to characterize this dichotomy. They include 'necessity' versus 'opportunity' entrepreneurs, 'real' versus 'quasi' entrepreneurs, 'replicative' or 'routine' entrepreneurs versus 'innovative' or 'high impact' or 'ambitious' entrepreneurs (Wennekers *et al.*, 2010: 173).

4 According to Maslow (1954), human motivation moves through a five-stage pattern of needs that has been represented in the form of a pyramid. First are physiological needs such as hunger, thirst and sleep. Second are security and safety needs such as a stable and predictable environment. Third are social or acceptance needs such as the sense of belonging. Fourth are self-esteem needs such as the need to feel respected. Fifth is the need for self-actualization or the fulfilment of individual abilities.

5 African economies grew by 5.1 per cent per year, on average, over the decade 2000–2010. This was twice the performance of the previous decade where average GDP growth was 2.5 per cent per year. While high commodity prices have played a role in Africa's recent growth performance, only one-third of growth in GDP was due to commodities, other sectors accounting for the rest. For example, between 2002 and 2007, hotels and restaurants grew by 8.7 per cent; finance by 8 per cent, transport and communications by 7.8 per cent and construction by 7.5 per cent (McKinsey Global Institute, 2010). Political and macroeconomic stability as well as microeconomic reforms are identified as the major factors behind Africa's recent growth.

6 See, for example, the recent review by Wennekers *et al.* (2010). Most recently, thanks to the World Bank's efforts in collecting comparable data on entrepreneurship across the world, some recent studies of entrepreneurship have integrated developing countries in their samples. For example, Djankov *et al.* (2002) analyse the cost of firm entry while Klapper and Love (2010) have recently analysed the effect of the global economic and financial crisis on entrepreneurship across the world. They find that the crisis had a significant negative effect on enterprise creation across the world.

7 Recent analyses of entrepreneurship have relied on the GEM database which started collecting systematic data on self-employment in 1999 with ten developed countries. Only recently have some African countries been covered by GEM (see www.gemconsortium.org).

8 The self-employed comprise own-account workers whether they work alone or use hired labour (Robson, 2007).

9 See Acs (2007).

10 Visit www.gemconsortium.org/about.aspx?page=ab_what_gem_is for information on the GEM.

11 About 60 per cent of African countries were implementing or had implemented economic liberalization programmes by the second half of the 1980s (UNCTAD, 2008).

12 Cross-country information on access to credit is very sparse. Existing empirical research in industrial organization both in developing and developed countries, shows that a limited number of entrepreneurs use credit in order to start their businesses. Credit is mostly accessed once the business has been established and proved to be viable (Nkurunziza, 2010).

13 In countries where the procedure to register a business is speedy and cheap, even 'small entrepreneurs' might choose to register their business and operate in the formal sector.

14 It is highly likely that many of these entrepreneurs operating in the informal sector are not captured by our measure of entrepreneurship as they do not register their firms.

15 The World Bank uses GNI per capita to define the four income groups but we use GDP per capita measured in 2005 PPP as this is the variable consistently used in the chapter.

Also, our group boundaries are close to but not exactly the same as those defined by the World Bank (see http://data.worldbank.org/about/country-classifications).

16 Measuring entrepreneurship by the number of business registrations may underestimate the number of entrepreneurs who establish their businesses in the informal sector.

17 Data on these variables is from the World Bank's Doing Business online database accessed on 11 September 2011 (www.doingbusiness.org/custom-query).

18 www.doingbusiness.org/press.

19 The African countries included are Burkina Faso, Ethiopia, Gabon, Ghana, Kenya, Madagascar, Malawi, Mauritius, Niger, Nigeria, Rwanda, Senegal, South Africa, Togo, Uganda and Zambia.

20 The Hausman (1978) test comparing random and fixed effects models cannot be performed with robust standard errors.

21 This could reflect the fact that the sample used is dominated by developing countries.

22 Given that we have estimated a semi-logarithmic model, the elasticity is derived as: coefficient times the inverse of the mean of entrepreneurship. This is –0.82/3.32. Using the median instead of the mean as the denominator returns an elasticity of 0.47.

23 The lower figure is calculated by assuming that on average limited liability firms have the country's overall average number of permanent employees per firm (small, medium and large) of 21.14. The higher bound assumes an average medium size for all limited liability firms, which is 34.82 permanent employees (figure for 2006, the latest year for which this information is available).

24 Data from www.doingbusiness.org/Custom-Query/rwanda.

25 See http://media.mit.edu/ventures/EPROM/whyafrica.html.

26 www.bbc.co.uk/news/14185334.

References

Acs, Z. (2007). 'How is Entrepreneurship Good for Economic Growth?' *Innovations*, 1 (1), 97–107.

Ahn, T. (2010). 'Attitudes toward Risk and Self-Employment of Young Workers', *Labour Economics*, 17 (2), 434–442.

Arenius, P. and Minniti, M. (2005). 'Perceptual Variables and Nascent Entrepreneurship', *Small Business Economics*, 24 (3), 233–247.

Audretch, D.B. and Thurik, A.R. (2001). 'What is New about the New Economy: Sources of Growth in the Managed and Entrepreneurial Economies', *Industrial and Corporate Change*, 10 (1), 267–315.

Ayyagari, M., Demirguc-Kunt, A. and Maksimovic, V. (2011). 'Small vs. Young Firms across the World: Contribution to Employment, Job Creation and Growth', Policy Research Working Paper 5631, World Bank.

Banerjee, A. and Newman, A. (1993). 'Occupational Choice and the Process of Development', *Journal of Political Economy*, 101 (2), 274–298.

Blanchflower, D. and Oswald, A. (1998). 'What Makes an Entrepreneur?' *Journal of Labour Economics*, 16 (1), 26–60.

Braguinsky, S., Klepper, S. and Ohyama, A. (2009). 'Schumpeterian Entrepreneurship', Atlanta Competitive Conference Paper.

Carree, M.A., van Stel, A.J., Thurik, A.R. and Wennekers, A.R.M. (2002). 'Economic Development and Business Ownership: An Analysis using Data of 23 OECD Countries in the Period 1976–1996', *Small Business Economics*, 19 (3), 271–290.

Carree, M.A., van Stel, A.J., Thurik, A.R. and Wennekers, A.R.M. (2007). 'The Relationship between Economic Development and Business Ownership Revisited', *Entrepreneurship and Regional Development*, 19 (3), 281–291.

Charman, A.J. and Petersen, L.M. (2009). 'An Investigation of Characteristics Distinguishing "Entrepreneurs" from the "Self-Employed" in South Africa', Paper presented at the Second Annual International Conference on Entrepreneurship, WITS Business School.

Chenery, H. and Syrquin, M. (1989). 'Three Decades of Industrialization', *World Bank Economic Review*, 3 (2), 145–181.

Djankov, S., La Porta, R., Lopez-de-Silanes, F. and Shleifer, A. (2002). 'The Regulation of Entry', *Quarterly Journal of Economics*, CXVII (1), 1–37.

Freytag, A. and Thurik, R. (2007). 'Entrepreneurship and its Determinants in a Cross-Country Setting', *Journal of Evolutionary Economics*, 17, 117–131.

Haltiwanger, J., Jarmin, R. and Miranda, J. (2009). 'Jobs Created from Business Startups in the United States', Kauffman Foundation.

Hausman, J.A. (1978). 'Specification Tests in Econometrics', *Econometrica*, 46, 1251–1271.

Hausmann, R., Hwang, J. and Rodrik, D. (2007). 'What You Export Matters', *Journal of Economic Growth*, 12 (1), 1–25.

Hessels, J., Suddle, K. and Mooibroek, M. (2008). *Global Entrepreneurship Monitor 2007*. Zoetermeer, Netherlands: EIM.

Ilmakunnas, P. and Kanniainen, V. (2001). 'Entrepreneurship, Economic Risks, and Risk Insurance in the Welfare State: Results with OECD Data 1978–93', *German Economic Review*, 2 (3), 195–218.

Kiggundu, M. (1997). 'Retrenchment Programs in Sub-Saharan Africa: Lessons for Demobilization', Bonn International Center for Conversion, Paper 10.

Kimhi, A. (2009). "Entrepreneurship and Income Inequality in Southern Ethiopia', *Small Business Economics*, 34 (1), 81–91.

Klapper, L. and Love, I. (2010). 'The Impact of the Financial Crisis on New Firm Registrations', Policy Research Working Paper 5444, World Bank, Washington, DC.

Klapper, L., Laeven, L. and Rajan, R. (2006). 'Entry Regulation as a Barrier to Entrepreneurship', *Journal of Financial Economics*, 82 (3), 591–629.

Lucas, R.E., Jr (1978). 'On the Size Distribution of Business Firms', *Bell Journal of Economics*, 9, 508–523.

McKinsey Global Institute (2010). 'Lions on the Move: The Progress and Potential of African Economies', McKinsey & Company.

Makura, M. (2008). *Africa's Greatest Entrepreneurs*. Cape Town: Penguin Books.

Maslow, A. (1954). *Motivation and Personality*. New York: Harper.

Nkurunziza, J.D. (2007). 'Generating Rural Employment in Africa to Fight Poverty', in Jomo Kwame Sundaram (ed.), *Towards Full and Decent Employment*. London: Zed Books Limited, 158–190.

Nkurunziza, J.D. (2010). 'The Distribution of Firm Size in Africa's Manufacturing Sector and its Implication for Industrial Policy', presented at NYU Africa House. Accessed at: www.nyu.edu/africahouse/upcomingevents/Nkurunziza_paper.pdf.

Noorderhaven, N., Thurik, R., Wennekers, S. and van Stel, A. (2004). 'The Role of Dissatisfaction and per Capita Income in Explaining Self-Employment across 15 European Countries', *Entrepreneurship Theory and Practice*, 28 (5), 447–466.

Parker, S. and Robson, M. (2004). 'Explaining International Variations in Entrepreneurship: Evidence from a Panel of OECD Countries', *Southern Economic Journal*, 71 (2), 287–301.

Roberts, L.P. and Robinson, P.B. (2010). 'Home-Based Entrepreneurs, Commercial Entrepreneurs and White-Collar Workers: A Comparative Study of Attitudes toward Self-Esteem, Personal Control and Business Growth', *Journal of Small Business and Entrepreneurship*, 23 (3), 333–353.

Robson, M. (2007). 'Explaining Cross-Country Variations in Entrepreneurship: The Role of Social Protection and Political Culture', *Comparative Labour Law and Policy Journal*, 28, 863–892.

SEED Initiative (2010). 'An Investigation into the Triple Bottom Line Performance of Micro and Small Social and Environmental Enterprises in Developing Countries: Establishing a Baseline for a Longitudinal Study', United Nations Environment Program, Nairobi.

Stephens, H.M. and Partridge, M.D. (2011). 'Do Entrepreneurs Enhance Economic Growth in Lagging Regions?' *Growth and Change*, 42 (4), 431–465.

The Whitaker Group (2011). *Frontier Africa.* Country Focus: Rwanda, 2.

UNCTAD (2008). 'Economic Development in Africa Report 2008: Export Performance following Trade Liberalization: Some Patterns and Policy Perspectives', New York and Geneva.

UNECA (2005). 'Economic Report on Africa 2005: Meeting the Challenges of Unemployment and Poverty in Africa', United Nations Publication, Addis Ababa.

Van Stel, A., Carree, M. and Thurik, R. (2005). 'The Effect of Entrepreneurial Activity on National Economic Growth', *Small Business Economics*, 24 (3), 311–321.

Verheul, I., Wennekers, A., Audretsch, B. and Thurik, R. (2003) 'An Eclectic Theory of Entrepreneurship: Policies, Institutions and Culture', in D. Audretsch (ed.), *SMEs in the Age of Globalization.* Cheltenham: Edward Elgar Publishing, 536–606.

Wennekers, S. (2006). 'Entrepreneurship at Country Level: Economic and Non-Economic Determinants', PhD Thesis, Erasmus Research Institute of Management.

Wennekers, S., van Stel, A., Carree, M. and Thurik, R. (2010). 'The Relationship between Entrepreneurship and Economic Development: Is It U-shaped?' *Foundations and Trends in Entrepreneurship*, 6 (3), 167–237.

Wennekers, S., van Stel, A., Thurik, R. and Reynolds, P. (2005). 'Nascent Entrepreneurship and the Level of Economic Development', *Small Business Economics*, 24 (3), 293–309.

White, H. (1980). 'A Heteroskedasticity-Consistent Covariance Matrix Estimator and a Direct Test for Heteroskedasticity', *Econometrica*, 48, 817–838.

Wooldridge, J. (2002). *Econometric Analysis of Cross-Section and Panel Data.* Cambridge, MA: The MIT Press.

World Bank (2011a). World Development Indicators 2011. Accessed at: http://data.worldbank.org/indicator/.

World Bank (2011b). *Enterprise Surveys.* Accessed at: www.enterprisesurveys.org.

Part II

External and Spatial Economies

5 Cereal Price Transmission from International to Domestic Markets in Africa[1]

Carolin Kouyaté, Stephan von Cramon-Taubadel, Friederike Greb, Nelissa Jamora and Nadine Würriehausen

Introduction

Motivated by the recent peaks in international food prices, we conducted a study to improve our understanding of the extent and speed of transmission of international cereal price changes to the domestic retail and wholesale level in developing and emerging countries (Greb *et al.*, 2012). Other than most recent studies on world-to-domestic price transmission (PT) we attempted to extract general lessons about the drivers of PT by estimating PT processes with a consistent set of price data (Food and Agriculture Organization of the United Nations Global Information and Early Warning System – FAO GIEWS) for a large number of countries using a uniform methodology. Based on this report, we use this study to set the focus specifically on PT results for African countries, which differ significantly from those in other regions or continents. In the sample, 35 of the 71 countries are in Africa and also roughly half of the 499 domestic price series.

The study has the following structure. In next section, we give a brief overview of the vector error correction model that we used for estimating our sample of measures of cereal PT. In the third section, we describe how we used the GIEWS dataset and present the results of African price pairs for each cereal product and before and after a structural break in July 2007. In a subsequent meta-regression analysis, in the fourth section we measure how much of the variation in the resulting samples of PT estimates can be attributed to factors that might be expected to influence the strength of PT. This is followed by a discussion of the results and the conclusion.

Method: The Vector Error Correction Model

The Structure of the Vector Error Correction Model

The study of PT for homogeneous commodities in space, or for a product as it is transformed along the stages of the marketing chain (e.g. wheat – flour – bread), has attracted the interest of agricultural economists for many decades (Meyer, 2004). Early empirical studies of PT were based on simple correlation and regression analyses that did not account for dynamics and lead-lag relationships in price data (for a survey, see Fackler and Goodwin, 2001). In the course of the

1980s, these methods were increasingly replaced by dynamic regression models that include lagged prices (e.g. Ravallion, 1986) and studies based on the concept of Granger causality (Gupta and Mueller, 1982). The emerging cointegration literature highlighted several pitfalls associated with the regression analysis of price data. In particular, since price data are often non-stationary, regression can lead to spurious results (Hassouneh *et al.*, 2012). The basic insight of the cointegration approach is that to avoid the pitfall of spurious regression one must test whether non-stationary prices series (also referred to as 'integrated' price series) are not only correlated with one another but are rather 'cointegrated'. Cointegrated means that there exists a linear combination of the non-stationary series that is itself stationary, in other words that the series share a common form of non-stationarity and cannot drift apart indefinitely.

Ardeni (1989) published the first study of PT on agricultural markets based on cointegration methods. It is fair to say that with the exception of a comparatively small literature based on so-called parity bounds models (Barrett and Li, 2002) today essentially the entire empirical PT literature draws on cointegration methods and, in particular, the so-called vector error correction model (VECM). The VECM is a re-parameterization of the standard vector autoregressive (VAR) model, which relates the current levels of a set of time series to lagged values of those series. A simple VECM that captures the interactions between international or world prices and domestic price takes the following form:

$$\Delta p_t^d = \varphi_1 + \alpha_1 \underbrace{(p_{t-1}^d - \beta_1 p_{t-1}^w)}_{\text{error correction term}} + \delta_1 \Delta p_{t-1}^w + \rho_1 \Delta p_{t-1}^d + \varepsilon_{1t} \tag{1a}$$

$$\Delta p_t^w = \varphi_2 + \alpha_2 \underbrace{(p_{t-1}^d - \beta_1 p_{t-1}^w)}_{\text{error correction term}} + \delta_2 \Delta p_{t-1}^w + \rho_2 \Delta p_{t-1}^d + \varepsilon_{1t} \tag{1b}$$

where
p_t^d is the domestic price;
p_t^w is the world price; and
φ, α, β, δ and ρ are parameters to be estimated.

In matrix notation, and allowing for more than one lag of the price difference terms, this VECM can be written compactly as:

$$\begin{bmatrix} \Delta p_t^d \\ \Delta p_t^w \end{bmatrix} = \begin{bmatrix} \varphi_1 \\ \varphi_2 \end{bmatrix} + \begin{bmatrix} \alpha_1 \\ \alpha_2 \end{bmatrix} [1 \beta_1] \begin{bmatrix} p_{t-1}^d \\ p_{t-1}^w \end{bmatrix} + \sum_{i=1}^{k} \begin{bmatrix} \delta_{1i} & \rho_{1i} \\ \delta_{2i} & \rho_{2i} \end{bmatrix} \begin{bmatrix} \Delta p_{t-i}^w \\ \Delta p_{t-i}^d \end{bmatrix} + \begin{bmatrix} \varepsilon_{1t} \\ \varepsilon_{2t} \end{bmatrix} \tag{2}$$

From the perspective of empirical PT analysis, the main advantage of the VECM over the VAR is that it separates the long-run equilibrium (or 'cointegrating') relationship between p^w and p^d – which is captured by the error correction term $(p_{t-1}^d - \beta_1 p_{t-1}^w)$ – from the short-run dynamics that ensure that any deviations from this long-run equilibrium are 'corrected' and thus only temporary. The key parameters in the VECM are β_1, which describes how one price reacts to changes in the other in the long run,[2] and the so-called 'adjustment' parameters α_1 and α_2. If p^w and p^d are cointegrated, then α_1 and α_2 must have negative and positive signs, respectively. If this is the case, then if for example p^d becomes too large relative to p^w and the error correction term is correspondingly positive, a decrease in p^d in the first equation of the VECM, and an increase in p^w in the second equation, will drive the prices back towards their long-run equilibrium. One-to-one PT in the long run requires that $\beta_1 = 1$, while $0 < |\alpha_i| \leq 1$, with large (small) values of α_1 and α_2 indicating that errors are corrected rapidly (slowly).[3]

We use a basic empirical strategy for estimating PT. The first step is to determine whether the individual price series p^w and p^d are both non-stationary (also referred to as 'integrated' or 'I(1)'). This is usually carried out using the ADF (Dickey and Fuller, 1979) and KPSS tests (Kwiatkowski *et al.*, 1992). If the prices are not both I(1), they cannot be cointegrated. If they are both stationary or 'I(0)' they can be studied using Auto-Regressive Distributed Lag (ARDL) models. If the series are both I(1), the null hypothesis that they are not cointegrated can be tested using a two-step OLS procedure proposed by Engle and Granger (1987) or a maximum likelihood procedure developed by Johansen (1988). If the null of no cointegration is rejected, the VECM in equation (2) can be estimated, again using methods proposed by Engel and Granger or Johansen. Finally, the resulting estimates of β and α are interpreted.

Limitations of the Vector Error Correction Model, and Alternatives

While the VECM underlies most empirical work in PT analysis, it is restrictive in some settings. In particular, the VECM in equation (2) is linear in two senses (Hassouneh *et al.*, 2012). First, it is linear in the sense that all of the parameters in the model are assumed to be constant over the entire sampling period. Second, it is linear in the sense that the dependent variables react linearly to changes in the independent variables. Numerous studies have shown that in many applications one or both of these types of linearity cannot be expected to hold (Hassouneh *et al.*, 2010; Serra and Goodwin, 2003; Serra *et al.*, 2006; von Cramon-Taubadel, 1998; von Cramon-Taubadel and Amikuzuno, 2012).

For our purposes, the first type of linearity is especially restrictive. The PT relationship that links an international price to a country's domestic market price need not be constant over time. Changes in the country's trade policy (for example, an increase or reduction of import tariffs) can alter the nature of the PT relationship, as can a switch from a net export to a net import position. Furthermore, spatial equilibrium theory (Takayama and Judge, 1971) predicts that short-run price adjustments due to arbitrage will take place only if the difference between international and domestic prices exceeds a threshold that is determined by transport and transaction costs (Barrett and Li, 2002). If the difference between prices is less than this threshold, there is no incentive for traders to engage in arbitrage, and prices can move independently of one another.

In such cases PT will be characterized by different so-called 'regimes' (for example, one regime before and one regime after an import tariff change; or one regime for the net export situation, and one for the net import situation). In recent years several models of regime-dependent PT have been developed and applied in the literature. Most of these can be described as piecewise linear models in which each regime is characterized by a standard VECM as in equation (2) above, and some trigger or transition mechanism determines when the model jumps from one regime to another. This trigger can be exogenous (e.g. coinciding with the date of a policy change) or endogenous (e.g. determined by whether the distance between the international and the domestic prices exceeds a certain threshold). Hassouneh *et al.* (2012) review a number of the regime-dependent PT models that are common in current research, including the threshold VECM (Goodwin and Piggott, 2001), the asymmetric VECM (von Cramon-Taubadel, 1998) and the smooth transition VECM (Teräsvirta, 1994).

Estimating regime-dependent PT models is considerably more complicated than estimating a standard VECM. Some of these models require additional exogenous variables in addition to the endogenous prices, for example information on the timing of policy changes or other exogenous shocks that lead to regime changes. Other regime-dependent models such as the threshold VECM can be estimated using prices alone, but require additional information and testing to determine the appropriate number of thresholds.[4] Finally, there is no unified testing framework for comparing these regime-dependent models with one another.

Authors who are interested in analysing PT in a specific product/country setting, or who use such a specific setting to illustrate a new regime-dependent PT model that they have developed or refined, can afford to engage in the additional data collection, specification, testing and interpretation that this entails. As outlined in 'Estimates of the long-run PT coefficient and the adjustment parameters', below, however, the FAO GIEWS data provide us with domestic price series for three main cereal products (maize, rice and wheat) in 71 countries. It is beyond the scope of this study to carry out detailed regime-dependent PT analysis for each of these individual settings. Instead, we are obliged to use a comparatively simple PT model, such as the VECM, the estimation of which can be automated to permit the analysis of a large number of domestic–international price pairs. We recognize that the simple VECM specification in (2) will not be appropriate for all of the domestic–international price pairs in the GIEWS data. The additional insights that can be generated by estimating PT for a large number of price pairs and then analysing the resulting cross-section sample of results come at the cost of a necessarily simple method of analysis that is not appropriate for each of these pairs individually.

In an attempt to deal with the shortcomings of the simple VECM, we propose an alternative method of analysis. To allow for at least one possible source of non-linearity we modify the basic VECM in equation (2) to include a structural break, which we postulate to have taken place in July 2007. This roughly corresponds to the beginning of the first agricultural price peak and the beginning of the recent phase of increased volatility on international commodity markets. Hence, we estimate the following model, which allows the nature of PT between international and domestic cereal prices to change with the onset of higher and more volatile price in recent years. The resulting specification is as follows, where the superscript * distinguishes between pre-break and post-break parameters:

$$\begin{bmatrix}\Delta p_t^d\\ \Delta p_t^w\end{bmatrix}=\begin{cases}\begin{bmatrix}\alpha_1\\ \alpha_2\end{bmatrix}[1\beta_1]\begin{bmatrix}p_{t-1}^d\\ p_{t-1}^w\end{bmatrix}+\sum_{i=1}^{k}\begin{bmatrix}\delta_{1i} & \rho_{1i}\\ \delta_{2i} & \rho_{2i}\end{bmatrix}\begin{bmatrix}\Delta p_{t-1}^d\\ \Delta p_{t-1}^w\end{bmatrix}+\begin{bmatrix}\varphi_1\\ \varphi_2\end{bmatrix}+\begin{bmatrix}\varepsilon_{1t}\\ \varepsilon_{2t}\end{bmatrix}, & t < July\ 2007\\ \begin{bmatrix}\alpha_1^*\\ \alpha_2^*\end{bmatrix}[1\beta_1^*]\begin{bmatrix}p_{t-1}^d\\ p_{t-1}^w\end{bmatrix}+\sum_{i=1}^{k}\begin{bmatrix}\delta_{1i}^* & \rho_{1i}^*\\ \delta_{2i}^* & \rho_{2i}^*\end{bmatrix}\begin{bmatrix}\Delta p_{t-1}^d\\ \Delta p_{t-1}^w\end{bmatrix}+\begin{bmatrix}\varphi_1^*\\ \varphi_2^*\end{bmatrix}+\begin{bmatrix}\varepsilon_{1t}^*\\ \varepsilon_{2t}^*\end{bmatrix}, & t \geq July\ 2007.\end{cases} \quad (3)$$

Equation (3) is thus a regime-dependent VECM that links two standard VECMs, one for the period prior to July 2007, and one for the period thereafter. To check whether July 2007 is a plausible cut-off, we applied the Gregory and Hansen (1996) test of the null of no cointegration against the alternative of cointegration with a possible regime shift to each domestic/international price pair in the GIEWS data. We obtained a distribution of break dates selected by the Gregory and Hansen test.[5] While there is evidence of regime shifts in some domestic/international price relationships in 2003/04 for rice and 2004/05 for maize, for all three products (rice, maize and wheat) by far the most regime shifts are indicated in 2007/08. July 2007 therefore appears to be a reasonable choice for the cut-off date in the regime-dependent VECM in equation (3).

Estimates of International–Domestic Cereals PT

Following the discussion of methods in the previous section, we follow a comprehensive approach to generate insights into the nature of international to domestic PT for major cereal products. Using the extensive FAO GIEWS price data set, we test whether the price series are cointegrated with a corresponding international reference price. For market pairs where this is the case we generate estimates of β and α using the VECM in equation (2) and the regime-dependent VECM in equation (3). This work is outlined in 'Estimates of the long-run PT coefficient and the adjustment parameters', below. In this analysis we consider maize, rice and wheat.

This approach has its advantages and disadvantages. As discussed above, the FAO GIEWS price data includes hundreds of price series. Hence, we are obliged to automate the estimation and work with simple uniform specifications that may not be appropriate in all cases. On this count estimates in the PT literature might be more reliable. Most studies in the literature only report a few PT estimates, typically for a single product and one or relatively few countries.[6] As a result, the estimates in other studies can be expected to reflect detailed work by authors who have a comprehensive understanding of the markets that they study, and who have undertaken careful specification searches, for example to determine appropriate lag-lengths for the VECMs that they estimate, etc.

The FAO GIEWS food price data set was established in 2009 as part of the FAO Initiative on Soaring Food Prices (ISFP).[7] The prices reported in GIEWS are collected from national official sources and non-official institutions. The GIEWS price series are monthly and most run through to the end of 2011; some start as early as 1995, others as late as 2008. We impose a minimum length of ten observations for a time series to be considered in our analysis and analyse PT between domestic and the following international prices:

- wheat – US No. 2 HRW, FOB Gulf of Mexico;
- rice – Thai 5 per cent, FOB Bangkok;
- yellow maize – US No. 2 yellow, FOB Gulf of Mexico;
- white maize – white maize, FOB Randfontein (South Africa).

The GIEWS data include a total of 57 domestic prices for wheat, 262 domestic prices for rice and 180 domestic prices for maize. GIEWS mainly provides results for countries in Africa, Asia/Pacific and Latin America, but only seven for Europe and none for North America (499 in total). To estimate the VECMs in equation (2) and (3) above with the GIEWS data a decision about the number of lags (k) to include must be reached. The Akaike Information Criterion (AIC – Akaike, 1974) indicates that $k=1$ in the great majority of cases, so for simplicity we employ one lag throughout.[8]

Cointegration

Table 5.1 presents information on the numbers and shares of international/domestic price pairs, which are found to be cointegrated according to the GIEWS estimates. Overall, the sample suggests that international and domestic prices are cointegrated more often for African markets (49 per cent) than for markets located in Asia, Pacific Region, Latin America, Europe and Asia (35 per cent). This tendency holds also the case for the estimates generated with allowing for a structural break at July 2007. Before the break 26 per cent of all African market pairs are cointegrated and 21 per cent of market pairs in other regions. In the period thereafter cointegration is found in 41 per cent of African price pairs and 28 per cent of price pairs in the rest of world.

We then compare results from only African countries with those from the rest of the world.[9] In Africa, there is less frequent evidence of cointegration for maize (28 per cent) than for rice (68 per cent) and wheat (41 per cent). The market pairs for maize in Africa display a slightly lower prevalence of cointegration

Table 5.1 The Prevalence of Cointegration in the PT Estimates

	Entire Period	*Before July 2007*	*After July 2007*
Africa	121 of 248 (49%)	45 of 170 (26%)	101 of 247 (41%)
Rest of the world	87 of 251 (35%)	44 of 214 (21%)	69 of 250 (28%)
Total/Σ_N	208 of 499 (42%)	89 of 384 (23%)	170 of 497 (34%)

Source: own calculations with GIEWS price data.

Notes
Cointegration is determined by Johansen Test with 5 per cent significance level. Rest of the world: Asia, Pacific Region, Latin America, Europe and Oceania.

than in other countries (34 per cent). However, in the results for rice and wheat we find a much higher share of cointegrated market pairs in Africa compared with non-African countries. In most cases, the share of cointegrated pairs in Africa is lower if we test for cointegration in the two regimes before and after July 2007.

Many series of the earlier regime dropped out of the estimation because of the low number of observations. Furthermore, some of the shorter price series may lead to fewer positive tests of cointegration. Especially for rice price pairs (e.g. Rwanda) there is sometimes evidence for cointegration for an entire price series but not as we would logically expect also for both regimes. Deviating price movements matter more in shorter series even if they are smoothed out in the long run and may thus distort the test. In other cases, the cointegration test allowing for a regime-switch in 2007 seems more appropriate than testing for the overall period as many results for maize price pairs suggest. Taking this into account the results imply somewhat more frequent cointegration after the start of the global food price crisis on maize in Cape Verde, Chad, Ethiopia, Niger, Togo and Uganda, on rice in Guinea-Bissau and on wheat in Sudan. Fewer maize markets in South Africa and Zimbabwe are cointegrated for the post-2007 period; this could indicate a certain degree of decoupling of local price levels from international prices.

Estimates of the Long-Run PT Coefficient and the Adjustment Parameters

The results point to relatively slow PT for all cereal products and regions. Table 5.2 summarizes the average estimates of the long-run PT coefficient β and of the adjustment parameters α_1 and α_2 and by cereal product. On average, the estimated β is 0.73 for international–domestic price pairs in African countries. This indicates that, on average, changes in international prices are transmitted by 73 per cent to domestic prices. As discussed above, the adjustment parameter from the first equation in (2) above is expected to be negative. The average speed of adjustment of local prices (α_1) is –0.27. This implies that it will take roughly

Table 5.2 Average Estimates of the Long-Run PT Coefficient and the Adjustment Parameters

	$\varnothing \beta$				$\varnothing \alpha_1$				$\varnothing \alpha_2$		
	Maize	*Rice*	*Wheat*	*All*	*Maize*	*Rice*	*Wheat*	*All*	*Maize*	*Rice*	*All*
Africa	0.75	0.75	0.58	0.73	–0.24	–0.29	–0.21	–0.27	–0.20	0.20	0.18
RoW	0.69	0.57	1.23	0.64	–0.25	–0.17	–0.13	–0.19	0.08	0.22	0.21
Total	0.72	0.67	0.81	0.69	–0.24	–0.24	–0.18	–0.24	–0.13	0.21	0.19

Source: own calculations with GIEWS price data.

Notes
Only significant coefficients for cointegrated market pairs are considered. The expected sign of α_1 is negative. None of the wheat estimates of α_2 were significant. RoW: rest of the world.

2.2 months to correct one-half of any disequilibrium that emerges due to unexpected price movements on international or domestic markets. A somewhat slower response is indicated by the average across all cereals for countries in other regions (average $\alpha_1=-0.19$, which corresponds to a half-life of 3.3 months). In addition, the average β is slightly smaller (0.64). In addition to the strong and above-average prevalence of cointegration with the world market price, also the largest long-run PT coefficients and the fastest price reaction was found for African rice markets. A total of 75 per cent of a price shock is transmitted in the long run, with half of the adjustment of local prices taking place within two months. The average long-run transmission of maize prices is equivalent but with a half-life of 2.5 months. However there is evidence that for a number of rice market pairs, the world market contributes to the adjustment in prices.

Price Reaction on Domestic Level and World Market Side

In most cases, we focus on the adjustment parameter from the first equation in (2) above, i.e. the equation that explains changes in domestic prices, because in the majority of all cases, only this α is statistically significant. In other words, the dynamics of international/domestic cereal PT are such that domestic prices adjust to deviations from the long-run price relationship, but international prices do not. The only notable exception to this rule is rice. If the adjustment parameters from the second equation in (2) above are considered, we find that these are in most cases insignificant, except for rice.[10] Specifically, there is evidence of a statistically significant reaction by international prices to disequilibrium between domestic and international prices in 121 African market pairs (45 per cent), of which 82 involve rice. Similar results were found for the other countries in our sample.

As pointed out above, the simple linear VECM is restrictive and probably not appropriate for many of the individual price pairs in the GIEWS data. Hence, a certain number of spuriously significant adjustment parameters for international prices can be expected. Nevertheless, the fact that significant adjustment parameters for international prices occur, if at all, almost exclusively for rice price pairs suggests that the determination of international rice prices differs fundamentally from the determination of international wheat and maize prices. These results confirm a very similar finding by Gilbert (2011). We can conclude that most countries are price takers on wheat and maize markets, but the evidence for rice is mixed.

PT Before and After July 2007

Table 5.3 contrasts average estimates of the coefficient of PT on cereal markets before and after the onset of the recent phase of price peaks and increased price volatility in mid-2007. If we compare the average estimates from the period prior to July 2007 with the average estimates from the period thereafter, PT has become stronger and faster for African–international price pairs, whereas the opposite is the case for the country group consisting of Asia, the Pacific Region, Latin America, Europe and Oceania.

Table 5.3 Average PT Parameters Estimated Before and After July 2007

	$\varnothing\beta$				$\varnothing\alpha_1$				$\varnothing\alpha_2$			
	Maize	*Rice*	*Wheat*	*All*	*Maize*	*Rice*	*Wheat*	*All*	*Maize*	*Rice*	*Wheat*	*All*
1	0.08	0.90	1.9	0.81	–0.29	–0.59	–0.06	–0.45	–0.32	0.12	0.49	0.03
2	0.59	0.90	25.28	3.07	–0.37	–0.29	–0.24	–0.32	–0.19	0.24	–	0.13
3	0.84	0.65	–	0.69	–0.49	–0.21	–	–0.29	0.47	0.03	–	0.06
4	0.70	0.27	1.63	0.42	–0.37	–0.24	–0.26	–0.28	0.16	0.14	–	0.14

Source: own calculations with GIEWS price data.

Notes

Only significant coefficients for cointegrated market pairs are considered. The expected sign of α_1 is negative. (1) Africa before July 2007, (2) Africa after July 2007, (3) RoW before July 2007, (4) RoW after July 2007.

On African maize and wheat markets the long-run PT coefficients (β) have increased considerably since mid-2007, from 0.08 to 0.59 and from 1.9 to 25.28, respectively.[11] On rice markets the average PT coefficient does not change after July 2007. The short-run adjustment coefficients (α_1) for maize and wheat have increased (in absolute terms), from –0.29 to –0.37 and from –0.06 to –0.24, respectively. However, at the same time the short-run adjustment coefficients for rice (α_1) have on average fallen, from –0.59 to –0.29. This suggests that PT has become more complete and faster since mid-2007 for maize and wheat. The extent of PT for rice does not change but the price reaction becomes slower for the second period. As discussed above, after July 2007 a considerable amount of the price reaction to shocks in the rice market takes place on the world market side. The average speed of adjustment (α_2) for rice has doubled. Overall PT becomes faster and more complete after July 2007 for all cereal price pairs in African markets if we take the world rice market reaction into account. However, these results must be interpreted with caution. The prevalence of outliers is high in particular in the post-July 2007 VECM results, presumably due to the short length of the available time series. Furthermore, here only coefficients of cointegrated market pairs are reported, with potential biases in the results, as discussed earlier.

Analysis of the Determinants of the Strength of PT

Method

The averages presented above hide considerable variation in the estimates of α and β for individual country/product combinations. To explain this variation, and thus to generate insights into the factors that influence the strength of PT from international to domestic markets, we estimate meta-regressions. In each regression a set of estimated parameters (αs or βs) is regressed on a set of covariates that might be expected to influence PT. These covariates are listed and described in Table 5.4 and cover geographic (e.g. landlocked), infrastructural (e.g.

Table 5.4 Covariates Used in the Meta-Regression of the Determinants of PT

Name	*Description*	*Source/Link*	*Expectation/Theory*
Commodity fixed effects	Wheat, maize, rice	–	Unobserved commodity-specific heterogeneity
Region fixed effects	Europe; East and South Africa; West and Central Africa; MENA and Asia; Oceania; Latin America	http://unstats.un.org/unsd/methods/m49/m49regin.htm	Unobserved region-specific heterogeneity
Landlocked	1 if country has no access to sea	Google maps	For landlocked countries, international trade must cross more borders
Trade openness	Total trade as a share of income, average 2006–10 (import + export/GDP)	World Bank Development Indicators	Open economies are better integrated into world markets and thus PT should be stronger
STE	1 for countries that have STEs	Literature	STEs interfere with trade and insulate the domestic prices from international fluctuations
Ease of trade	Ease of trading across borders, between 0 (worst) to 1 (best)	World Bank, Doing Business, Ease of Trading across borders	Transaction costs reduce PT
Logistics	Logistics performance index of quality of trade and transport-related infrastructure between 1 (worst) to 5 (best)	World Bank 2007	Better logistics mean lower costs of trade and higher PT
Net importer	Net cereal import ratio (export–import, 3 year average 2009–11) to domestic consumption	USDA, PSD Online	If the share of staple imports in domestic consumption is high, more is undertaken to insulate domestic markets
Retail	1 if domestic price is measured at the retail rather than a more upstream level	Literature/GIEWS	The farther 'inland' a domestic price is measured, the weaker its link to international prices

logistics), institutional (e.g. state trading enterprises, STEs) and market or commodity specific factors (e.g. net importer). We include dummy variables for cereals (omitting rice) and regions (omitting Asia/Pacific) to capture any corresponding fixed effects.

Results

We first present the results of logit regressions that predict whether pairs of international and domestic prices are cointegrated. The dependent variable equals 1 when the two prices are cointegrated, and 0 otherwise, and this variable is explained using the covariates listed in Table 5.4 – for example whether the country in question is landlocked, whether it has an STE for cereals, etc.

Maize and wheat are less likely to be cointegrated with the corresponding international prices than rice prices are (by roughly 30 and 20 per cent, respectively), and domestic prices in East and South Africa, West and Central Africa and Latin America are more likely to be cointegrated with international prices (by 25, 32 and 19 per cent, respectively). As we would expect, if an STE is responsible for trading the product in question, the probability of cointegration falls by almost 22 per cent. If the domestic price being considered is a retail price, the probability that it is cointegrated with international prices falls by almost 13 per cent. This result is plausible, as retail prices are further removed from international prices than wholesale or border prices. Improvements in logistics have a surprising negative impact on the probability of cointegration between domestic and international prices. Ease of trade has the expected positive impact, and being landlocked the expected negative impact on the probability of cointegration, but neither of these effects is significant. A high net import ratio may lead to more policy intervention to insulate domestic markets from international price movements, however this is not reflected

Table 5.5 Logit Regression of Cointegration Status on Factors That Might Influence PT

Covariate	*Entire Period*	*Before July 2007*	*After July 2007*
Maize	–0.296***	0.044	–0.269***
Wheat	–0.202***	–0.151	–0.130*
East and South Africa	0.251**	0.091	0.310***
West and Central Africa	0.321***	0.093	0.388***
Europe	0.189	–0.175***	0.163
Latin America	0.189**	–0.041	0.286***
Trade openness	0.000	0.002	0.000
Net importer	0.035	0.033	0.136
STE	–0.216***	0.283	0.009
Retail	–0.126**	0.064	–0.127**
Ease of trade	0.395	0.245	0.509
Logistics	–0.527***	–0.152	–0.460***
Landlocked	–0.125	–0.074	0.119

Notes
*, ** and *** refer to significance at the 10, 5 and 1 per cent levels, respectively. Marginal effects rather than coefficients are reported.

in the results. Most of these results also hold if only the time period after July 2007 is considered. However, if the period prior to July 2007 is considered the logit regression is much less informative. This is probably due to the fact that many GIEWS price series are very short prior to July 2007, leaving too few observations for dependable cointegration testing. Hence, the logit regression for the pre-July 2007 period is based on fewer and less trustworthy test results.

Meta-regression results for individual estimates of α and β are summarized in Tables 5.6 and 5.7. Table 5.6 presents results for the GIEWS estimates of α and β from *all* domestic/international price pairs. Moreover, in Table 5.7 the GIEWS estimates are based only on α and β from *cointegrated* domestic–international price pairs.

The meta-regressions in Table 5.6, which are based on all estimates of α and β, are generally quite similar to the corresponding meta-regressions in Table 5.7, which are based only on estimates of α and β from cointegrated domestic–international price pairs. For example, in both tables we see in the second column that α is roughly seven percentage points more negative for maize prices than for rice and wheat prices, suggesting that PT on maize markets is somewhat more rapid. This supports the finding in Table 5.2 that αs for maize tend to be somewhat larger (in magnitude).[12] Indeed, this result is also corroborated by results that are based only on non-cointegrated price pairs (not reported here). Here the estimated coefficient for maize indicates that α is roughly eight percentage points more negative for maize prices.

Similar parallels can be found across both tables for example for the West and Central Africa fixed effect (–5.1 percentage points in Table 5.6, –3.1 percentage points in Table 5.7) and for the ratio of net imports to consumption (5.4 and 5.3 percentage points less error correction according to the results in Tables 5.6 and 5.7).[13] Some parallel findings are counter-intuitive, however. In particular, in both Table 5.6 and Table 5.7 we see that improvements in logistics are associated with large (less negative) values of α, and therefore with slower PT.

Moving to the results for the pre-July 2007 period, we again see many parallels between Tables 5.6 and 5.7. In particular, both tables display evidence of significantly more negative αs (and therefore more rapid PT) for East and South Africa and West and Central Africa, for Latin America, for more trade open countries and, surprisingly, for countries with STEs. In the post-July 2007 period, the results in both tables point to significantly more negative αs for maize and wheat, and for West and Central Africa.[14]

These parallels are less apparent for the meta-regressions in Tables 5.6 and 5.7 that explain the variation in the βs. Overall, the meta-regressions indicate that the selected covariates are able to explain a larger proportion of the variance in the adjustment parameters (the αs) than of the variance in the long-run PT coefficients (the βs). The meta-regressions for the estimates of β generally produce fewer significant coefficients, and they also produce many coefficients that are implausibly large, especially in the pre- and post-July 2007 subsamples. Since β is expected to be close to 1, it is difficult for example to interpret coefficients that suggest that β increases by over five for price pairs involving wheat (see the second column of Table 5.6).

Table 5.6 Estimated Coefficients for the Meta-Regressions (All)

Covariate	*Entire Period*		*Before July 2007*		*After July /2007*	
	α	β	α	β	α	β
Intercept	–0.323***	–0.712	0.265	–2.765	–0.082	4.230
Maize	–0.067***	0.131	–0.033	–0.046	–0.137***	0.719
Wheat	0.002	0.491**	–0.025	5.088**	–0.112***	5.091***
East and South Africa	–0.013	0.148	–0.339***	2.360	0.004	3.164
West and Central Africa	–0.051*	0.148	–0.408***	2.216	–0.149***	2.648
Europe	0.038	0.644	–0.050	–0.033	0.025	3.108
Latin America	0.008	0.252	–0.356***	2.275	–0.005	3.722**
Trade openness	0.000	0.000	–0.004***	0.077**	0.000	–0.008
Net importer	0.054**	–0.227	0.014	0.102	–0.004	0.362
STE	0.031	0.390*	–0.244***	–3.216	0.019	–1.115
Retail	0.002	0.197	–0.025	–2.418	–0.020	1.095
Ease of trade	–0.035	1.303	0.197	–7.242	–0.173	9.935
Logistics	0.094***	–0.013	–0.023	0.878	0.054	–6.168***
Landlocked	0.023	0.447*	–0.076	–1.765	0.048	0.316
R^2	0.170	0.041	0.225	0.052	0.210	0.072

Notes
All meta-regressions estimated using OLS. *, ** and *** refer to significance at the 10, 5 and 1 per cent levels, respectively. Result based on estimates of α and β using all international–domestic price pairs.

Table 5.7 Estimated Coefficients for the Meta-Regressions (Cointegrated)

Covariate	*Entire Period*		*Before July 2007*		*After July 2007*	
	α	β	α	β	α	β
Intercept	–0.262*	0.725	0.718	–0.504	0.045	–5.871
Maize	–0.069**	0.057	–0.068	0.009	–0.167***	–1.441
Wheat	0.034	0.146	–0.591	0.279	–0.170**	8.762**
East and South Africa	–0.033	–0.017	–0.778***	–0.178	–0.041	5.596
West and Central Africa	–0.031	–0.008	–0.977***	0.024	–0.184**	3.069
Europe	0.078	0.393	–	–	0.130	5.941
Latin America	–0.015	0.142	–1.043***	0.300	–0.023	4.023
Trade openness	0.000	0.001	–0.008***	0.004	0.000	0.000
Net importer	0.053	–0.160	0.278	–0.900*	–0.005	0.720
STE	–0.023	0.141	–0.826***	–0.038	0.043	–2.963
Retail	–0.020	0.004	0.008	–0.094	–0.054	1.546
Ease of trade	0.118	0.433	0.882	–0.826	0.148	3.976
Logistics	0.038	–0.282	–0.006	0.504	–0.113	–0.152
Landlocked	0.008	0.156	–0.089	0.211	0.143**	1.633
	0.101	0.032	0.489	0.212	0.265	0.119

Notes

The sample before July 2007 includes too few observations for Europe to permit estimation. *, ** and *** refer to significance at the 10, 5 and 1 per cent levels, respectively. Results based on estimates of α and β only from cointegrated international/domestic price pairs.

In summary, the meta-regressions for the αs do generate a few signals. In particular, there is strong evidence of more rapid PT for maize across all of the GIEWS results regardless of what period is considered and whether cointegrated and/or non-cointegrated results are considered. Similarly, evidence of more rapid PT in Latin America appears repeatedly in Tables 5.6 and 5.7. There is weaker evidence for a positive relationship between trade openness and the speed of PT, and a negative relationship between net import ratios and PT. Before July 2007, it appears that PT was stronger in the presence of STEs, and when estimation is carried out without allowance for a break in July 2007, it appears that better logistics are associated with slower PT. These last two results run counter to our a priori expectations. The meta-regressions for the βs have lower explanatory power than those for the αs, and they fail to produce many robust and plausible results.[15]

Discussion

The results provide evidence that international cereal price changes are transmitted more frequently, stronger and faster to domestic markets in African countries compared with other countries of the sample. Roughly every second cereal price is cointegrated with the international reference price whereas this is only the case for 35 per cent of the price pairs in Asia, Pacific Region, Latin America, Europe and Oceania. Furthermore, the results point to relatively slow PT for all cereal products and regions, but with the main part of a price change being transmitted in the long run. Overall, the estimates for markets in Africa point to average long-run PT coefficients of roughly 0.73 and average adjustment parameters of roughly 0.27. This suggests that on average 73 per cent of a change in international prices will be transmitted to domestic markets, and that it takes approximately 2.2 months for one-half of a given price shock on international cereal markets to be transmitted to domestic markets. In non-African countries, 64 per cent of an international price change is transmitted in the long run with half of the price response within 3.3 months.

African rice markets show the highest share of cointegrated price pairs (68 per cent), the largest long-run PT coefficient and the fastest price reaction. For wheat and maize it is mostly the domestic prices that react to disequilibrium between themselves and the corresponding world reference prices. But in the case of rice, more than 60 per cent of all price pairs display international price reactions to disequilibrium as well. This becomes even more apparent when comparing the period before and after July 2007 where we find evidence for a shift from predominantly domestic price reactions to mainly reactions of the world market price. Hence, the determination of international prices for rice appears to differ fundamentally from that for wheat and maize. The reasons for this difference would be an interesting topic for future research. On maize markets there is evidence for a change in PT dynamics indicated by cointegration variations in combination with a stronger and faster PT to the domestic level after July 2007. This could be interpreted as evidence of a certain degree of decoupling of local markets from international prices in some countries, with other countries left stronger affected by international price changes. With a number of caveats we find that PT has become stronger for local markets in Africa after the onset of the recent phase of price peaks and increased price volatility in mid-2007. The results suggest that the opposite is the case for the country group consisting of Asia, the Pacific Region, Latin America, Europe and Oceania.

The differences between African countries and countries in other regions persist also after controlling for a number of economic, political, geographical covariates, as well as infrastructure and trade variables.[16] However, the analysis generates a number of insights into the drivers of PT from international to domestic cereal markets. Employing meta-regression analysis to explain variations in long-run PT coefficients (β) between domestic and international prices fails to generate compelling results. The meta-regressions for the adjustment parameters (α) do produce some more suggestive results. All other things being equal, there is some evidence of more rapid PT for maize than for wheat and rice, and more rapid PT in West and Central Africa and East and South Africa than in other regions. An increasing ratio of net imports to domestic consumption is associated with slower PT, which may be an indication of increased intervention on politically more sensitive markets. There is evidence that trade openness is positively associated with the speed of PT, but this effect is only significant in the pre-July 2007 period. In this period there is also robust evidence that the presence of an STE is associated with more rapid PT. Finally, there is some puzzling indication that improved logistics is correlated with slower PT.

The results presented here must be interpreted with caution. First, a lack of cointegration between two prices does not necessarily mean that there is no PT between them (McNew and Fackler, 1997). The underlying PT relationship may be characterized by regime-dependence, for example as a result of policy intervention or shifts between net import and net export positions. Hence, failure to find evidence of cointegration might be due to a failure to test for the right type of cointegration. The strength of the GIEWS price data is that it provides broad and consistent coverage of a large number of country/product combinations. However, the sheer number of price series available in GIEWS means it is not possible to implement a detailed modelling strategy for each individual series. Instead, we must resort to a uniform modelling strategy that can be automated. We have estimated one slightly more flexible VECM that allows for a regime shift in July 2007, but this is no substitute for careful, case-by-case specification and estimation of an appropriate model for each individual price pair. Second, the GIEWS price series are quite short. Few series have more than 150 monthly observations, and many have considerably fewer. It is reasonable to expect that the nature of cereal PT from international to domestic markets has changed in recent years as prices have increased and become more volatile, and some of the results that we produce with the GIEWS data appear to confirm this expectation. There are, however, only roughly 55 monthly observations available for the period since 2007.

Additional work might lead to additional or more robust insights into PT. First, the simple VECM employed to estimate the GIEWS price data might be made somewhat more flexible. It could be modified to allow for asymmetric PT, i.e. to test whether increases in international prices are transmitted to domestic prices in the same manner as decreases (von Cramon-Taubadel, 1998). The results of the simple non-parametric analysis of agreement in the direction of international and domestic price changes suggests that increasing international prices are being transmitted more often to domestic prices than decreasing international prices. Alternatively, it might be possible to estimate threshold VECMs (TVECMs) with the GIEWS data (Goodwin and Piggott, 2001; Greb *et al.*, 2011). The TVECM can account for phases with and without trade and trade reversals and by distinguishing between these phases or regimes provide better estimates of PT parameters.

Notes

1 Paper presented at the African Economic Conference 2012 in Kigali, Rwanda (30 October to 2 November 2012). This chapter is based on a report prepared for the Rural Policies Thematic Group, the Agriculture and Rural Development Department, and the Poverty Reduction and Equity Unit of the World Bank, under the supervision of the World Bank Senior Economist Sergiy Zorya. The opinions and conclusions expressed in the report and this study do not necessarily represent those of the World Bank.

2 If estimation is based on prices in logarithms then β_1 can be interpreted as the long-run elasticity of PT.

3 The speed of error correction captured by the magnitude of an adjustment parameter must be interpreted relative to the frequency of the data that is used to estimate it. An α of 0.4 estimated with annual data implies that 40 per cent of any deviation from long-run equilibrium is corrected within the space of one year. An α of 0.25 estimated with monthly data is smaller in magnitude but would nevertheless lead to over 95 per cent correction of any deviation from long-run equilibrium in the course of one year. Some authors transform αs into so-called half-lives that indicate how many units of time are required for the correction of one-half of a deviation from the long-run equilibrium. An α of 0.25 estimated with monthly data corresponds to a half-life of 2.41 months.

4 Furthermore, Greb *et al.* (2011) demonstrate that the maximum likelihood method used to estimate threshold VECMs in the literature to date is biased.

5 Detailed results can be obtained from the authors.

6 A list of all studies can be obtained from the authors.

7 We are grateful to David Hallam for providing us with this data in electronic form.

8 Detailed results can be obtained from the authors.

9 Detailed results can be obtained from the authors.

10 Detailed results can be obtained from the authors.

11 The implausibly large average PT elasticity result is caused by an outlier for an Ethiopian wheat market with an estimated β of 166.8 after July 2007.

12 In Table 5.2 we consider only significant coefficients.

13 Similar results were found for not cointegrated price pairs.

14 Similar results were found for not cointegrated price pairs.

15 We also experimented with weighted meta-regressions that account for the fact that some countries are more prevalent in the GIEWS data than others. These meta-regressions did not generate any additional insights.

16 Regressions on an income variable did not produce any significant results.

References

Akaike, H. (1974). A new look at the statistical model identification. *IEEE Transactions on Automatic Control* 19: 716–723.

Ardeni, P.G. (1989). Does the law of one price really hold for commodity prices? *American Journal of Agricultural Economics* 71: 661–669.

Barrett, C. and Li, J. (2002). Distinguishing between equilibrium and integration in spatial price analysis. *American Journal of Agricultural Economics* 84: 292–307.

Dickey, D.A. and Fuller, W.A. (1979). Distribution of the estimators for autoregressive time series with a unit root. *Journal of the American Statistical Association* 74: 427–431.

Engle, R.F. and Granger, C.W.J. (1987). Cointegration and error-correction: representation, estimation and testing. *Econometrica* 55: 251–276.

Fackler, P.L. and Goodwin, B.K. (2001). Spatial price analysis. In: Gardner, B. and Rausser, G. (eds), *Handbook of Agriculture Economics*, Vol. 1: 971–1024. Amsterdam: Elsevier Science BV.

Gilbert, C.L. (2011). Grain price pass-through, 2005–2009. In: Prakash, A. (ed.), *Safeguarding Food Security in Volatile Global Markets*. Rome: FAO. www.fao.org/docrep/013/i2107e/i2107e07.pdf.

Goodwin, B.K. and Piggott, N.E. (2001). Spatial market integration in the presence of threshold effects. *American Journal of Agricultural Economics* 83(2): 302–317.

Greb, F., Jamora, N., Mengel, C., von Cramon-Taubadel, S. and Würriehausen, N. (2012). Price transmission from international to domestic markets. Discussion paper of the Courant Research Centre 'Poverty, Equity and Growth in Developing Countries: Statistical Methods and Empirical Analyses' No. 125. Georg-August-University, Göttingen.

Greb, F., von Cramon-Taubadel, S., Krivobokova, T. and Munk, A. (2011). Threshold estimation in price transmission analysis. Discussion paper of the Courant Research Centre 'Poverty, Equity and Growth in Developing Countries: Statistical Methods and Empirical Analyses' No. 103. Georg-August-University, Göttingen.

Gregory, A.W. and Hansen, B.E. (1996). Residual-based tests for cointegration in models with regime shifts. *Journal of Econometrics* 70: 99–126.

Gupta, S. and Mueller, R. (1982). Analyzing the pricing efficiency in spatial markets: concept and applications. *European Review Agricultural Economics* 9: 301–312.

Hassouneh, I., Serra, T. and Gil, J.M. (2010). Price transmission in the Spanish bovine sector: the BSE effect. *Agricultural Economics* 41: 33–42.

Hassouneh, I., von Cramon-Taubadel, S., Serra, T. and Gil, J.M. (2012). Recent developments in the econometric analysis of price transmission. TRANSFOP (Transparency of Food Pricing) Working Paper No. 2. www.transfop.eu.

Johansen, S. (1988). Statistical analysis of cointegrating vectors. *Journal of Economic Dynamics and Control* 12: 231–254.

Kwiatkowski, D., Phillips, P., Schmidt, P. and Shin, Y. (1992). Testing the null hypothesis of stationarity against the alternative of a unit root. *Journal of Econometrics* 54: 159–178.

McNew, K. and Fackler, P.L. (1997). Testing market equilibrium: is cointegration informative? *Journal of Agricultural and Resource Economics* 22(2): 191–207.

Meyer, J. (2004). Methoden zur Analyse von Preistransmissionsprozessen. Dissertation, Georg-August-University, Göttingen.

Ravallion, M. (1986). Testing market integration. *American Journal of Agriculture Economics* 68: 102–109.

Serra, T. and Goodwin, B.K. (2003). Price transmission and asymmetric adjustment in the Spanish dairy sector. *Applied Economics* 35: 1889–1899.

Takayama, T. and Judge, G.G. (1971). *Spatial and Temporal Price Allocation Models*. Amsterdam: North-Holland.

Teräsvirta, T. (1994). Specification, estimation, and evaluation of smooth transition autoregressive models. *Journal of the American Statistical Association* 89: 208–218.

von Cramon-Taubadel, S. (1998). Estimating asymmetric price transmission with the error correction representation: an application to the German pork market. *European Review of Agricultural Economics* 25: 1–18.

von Cramon-Taubadel, S. and Amikuzuno, J. (2012). Seasonal variation in price transmission between tomato markets in Ghana. *Journal of African Economies* 21(4): 669–686.

6 Impacts of Regional Trade Agreements on Trade in Agrifood Products

Evidence from Eastern and Southern Africa

Albert Makochekanwa

Introduction

Although the world has witnessed increased economic interdependence and a rapid increase in regionalism which has resulted in proliferation of regional trade agreements (RTAs), literature does not provide conclusive results of the welfare effects of these RTAs (Jayasinghe and Sarker, 2007) both to participating member countries and also to the world at large. One branch of literature considers RTAs, not only as reducing welfare both to participating countries and the to world at large, but also as "stumbling blocks" to multilateral free trade (Bhagwati, 1998; Panagaria, 2000). On the other hand, the other branch of literature supports RTAs as raising welfare both for member countries, and the for world at large, thus acting as "building blocks" to multilateral free trade (Summers, 1991; Ethier, 1998). This controversy on the impacts of RTAs is inherently an empirical issue and mainly a result of the fact that the net welfare effect will normally depend on the relative magnitudes of trade creation and trade diversion effects. Moreover, the net effect of trade creation and diversion may vary across commodities within the same RTA, between RTAs and over time (Jayasinghe and Sarker, 2007).

Trade in agrifoods at any level of cooperation, from bilateral, to regional, to inter-region and to multilateral remains more complex than any other sector and varies across agreements (Aksoy, 2004). Thus, comparing trade in agrifoods and other sectors, it can be noted that even though negotiations at RTAs and WTO/GATT (World Trade Organization/General Agreement on Tariffs and Trade) have generally reduced existing tariffs on industrial products, tariffs on agrifoods are still relatively high, thus resulting in subdued trade in such products even within some RTAs. The situation is even made worse by agriculture protection which still exists (at WTO negotiation level), for instance, in the form of export subsides, special safeguards, amber-box and blue-box provisions of the Uruguay Round Agreement on Agriculture (URAA). These provisions complicate liberalization in agricultural trade given that a number of countries rely on them. Thus, even countries that are members of a given RTA, average preferential tariffs for agricultural products are still high in most of these trade blocs.

While a number of empirical studies have been done on the impacts of RTAs, most studies were done either at aggregate level or for manufacturing products (for instance, Clausing, 2001; Krueger, 2000) with the effects of RTAs on trade in agrifood products still to be investigated rigorously, especially in the eastern and southern Africa region. This void motivates this study which focuses on the impacts of RTAs on trade of major agrifood products deemed to be important for the region's food security. The eastern and southern Africa region analysed in this study features three regional economic communities (RECs), namely the Common Market for Eastern and Southern Africa (COMESA), the East African Community (EAC) and the Southern African Development Community (SADC).

To achieve its objectives, the study's investigation relies both on statistical trade-related indices and on an econometric gravity trade model. In both cases, a disaggregated agrifood data level was used. The three major agrifood commodities analysed are: maize, rice and wheat. These commodities were selected mainly because of their importance in the food security basket of the region. Changes in two trade-related indices, namely intra-trade index and production complementarity index, infer the extent of intra-regional trade in the above three commodities in the three RECs.[1] On the econometric side, an extended gravity model was employed to determine the extent of intra-regional trade creation and trade diversion impacts for the three commodities separately.

Background to RTAs in Eastern and Southern Africa

The COMESA

The COMESA[2] started as a preferential trade area (PTA) in 1980 and later turned into a common market in 1993. The aim of COMESA is to promote sustainable economic and social development for all its member countries through enhanced cooperation leading to regional integration especially in the areas of trade, customs, infrastructure (transport and communications), science and technology, agriculture and natural resources. The main objectives of COMESA in the area of trade, among others include the creation of a free trade area (FTA); the establishment of a customs union (CU) and eventual establishment of a monetary union (MU).

The COMESA FTA was launched in October 2000 with nine participating states, after 16 years of gradual reduction of tariffs on intra-COMESA trade.[3] In November 2007, 13 countries were participating in the FTA; other member states had carried out tariff reductions of between 10 and 80 per cent. The region launched its CU in 2009, though with few members signing into the newly created CU.

COMESA cooperates with other regional organizations to liberalize trade. A Joint Task Force has been set up with the EAC and the SADC to harmonize their trade liberalization programmes and eventually form the COMESA–EAC–SADC tripartite FTA.

The EAC

The EAC is the regional intergovernmental organization of Kenya, Uganda, Tanzania, Rwanda and Burundi. The Treaty for the Establishment of the East African Community was signed on 30 November 1999 and entered into force on 7 July 2000, initially with three members, Kenya, Uganda and Tanzania, with Rwanda and Burundi joining in 2007.

The EAC aims at widening and deepening cooperation among the partner states in, among others, political, economic and social fields for their mutual benefit. To this extent the EAC countries established a CU in 2005 and a common market in 2010.

The SADC

The SADC[4] began in 1980 as a loose alliance of nine majority-ruled states in southern Africa known as the Southern African Development Coordination Conference (SADCC), with the main aim of coordinating development projects in order to lessen economic dependence on the then apartheid South Africa. It changed from a Coordinating Conference into a Development Community (SADC) in 1992. The community vision is that of a common future, a future within a regional community that will ensure economic well-being, improvement of the standards of living and quality of life, freedom and social justice, and peace and security for the people of southern Africa.

The region's Protocol on Trade mainly deals with all the trade issues of the Community. The specific objective of this protocol which directly deals with intra-trade as stated in Article 2 is "To further liberalize intra-regional trade in goods and services on the basis of fair, mutually equitable and beneficial trade arrangements, complimented by Protocols in other areas."

The region has been trading as a PTA[5] since its inception in 1980. However, based on the implementation of the agreed tariff phase down commitments between 2000 and 2007, SADC attained the FTA[6] as of January 2008, though the formal FTA launch was done at a regional Heads of State Summit, which was held at Johannesburg, South Africa in August 2008. The creation of an FTA, in principle, saw up to 85 per cent of intra-SADC trade flows duty free, with the remaining 15 per cent consisting of sensitive products to be liberalized by 2012 (SADC Secretariat, 2003). According to the region's Regional Indicative Strategic Development Plan's (RISDP) roadmap, SADC FTA is followed by a CU (which was supposed to have been into effect from 2010, but has been delayed), common market in 2015, MU in 2016 and, finally, economic union, in 2018.

Objectives

Given the brief introduction and background, the main question that the study will seek to answer is: Have RTAs in the three RECs promoted intra-regional agrifood trade? The study's objective will be to analyse the impacts of RTAs on intra-trade in three selected agrifood products in the three RECs. The empirical analyses have been done for the years 2005 to 2010 across the three RECs.

Literature Review

Empirical studies analysing the impacts of RTAs have employed a range of techniques, ranging from simple descriptive and statistical approaches to complex computable general equilibrium (CGE) modelling, with econometric approaches in-between. Since this study employs statistical and econometric approaches, empirical review will therefore be limited to these two approaches. Furthermore, given that the econometric approach dominates most studies, this section will review more studies which employed econometric techniques than those which employed statistical methodologies.

The main objective of Sunde *et al.*'s (2009) study was to investigate the determinants of intra-industry trade (IIT) between Zimbabwe and its SADC regional trade partners. To achieve its objectives, the paper employed a modified gravity model equation which included an IIT index as one of the explanatory variables. After employing the ordinary least squares (OLS) technique, the paper found per capita income, trade intensity, distance, exchange rate and gross domestic product (GDP) as the main reasons which explained IIT between Zimbabwe and its SADC trading partners. The research also found that most countries in SADC traded more or less the same goods and this, according to the study, was mainly a function of past development that these countries were subjected to during the colonial era which resulted in the establishment of similar economic structures and per capita incomes that were more or less the same.

Using a statistical analysis approach, Kalaba and Tsedu (2008) evaluated the performance of intra-SADC trade since the implementation of the Trade Protocol covering the period 2000 to 2006 mainly at aggregate level. Specifically, the paper assessed performance of intra-SADC trade by zeroing in on intra-SADC export share, comparing intra-SADC share with other regional blocs and intra-country trade share. The research's results showed that, irrespective of remarkable growth in total exports between 2000 and 2006, intra-SADC trade remained weaker. Comparing SADC intra-trade with other regional blocs, the study concluded that SADC was lagging behind most regions. In fact, during the implementation period, statistical figures showed that SADC's growth of extra-regional trade was even greater than with fellow members. Lastly, the study found out that more than two-thirds of total trade within the region was conducted via South Africa.

Jayasinghe and Sarker (2007) employed an extended gravity model to investigate the effects of North American FTA (NAFTA) on trade in six agrifood commodities (red meat, grains, vegetables, fruits, sugar and oilseeds) for the period 1985–2000. The study's results suggested that intra-trade in red meat, vegetables, grains and sugar significantly increased among the NAFTA members during the study period, with accelerated increases in the first two products, that is, red meat and vegetables. Overall, the study revealed that NAFTA countries traded more with each other than they traded with non-member countries mainly as a result of one of the following two reasons: either because the reduction of intra-NAFTA tariffs has created new trade or because trade has been diverted from the rest of the world to intra-NAFTA channels.

Karim and Ismail's (2007) study quantified the potentials of intra-regional agricultural trade in the COMESA region using Sudan, Egypt and Kenya as case studies. The paper employed a plethora of trade-related indices including instability index, production similarity index, comparative production performance index, export similarity index and revealed comparative advantage. The study found that there was scope for potential trade in agricultural trade among the regional members. Specifically, the instability indices of production in cereals, pulses, and roots and tubers were more stable at the regional level than at the national level. The results of the production similarity index indicated differences in production patterns of the three countries. Export similarity indices results showed that countries were dissimilar in their export patterns. Revealed comparative advantage indices for each country were generally higher for dominant export products. As dominant products differ among the countries the pattern of specialization differs considerably among these countries, and, therefore, there is a potential for expanding intra-regional trade in the region. The paper concluded that the government policies of COMESA member countries, especially Sudan, should pay more emphasis to encourage integrating their markets regionally to benefit from potential trade and comparative advantage existing in the region.

The study by Rojid (2006) focused mainly on investigating two important issues regarding regional integration; first, the extent to which COMESA was a building or stumbling block and, second, estimation of trade potentials within the COMESA region for COMESA members. The paper employed a gravity trade model using a Tobit estimation technique. The results of the study led the author to conclude that, for the 21-year period (1980 to 2001), COMESA was a building block and that the region liberalized trade more internally than it diverted trade from the rest of the world. On the issue of export trade potential, the results suggested that trade potential within the region was limited given that most member states of the group were overtrading within the region.

Molinari (2003) employed a gravity trade model for eight broad European Union (EU) trade sectors with the main objective of investigating the level and trends of sectoral integration effects within the economic bloc's member countries since the 1970s. Among other determinants of sectoral trade within the region, trade integration effects in the form of preferential trade arrangements such as the EU, European FTA (EFTA) and NAFTA were found to be positively related to trade.

The study by Chauvin and Gaulier (2002) was motivated by SADC's launch of the regional tariff schedule phase down as part of the implementation of the regional Trade Protocol. The main objective of the paper was to analyse the potential benefits of this liberalization initiative and the potential of increasing intra-SADC to member states especially given that the economic structure existing among its participating members was more or less the same. The study employed both statistical and econometric approaches. The statistical approach was mainly calculation of three trade-related indices: export diversification indices, revealed comparative advantages and trade complementarity indices. On the other hand, the econometric approach utilized the gravity trade model. Given that SADC countries had concentrated and similar comparative advantages, the research's statistical and econometric analyses suggested that the room for further trade within SADC was limited.

Methodology

Conceptual Framework

The impacts of RTAs on trade on agrifood products can be analysed within the Vinerian framework, among others. Following Jacob Viner (1950), whenever countries form an RTA, there are basically two possible consequences. First, costly produced products within the RTA union may displace similar lower cost produced products from countries outside the union, thus diverting trade from more efficient producers. This is the negative trade diversion effect. The second possibility is that lower cost imports from another member may displace domestic production in one member country, resulting in creation of new trade among members. This is the positive impact called trade creation. Additionally, establishment of an RTA may alter the relative prices of members' imports, leading to an expansion of consumption in the domestic market. Thus, trade creation can be considered as having two composite effects: a production effect and a consumption effect.

Generally, following the Vinerian contribution in the 1950s, trade creation and trade diversion effects have been investigated in a static framework (Jayasinghe and Sarker, 2007). Table 6.1 provides a summary of the general effects of RTA in the form of both trade creation and trade diversion. The table summarizes the spectrum of potential benefits and costs of regional trade integration, from an FTA to higher dimension of regionalism above CU.

Analytical Framework

The study used two methodologies to achieve its objectives. First, the research employed statistical analysis in which two trade-related indices were calculated to see the annual and/or range changes in intra-trade among member states of the three RECs under study. Second, the research employed an extended gravity trade model mainly to see whether the COMESA and SADC FTAs, and the EAC CU either created trade or diverted trade among the participating member countries.

Trade Related Indices

CHANGES IN INTRA-REGIONAL AGRIFOOD TRADE

This statistical index traces changes in movements in intra-regional agrifood trends and intra-regional trade relative to total trade. Since the study analysis was a five-year period, 2005 was used as a base year while 2010 was used to gauge the degree to which intra-regional trade in agriculture has changed over the years.

Table 6.1 Potential Benefits and Costs of Regional Trade Integration

Potential Benefits: Advantages	*Potential Loss/Costs: Disadvantages*
Trade Creation	
Trade creation and trade diversion for home country conditional on elasticities of demand and supply, changes in tariffs, elasticities of substitution	
• Lower price imports from partner • Higher consumer surplus • Greater variety of goods • Saving on real resources • Users of imported inputs may expand business (positive production effect) • Possible increase in exports to partners • Reduced cost of trading due to preferential access (reduced NTBs) • Increased FDI if opportunities arise due to harmonized, credible policy environment over a larger market	• Local producers of similar goods may be competed out (or temporarily dislocated) – a negative production effect and loss of employment • Loss of tariff revenue from positive to zero tariff • Cost of enforcing rules of origin (FTA)
Trade Diversion	
Note: Some industries/sectors may reap some benefits outlined above, *but costs are dominant*	• Higher price imports from partner countries, loss of consumer surplus (reduced welfare) • Local producers under pressure • Loss of FDI if trade diversion arises (specific areas) • Loss of tariff revenue from positive to zero tariff • Cost of enforcing rules of origin (FTA)

Trade and Development (intra-union specialization) ***Dynamic Gains, especially CU and Higher***	

• Increased competition (competitiveness on price and quality counts)
• Economies of scale due to larger market, lower unit costs
• Spillover effects, e.g. transfer of know-how
• Pooling of investment resources for basic "hard" regional infrastructure (education and research in identified areas)
• Harmonized commercial policies, incentives, macroeconomic policies to lead to:
  • Accelerated intra-regional trade if intra-regional comparative advantages are developed into complementarities in supply and demand at regional level
  • Credibility and certainty attracting FDI
  • Bargaining power for bloc in global trading system
  • Employment generation
  • Increased productivity and exports to region and other areas
	Situational and most likely short-term dislocation of local private business/employment for some industries/sectors

Source: Lyakurwa *et al.* (1997).

Notes
NTB – non-tariff barrier; FDI – foreign direct investment.

PRODUCT COMPLEMENTARITIES

The degree to which eastern and southern Africa member countries' imports from other member states complement domestic production/consumption (from the point of view of importing member countries) provides a barometer of the extent to which intra-regional trade will be beneficial to all member countries, and hence promoted. In a situation where there is high trade complementarity in agricultural product trade within the region, it follows that more trade will be expected to increase especially when the region becomes a fully functional FTA. As pointed by Khandelwal (2005: 13), "product complementarities between countries are an important indicator of the potential for expansion of intraregional trade".

This study therefore calculated bilateral complementarity indices in agrifood trade for the three RECs' member states. Again, 2005 was used as a base year while 2010 was used to gauge the degree to which intra-regional trade in agriculture has changed over the years.

For two trading countries, *i* and *j*, the algebraic bilateral product complementarity index for the agricultural products, *a*, following Tsikata (1999), is given by:

$$C_{aij} = 100 - \sum_{i} \left(\left| M_{aij} - X_{aij} \right| \div 2 \right) \quad (1)$$

where X_{aij} represents the share of agricultural good *a* in the total exports of country *i* to country *j*, and M_{aij} represents the share of agricultural good *a* in the total imports of country *j* from country *i*. The computed index values will vary between zero and 100, where zero implies no complementarity between countries *i* and *j*'s trade in agrifood products, while a value of 100 would imply perfect match between the exports and imports of the two trading countries. As pointed out before, higher index values would imply high potential benefits in intra-regional agrifood trade during the implementation of the Protocol, with lower values implying low potential benefits.

Gravity Trade Model

The effects of the implementation of FTA or a CU on trade on agrifood products can also be analysed using a gravity trade model. Whilst the gravity model[7] has been used in a number of fields of studies such as human migration and investment flows across countries, its application in international trade seems to dominate its overall use. In its trade application, Tinbergen (1962) and Poyhonen (1963) were the first independently to apply this methodology in their analysis of international trade flows. The gravity trade model borrows from Newton's (1687) "Law of Universal Gravitation".[8] Newton's theory postulates that the force of attraction between two separate entities *i* and *j* is a positive function of the entities' respective masses and inversely related to the squared distance between the objects. In analysing trade using the same gravity principle, the entities are replaced by a pair of countries, while the countries' masses are proxied by the respective GDP with distance replaced by a variable representing resistance (which in most cases is the actual distance between the pair of trading countries). Thus, in its original algebraic representation, and analogous to Newton's representation, the gravity model for agrifood trade can be depicted by equation (2):

$$trade_{ija} = A\frac{(GDP_i GDP_j)^{b_1}}{(distance_{ij})} \qquad (2)$$

where $trade_{ija}$ is the bilateral trade between country i and j in agriculture products, a; GDP_i and GDP_j are the countries' respective income; $distance_{ij}$ is the distance between the two trading partners and A is a constant. Taking logarithms to gravity model equation (2) results in the following representation:

$$\ln(trade_{ijat}) = A + \beta_1 \ln GDP_{it} + \beta_2 \ln GDP_{jt} + \beta_3 \ln(distance_{ij}) + \beta_4 X_{ij} + \varepsilon_{ij} \quad (3)$$

In equation (3), A, β_1, β_2 and β_3 are coefficients to be estimated, while ε_{ij} is the error term which captures other shocks and chance events which might influence agrifood bilateral trade between the two trading partners. In the above equation X_{ij} represents other possible variables used in international trade literature. Thus, equation (3) represents the basic gravity trade model where income is predicted to affect positively bilateral trade, while distance will be expected to have a negative effect on bilateral trade.

Whilst all trade researchers agree to the empirical model specification represented in equation (3), i.e. that trade is the dependent variable while GDPs and distance are the core explanatory variables, contention still exists on which other variables are to be included in the extended gravity trade model. As a result of this contention, Ghosh and Yamarik (2004) provided a list of 49 variables (one dependent and 48 independent variables) which have been used in literature to estimate the gravity trade model, though in various combinations. Among the multitudes of possible explanatory variables, an RTA variable, in the form of a dummy has been one of such potential variables. According to Jayasinghe and Sarker (2007), the RTA dummies enable us to isolate the two distinct effects, trade creation and trade diversion that RTAs may exert on trade flows. Thus, a RTA variable has, among other things, been included to estimate the possible amount of trade creation and trade diversion emanating from RTA between participating member countries.

To this end, this study will follow Frankel *et al.* (1995), and Jayasinghe and Sarker (2007) gravity model specifications, and estimate the following gravity model:

$$\begin{aligned}\ln(trade_{ijat}) = A + \beta_1 \ln GDP_{it} + \beta_2 \ln GDP_{jt} + \beta_3 \ln(distance_{ij}) + \beta_4 \ln P_{it} + \\ \beta_5 \ln P_{jt} + \beta_6 COMESA_{ij} + \beta_7 COMESA0_{ij} + \beta_8 EAC_{ij} + \\ \beta_9 EAC0_{ij} + \beta_{10} SADC_{ij} + \beta_{11} SADCO_{ij} + \beta_{12} lan_{ij} + \\ \beta_{13} border_{ij} + \varepsilon_{ij}\end{aligned} \qquad (4),$$

and $i = 1, 2, 3; j = 1, \ldots, n$

where:
$COMESA_{ij}$ = 1 if *j* is a member of COMESA, 0 otherwise;
$COMESA0_{ij}$ = 1 if *i* is a net importer from a non-member *j*, 0 otherwise;
EAC_{ij} = 1 if *j* is a member of EAC, 0 otherwise;
$EAC0_{ij}$ = 1 if *i* is a net importer from a non-member *j*, 0 otherwise;
$SADC_{ij}$ = 1 if *j* is a member of SADC, 0 otherwise;
$SADCO_{ij}$ = 1 if *i* is a net importer from a non-member *j*, 0 otherwise.

In equation (4), $trade_{ijat}$ is the current US dollar value of total bilateral trade (exports plus imports) between country *i* and country *j* in year *t* in one of the six agrifood products. GDP_{it} and GDP_{jt} are nominal GDPs of country *i* and country *j* in year *t* in US dollars. P_{it} and P_{jt} are country *i* and country *j*'s respective populations. Lan_{ij} represents the countries' respective language(s), while $border_{ij}$ indicates whether trade partners, country *i* and country *j*, share a common border or not. Variable $distance_{ij}$ is the weighted distance (as opposed to the simplest measure of geo-distance which considers only the main city of the country) in kilometres between country *i* and country *j*. Weighted distance is used because the study considered that some capital cities are not populated enough to represent the "economic centre" of the country. Thus, the weighted distance measures use city-level data to assess the geographic distribution of population inside each nation. The idea is to calculate distance between two countries based on bilateral distances between the largest cities of those two countries, those inter-city distances being weighted by the share of the city in the overall country's population (www.cepii.fr).

Following studies by both Frankel *et al.* (1995), and Jayasinghe and Sarker (2007), this chapter defines two dummy variables: (i) regional bloc dummy and (ii) an openness dummy. Thus, $COMESA_{ij}$ represents the existence of an RTA between country *i* and country *j* in equation (4). In interpreting the effect of this dummy, a positive and statistically significant estimated coefficient of the regional bloc in a particular product equation and estimation period implies that the intra-regional trade has been stimulated by the implementation of COMESA FTA. In this case, the estimated coefficient will be indicating the amount of additional trade, beyond the level their economic and geographic characteristics would allow, that had taken place among COMESA countries as a result of the implementation of the region's FTA. This, according to Aitken (1973) and Endoh (1999), means the coefficient will be interpreted to reflect trade creation effects of COMESA FTA implementation. The coefficients of EAC_{ij} and $SADC_{ij}$ are interpreted the same.

$SADCO_{ij}$ dummy on the other hand captures the degree of openness of SADC members' imports from the rest of the world. The dummy takes a value of one if a member is a net importer from the rest of the world (the importer is a member of SADC while the exporter is not in SADC) and zero otherwise. This dummy variable reflects any trade diversion occurring in the respective SADC states' import structure. The estimated coefficient of this variable indicates the degree to which SADC countries under- or over-imported from the rest of the world relative to the predictions of the standard gravity model. As such, in the case where the coefficient of this variable is negative and statistically significant, it indicates the extent to which SADC countries are under-importing from the rest of the world. More generally, it implies that an RTA member has reduced its net imports from the rest of the world relative to its net exports to the rest of the world (Eichengreen and Irwin, 1998; Frankel, 1997). Thus by focusing on the effects of the two dummy variables, a separation of the cases where SADC is trade creating only (i.e. it caused intra-regional trade to increase above average levels without changes in openness to non-members' trade) from those where SADC's increase in intra-region trade comes at the expense of non-members' exports to the bloc countries can be done. The latter effect can be identified as trade diversion. The coefficients of $COMESA0_{ij}$ and $EAC0_{ij}$ are interpreted the same.

In interpreting the estimated coefficients, given the double-logarithmic specification of the estimated function, the parameter estimates on the GDP_i, GDP_j, P_i, P_j and distance variable can be interpreted as elasticities. For instance, in equation (3), β_2 shows the percentage change in $trade_{ijat}$ induced by a 1 per cent change in GDP_j, *ceteris paribus*. Given that the two RTA dummies cannot be expressed in log form, the parameter estimates of β_6 and β_7 (from equation (3)) need to be interpreted with care. The percentage effect of the dummy variable is calculated following Halvorsen and Palmquist (1980).[9] Thus for illustrative purposes, if the coefficient estimate of the SADC dummy variable in Equation (3) is β_6, this will indicate that two SADC members traded an extra $\{\mathbf{exp}(\boldsymbol{\beta}_6)-1\} \times 100\%$ relative to the amount they traded with a non-SADC state. In other words, this will imply that the mean (or average) trade between two SADC members is higher than their mean trade with the rest of the world by $\{\exp(\boldsymbol{\beta}_6)-1\} \times 100\%$. It is however important to note that the benchmark is when a member country trades with a non-member country. Likewise, the *SADCO* parameters ($\boldsymbol{\beta}_7$) need to be interpreted with care. For instance, if the estimated coefficient, $\boldsymbol{\beta}_7$, is negative, total trade for a given product at disaggregated level of a SADC member (where the SADC member is a net importer) with a non-SADC partner is $\{\exp(-\beta_7)-1\} \times 100\%$ less than its net exports to non-members.

With regard to factors and variables that determine exports in the gravity trade model framework, there is a pool of potential variables, besides the three core variables of importer GDP, exporter GDP and distance, which explain the direction of exports. As pointed out before, Ghosh and Yamarik (2004) indicate that there are around 48 factors that have been used in gravity trade model literature which seek to explain the direction of exports.[10] Thus the following are the determinants found in literature and the ones that are used in this study. GDP of the exporting country measures the production capacity of the country, with more production expected to boost exports. A priori, a positive correlation is expected between this variable and exports. The importing country's GDP, as a variable, measures the absorption capacity, with higher GDP implying more import demand. A positive relationship is expected between GDP of the importing country and exports of the reporting country. The distance variable imposes trade costs and, as such, it is expected to affect exports negatively. The impact of population as a variable is indeterminate. On one hand, larger population means a country is more diversified and self-sufficient implying a negative impact on exports. On the other hand, larger population allows economies of scale in production resulting in more exports, and hence positively contributing towards a country's exports. The impact of inflation is also indeterminate, with higher inflation causing citizens to circumvent high cost of living by importing. In this case, a positive relationship is expected between imports and inflation. On the other hand, higher inflation may also result in consumers scaling down their purchases including imports. With regards to dummy variables, common language means communication efficiency resulting in increased trade. Thus a positive sign is expected on the common language variable. Sharing a common border reduces transport costs and thus a positive correlation is expected between trade and common border. Lastly, RTA dummies are expected to be positively correlated with trade given that RTAs are formed to improve trade among participating member countries.

Data Description

The study concentrated on agrifood trade for the period covering 2005 to 2010. This period was selected as it covers the time when all the three RECs were trading roughly at least as FTAs. GDP and population figures used in this study are taken from the IMF database. The weighted distance between countries' major economic cities, as well as information partners' languages and border are all taken from www.cepii.fr. The yearly statistical trade figures for each country's agrifood exports by destination and imports by source (up to HS6 digit level) are taken from the World Bank's World Integrated Trade Solutions (WITS) database. The database classifies statistical data according to the Harmonized Commodity Description and Coding (HS) System.

The agrifood commodities analysed in this study are classified under three different categories according to HS codes as contained in the WITS database. They are maize corn (HS 1005), rice (HS 1006) and wheat (HS 1001).

Estimated Results and Inferences

Computed Changes in Intra-Regional Agriculture Trade

Table 6.2 shows the shares of each reporting COMESA or EAC or SADC member countries' trade to its respective regional bloc. The table reports shares for countries that have reported data between 2005 and 2010. Across the rows are the reporting country's average trade (export plus imports divided by two) of which the share of what is traded with respective regional bloc(s) in question is calculated. Along the columns are the three products for which the analysis is carried out. Each cell in the table at the intersection of a country and a product contains two numbers. The top number shows the share of average trade of a given product of the reporting trading country (on the corresponding row) to respective regional bloc(s) (e.g. COMESA, EAC or SADC (SACU))[11] in the total average trade of that exporting country for the year 2005. The second number, in parentheses, is the share in the year 2010. In some cells there are arrows pointing downwards or upwards. These arrows indicate the direction of change in shares between 2005 and 2010. In a cell where there is no arrow, it implies that the share in the two periods was the same. Lastly, "n.a." implies that the exporting country did not export the particular product in the year in question, with a cell figure of zero (0, 0) implying that the exporting country did not export to the respective region(s) of which it is a member, though it exported to other non-regional trade partners.

The tabulated results show that, for example, in 2005, Zimbabwe's average maize trade which was destined to both COMESA and SADC regions accounted for 92 per cent of its total trade. In 2010 its share destined towards these two trading blocs had gone up to 98 per cent. Thus, Zimbabwe's intra-COMESA and intra-SADC trade in maize during the period under review, based on this indicator increased.

Namibia, Rwanda, Tanzania and Zimbabwe are the four countries whose intra-regional trade across the three products increased during the period reviewed. These are the countries which have integrated the most as they managed to increase intra-regional trade amongst their respective regional trade blocs for all the three agrifood products more than other countries. For instance, in 2005, Namibia traded 71 and 28 per cent of total rice and wheat with SADC and SACU regions (the two regional blocs to which it is a member), respectively, but, as of 2010, the respective shares have increased 90 and 47 per cent.

On the other hand, Burundi, Malawi and Sudan are the countries whose intra-regional trade in at least two of the three products has declined. For instance, in 2005, Burundi traded 100 and 99 per cent of total maize and rice to COMESA and EAC regions (the two regional blocs to which it is a member), respectively, but, as of 2010, the respective shares have declined to 98 and 17 per cent. This implies that, despite the fact that the country is a member of COMESA FTA and EAC CU, the country's trade with members in these regions in maize and rice declined. In other words, Burundi's integration into these regions for these two products, based on this indicator, has declined between 2005 and 2010.

For Swaziland, being a member for the three RECs, namely COMESA, SADC and SACU, did not have any new effect given that the country had already been trading 100 per cent of all the three agrifood products with members from these three regions. The country's performance integration in these three products may, however, be due mainly to the SACU integration effect, as a larger proportion of the country's three agrifood products were traded with the SACU region.

Product Complementarities

Table 6.3 presents product complementarity indices (PCIs) for countries from the three RECs for which data was readily available. These indices are calculated to individual countries and also an average index is provided. Given the paucity of data at product level, especially at HS4 or HS6, the section calculated the PCIs for agricultural commodities as a whole.

Table 6.2 Changes in Intra-Regional Trade Share 2005 and 2010

	Country/ Product	*Regional Bloc(s)*	*Percentage Destined for Respective Regional Blocs*		
			Maize	*Rice*	*Wheat*
1	Botswana	SADC/SACU	100 (100)	99 ↓ (97)	100 (100)
2	Burundi	COMESA/EAC	100 ↓ (98)	99 ↓ (17)	100 ↓ (7)
3	Comoros	COMESA/SADC	71 ↓ (16)	0.3 ↑ (26)	0.0 (0.0)
4	Kenya	COMESA/EAC	42 ↓ (29)	20 ↓ (11)	0.3 ↑ (1.0)
5	Madagascar	COMESA/SADC	98 ↓ (78)	0.04 ↑ (2.6)	0.0 ↑ (0.9)
6	Malawi	COMESA/SADC	100 (100)	14 ↓ (69)	16 ↓ (2.0)
7	Mauritius	COMESA/SADC	0.4 ↑ (12)	0.2 (0.2)	0.0 (0.0)
8	Mozambique	SADC	94 ↑ (99)	0.8 ↑ (4)	1.0 ↑ (1.1)
9	Namibia	SADC/SACU	95 ↑ (97)	71 ↑ (90)	28 ↑ (47)
10	Rwanda	COMESA/EAC	8 ↑ (100)	44 ↑ (78)	0.0 ↑ (12)
11	South Africa	SADC/SACU	73 ↓ (17)	1.2 ↑ (2.8)	3.0 ↑ (2.0)
12	Sudan	COMESA	0.4 ↓ (0.3)	89 ↓ (60)	0.0 (0.0)
13	Swaziland	COMESA/SADC/SACU	100 (100)	100 (100)	100 (100)
14	Tanzania	SADC/EAC	83 ↑ (94)	11 ↑ (96)	25 ↓ (4)

Table 6.2 Continued

	Country/ Product	*Regional Bloc(s)*	*Percentage Destined for Respective Regional Blocs*		
			Maize	*Rice*	*Wheat*
15	Uganda	COMESA/EAC	69 ↑ (93)	10 ↑ (96)	7.0 ↓ (3.0)
16	Zambia	COMESA/SADC	89 ↑ (98)	57 ↓ (36)	78 ↑ (100)
17	Zimbabwe	COMESA/SADC	92 ↑ (98)	22 ↑ (32)	20 ↑ (26)

Source: author.

For almost all tabulated countries, the average PCIs were concentrated between 40 and 50. However, when one considers the individual reporter countries' indices, the picture becomes very varied. For instance, Botswana and Rwanda's PCI values were relatively high, and were above 50 for 19 and 20 countries, respectively, out of the 26 countries' trading partners, signifying that the countries these two countries' trade in agriculture commodities complimented (in consumption) that of other trading partners from the three regional blocs in 2010.

Given that regional staple foods are mainly the three commodities analysed in this chapter, it follows that higher PCIs presented in Table 6.3 are thus signifying complementarity in consumption as opposed to complementarity in production. These higher PCIs also indicate that the region has even higher potential for intra-regional trade in these agrifoods.

Gravity Trade Model Result Estimations

The study estimated a pooled time-series, cross-sectional regression for the whole period 2005 to 2010. Although the chapter employed the panel data approach, measuring fixed or random effects is problematic under the current approach given that the study's main objective is to measure the intra-regional trade and openness to trade.[12] This view or approach is supported by Jayasinghe and Sarker (2007).

Table 6.4 contains the estimated gravity results for the three commodities traded by countries from COMESA, EAC and SADC regional blocs. Coefficients of the estimated standard gravity model are discussed first, followed by a discussion of intra-region and extra-region impacts of the three RECs' respective FTAs and/or CU (in the case of EAC). The adjusted R^2 ranges from 0.41 for maize to 0.49 for rice. The estimated importer's GDP and exporter's GDP coefficients generally have the expected positive sign in most equations and are,

Table 6.3 Product Complementarity Indices

Country	*Code*	*AGO*	*BWA*	*BDI*	*COM*	*ZAR*	*DJI*	*EGY*	*ERI*	*ETH*	*KEN*	*LSO*	*LBY*	*MDG*	*MWI*	*MUS*	*MOZ*	*NAM*	*RWA*	*SYC*	*ZAF*	*SDN*	*SWZ*	*TZA*	*UGA*	*ZMB*	*ZWE*	*Ave*
Botswana	BWA	48	–	54	62	25	63	52	62	67	53	60	58	53	56	24	59	24	56	58	18	54	57	55	56	48	46	50
Burundi	BDI	53	74	–	59	50	50	45	52	84	39	79	49	56	50	43	50	55	51	50	43	52	47	45	49	48	51	53
Djibouti	DJI	43	61	48	55	40	–	46	45	51	42	64	42	48	43	51	43	46	41	52	46	44	57	43	39	43	40	47
Egypt	EGY	31	53	29	49	35	38	–	50	42	37	62	39	37	28	41	39	35	42	40	34	29	48	41	31	26	31	38
Ethiopia	ETH	28	45	39	47	29	34	30	55	–	30	79	27	31	32	26	31	40	48	40	30	33	50	32	29	31	33	38
Kenya	KEN	28	30	35	53	31	36	29	39	34	–	39	27	47	32	31	34	42	44	33	27	29	32	33	36	27	30	34
Madagascar	MDG	34	54	43	56	36	47	41	51	46	36	48	36	–	34	36	39	54	50	40	36	38	51	39	34	30	38	42
Malawi	MWI	38	38	45	40	30	33	34	63	47	31	49	29	35	–	58	30	28	50	38	27	30	49	29	27	22	32	37
Mauritius	MUS	21	25	29	33	26	35	29	36	33	26	48	26	28	27	–	28	36	35	24	25	29	33	27	24	26	25	29
Mozambique	MOZ	35	61	41	66	27	47	34	75	46	29	80	28	72	37	39	–	67	37	43	32	37	45	31	36	26	32	44
Rwanda	RWA	57	68	51	68	52	58	40	59	72	50	76	54	64	55	54	51	60	–	60	33	58	45	33	49	53	38	54
South Africa	ZAF	42	40	43	53	33	49	33	57	52	37	44	42	49	41	39	42	47	51	52	–	39	56	43	48	38	36	44
Sudan	SDN	37	40	44	89	39	47	39	83	84	41	92	41	86	42	75	43	47	43	34	45	–	88	41	44	42	42	53
Tanzania	TZA	44	43	49	59	36	53	32	56	54	34	57	38	48	39	30	37	44	49	46	27	43	51	–	39	29	36	43
Uganda	UGA	35	49	42	51	36	41	36	36	44	35	58	35	40	31	38	36	46	46	43	31	32	45	35	–	28	34	39
Zambia	ZMB	42	69	46	64	24	47	24	66	54	23	67	45	54	53	47	27	46	60	60	19	56	62	47	50	–	27	46
Zimbabwe	ZWE	48	49	49	65	46	56	42	65	55	46	64	49	48	48	48	47	42	50	56	31	54	40	48	48	36	–	49

Source: author calculations.

Notes
AGO – Angola; COM – Comoros; ZAR – Democratic Republic of Congo (DRC); ERI – Eritrea; LSO – Lesotho; LBY – Libya; NAM – Namibia; SYC – Seychelles; SWZ – Swaziland.

Table 6.4 Gravity Regression Results of SADC Trade in Six Commodities, 2005–2010

Variable/Product	*Maize*	*Rice*	*Wheat*
GDP importer	0.22 (1.9)**	0.41 (4.7)***	0.25 (1.5)
GDP exporter	0.95 (6.8)***	0.61 (8.2)***	0.40 (1.9)**
Population importer	0.32 (2.3)**	0.67 (7.7)***	–
Population exporter	–0.11 (2.70)***	–	0.80 (3.29)***
Inflation importer	0.18 (2.5)**	0.09 (1.3)	–
Inflation exporter	–	–0.06 (–1.5)	–0.50 (–4.9)***
Distance	–0.18 (–2.9)**	–0.49 (–2.1)**	–0.83 (–5.4)***
Common border	1.1 (2.5)**	–	3.27 (3.42)***
COMESA (regional dummy)	7.2 (5.4)***	1.89 (1.6)*	0.27 (1.0)
COMESA0 (openness dummy)	5.4 (3.9)***	2.17 (2.0)**	1.34 (1.4)
EAC (regional dummy)	2.2 (2.9)***	–	–18.9 (–4.2)***
EAC0 (openness dummy)	–	–0.99 (–1.4)	–24.1 (–4.8)***
SADC (regional dummy)	0.51 (0.4)	3.37 (1.9)*	8.56 (4.02)***
SADC0 (openness dummy)	–2.6 (–2.3)**	3.0 (1.5)	3.78 (2.0)**
R^2	0.44	0.49	0.41
No. of observations	1,182	1,404	756

Notes
***, ** and * significant at 1, 5 and 10 per cent level respectively. t-statistics in parentheses.

in most equations, significant at the 1 per cent level. For instance, a unit percentage increase in importer GDP will result in increased maize trade by 0.22 per cent, while the same percentage rise will cause a 0.40 per cent increase in trade of wheat. Across all the tabulated results, the estimated coefficients range from 0.22 to 0.41 and 0.40 to 0.95 for importer and exporter GDPs, respectively.

Thus, the result shows that there is a statistically significant positive relationship between bilateral trade and incomes of partners. Generally, these results are consistent with the findings of other studies such as Makochekanwa *et al.* (2010), Jayasinghe and Sarker (2007), Frankel and Wei (1998) and Gilbert *et al.* (2001), among others.

The parameter estimates of both importer and export populations for the model are in most cases positive and statistically significant for the three products under study. Thus, for maize and rice, larger population size in the importer countries encourages more trade between partners, with larger population size or the importing country meaning increased consumption, hence increased imports. On the other hand, in the case of maize, large population size in the exporting country reduced exports as local demand was given first priority. The estimated coefficients for P_i and P_j can thus take either a positive or a negative sign and such findings were also reported in previous studies such as Eita and Jordaan (2007).

The effect of importer inflation is positive on maize, indicating that inflation in importing countries will stimulate consumers to try to avoid domestic inflation by substituting local goods with imports. Thus, in this scenario, a 1 per cent rise in the inflation rate in importer countries increases demand for maize imports by 0.18 per cent. On the other hand, the inflation rates of exporting countries have a negative impact on the wheat trade, with a 1 per cent increase causing a decline in demand for wheat of 0.50 per cent.

In all the tabulated results, bilateral distance has a negative effect on trade with the magnitude differing across products and time. As theoretically expected, the parameter estimates of the distance variable are negative and statistically significant, at least, at the 5 per cent level during the period of the study irrespective of the products. For all products, results indicate that the volume of trade in each of the selected commodities diminishes as distance increases. For instance, a unit increase in distance will reduce trade by a magnitude of 0.18 per cent for maize, 0.49 per cent in the case of rice and 0.83 per cent for wheat. Thus, the coefficients for our distance variable seem to take a wide range for the three commodities. The estimated effects of distance on bilateral trade in agrifood commodities presented in this study confirm the findings of Bikker (1987) and Boisso and Ferrantino (1994) among others. This result is similar to the findings of Jayasinghe and Sarker (2007), among others.

The coefficients of having a common border are positive and statistically significant, at least at the 5 per cent level of significance, in the cases of maize and wheat in which they are reported. This, as said before, is according to theoretical expectations which assumes that countries that share the same language and also share a common border are more likely to trade with each other than countries which have different languages and that do not share a common border.

Regional Dummy Effects

Empirical results shown in Table 6.4 suggest that there is a significant positive effect for all the three regional blocs (CMESA, EAC and SADC) on trade in maize during the study period. The calculated percentage change of the estimated bloc and openness coefficients of the three respective RECs and for the selected commodities are reported in Table 6.5, panels A through to C.

The estimated coefficient COMESA regional dummy is positive (Table 6.5) across the three agriculture products, although it is not significant for the case of wheat. This positive sign suggests that COMESA FTA has resulted in more regional trade in both maize and rice being conducted within the region, than when it is compared to the rest of the world (RoW). Specifically, Panel A of Table 6.5 indicates that two COMESA member states traded 566 per cent more than they traded with RoW on an annual average between 2005 to 2010. The trade bias was even higher in the case of maize where countries traded around 138,791 per cent more than they traded with RoW. The fact that these regional members traded very much amongst themselves when compared to RoW is understandable given the nature of the product, maize, which is bulky in nature, hence relatively expensive to transport (higher per tonnage transportation costs) and thus traders prefer to buy from nearby regional countries.

With regard to the estimated coefficient for the EAC regional dummy, here the dummy has a positive sign on maize and a negative sign on wheat, and these coefficients are both significant at the 1 per cent level. The calculated percentages for maize and wheat for the EAC dummy are presented in Panel B of Table 6.5. In the case of maize, the tabulated percentage indicates that two EAC members traded 839 per cent more among themselves than with RoW. In the

Table 6.5 Percentage Changes in Estimated Bloc and Openness Coefficients of SADC

Panel A: COMESA

Variable	*Maize*	*Rice*	*Wheat*
COMESA	138,791	566	31
COMESA0	22,390	781	283

Panel B: EAC

Variable	*Maize*	*Rice*	*Wheat*
EAC	839	n.a.	–100
EAC0	n.a.	–63	–100

Panel C: SADC

Variable	*Maize*	*Rice*	*Wheat*
SADC	66	2,816	524,729
SADC0	–93	1,847	4,271

case of wheat, two EAC countries traded 100 per cent less among themselves than they traded with RoW during the period 2005 to 2010. The negative coefficients on wheat imply that trade in this product was generally below the expected level of trade especially in a dispensation of zero tariff reduction under the CU.

Panel C of Table 6.5 presents the calculated percentages for the SADC regional dummy on maize, rice and wheat. All the SADC dummy coefficients are positive (see Table 6.4) and calculated percentages are also positive. For instance, two SADC countries traded 66 per cent more than they traded with RoW on an annual average during the period 2005 to 2010. The percentage of trade among SADC member states was even extremely high in the case of wheat, and this is understood given that most countries get a larger position of their wheat requirements from South Africa, which is an SADC FTA member country.

Trade Diverting Effects of RECs

Tracing the level of changes in the regional openness dummies (*COMESA*0, *EAC*0 and *SADCO*) can provide clues into the presence of trade diversion effects. This will provide us with information as to whether there were reductions in the level of imports by regional members in each of the three RECs from non-members relative to the level of exports by countries from each region to non-members over time. In this section, the study is interested in the level of the openness coefficient. As before, the relevant results are reported in Table 6.4 with Table 6.5 presenting the calculated percentage changes.

The estimated coefficients of the COMESA openness dummy are positive on all the three products, although it is insignificant on wheat. These (positive sign) results suggest that the imports of these commodities into the COMESA region from non-member states in RoW were higher than the gravity model would predict. During the period under review, net imports by a COMESA country from non-members was about 22,390 per cent, 781 per cent and 283 per cent higher for maize, rice and wheat, respectively, than its net exports to non-members.

In the case of the EAC the estimated openness coefficients are negative, although one (wheat) is statistically significant (Panel B, Table 6.5). The calculated percentages show that COMESA member countries imported 63 per cent and 100 per cent less rice and wheat, respectively, from RoW during the 2005–2010 period. There is clear evidence of trade diversion in these two products under COMESA regional integration.

The results on the SADC openness dummy shows positive coefficients on rice and wheat and a negative sign on maize, although the coefficient on rice is not significant. The positive sign on wheat suggests that the imports of these commodities into the SADC region from non-member states in RoW were higher than the gravity model would predict. During the period under review, net imports by a SADC country from non-members was about 4,271 per cent higher for wheat than its net exports to non-members. The situation is however different in the case of the maize trade. The calculated percentage shows that SADC member countries imported 93 per cent less rice from RoW during the 2005–2010 period.

Conclusion

The research analysed the impact of FTA arrangements in three RECs, namely the COMESA, the EAC and the SADC, on trade in three agrifood products, namely maize, rice and wheat, for the period covering 2005 to 2010. The study relied both on trade-related indices and also on the gravity trade model.

Changes in intra-regional trade shares shows that Namibia, Rwanda, Tanzania and Zimbabwe are the four countries whose intra-regional trade across the three products increased during the period reviewed. On the other hand, Burundi, Malawi and Sudan are the countries whose intra-regional trade in at least two of the three products has declined.

The results from the gravity trade model show that all the traditional variables, that is, GDP for exporter and importer countries as well as distance, have expected theoretical signs. Population size, which was an added variable, carries both positive and negative signs, as expected by theory. The coefficients on all variables of interest, that is COMESA, EAC and regional dummies, shows that, with the exception of wheat trade in EAC, the estimated coefficients for these regional dummies in all other RECs and commodities is positive and statistically significant; indicating that intra-regional trade in those regions and for such commodities is above the predicted level of the standard gravity model.

The coefficients of the *COMESA*0, *EAC*0 and *SADCO* dummy variables which provide information on the presence of trade diversion effects vary across regional blocs and also across the products. For instance, the estimated coefficients of *COMESA*0 across the three products are positive and statistically significant, suggesting that imports of these commodities into COMESA member states from non-member states in RoW were higher than the gravity model would predict.

Notes

1 The analysis is *only* limited to countries participating in COMESA and SADC FTAs, and the EAC CU.

2 The treaty establishing COMESA was signed on 5 November 1993 at Kampala (Uganda) and was ratified on 8 December 1994 at Lilongwe (Malawi). It has 19 member countries: Burundi, Comoros, DRC, Djibouti, Egypt, Eritrea, Ethiopia, Kenya, Libya, Madagascar, Malawi, Mauritius, Rwanda, Seychelles, Sudan, Swaziland, Uganda, Zambia and Zimbabwe.

3 COMESA was formed in 1994 as a successor to the PTA. Tariff reduction had started in 1984 within the framework of the PTA, but was accelerated with the formation of COMESA.

4 The current SADC member states are: Angola, Botswana, DRC, Lesotho, Madagascar, Malawi, Mauritius, Mozambique, Namibia, South Africa, Swaziland, Tanzania, Zambia and Zimbabwe.

5 It is the loosest form of economic integration, which liberates trade among member countries by *lowering* of trade barriers against imports from other member countries while trade barriers against non-member countries are maintained. As such, PTAs place non-member countries at a competitive disadvantage, and divert trade from them towards member countries. This is because the duty-free (even with high production costs) imports from within members may become cheaper than duty-paid (but with lower production costs) imports from non-members.

6 In this group, member countries *remove* both tariff and non-tariff barriers when trading with each member state. Nevertheless, each member country retains its own set of trade barriers (including customs duties) against non-member countries; and these trade barriers normally vary from one member to another. Similarly, a member may retain a separate set of barriers against imports from different non-member countries.

7 Frankel (1997) and Deardorff (1998), among others, provide theoretical micro foundations of the gravity trade model and Frankel (1998: 2) pointed out that the gravity equation has recently "gone from an embarrassment of poverty of theoretical foundations to embarrassment of riches".

8 Following Newton's (1687) "Law of Universal Gravitation", classical gravity theory states that the attractions force F_{ij} between two entities i and j is proportional to their respective masses m_i and m_j and inversely proportional to the squared distance d_{ij}^2 between these entities. This law is formalized as:

$$F_{ij} = G\frac{M_i M_j}{D_{ij}^2}$$

where F_{ij} is the attractive force;
M_i and M_j are the respective two countries' masses;
$D2_{ij}$ is the distance between the two objects;
G is a gravitational constant depending on the units of measurement for mass and force.

9 Following Halvorsen and Palmquist (1980), if the estimated coefficient is say β_6, change in the value of a given total product trade at disaggregated level (i.e. $trade_{ijat}$) can be calculated for change of dummy variable from zero to one using the following formula: $(trade_{ijat(1)} - trade_{ijat(0)}) / trade_{ijat(0)} = e^{\beta 2} - 1$.

10 This study has experimented with a number of possible variables in each of the six product gravity models and the ones presented in this section are the most significant ones.

11 The Southern African Customs Union (SACU) is the oldest existing customs union in the world and is composed of five countries of Southern Africa namely Botswana, Lesotho, Namibia, South Africa and Swaziland. Its headquarters is in the Namibian capital Windhoek.

12 Fixed/random effects estimations do not allow inclusion of dummy variables (such as the COMESA, EAC and SADC dummies).

References

Aitken, N.D. 1973. "The Effects of the EEC and EFTA on European Trade: A Temporal Cross-Section Analysis", *American Economic Review*, 63(5): 881–892.

Aksoy, M.A. 2004. "Global Agricultural Trade Policies". In: M.A. Aksoy and J.C. Beghin, eds, *Global Agricultural Trade and the Developing Countries*. Oxford: Oxford University Press and the World Bank.

Bhagwati, J. 1998. "Trading Preferentially: Theory and Policy", *Economic Journal*, 108(449): 1128–1148.

Bikker, J. 1987. "An International Trade Flow Model with Substitution: An Extension of the Gravity Model", *KYKLOS*, 40(3): 315–337.

Boisso, D. and M. Ferrantino. 1994. "Economic and Cultural Distances in International Trade: An Empirical Puzzle", US International Trade Commission, Washington DC.

Chauvin, S. and G. Gaulier. 2002. "Regional Trade Integration in Southern Africa", CEPII Working Paper No. 12.

Clausing, K.A. 2001. "Trade Creation and Trade Diversion in the Canada-United States Free Trade Agreement", *Canadian Journal of Economics*, 34: 677–696.

Deardorff, A. 1998. "Determinants of Bilateral Trade: Does Gravity Work in a Neoclassical World?" In: J. Frankel, ed., *The Regionalization of the World Economy*. Chicago, IL: University of Chicago Press.

Eichengreen, B. and D. Irwin. 1998. "The Role of History in Bilateral Trade Flows". In: J. Frankel, ed., *The Regionalization of the World Economy*. National Bureau of Economic Research. Chicago, IL: University of Chicago Press.

Eita, J.H. and A.C. Jordaan. 2007. "South Africa Exports of Metal and Articles of Base Metal: A Gravity Model Approach", *Journal of Studies in Economics and Econometrics*, 31(3): 81–96.

Endoh, M. 1999. "Trade Creation and Trade Diversion in the EEC, the LAFTA and the CMEA", *Applied Economics*, 31: 207–216.

Ethier, W. 1998. "The New Regionalism", *Economic Journal*, 108: 1149–1161.

Frankel, J. 1997. "Regional Trading Blocs in the World Economic System", Institute for International Economics, Washington DC.

Frankel, J. (ed.). 1998. *The Regionalization of the World Economy*, Chicago, IL, London: University of Chicago Press.

Frankel, J.A. and S.J. Wei. 1998. "Regionalization of World Trade and Currencies: Economics and Politics". In: J. Frankel, ed., *Regionalization of the World Economy*. NBER Project Report. Chicago, IL: University of Chicago Press.

Frankel, J.A., E. Stein and S.J. Wei. 1995. "Trading Blocs and the Americas: The Natural, the Unnatural, and the Super Natural", *Journal of Development Economics*, 47: 61–95.

Ghosh, S. and S. Yamarik. 2004. "Are Regional Trading Arrangements Trade Creating? An Application of Extreme Bounds Analysis", *Journal of International Economics*, 63: 369–395.

Gilbert, J., R. Scollay and B. Bora. 2001. "Assessing Regional Trading Arrangements in the Asia-Pacific", Policy Issues in International Trading and Commodities Study Series No. 15, United Nations Conference on Trade and Development, New York.

Halvorsen, R. and R. Palmquist. 1980. "The Interpretation of Dummy Variables in Semilogarithmic Equations", *American Economic Review*, 70: 474–475.

Jayasinghe, S. and R. Sarker. 2007. "Effects of Regional Trade Agreements on Trade in Agrifood Products: Evidence from Gravity Modeling Using Disaggregated Data", *Review of Agriculture Economics*, 30(1): 61–81.

Kalaba, M. and M. Tsedu. 2008. "Implementation of the SADC Trade Protocol and the Intra-SADC Trade Performance", Trade and Industrial Policy Strategy (TIPS), South Africa.

Karim, I.E.E.A. and I.S. Ismail. 2007. "Potential for Agricultural Trade in COMESA Region: A Comparative Study of Sudan, Egypt and Kenya", *African Journal of Agricultural Research*, 2(10): 481–487.

Khandelwal, P. 2005. "COMESA and SADC: Prospects and Challenges for Regional Trade Integration", UNU-CRIS Occasional Papers, 0-2005/1.

Krueger, A.O. 2000. "Trade Creation and Trade Diversion under NAFTA", NBER Working Paper No. W7429, National Bureau of Economic Research, Cambridge MA.

Lyakurwa, W., A. McKay, N. Ng'eno and W. Kennes. 1997. "Regional Integration in Sub-Saharan Africa: A Review of Experiences and Issues". In: A. Oyejide, I. Elbadawi and P. Collier, eds, *Regional Integration and Trade Liberalization in Sub-Saharan Africa, Vol. 1: Framework, Issues and Methodology Perspectives*. London: Macmillan Press Ltd.

Makochekanwa, A., J. Maringwa and E. Mahembe. 2010. "The Impacts of SADC Trade Protocol Implementation on Trade in Agrifood Products", *African Integration Review*, 4(1): 107–156.

Molinari, A. 2003. "Sectoral Border Effects: Analysing Implicit EU Trade Integration", University of Sussex.

Panagariya, A. 2000. "Preferential Trade Liberalization: Traditional Theory and New Developments", *Journal of Economic Literature*, 38: 287–331.

Poyhonen, P. 1963. "A Tentative Model for the Volume of Trade between Countries", *Weltwirtschaftliches Archiv*, 90: 23–40.

Rojid, S. 2006. "COMESA Trade Potential: A Gravity Approach", *Applied Economic Letters*, 13: 947–951.

SADC Secretariat. 2003. "Regional Indicative Strategic Development Plan". Gaborone, Botswana. Available at: www.sadc.int/index.php/download_file/31/542/.

Summers, L. 1991. "Regionalism and World Trading System", *Policy Implications of Trade and Currency Zones: A Summary of the Bank's 1991 Symposium*. Kansas City, MO: Federal Reserve Bank of Kansas City.

Sunde, T., C. Chidoko and J. Zivanomoyo. 2009. "Determinants of Intra-Industry Trade between Zimbabwe and its Trading Partners in the Southern African Development Community Region (1990–2006)", *Journal of Social Sciences*, 5(1): 16–21.

Tinbergen, J. 1962. "An Analysis of World Trade Flows". In: J. Tinbergen, ed., *Shaping the World Economy*. New York: Twentieth Century Fund.

Tsikata, Y. 1999. "Southern Africa: Trade, Liberalization and Implications for a Free Trade Area", TIPS Annual Forum. Available at: www.acp-eutrade.org/documents/113_tsikata_tips.pdf.

Viner, J. 1950. "The Customs Unions Issues", Carnegie Endowment for International Peace, New York. Available at: www.cepii.fr/anglaisgraph/bdd/distances.htm.

7 Export Diversification and Intra-Industry Trade in Africa[1]

Siope Vakataki 'Ofa, Malcolm Spence, Simon Mevel and Stephen Karingi

Introduction

In January 2012, the African Union Summit of African Heads of State and Government endorsed the theme of Boosting Intra-African Trade, paving the way towards fast-tracking a Continental Free Trade Area (CFTA) with a tentative timeframe of 2017. The January 2012 decision mandated UNECA (United Nations Economic Commission for Africa), AUC (African Union Commission), AfDB (African Development Bank) and Member States to collaborate closely towards the implementation of relevant action plans at the national, regional and continental levels on boosting intra-African trade and the establishment of the CFTA. In particular, the January 2012 Summit recognized the low level of trade between African countries and called upon Member States, regional economic communities (RECs) and the AUC to promote industrial development policy and value addition to diversify African economies and thereby move away from heavy reliance on traditional primary exports.

It is against this backdrop that this study attempts to contribute to the current trade policy dialogue on boosting intra-African trade in four aspects. First, the study examines patterns of export diversification for African economies. Second, a measure of intra-industry trade (IIT) for African economies is estimated. IIT is understood as simultaneous import and export of similar but differentiated goods. Third, the study evaluates potential linkages between export diversification and IIT in Africa. Informed by the patterns of trade in African economies, constraints towards export diversification and IIT are discussed and ways to overcoming these constraints are explored.

The chapter begins by briefly discussing the theoretical underpinnings behind IIT and export diversification. Second, it presents the evolution and status of IIT and export diversification in Africa. Third, it attempts to examine the linkages between IIT and export diversification as well as exploring potential pathways to enhancing IIT and/or export diversification in Africa. Fourth, the chapter discusses constraints to IIT and export diversification in Africa. Finally, policy recommendations are formulated to conclude the chapter.

Theoretical Underpinnings of Export Diversification and IIT

Export Diversification

Export expansion can be either through the extensive margin – new products or new markets – or the intensive margin – more of current products. Export diversification is therefore understood as the expansion of exports due to new products or new markets – extensive margin. Amurgo-Pacheco and Pierola (2007) provide a useful narrower definition by discussing a geographic dimension with export diversification via the extensive margin in the export of new products to existing markets, old products to new markets and new products to new markets.

Why is export diversification important for Africa? Export diversification – and economic diversification in general – build the resilience of poorer countries to face external economic shocks. Diversification is more relevant today to Africa as the impact of the global financial crisis has affected both rich and poor economies globally. For Africa, with its high dependence on primary commodities and which faces fluctuating world prices on most primary goods, there is a need to pursue developmental strategies which promote export diversification. In addition, Africa requires high and sustained growth to help combat poverty. Export diversification is widely seen as a positive trade objective in sustaining economic growth (Brenton *et al.*, 2007). Delgado (1995) argued that diversifying the agricultural export base and diversifying the economy across sectors are central to the long-run growth strategies in Africa given the high concentration ratio of agricultural exports (food and beverages typically account for well over half of merchandise exports in non-oil exporting African countries). Moreover, there is convergence in the developmental literature that growth requires structural transformation (primary – manufacturing – services trade), hence African economies must diversify their production base into high value-added production in order to achieve sustained economic growth.[2] Diversification is sometimes claimed to be important not just for resource-rich countries, but as a pre-requisite for economic growth (UNECA and AUC, 2007).

Almost every theory of international trade predicts that a larger economy will export more in absolute terms than a smaller economy. Nevertheless, trade theories differ in predicting how relatively larger economies export more (Hummels and Klenow, 2005). One strand of literature emphasizes export expansion through the intensive margin, based on seminal work by Armington (1969). Brenton *et al.* (2007) has argued that low income countries focus on greater differentiation of existing products rather than attempting to diversify directly into new export categories. On the other hand, some have argued for the expansion of exports via the extensive margin, based on the influential work of Krugman (1980). However, Hummels and Klenow (2005) argue that neither the intensive margin hypothesis by Armington (1969) nor Krugman's extensive margin hypothesis fully explain international trade patterns in developing countries, and provided an empirical framework dividing trade expansion into both intensive and extensive. The authors argued that consumer preferences for variety increases as economic development increases, thereby providing an incentive for export expansion in the extensive margin. Their study found that larger economies export higher volumes of each good (intensive margin), export a higher variety of goods (extensive margin)[3] and export higher quality goods.

Imbs and Wacziarg (2003) found that the process of diversification follows a two-stage process (U-shape relationship), in which growth in the early stages of development is accompanied by diversification, until a turning point upon which the trend reverses towards increasing specialization once more. Few African economies are at the level of development associated with the turning point towards specialization, suggesting that further growth on the continent can lead to greater diversification. This study adopts a measure of GDP per capita, and there is faint evidence of this relationship in Africa, although oil-exporting economies with relatively large GDPs but with poorly diversified exports are anomalies inconsistent with the two-stage diversification hypothesis. A recent finding (Karingi and Spence, 2011) suggests that many African countries are currently engaged in export activities (export sophistication) not commensurate with their level of development and hence associated with significant opportunity costs.

The export sophistication[4] (EXPY) measures weighted goods according to the income of the exporting countries (Hausmann *et al.*, 2007) arguing that future growth is significantly influenced by current export sophistication. Countries such as Liberia, Madagascar or Egypt can be thought of as exporting products that are richer than they are, and as such can expect higher growth in the future. Imbs and Wacziarg's (2003) U-shape relationship was later verified for developing countries by Cadot *et al.* (2008). The latter study suggests that growth at the income levels of most African economies should prompt diversification. As developing economies grow, consumption patterns change through Engel effects, that is, increased demand for a greater variety of goods as income rises. A rising middle class in Africa is likely to demand a larger variety of goods (AfDB, 2011). UNECA's work on export diversification has reiterated the justifications for diversification with respect to growth dynamics (UNECA and AUC, 2007, 2011; Karingi and Spence, 2011).

Ben Hammouda *et al.* (2006) offer a richer analysis of the diversification regimes in Africa, and found that there is little economic diversification despite prolonged periods of peace and stability. Some African economies remain poorly diversified, such as Burkina Faso and the Seychelles. Also, some African economies – for instance, Mozambique and Malawi – started the process but have not made any significant breakthrough in diversifying agricultural products and are yet to diversify into the higher value activities. Nonetheless, the authors found that some African economies with deepened diversification are engaging in structural transformation in a sustainable manner. Tunisia's horizontal diversifications into high value activities and Madagascar's capture of vertical value chains in clothing and apparels are examples. However, the study also found other African economies that were backsliding in the diversification process. Typically, the reason why African economies have attempted to move into new sectors is due to rising commodity prices which leads to an ever-increasing concentration of exports, enclave economies and Dutch disease effect.[5] Guinea-Bissau and Angola can be categorized by this regime. Lastly, the study found that countries which went through conflicts see their diversification prospects negatively impacted. Some countries which had undergone instability, such as Liberia, Sierra Leone and the Democratic Republic of the Congo, have had positive diversification outcomes when they became more stable.

Export diversification through product differentiation in Africa has not been subject to extensive economic scrutiny. Brenton *et al.* (2007) articulate a convincing case for low income countries to focus on greater differentiation of existing products, rather than attempting to diversify directly into new export categories. This stems from the observation that export growth at the intensive margin is far more significant for developing countries than that at the extensive margin (i.e. export growth is dominated by intensifying trade in existing products rather than undertaking new export activities – see Amurgo-Pacheco and Pierola, 2007; Brenton and Newfarmer, 2009). This may be linked to the fact that the gains from developing new goods for export are socialized through information spillovers, yet the costs are private, leading to a sub-optimal level of innovation (Hausmann and Rodrik, 2003).

Moreover, when developing countries do undertake extensive expansion, the survival rate is very low. With imperfect information firms are *ex ante* unaware of the profitability of entering foreign markets, and evidence suggests that Africa is particularly poor at sustaining export relationships once they are created. Besedes and Prusa (2007) show that African exports would have had a three percentage points higher growth rate if they had South Korea's survival compared to a 1.8 percentage points higher growth rate if they had South Korea's deepening (growth of trade in surviving relationships). For Malawi, just 35 per cent of export flows survive beyond one year (Brenton *et al.*, 2007). Investing in improving the quality of existing products is further warranted on the grounds that rich countries import more from countries that produce higher quality goods (Hallak, 2006). In the policy framework of new structural economics (Lin, 2010) export diversification is best achieved by focusing on existing comparative advantage, where industries are competitive, leading to the capture of economic rents for reinvestment and subsequent upgrading of endowments structures.

While this is suggestive of a need to prioritize intensive expansion through greater differentiation, Klinger and Lederman (2006) and Cadot *et al.* (2008) show that the process of diversification (as opposed to export growth) in low income countries is driven from inside the frontier innovation (emulations) and extensive expansion, suggesting that African countries should undertake new export activities if they are to succeed in diversifying exports, but that they should be in industries in which there is already existing expertise. In practice, the dichotomy between intensive and extensive expansion is of little prescriptive utility as export growth and diversification require the upgrading of production of existing exports and the undertaking of new export activities. This implies that African economies need to explore dynamic comparative advantages[6] when promoting diversification. These are potential sectors outside Africa's main comparative advantage sectors of primary commodities and fuel. The role of developing the manufacturing sector, therefore, is of crucial importance. Structural adjustment is a costly exercise and therefore identifying the potential success sectors is essential.

The quality of institutions also matters for diversification. Rauch (2007) presents a model in which institutional reforms are conducive to allowing firms to enter higher value production activities and improve the results of trade liberalization relative to those targeted towards lower value production. Tybout (2000) found that differences between manufacturing efficiency in developing country firms relative to developed country counterparts are driven by low incomes in target markets, detrimental macro-policies, high transportation costs, bureaucracy and poor rule of law. Given the rising incomes and improved macro-stability in many African economies, transportation costs and improved rule of law emerge as policy priorities. Improving intellectual property rights, in particular, can help to privatize some of the positive externalities generated by new exporters which lead to sub-optimal innovation (Hausmann and Rodrick, 2003). Greater adherence to international metrology standards is crucial to ensure that differentiated goods can be assessed on a level playing field. With respect to infrastructure, its negative impact on trade costs is well established (Freund and Rocha, 2010; Limao and Venables, 2001). Cheaper international transit is also associated with extensive expansion (Dennis and Shepard, 2007; Pearson, 2010), while recent evidence from Eastern Europe shows it is also a driver of product quality (Harding, 2009). Karingi and Spence (2011) also found infrastructure to be a significant determinant both of productivity and of export sophistication in the African context.

Overall, while the literature on export diversification has argued for the prioritization of intensive or extensive margins respectively or both, we put forward an argument that there is a case for African countries to pursue export expansion through the intensive margin – through product differentiation – and also the extensive margin conditional on existing industries' competitiveness to compete in foreign markets.

IIT

Classical and neo-classical trade theories hypothesize that trade occurs because of differences between economies and the subsequent prospect of gains from specialization. The eighteenth century economist Adam Smith developed the theory of absolute advantage and was the first to argue that free trade led to prosperity. Two influential theories on international trade have been developed based on Smith's absolute advantage theory. The first was David Ricardo's comparative advantage theory in the early nineteenth century, and later in the mid-twentieth century, two Swedish economists, Eli Heckscher and Bertil Ohlin, developed the Heckscher–Ohlin theory of international trade.

According to Ricardian comparative advantage, countries produce and export commodities in which they have a relative cost advantage and import those commodities in which they have a relative cost disadvantage. The Ricardian model explained that specialization based on differences in labour productivity using different technologies determines a country's comparative advantage. The Heckscher–Ohlin trade model extended the Ricardian model to show that countries specialize and export products that use their abundant and cheap factors of production and import products that use the countries' scarce (and therefore costly) factors. Hence, factor endowments (capital, land and labour) determine a country's comparative advantage.

However, a new trade pattern has emerged in most developed countries – increased IIT – of which the classical theories of Smith, Ricardo and Heckscher–Ohlin could not fully account for. Moreover, the classical trade theories above emphasized that firms have homogeneous productivity and thus are expected to trade in similar quality goods, which is no longer the case today. Balassa (1966) and Grubel (1967) were among the first to observe tendencies towards trade of similar but differentiated products – IIT – rather than specialization, in the trading patterns of the European Economic Community. Their work heralded the search for new theories of international trade capable of explaining the phenomenon of IIT. Of the new trade theories, Krugman (1979, 1980) and Lancaster's (1980) monopolistic competition models are among the best known. They introduce two key assumptions: increasing returns to scale and consumers' love for variety. Under the assumption of increasing returns to scale, large firms have a cost advantage over smaller firms and monopolistic competition ensues. Opening up to trade means firms can serve a larger market and hence reduce costs and consumers can benefit from an increased range of varieties. Increased competition may also force prices down but consequently forcing smaller firms out of the market. Brander and Krugman (1983) add that IIT may take place even in instances in which goods are homogeneous. Domestic monopolists may enter foreign markets at a lower price than that charged for goods at home leading to the prospect of 'reciprocal dumping': two-way trade in the same product, even if the goods are identical, the initial prices are equal and trade is costly.[7]

Theories of economic geography add another possible explanation for IIT. The role of external returns to scale is more explicit here. The argument is that geographical location of firms leads to the development of clusters with technological and pecuniary externalities and external economies of scale. The success of the gravity model of trade flows also underlines that distance matters, and proximity to markets is a significant determinant of trade (gravity models also reflect the Linder hypothesis, which proposes that trade often occurs between similar sized economies – see Linder, 1961). Lastly, geographically fragmented production sees different stages of the value change dispersed across countries according to factor endowments or labour productivity. This can occur within multinational firms or between firms at different levels of the supply chain. Ethier (1982) presents a model through which restricted trade in intermediate goods requires final good production to be located near to intermediate goods, explaining the emergence of industrial clusters.

Debaere (2005) shows that new trade theory does not hold for non-OECD (Organisation for Economic Co-operation and Development) countries where many of the key assumptions – namely mature industries capable of realizing economies of scale and trading highly differentiated goods – do not reflect realities of African economies. Somewhat crudely we can say that factor endowments determine North–South trade in line with the Heckscher–Ohlin framework, with new trade theories offering insights into North–North trade.

However, IIT is emerging as vital to our understanding of South–South trade. Indeed, UNCTAD (2011) suggests three different analytical frameworks of South–South trade in which IIT is pivotal. First, the flying geese model (Akamatsu, 1962) of regional industrialization allowed East Asian economies to dovetail on the success of regional leaders. IIT here is a mechanism for learning, as low-flying geese import more sophisticated goods from their neighbours at first as a means of acquiring production know-how which allows for their manufacture for reverse export. Second, new-centre-periphery patterns envisage that African countries may be subject to foreign direct investment flows in the shape of large multinational corporations which engage in intra-firm, IIT, but bring little in terms of diversification or development. Third, the emergence of regional growth poles may lead to external economies of scale and agglomeration economies, allowing for product differentiation and IIT. We may add a fourth analytical framework in the shape of regional value chains. In a Ricardian perspective of IIT, relatively capital-intensive economies can specialize in the production of finished products, the intermediate inputs for which can be offshored to relatively labour abundant economies thereby generating regional value chains (Falvey, 1981; Hirchberg *et al.*, 1994). The importation of raw materials for processing and subsequent re-export is an example of vertical IIT, that in which the traded goods differ by quality, rather than horizontally differentiated goods which differ by price (Fontagné and Freudenberg, 1997).

The Status and Evolution of Export Diversification and IIT in Africa

Export Diversification Index for Africa

This section evaluates the evolution and status of African economies' export diversification patterns. A Normalised Herfindahl–Hirschman index (see Hirschman, 1964; UNECA and AUC, 2007) is used to estimate export diversification (or concentration), and is given by:

$$H = \sqrt{\frac{\sum_{i=1}^{N}\left(\frac{x_i}{\sum_{i=1}^{N} x_i}\right)^2 - \sqrt{\frac{1}{N}}}{1-\sqrt{\frac{1}{N}}}}$$

where x_i is the exports of product i, and N is the number of products considered. The index H denotes values $0 \geq H \leq 1$; an index value closer to one represents extreme concentration (low export diversification) and value close to zero attests of high diversification.

The normalized Herfindahl–Hirschman index is computed using the BACI dataset (Gaulier and Zignago, 2010) created by the Centre d'Études Prospectives et d'Informations Internationales (CEPII). The BACI dataset reconciles the trade flows reported to UN COMTRADE by exporters and importers at the Harmonized System six-digit level (HS6), vastly improving the reliability of the data coverage vis-à-vis the original dataset. The database covers more than 200 countries and 5,000 products. We use the nomenclature Harmonised System 1996, which covers the years 1998 to 2009. Data is currently available for 51 of the 56 economies in the dataset. Western Sahara and St. Helena are omitted leaving a sample of 49. The Southern African Customs Union (SACU) is reported as one entity in the dataset. Hence, the external trade of its members (Botswana, Lesotho, Namibia, South Africa and Swaziland) is grouped together making it impossible to examine IIT between members (see Visser, 2001; Cattaneo and Fryer, 2003; TIPS and AusAid, 2006, for analysis of intra-industry between Southern African countries).[8]

Aggregating regional trade flows, we find that Africa lags behind other regions in terms of export diversification, and is actually moving towards further concentration in the products it exports over the period 1998–2009. Given the prominent role of fuel in Africa's total exports, the rising fuel price over the period is one explanatory factor (a higher oil price increases the value of oil exports relative to non-oil exports and hence the export basket is more concentrated).

Figure 7.1 reports the normalized Hirschman index for 49 African economies in 2009 with full results for each year in the period 1998–2009 presented in the Appendix (Table 7.3). The most striking observation is the large heterogeneity in the concentration of exports, and a broadly uniform distribution across that

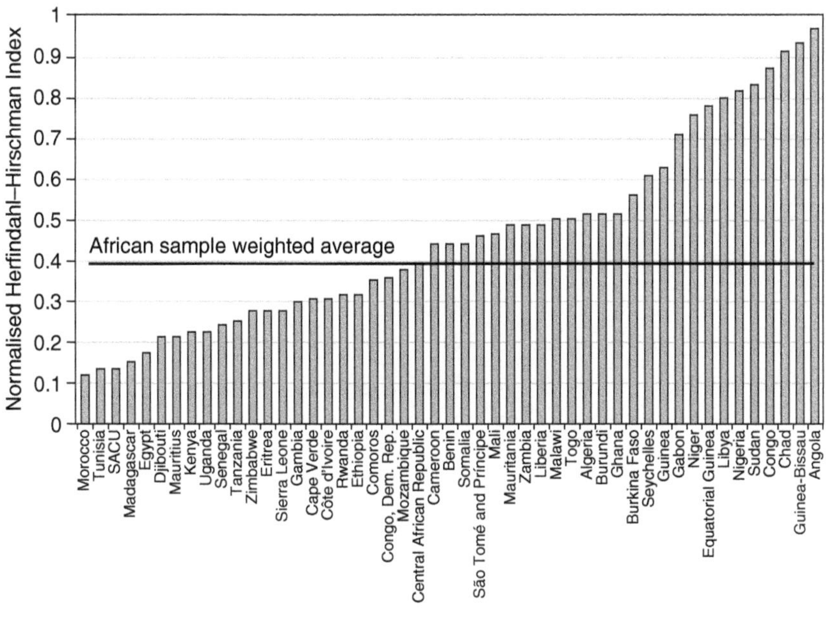

Figure 7.1 Normalized Herfindahl–Hirschman Index, 2009

Source: author's estimates using the BACI dataset.

concentration. Therefore, while it is true that Africa lags behind other regions with respect to export diversification, to say that African economies are poorly diversified masks the vast range of diversification regimes.

What explains this heterogeneity? Given the large number of small economies in Africa, one may expect that the size of the economy would limit the ability to export a large spectrum of goods, but there is no apparent correlation between GDP and diversification. Imbs and Wacziarg (2003) found that diversification follows a two-stage process. Growth in the early stages of development is accompanied by diversification until a turning point when the trend reverses towards increasing specialization once more in a relationship replicated for exports by Klinger and Lederman (2006), albeit at a slightly higher turning point. Few African economies are at the level of development associated with the turning point towards specialization, suggesting that further growth can lead to greater diversification. Each study adopts a measure of GDP per capita, and there is faint evidence of this relationship in Africa, although oil exporting economies with relatively large GDPs and poorly diversified exports are anomalies inconsistent with the two-stage diversification hypothesis.

Turning to diversification trends, Figure 7.2 plots the normalized Hirschman index in 1998 against that in 2009. Those to the right of the line have succeeded in diversifying their exports, whereas those to the left have moved towards further concentration, with the distance from the line an indication of the magnitude of the shift. There are a number of phenomena that can be ascertained from this picture. First, some African economies have managed significantly to diversify exports over the 12-year period. These include Burundi, Central African Republic, Comoros, the Democratic Republic of the Congo, Egypt, Eritrea, Ethiopia, Gambia, Mali, Rwanda, Sierra Leone and Uganda. Second, other African economies have witnessed a shift towards concentration of exports when comparing 1998 and 2009. Angola, Cameroon, Chad, Congo, Ghana, Guinea, Guinea-Bissau, Niger, Togo and Sudan are in this category. Overall, it appears

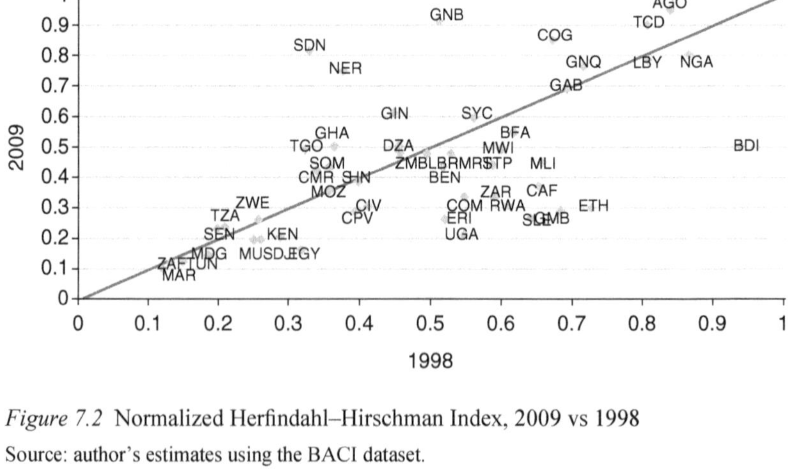

Figure 7.2 Normalized Herfindahl–Hirschman Index, 2009 vs 1998

Source: author's estimates using the BACI dataset.

that those countries which were heavily concentrated in 1998 remain so in 2008, lending support to the 'resource curse' explanation, a feature of which is the emergence of enclave economies which undermine the very process of structural transformation. Similarly, already diversified economies cannot be expected to diversify further (although Kenya and Egypt have succeeded in this endeavour).

IIT Index for Africa

This section unpacks the current status of IIT in Africa. It employs the Grubel–Lloyd index (Grubel and Lloyd, 1975), an accepted measure of the proportion of total trade which is intra-industry in nature, defined as:

$$GLI_j = \frac{\sum_{i=1}^{N}\left[(x_i + m_i) - |x_i - m_i|\right]}{\sum_{i=1}^{N}(x_i + m_i)} = 1 - \frac{\sum_{i=1}^{N}|x_i - m_i|}{\sum_{i=1}^{N}(x_i + m_i)}$$

where *GLI* is the Grubel–Lloyd index for country *j*, which is scaled between zero (no IIT) and one (all trade is intra-industry); and x_i and m_i represent country *j*'s exports and imports of product *i* respectively; and *N* is the total number of product lines.[9]

From existing research we know that IIT in Africa is low compared to other regions. A study by de Ferranti *et al.* (2002) showed that while the proportion of African trade which is intra-industry in nature has increased from 1980 to 1998, the share of IIT in total trade still lags behind all other regions.

The BACI dataset used to calculate the normalized Herfindahl–Hirschman index above can also be utilized to compute the Grubel–Lloyd index for the 49 African economies identified. The Grubel–Lloyd index is extremely sensitive to the level of data aggregation, with analysis at the six-digit level allowing for the narrowest definition of industry available – meaning that only simultaneous import and export of goods in the same product line are deemed intra-industry.

Brülhart's (2008) study, based on bilateral trade flows, defines IIT as the simultaneous exports and imports of a given product between pairs of countries. Our analysis employs a multilateral approach with trade aggregated across all partners and IIT is said to be present as long as there is simultaneous exportation and importation of the given product. This approach is preferred for two reasons. First, while there is certainly further scope for diversification in Africa's trading relationships, the imperative to diversify its products as outlined above is more pressing and may well be a precursor to diversification of partners. As such, we define export diversification in terms of products, not partners. Hence, a similar definition of IIT is appropriate. Second, and somewhat more pragmatically, under Brülhart's (2008) bilateral methodology, no African economy was said to have IIT greater than 5 per cent of total trade and for numerous other African economies, there was virtually no IIT. This provides very little scope for further analysis relative to the multilateral approach which by definition returns a larger value of IIT. Comparative analysis among the world's regions is not undertaken here, but we know from existing surveys (Brülhart, 2008; World Bank, 2003;

UNCTAD, 2011) that IIT in Africa is low relative to other regions. Lastly, Grubel–Lloyd indices are computed across the seven broad economic categories (BECs) to provide insight into variations in IIT across product categories.[10]

The Grubel–Lloyd index for each African country is reported in Table 7.1. The first observation is that IIT is generally rather low at around 10 per cent for the average African economy. For 32 of the countries in our sample of 50, however, IIT is below average, and for eight economies the level of IIT is less than 2 per cent. With the average skewed by the strong performance of a handful of countries the median rate of IIT in a meagre 5 per cent. Turning to the strong performers, there are eight economies in which IIT exceeds 20 per cent of total trade. The finding that Equatorial Guinea enjoys the largest rate of IIT in Africa is somewhat surprising given that its external trade is highly concentrated in fuels. Indeed, analysis of IIT by BEC reveals that out with BEC 3, that pertaining to fuels and lubricants, IIT is in fact very low. This result can be attributed to the lack of refinery capacity in Equatorial Guinea, requiring the exporting and re-importing of its petroleum products. When BEC 3 is removed from the analysis, Equatorial Guinea falls from the top of the stack to third from the bottom. This pattern is repeated, albeit to a lesser extent, for Cameroon, Niger, Libya and Côte d'Ivoire. For trade flows excluding BEC 3, those countries with the highest Grubel–Lloyd indices are SACU (31 per cent), Tunisia (27 per cent), Uganda (20 per cent), Mauritius (18 per cent) and Egypt (17 per cent).

Closer scrutiny of IIT in BEC 3 shows there are a range of countries exhibiting high IIT while the majority show relatively low IIT. Some oil exporters, including Côte d'Ivoire, Egypt and Equatorial Guinea, show large shares of IIT in fuels indicating re-imports of exported products. However, most African oil exporters such as Algeria, Angola, Chad, Congo, Gabon, Libya, Nigeria and Sudan have very low IIT indices. This general pattern reflects the well-established comparative advantages of African economies, with the pattern replicated for BEC 7 (good not specified elsewhere) which includes metals.

With the exception of extractive industries (BEC 3 and BEC 7), there is relatively little variance in IIT across BECs: countries with low IIT have low IIT in each category, and countries with high IIT have high IIT in each category. Rwanda is a notable exception which has low IIT in all categories except BEC 5 – transport equipment and parts and accessories – for which the Grubel–Lloyd index is 37 per cent. It is interesting to note, however, that the two entities with the highest IIT, SACU and Tunisia, have considerably higher IIT in higher value-added activities (BEC 4–6). This is suggestive of a possible threshold effect through which IIT is relatively constant across product lines until a particular threshold, after which there is little scope for further IIT in low value-added activities but IIT continues to grow in higher value-added activities which have more scope for differentiation. Given the low level of IIT in Africa, it is not possible to test such a hypothesis, however, and it remains highly speculative.

The reasons for the generally low levels of IIT are suggested by the theory discussed in the second section of the chapter, above. First, the small size of many African economies is insufficient to generate meaningful economies of scale to overcome trade costs. Indeed, a positive relationship between income and IIT implies that larger economies may be able to benefit from economies of scale which in turn leads to deeper IIT. Note that such a positive relationship is slightly undermined, however, by a cluster of high income countries for which there is little IIT owing to the concentration of oil exports in their trade regimes (these countries include Algeria, Angola, Libya, Nigeria and Sudan). Of course, this primary commodity concentration means that export structures are similar across countries with a focus on low value-added, poorly differentiated exports. The lack of a mature manufacturing sector in most countries means there is little trade in finished products, so there are few African varieties of manufactured goods for consumers to choose from. The positive relationship between the share of manufacturing in GDP and IIT implies that the greater scope for economies of scale and differentiation in the manufacturing sector can lead to IIT.

Second, trade costs are prohibitively high, and those African economies which have developed industrial bases are geographically dispersed, making IIT costly. Third, intellectual property right development is poor[11] meaning that the incentive to differentiate goods through branding in African economies is not well protected. Not one African brand was featured in the top 100 most valuable global brands in a recent survey (Interbrand, 2011). Similarly, there are very few African multinational firms relative to other regions – many of which are concentrated in extractive industries – implying that intra-firm (intra-industry) trade is virtually non-existent.[12]

Last, a bias against domestic goods has been observed in many African countries, with some research indicating a preference for imports from technologically more advanced countries (Agbonifoh and Elimimian, 1999; Okechuku and Onyemah, 1999; Opoku and Akorli, 2009). This preference for goods not made in Africa means that differentiated goods that are produced on the continent are less preferred, with the origin of the product often more important than its price or other attributes.[13] When we compare intra-African and IIT to that with all trading partners, it shows that the economies with the largest total IIT, Tunisia (28 per cent) and SACU (28 per cent) have relatively low intra-African IIT implying that their IIT is dominated by trade with trading partners located outside Africa. This is not consistent with the trend, however, with most African economies undertaking more IIT with each other than they do with external partners. Geographical proximity is one possible explanation, as is the observation that intra-African trade contains more value added, and hence more differentiated goods, than that with the rest of the world (wa Gĩthĩnji and Adesida, 2011). Members of the East African Community (EAC) in particular enjoy higher intra-African IIT than that with all partners. In addition, we find that Uganda (32 per cent), Zambia (20 per cent), Tanzania (18 per cent), Kenya (18 per cent), Mauritius (18 per cent), Senegal (17 per cent), Sierra Leone (16 per cent) and Zimbabwe (15 per cent) are among the highest intra-African IIT economies (excluding BEC 3).

Analysis thus far has been concerned with IIT in 2009, the most recent year for which data is available. With Africa's share of world trade increasing from

Table 7.1 Grubel–Lloyd Index by BEC, 2009

Country	*Grubel–Lloyd Index*		*Grubel–Lloyd Index by BEC*							*Grubel–Lloyd Index Excluding BEC 3*	
	Rank	*Grubel–Lloyd*	*BEC 1*	*BEC 2*	*BEC 3*	*BEC 4*	*BEC 5*	*BEC 6*	*BEC 7*	*Rank*	*Grubel–Lloyd*
Equatorial Guinea	1	0.544	0.000	0.002	0.638	0.009	0.017	0.004	0.000	47	0.007
Tunisia	2	0.289	0.117	0.227	0.447	0.413	0.295	0.223	0.022	2	0.267
SACU	3	0.286	0.205	0.231	0.171	0.348	0.570	0.378	0.404	1	0.306
Senegal	4	0.252	0.126	0.205	0.592	0.115	0.146	0.230	0.199	6	0.166
Côte d’Ivoire	5	0.227	0.039	0.148	0.605	0.161	0.231	0.162	0.854	15	0.105
Egypt	6	0.222	0.121	0.190	0.459	0.110	0.122	0.313	0.022	5	0.173
Uganda	7	0.206	0.189	0.196	0.274	0.220	0.227	0.147	0.034	3	0.196
Mozambique	8	0.204	0.201	0.067	0.607	0.151	0.102	0.080	0.010	12	0.112
Cameroon	9	0.196	0.014	0.032	0.613	0.068	0.021	0.058	0.003	28	0.033
Mauritius	10	0.175	0.171	0.185	0.108	0.214	0.101	0.184	0.059	4	0.179
Kenya	11	0.164	0.098	0.167	0.206	0.159	0.158	0.218	0.028	8	0.156
Liberia	12	0.152	0.026	0.004	0.030	0.015	0.175	0.073	0.024	7	0.159
Zambia	13	0.144	0.126	0.149	0.094	0.156	0.174	0.085	0.056	9	0.147
Morocco	14	0.139	0.079	0.121	0.134	0.185	0.174	0.157	0.003	10	0.139
Niger	15	0.130	0.016	0.014	0.764	0.037	0.016	0.010	0.000	39	0.019
Djibouti	16	0.123	0.138	0.080	0.579	0.057	0.215	0.044	0.107	14	0.106
Seychelles	17	0.120	0.202	0.047	0.621	0.122	0.019	0.066	0.000	13	0.110
Zimbabwe	18	0.105	0.086	0.146	0.015	0.086	0.060	0.075	0.016	11	0.113
Tanzania	19	0.099	0.105	0.085	0.113	0.114	0.080	0.136	0.187	17	0.097
Sierra Leone	20	0.098	0.028	0.053	0.051	0.167	0.243	0.113	0.000	16	0.101
Madagascar	21	0.085	0.080	0.059	0.211	0.113	0.105	0.056	0.458	19	0.075
Rwanda	22	0.071	0.036	0.037	0.015	0.072	0.372	0.038	0.004	20	0.075
Malawi	23	0.071	0.040	0.084	0.007	0.071	0.090	0.078	0.002	18	0.075
Libya	24	0.060	0.008	0.016	0.085	0.010	0.005	0.002	0.000	46	0.010

Gambia	25	0.052	0.031	0.080	0.004	0.035	0.062	0.059	0.000	21	0.055
Burundi	26	0.048	0.047	0.012	0.530	0.058	0.145	0.038	0.000	24	0.043
São Tomé and Príncipe	27	0.046	0.006	0.019	0.227	0.044	0.041	0.031	0.000	38	0.022
Togo	28	0.041	0.017	0.090	0.001	0.016	0.004	0.014	0.000	22	0.044
Ethiopia	29	0.036	0.043	0.015	0.000	0.061	0.075	0.043	0.000	25	0.041
Nigeria	30	0.034	0.010	0.048	0.027	0.059	0.040	0.067	0.084	23	0.044
Sudan	31	0.033	0.026	0.007	0.055	0.033	0.022	0.004	0.024	41	0.018
Eritrea	32	0.031	0.007	0.050	0.000	0.047	0.044	0.036	0.000	27	0.034
Algeria	33	0.029	0.041	0.026	0.025	0.018	0.070	0.012	0.000	29	0.033
Ghana	34	0.029	0.025	0.027	0.074	0.027	0.015	0.029	0.000	34	0.026
Somalia	35	0.028	0.036	0.007	0.004	0.010	0.068	0.028	0.148	32	0.029
Mali	36	0.028	0.005	0.032	0.071	0.047	0.006	0.016	0.000	36	0.023
Burkina Faso	37	0.028	0.035	0.023	0.001	0.037	0.051	0.056	0.000	30	0.032
Angola	38	0.022	0.002	0.027	0.019	0.052	0.016	0.007	0.003	33	0.028
Gabon	39	0.022	0.011	0.007	0.014	0.050	0.118	0.036	0.000	31	0.029
Central African Republic	40	0.021	0.025	0.009	0.000	0.059	0.028	0.010	0.000	37	0.022
Cape Verde	41	0.020	0.020	0.006	0.000	0.034	0.020	0.049	0.030	35	0.023
Congo	42	0.019	0.005	0.008	0.021	0.033	0.029	0.008	0.005	43	0.016
Comoros	43	0.017	0.002	0.009	0.000	0.032	0.040	0.010	0.146	42	0.018
Guinea	44	0.016	0.028	0.009	0.001	0.052	0.021	0.006	0.000	40	0.018
Congo, Dem. Rep.	45	0.015	0.012	0.010	0.014	0.033	0.037	0.018	0.000	44	0.015
Chad	46	0.013	0.081	0.012	0.002	0.044	0.065	0.020	0.000	26	0.038
Guinea-Bissau	47	0.010	0.005	0.026	0.000	0.034	0.012	0.019	0.000	45	0.013
Benin	48	0.007	0.003	0.003	0.031	0.011	0.001	0.013	0.000	49	0.005
Mauritania	49	0.005	0.005	0.002	0.000	0.013	0.018	0.009	0.000	48	0.005
Median	–	0.050	0.030	0.029	0.041	0.055	0.061	0.044	0.002	–	0.039
Weighted average	–	*0.147*	*0.082*	*0.139*	*0.146*	*0.163*	*0.201*	*0.178*	*0.177*	–	*0.147*

2.1 per cent in 1998 to 3.2 per cent in 2009 (UNECA and AUC, 2011) it is of interest to identify whether the observed trade growth is intra-industry or inter-industry. Figure 7.3 compares Grubel–Lloyd indices in 1998 and 2009 revealing that for the vast majority of African economies IIT is greater in the latter year than the former.

Hamilton and Kniest (1991, p. 360) uncovered a conceptual problem in comparing Grubel–Lloyd indices over time periods in this way: 'An increase in inter-industry trade flows will show up as an increase in the Grubel-Lloyd index of IIT when the increase in inter-industry trade acts to reduce the trade imbalance in the sector being measured.' A measure of marginal IIT has since been developed to capture the proportion of the increase in imports or exports of a particular industry which is matched by an increase of exports or imports of the same industry. As a dynamic indicator, it also provides insights into the process of export diversification that forms the subject of present interest. The favoured measure of Marginal Intra-industry Trade (MIIT) is that first put forth by Brülhart (1994) and given by:

$$MIIT_{ijt} = 1 - \frac{\sum_{i=1}^{N} \left| \Delta_t x_{ij} - \Delta_t m_{ij} \right|}{\sum_{i=1}^{N} \left(\left| \Delta_t x_{ij} \right| + \left| \Delta_t m_{ij} \right| \right)}$$

which can be aggregated across industries as follows:

$$MIIT_{jt} = \sum_{i=1}^{N} w_{ijt} MIIT_{ijt}$$

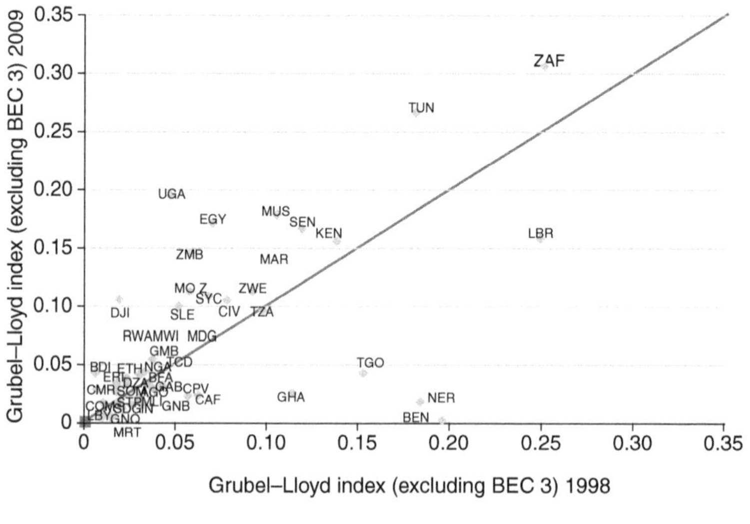

Figure 7.3 African Economies' Intra-Industry Trade Over Time, 1998 vs 2009

Source: author's estimates using the BACI dataset.

where w_{ijt} is the weight of each industry exports and imports in total trade, given by:

$$w_{ijt} = \frac{|\Delta_t x_{ij}| + |\Delta_t m_{ij}|}{\sum_{i=1}^{N} \left(|\Delta_t x_{ij}| + |\Delta_t m_{ij}| \right)}$$

and $\Delta_t x_{ij}$ represents the change in exports between two points in time t for country j in product i respectively; and N is the total number of product lines. Similarly, $\Delta_t m_{ij}$ represents the change in imports between two points in time t for country j in product i. As with the Grubel–Lloyd index, a value of zero shows no marginal IIT while an index of one indicates that all of the observed trade growth is intra-industry in nature.

Table 7.2 reports the marginal IIT over the period 1998–2009. Given that IIT in 2009 remained low for many African economies, it is not surprising that the trade expansion in these economies has been dominated by inter-industry trade. The high MIIT reported by Equatorial Guinea draws attention to the bias caused by fuels. Outwith BEC 3, Equatorial Guinea's trade expansion contained virtually no IIT. Consulting the final column, that which reports MIIT excluding BEC 3, we see that only five African economies can attribute more than 15 per cent of (non-oil) trade growth to IIT: SACU, Tunisia, Uganda, Senegal and Egypt. For SACU and Uganda, MIIT is high in transport equipment (BEC 5), while Tunisia's MIIT has been driven by capital goods (BEC 4) and food and beverages (BEC 1). Thereafter, as was the case for the Grubel–Lloyd index reported above, results appear to be broadly uniform across economic categories with high MIIT in transport equipment for Djibouti, Rwanda, Sierra Leone and Ghana clear exceptions.

Linking IIT and Export Diversification in Africa

To recap, based on the statistics of the status of IIT and export diversification in Africa, we found that IIT and export diversification in Africa lagged behind other regions. In addition, while it was found that a few African economies did improve IIT and export diversification over the period, there is a clear pattern towards sustaining inter-industry trade (which predominantly reflects Africa's high dependence on primary exports) and product concentration. Also, as expected, oil-exporting countries play a crucial role in sustaining product concentration figures for Africa. With these trends in mind, this section sets out to explore the relationship between intra-industry and export diversification in Africa.

Empirical literature on IIT is suggestive of a strong link with export diversification. De Ferranti *et al.* (2002) find a robust positive relationship between IIT and export diversification in Latin America, as does Petersson (2005) in South Africa. It is intuitive that export diversification may increase IIT if the new product lines undertaken allow for mutual exchange with trading partners. In this case, diversification expands IIT. Diversification may also allow for the movement of capital towards industries in which economies of scale have not yet been realized thereby further expanding the opportunities for IIT.

Table 7.2 Marginal IIT by BEC, 2009

Country	*MIIT*		*Marginal IIT by BEC*							*MIIT Excluding BEC 3*	
	Rank	*Grubel–Lloyd*	*BEC 1*	*BEC 2*	*BEC 3*	*BEC 4*	*BEC 5*	*BEC 6*	*BEC 7*	*Rank*	*Grubel–Lloyd*
Equatorial Guinea	1	0.558	0.000	0.002	0.654	0.008	0.018	0.004	0.000	49	0.006
Tunisia	2	0.290	0.099	0.225	0.463	0.392	0.274	0.219	0.021	2	0.261
SACU	3	0.260	0.193	0.212	0.188	0.287	0.508	0.320	0.305	1	0.274
Côte d'Ivoire	4	0.251	0.033	0.153	0.617	0.161	0.178	0.123	0.852	10	0.108
Cameroon	5	0.248	0.013	0.026	0.812	0.078	0.025	0.064	0.003	32	0.032
Senegal	6	0.244	0.151	0.190	0.550	0.101	0.135	0.226	0.010	4	0.166
Uganda	7	0.225	0.208	0.204	0.307	0.237	0.271	0.157	0.029	3	0.213
Egypt	8	0.219	0.114	0.172	0.466	0.135	0.113	0.277	0.002	5	0.163
Mozambique	9	0.207	0.184	0.069	0.603	0.145	0.110	0.078	0.005	11	0.108
Zambia	10	0.141	0.110	0.147	0.091	0.161	0.163	0.067	0.040	6	0.144
Morocco	11	0.140	0.093	0.123	0.124	0.195	0.172	0.134	0.002	7	0.142
Kenya	12	0.133	0.098	0.137	0.093	0.150	0.135	0.187	0.020	8	0.139
Mauritius	13	0.133	0.090	0.141	0.164	0.170	0.097	0.142	0.165	9	0.131
Djibouti	14	0.121	0.137	0.075	0.590	0.052	0.232	0.040	0.107	12	0.103
Seychelles	15	0.112	0.176	0.040	0.866	0.050	0.014	0.082	0.236	16	0.082
Niger	16	0.099	0.033	0.083	0.305	0.035	0.053	0.059	0.000	21	0.060
Zimbabwe	17	0.096	0.062	0.140	0.007	0.070	0.063	0.073	0.001	13	0.103
Sierra Leone	18	0.087	0.007	0.054	0.053	0.150	0.211	0.107	0.000	14	0.090
Tanzania	19	0.087	0.107	0.073	0.099	0.095	0.071	0.108	0.140	15	0.085
Malawi	20	0.072	0.040	0.094	0.000	0.070	0.091	0.060	0.002	17	0.078
Madagascar	21	0.071	0.072	0.042	0.121	0.106	0.116	0.056	0.222	20	0.066
Rwanda	22	0.070	0.031	0.035	0.020	0.071	0.401	0.036	0.004	18	0.072
Liberia	23	0.065	0.027	0.024	0.001	0.015	0.074	0.073	0.000	19	0.067
Libya	24	0.063	0.006	0.014	0.092	0.011	0.004	0.002	0.000	47	0.009
Ghana	25	0.057	0.020	0.022	0.020	0.027	0.394	0.023	0.000	22	0.059
Benin	26	0.051	0.007	0.102	0.028	0.015	0.001	0.041	0.000	23	0.053

Burundi	27	0.049	0.081	0.011	0.482	0.055	0.156	0.034	0.000	24	0.047
São Tomé and Príncipe	28	0.046	0.014	0.020	0.231	0.036	0.024	0.030	0.000	38	0.022
Gambia	29	0.042	0.023	0.059	0.000	0.037	0.021	0.055	0.000	25	0.044
Ethiopia	30	0.038	0.052	0.014	0.000	0.065	0.090	0.041	0.000	26	0.044
Togo	31	0.036	0.023	0.053	0.002	0.041	0.024	0.024	0.000	29	0.037
Algeria	32	0.033	0.051	0.026	0.028	0.020	0.093	0.015	0.000	28	0.039
Sudan	33	0.033	0.022	0.006	0.055	0.036	0.023	0.004	0.023	43	0.017
Central African Republic	34	0.031	0.088	0.008	0.000	0.061	0.067	0.017	0.000	31	0.032
Somalia	35	0.030	0.039	0.007	0.005	0.010	0.070	0.031	0.148	33	0.031
Nigeria	36	0.028	0.012	0.047	0.016	0.060	0.041	0.054	0.007	27	0.043
Burkina Faso	37	0.027	0.028	0.022	0.000	0.040	0.042	0.060	0.000	34	0.031
Eritrea	38	0.021	0.020	0.024	0.000	0.022	0.022	0.020	0.000	39	0.022
Angola	39	0.021	0.001	0.030	0.017	0.053	0.017	0.007	0.003	35	0.029
Cape Verde	40	0.020	0.019	0.009	0.000	0.035	0.017	0.047	0.025	37	0.023
Congo, Dem. Rep.	41	0.019	0.012	0.018	0.015	0.033	0.043	0.019	0.000	40	0.020
Gabon	42	0.019	0.011	0.009	0.008	0.040	0.038	0.065	0.016	36	0.024
Congo	43	0.018	0.011	0.010	0.019	0.030	0.031	0.009	0.005	42	0.017
Comoros	44	0.017	0.002	0.010	0.000	0.026	0.045	0.013	0.148	41	0.018
Guinea	45	0.013	0.035	0.004	0.000	0.034	0.023	0.017	0.000	45	0.015
Chad	46	0.012	0.082	0.008	0.001	0.044	0.089	0.025	0.000	30	0.037
Mali	47	0.012	0.008	0.008	0.001	0.047	0.007	0.013	0.000	46	0.012
Guinea-Bissau	48	0.010	0.007	0.019	0.000	0.041	0.012	0.021	0.000	45	0.013
Mauritania	49	0.006	0.005	0.002	0.000	0.021	0.023	0.009	0.000	48	0.007
Median	–	0.054	0.032	0.028	0.024	0.049	0.065	0.044	0.002	–	0.044
Weighted average	–	*0.10*	*0.057*	*0.077*	*0.138*	*0.092*	*0.087*	*0.101*	*0.427*	–	*0.083*

Figure 7.4 shows a positive correlation between export diversification and IIT for African economies, after isolating BEC 3. While at this point we have not established causation, the positive correlation – a formal linkage between the two variables of interest for African economies is established – allows us to explore potential pathways towards strengthening the growth of the two variables of interest.

A closer examination of the African economies sample reveals that, over the 12-year period (1998–2009), the top ten exporters expanded exports through the intensive margin. Two policy implications are worth mentioning. First, the existing primary product concentration of African exports, coupled with the rising demand for these commodities from developing economies in Asia, has meant that export expansion has occurred in these industries (exporting more volume of existing export products). Second, the gradual increase in prices of oil and other primary commodities in recent times amplify the intensive margin increase as the trade growth is measured in value terms. Nonetheless, a few African economies have managed to expand exports over the ten-year period at the extensive margin, namely Egypt, Nigeria, Libya and Equatorial Guinea.

The second section of the chapter emphasized the need for greater product differentiation to engender extensive expansion and stimulate IIT and there is evidence of some success stories with respect to diversification through differentiation. For instance, Mali's fresh mango export volumes increased six-fold between 1993 and 2008 (Sangho *et al.*, 2010). Coffee washing began in Rwanda in 2000 and by 2009 washed coffee exports accounted for 23 per cent of coffee exports and 32 per cent of coffee revenue in 2009 (export volumes stayed

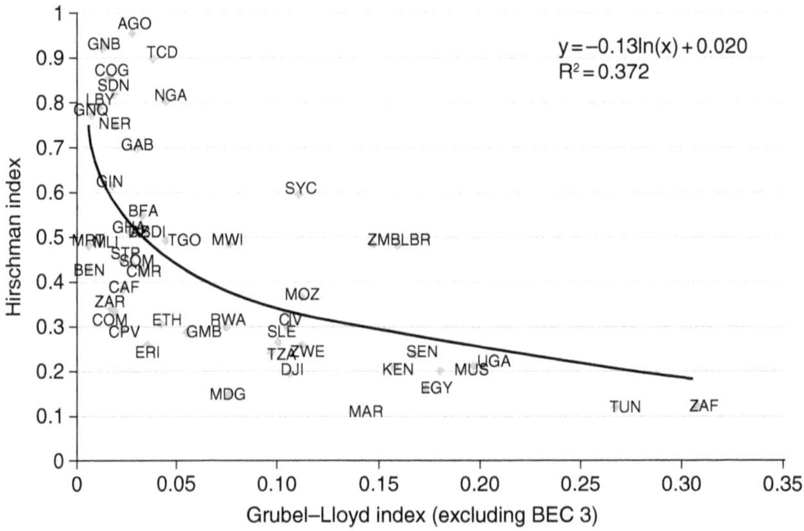

Figure 7.4 Africa's Export Diversification and Intra-Industry Trade, 2009

Source: author's estimates using the BACI dataset.

constant but revenues were up over the period owing to the quality enhancements). In addition, Uganda has recently started exporting washed, roasted and packed coffee as a finished product to the UK and US markets (Easterly and Reshef, 2010). The alcoholic beverage market is one in which greater differentiation is leading to active competition, led by firms including SABMiller South Africa, the Distil Group and Nigerian Brewers. While we find vibrant competition within several African economies, preliminary estimates between alcoholic beverage differentiation and IIT in Africa was not significant.[14] Early entrance into other African markets in which brands are not well established present a unique opportunity to engender customer relationships and brand loyalties given that consumer spending is expected to almost double to US$1.4 trillion in 2020 compared to today (McKinsey, 2010).

As these cases exemplify, the agro-food sector is perhaps the most ripe for product differentiation given its prominence in many African economies and its relevance for Africa's poverty reduction agenda. Indeed, many African economies are currently net food importers, and domestic processing of food products (and possible capturing economies of scale therein) will be imperative to addressing Africa's growing populations' food demand. The African Agribusiness and Agro-Industries Development Initiative (3ADI), part of NEPAD's (New Partnership for Africa's Development) Comprehensive Africa Agriculture Development Programme, aims to have an agriculture sector in Africa which, by the year 2020, is made up of highly productive and profitable agricultural value chains such that by 2020 more than 50 per cent of the continent's food products sold in local and national markets will be in processed form. At present, there are a number of mechanisms through which agro-food products can be differentiated towards this end. Voluntary sustainability initiatives in forestry, coffee, tea, cocoa and banana industry sectors have been successful at differentiating goods, with subsequent sales increases in excess of that experienced by conventional markets (IISD and IIED, 2010). Of course, the social dimension of schemes including fair trade aims to provide farmers with a surplus for re-investment and possible diversification.

Adhering to quality standards is a further option. The certification of Mali's mangoes as organic was one success factor with regard to exporting to Europe, where organic products are enjoying increased demand. The intuition behind differentiation of this kind is that buyers rely on formal institutions and quality standards to allow them to choose goods differentiated by quality. Geographic indicators are another means of differentiation, and have been successfully employed in the South African wine market and protected under TRIPS (Trade Related aspects of Intellectual Property Rights). Differentiation by country of origin through schemes including 'Proudly South African', Uganda's 'Gifted by Nature' and Nigeria's 'Heart of Africa' also has the advantage of a targeting bias towards imported goods from more developed countries.

Thus far, analysis has been limited to trade in goods only, but the increasing role of trade in services offers further opportunities for differentiation, diversification and IIT. For example, the arts and entertainment industry is a key service sector capable of driving greater diversification. The production of and subsequent trade in films, literature, music and broadcast services relies on a multiplicity of inputs and contains linkages to complementary services and physical inputs, including publishing, technical equipment and financial, legal, advertising and travel services. The film and television industry is exemplary here. Several studies have applied the value chain concept to film production (OECD, 2008; Eliashberg *et al.*, 2006; Joffe and Jacklin, 2003, for the Southern African Development Community region) and South Africa estimates that the economic multiplier of direct film spend is 2.5 (Joffe and Newton, 2008). Nigeria is now ranked second in global film production behind India, benefiting from low-cost digital formats, a high share of Nigerian ownership (97 per cent of 139 distribution companies are almost entirely Nigerian owned) and informal distribution networks to the growing African market (UNESCO, 2009). The *New York Times* estimates the industry is now worth US$500million.[15] This is an excellent example of the value of external economies of scale and agglomeration and simultaneous backward and forward linkages leading to IIT and diversification. African authors and musicians are now globally recognized and are amongst the most competitive African exports. Nonetheless, creative industries face a number of challenges, including restrictions on foreign ownership of media (which often impedes the generation of regional markets), lack of multinational indigenous distribution firms and an ongoing preference for imported content (Balancing Act, 2012).

Financial services is a dynamic and growing sector traded globally. It remains a valuable source of revenue for financial and other institutions engaged in various economic activities across the globe. Within the last decade, African countries' financial markets have expanded, with a noted increase in the number of commercial banks operating in countries like Zambia, and measures have also been taken to reduce government ownership or privatize state-owned banks such as in Malawi (World Bank, 2010b). Diversification in the financial services depends on the full range of banking and non-banking financial services, i.e. insurance, the stock and bond exchange market, all of which equally depend largely on the full liberalization of the financial industry. UNCTAD (2001) stated that aside from the efforts of the South African financial services sector in boosting IIT in Africa, Nigerian banks have also been expanding their presence throughout much of Africa, injecting capital into the African economy by introducing new products and new managerial and technological skills, and expanding lending and savings mobilization.

Constraints on Export Diversification and IIT in Africa

In addition to the inherent disadvantages – heavy reliance on few primary commodities, infrastructure inadequacy and the Dutch disease dilemma of most African economies discussed in the second section of the chapter, there are other factors constraining the development of export diversification and IIT in Africa. This section attempts to outline those constraints. The section is divided into two; first, it discusses tariffs and non-tariff barriers on trade in goods before considering, second, non-tariff measures on trade in services.

Tariffs and Non-Tariff Barriers on Trade in Goods

A study by ECA, AUC and AfDB (2012) examined tariff barriers of 53 African economies based on data for 2004 computed from the MAcMap-HS6v2 database,[16] using the TASTE software.[17] The analysis shows that African economies face higher tariff rates on their exports within Africa compared to the rest of the world.

On average, African economies face a 8.7 per cent tariff when exporting to their African partners, compared to a 2.6 per cent average tariff faced by African economies when exporting to the rest of the world. This is due to Sub-Saharan Africa benefiting from preferential market access when exporting to foreign markets, thanks to various agreements concluded with the European Union, under the 'Everything but Arms' (EBA) initiative, with the United States via the African Growth and Opportunity Act (AGOA) and with certain developed countries through the General System of Preferences (GSP). This trend is also consistent by major product groups (agricultural and food products, primary products and other industrial products) providing some support towards the case for a continental free trade to lower trade barriers among African member countries.

In addition, the removal of tariff barriers imposed on imports of intermediate goods crucial for the development of the manufacturing sector across African economies is critical. A study by Laird *et al.* (2006) indicates applied tariffs[18] by stage of processing (primary, intermediate and final). This information indicates that the least developed countries – 33 of them being from Africa – impose the highest average applied tariffs on their imports of intermediate goods from the rest of the world (18 per cent compared to 9.1 per cent imposed by developing countries and 3 per cent by developed countries). However, intermediate goods are vital inputs to be used in the production process allowing for production and export of goods of higher value-added. Therefore, we can legitimately expect that, if the least developed countries in Africa reduce tariffs imposed on their imports of intermediate goods, African countries could significantly enhance their export diversification and IIT as well as their overall contribution to intra-African trade.

An assessment of constraints on African exports by UNECA, AU and AfDB (2010) based on a gravity model highlighted several supply-side constraints. Three are worth mentioning here. First, the study identified the nature of African economies – small, high tariff imposed by African countries, landlocked, high transportation cost, high dependence on primary products, low export diversification, low IIT – and lack of progress towards regional economic integration as constraints towards Africa boosting intra-African trade. Second, the poor condition of trade-related infrastructure was identified as a major constraint on trade in Africa. Poor infrastructure (roads and telecommunications) increases transportation time and costs, and timely and affordable diffusion of market information is impossible in some parts of Africa due to isolation and lack of effective telecommunications infrastructure. The length of paved roads as a percentage of total roads in Africa is about five times less than that of high income OECD countries, whereas telephone coverage (proxied by telephone mainlines per 1,000 people) is generally low (28.4) compared to 574.1 of OECD high income countries. Telephone coverage is even lower in Sub-Saharan Africa (excluding South Africa) with 8.4 per cent.

Third, other supply-side constraints include an effective trade export promotion strategy, as well as efficient bureaucracies to service exporters are lacking. Customs authorities in many African countries are inefficient with frequent delays when goods cross borders. It is estimated that each day of delay reduces the export volume by about 1 per cent. At this rate, if Uganda reduces its factory-to-ship time from the current level of 58 days to 27 days, its exports would increase by 30 per cent (Njinkeu and Fosso (2006) in UNECA, AU and AfDB, 2010).

Another useful measure of trade constraint is based on pioneering efforts of James Anderson and Peter Neary in the 1990s and further refined by Kee *et al.* (2009), with the construction of an 'Overall Trade Restrictiveness Indices – OTRI'. This index tries to estimate the level of constraints on exports of African countries to the whole world (including African countries). The OTRI captures the trade policy of a country by calculating the uniform tariff that will keep its overall imports at the current level when the country in fact has different tariffs for different goods.[19] A second indicator used is Market Access-OTRI (MA-OTRI) which provides an aggregate percentage of the level of barriers encountered by each country's exporters when selling in other countries. The MA-OTRI reflects the effect of trade policies on exporters' access to markets which is different across trading partners and geographic regions, in part because of trade preferences and also because of composition of trade (World Bank and IMF, 2009). It should be noted that OTRI and MA-OTRI do not mirror trade barriers perfectly.[20]

We look first at the constraints on home country imports, reflected by OTRI which proxy the degree of domestic inefficiency of industries due to domestic trade distortionary policies (Kee *et al.*, 2009). Of the 32 African economies listed, five did not have data. An adjusted simple average[21] shows that for the 27 African economies for which data was available in 2009 the overall trade restrictiveness was 16 per cent. Two interesting observations warrant attention on OTRI. First, while the majority of African economies in the sample have overall trade restrictiveness below the average of 16 per cent, some African economies have high overall trade restrictiveness indices – Tanzania (52.9 per cent), Senegal (41.2 per cent), Algeria (36.4 per cent), Egypt (35 per cent), Sudan (27.3 per cent) and Côte d'Ivoire (25.7 per cent). Second, some African economies show extremely low overall trade restrictiveness indices – Botswana (0.6 per cent), Namibia (1.1 per cent), South Africa (4.3 per cent), Zambia (5.7 per cent) and Kenya (7.1 per cent) – suggesting that these countries have rather liberal trade regimes.

Looking further to the constraints on the two industry sectors of agriculture and manufacturing for each African economy in the sample, we find that the adjusted simple average OTRI for the agriculture sector in our African economies sample is extremely high at 22 per cent, reflecting the protectionist trade interest of most African economies on agriculture.[22] On the other hand, we find that the manufacturing sector faces an average of 14 per cent OTRI with the exception of Tanzania which shows a 55.4 per cent OTRI on manufacture.

Moving on to the MA-OTRI – an aggregate percentage of the level of barriers encountered by each country's exporters when selling in other countries – the overall market access adjusted simple average is 13 per cent. Three observations are worth noting. First, on average, African economies face lower constraints imposed by other countries (MA-OTRI, adjusted simple average of 13 per cent) compared to the constraints imposed by the African economies themselves on their imports from their partners (OTRI adjusted simple average of 16 per cent). This trend is suggestive that barriers to trade imposed by African economies themselves to their own respective industry sectors (particularly agriculture and manufacturing) are extremely high, which may have a negative implication through lower efficiency and productivity on export competitiveness. Second, while the majority of African economies face fewer barriers on their exports than the world average (13 per cent), some of them – including Togo (34.7 per cent), Mauritius (34.1 per cent), Uganda (26.1 per cent), Ghana (24.7 per cent) and Kenya (23.3 per cent) – encounter high constraints when exporting to other countries. Third, African agricultural exports face high protection from other countries. This is especially the case for agricultural exports from Mauritius (81.4 per cent), Burkina Faso (55.9 per cent), Cameroon (48.6 per cent), Tunisia (45.6 per cent), Togo (43.8 per cent) and Burundi (40.6 per cent). On the other hand, African exports of manufactured products face fewer constraints with an adjusted simple average of 7 per cent, compared to a 29 per cent average for agriculture exports.

Overall, the agriculture sector for the African sample is highly protected and the data shows that African countries have high trade barriers (both tariffs and non-tariff barriers) compared to manufacturing. In addition, when comparing barriers from Africa to the rest of the world, African economies faced much higher protection on tariffs for goods exported within African compared to those exported to the rest of the world. Also, while the non-tariff barriers level varies significantly among African countries, it seems generally to play a major role on hindering exports within Africa and outside.

Non-Tariff Barriers on Trade in Services

Constraints on trade in services in Africa are less pronounced than those on trade in goods. A World Bank survey, assessing applied trade policies in five services sectors – financial services, telecommunications, retail, professional services and maritime transport, of 102 economies, including 22 African countries in 2007 and 2008 – shows that, on average, the African sample's countries have relatively liberal trade in services policies. While the African sample is above the world's average, we find that South Asia, East Asia and the Pacific, and the Middle East and North Africa have more restrictive trade in services policies than the African sample.

The survey, however, claims that there is significant variation among African economies – Madagascar and Mauritius are found to have very liberal trade policies in services while Ethiopia has the highest restrictiveness not only in the African sample but for the whole surveyed sample. Nevertheless, only 22 African economies out of 54 were included in the survey, which is less than half the number of African countries. In addition, the survey does not provide the list of African countries surveyed. There is very limited data on applied policies governing trade in services in developing countries and this is certainly an area to explore for future research.

To summarize this section, with respect to constraints on trade in goods, we find that the agriculture sector is highly protected and the data shows that African countries have high trade barriers (both tariffs and non-tariff barriers) compared to manufacturing. In addition, when comparing trade barriers in goods within African countries and between Africa and the rest of the world, we find that African economies faced much higher tariff barriers on goods exported to African partners than on goods exported to the rest of the world.

Also, while the non-tariff barriers level varies among African countries, it plays a major role in hindering exports within Africa and outside. Nonetheless, while data on constraints for trade in services is limited for Africa, we find a preliminary study by the World Bank showing less pronounced constraints compared to Asia and Latin America. However, this preliminary survey should be interpreted with some caution as further studies in the country level for all African countries is needed, subject to data availability.

The main implication of high barriers to trade within Africa is that it deters the potential for export diversification among African countries. In addition, high tariffs on intermediate goods across Africa, which are vital for the growth and development of the manufacturing sector, further hamper the diversification of exports from primary commodities to higher value products. The next section concludes the chapter with some policy recommendations.

Concluding Remarks and Policy Implications

Based on the computation of Grubel–Lloyd indices (IIT) and Herfindahl–Hirschman indices (export diversification) for 49 African countries, three findings are worthy of attention. First, we found that, in general, the African sample has extremely low export diversification and IIT patterns. However, within the African sample, we find significant heterogeneity in export diversification patterns. Second, over the period 1998–2009, we find that the African sample shows a gradual move towards product concentration (lack of export diversification). Further, Africa is lagging behind other major regions (Asia, Pacific and the Americas) in terms of export diversification. Third, there is a positive correlation between IIT and percentage of manufacturing in GDP, suggesting that an increase in manufacturing production has a positive effect on IIT and vice versa. In addition, the economies with the largest total IIT (Tunisia and SACU) have relatively low intra-African IIT, meaning that for these African economies IIT mainly takes place with external trading partners located outside the continent.

In terms of the linkages between IIT and export diversification in the African sample, we found that an increase in export diversification is positively correlated to IIT and vice versa.

The chapter identified three key constraints to export diversification and IIT in Africa. First, while African countries have a comparative advantage on primary commodities (including agricultural products), the average tariff barriers faced by African exports of agricultural products are quite high. In addition, African the least developed countries impose very high tariffs on their imports of intermediate goods that are crucial for the expansion of IIT and export diversification in Africa. Second, we find that Africa encounters higher average tariff rates on goods traded within the continent than when exported to the rest of the world. Third, constraints in trade in services are less pronounced. These constraints need to be addressed in a systematic manner, ensuring that efforts towards boosting export diversification and IIT in Africa are undeterred.

In light of these preliminary findings, three policy implications deserve emphasis. First, the low export diversification and IIT for most African economies emphasizes the need to facilitate trade in the extensive margin. However, export expansion through the intensive margin should equally be promoted and supported. Trade facilitation may include hard and soft infrastructure. Greater product differentiation represents one possible pathway to simultaneously increasing IIT and export diversification. Second, the low export diversification and intra-industry for Africa implies that there are real constraints to trade among African economies which need to be addressed. The issue of tariff and non-tariff barriers to trade needs to be addressed in order to facilitate trade. In particular, there is the need to ensure that African exporters have the capacity to meet trade standards necessary to permit their exports within Africa as well as outside Africa. The development of the regional labelling programmes that enhance the environmental profile of African products and improve their market access is a commendable effort by the African Regional Organization for Standardization (ARSO) and the United Nations Environmental Programme (UNEP). The Continental Free Trade Area (CFTA) and the regional integration agenda have a critical role to play in that respect. Third, the liberalization of the financial sector (among other services sectors) is key in ensuring the growth of exports of goods and services in Africa.

This study is best understood as a prolegomenon to the assessment of IIT and export diversification in Africa. IIT is not yet a key issue for African economies, but if they sustain their current growth trajectories it will become increasingly relevant. As such, this chapter describes some of the pressing issues surrounding IIT, and the policy interventions to embrace better as a pillar of the export diversification paradigm. Future research would be well placed for closer scrutiny of bilateral IIT and disaggregated horizontal and vertical IIT. We also need a better understanding of the role of domestic, regional and international firms in intra-industry cross-border trade, and identification at the national level of key sectors in which IIT is expanding and why. Furthermore, firm level data would allow for greater scrutiny of the implication of so-called 'New-New Trade Theory' (NNTT) and its implications for export diversification and IIT in Africa. Similarly, more disaggregated data on trade in services would allow for deeper understanding of IIT in service sectors, and its relevance for wider export diversification.

Appendix

Table 7.3 Export Diversification of 49 African Economies (Normalized Herfindahl–Hirschman Index), 1998–2009

	1998	*1999*	*2000*	*2001*	*2002*	*2003*	*2004*	*2005*	*2006*	*2007*	*2008*	*2009*
Algeria	0.5	0.4	0.5	0.4	0.5	0.5	0.6	0.6	0.6	0.6	0.5	0.5
Angola	0.8	0.8	0.9	0.9	0.9	0.9	1.0	0.9	1.0	1.0	1.0	1.0
Burundi	0.9	0.8	0.8	0.7	0.5	0.6	0.6	0.6	0.4	0.4	0.4	0.5
Cameroon	0.3	0.3	0.4	0.4	0.4	0.4	0.4	0.4	0.5	0.5	0.5	0.4
Cape Verde	0.4	0.3	0.4	0.3	0.3	0.2	0.2	0.4	0.4	0.4	0.4	0.3
Central African Republic	0.7	0.7	0.7	0.5	0.6	0.4	0.4	0.5	0.3	0.3	0.3	0.4
Chad	0.8	0.8	0.7	0.8	0.7	0.7	0.8	0.7	0.9	0.9	0.9	0.9
Comoros	0.5	0.4	0.5	0.6	0.5	0.7	0.5	0.4	0.3	0.3	0.3	0.3
Congo	0.7	0.7	0.7	0.7	0.8	0.7	0.7	0.8	0.9	0.8	0.8	0.9
Congo, Dem. Rep.	0.6	0.7	0.6	0.6	0.7	0.5	0.5	0.5	0.4	0.4	0.4	0.3
Benin	0.5	0.6	0.5	0.5	0.4	0.5	0.5	0.5	0.4	0.4	0.4	0.4
Equatorial Guinea	0.7	0.7	0.8	0.9	0.9	0.9	0.9	0.9	0.9	0.9	0.8	0.8
Ethiopia	0.7	0.6	0.6	0.3	0.3	0.3	0.3	0.3	0.3	0.3	0.3	0.3
Eritrea	0.5	0.4	0.2	0.2	0.2	0.1	0.2	0.3	0.2	0.7	0.3	0.3
Djibouti	0.3	0.3	0.2	0.2	0.2	0.3	0.2	0.1	0.2	0.4	0.3	0.2
Gabon	0.7	0.7	0.8	0.8	0.8	0.8	0.7	0.8	0.7	0.7	0.7	0.7
Gambia	0.7	0.6	0.3	0.3	0.3	0.3	0.3	0.3	0.4	0.3	0.4	0.3
Ghana	0.4	0.3	0.3	0.3	0.4	0.4	0.4	0.3	0.4	0.4	0.4	0.5
Guinea	0.4	0.5	0.4	0.4	0.4	0.5	0.5	0.5	0.4	0.5	0.4	0.6
Côte d'Ivoire	0.4	0.4	0.4	0.3	0.4	0.4	0.3	0.3	0.3	0.3	0.3	0.3
Kenya	0.3	0.3	0.3	0.3	0.2	0.2	0.2	0.2	0.2	0.2	0.2	0.2
Liberia	0.5	0.5	0.4	0.5	0.4	0.6	0.5	0.5	0.4	0.5	0.4	0.5
Libyan Arab Jamahiriya	0.8	0.8	0.8	0.8	0.8	0.8	0.9	0.9	0.9	0.9	0.9	0.8
Madagascar	0.2	0.2	0.2	0.2	0.3	0.3	0.2	0.2	0.2	0.2	0.2	0.1

Malawi	0.6	0.5	0.5	0.6	0.5	0.5	0.4	0.5	0.5	0.4	0.4	0.5
Mali	0.7	0.6	0.5	0.5	0.7	0.7	0.6	0.7	0.7	0.7	0.7	0.5
Mauritania	0.5	0.5	0.4	0.4	0.4	0.4	0.4	0.4	0.5	0.4	0.4	0.5
Mauritius	0.3	0.2	0.2	0.2	0.2	0.2	0.3	0.2	0.2	0.2	0.2	0.2
Morocco	0.1	0.1	0.1	0.1	0.1	0.1	0.1	0.1	0.1	0.1	0.2	0.1
Mozambique	0.4	0.3	0.3	0.5	0.5	0.5	0.5	0.5	0.5	0.5	0.4	0.4
Niger	0.4	0.4	0.5	0.3	0.3	0.4	0.3	0.3	0.4	0.4	0.3	0.8
Nigeria	0.9	0.9	0.9	0.9	0.8	0.9	0.9	0.9	0.9	0.9	0.8	0.8
Guinea-Bissau	0.5	0.6	0.6	0.8	0.6	0.8	0.7	0.9	0.8	0.9	0.9	0.9
Rwanda	0.6	0.7	0.6	0.6	0.5	0.4	0.6	0.4	0.4	0.3	0.4	0.3
São Tomé and Príncipe	0.6	0.3	0.3	0.3	0.5	0.6	0.4	0.5	0.4	0.4	0.5	0.5
Senegal	0.2	0.2	0.2	0.2	0.2	0.2	0.2	0.2	0.2	0.2	0.3	0.2
Seychelles	0.6	0.6	0.7	0.6	0.5	0.6	0.5	0.4	0.5	0.5	0.5	0.6
Sierra Leone	0.6	0.4	0.4	0.4	0.3	0.5	0.5	0.6	0.4	0.4	0.3	0.3
Somalia	0.4	0.4	0.5	0.2	0.3	0.3	0.3	0.4	0.3	0.3	0.3	0.4
SACU	0.1	0.1	0.1	0.1	0.1	0.1	0.1	0.1	0.1	0.1	0.1	0.1
Zimbabwe	0.3	0.3	0.2	0.3	0.2	0.3	0.2	0.2	0.2	0.2	0.2	0.3
Sudan	0.3	0.4	0.5	0.6	0.5	0.6	0.6	0.6	0.6	0.9	0.9	0.8
Togo	0.3	0.3	0.3	0.2	0.2	0.2	0.3	0.2	0.3	0.3	0.5	0.5
Tunisia	0.1	0.1	0.1	0.1	0.1	0.1	0.1	0.1	0.1	0.1	0.1	0.1
Uganda	0.5	0.5	0.4	0.3	0.3	0.3	0.2	0.2	0.2	0.2	0.2	0.2
Egypt	0.3	0.3	0.3	0.2	0.2	0.2	0.2	0.2	0.2	0.2	0.2	0.2
Tanzania, United	0.2	0.2	0.2	0.2	0.2	0.3	0.3	0.3	0.2	0.2	0.2	0.2
Republic of Burkina Faso	0.6	0.6	0.6	0.5	0.5	0.7	0.7	0.8	0.7	0.7	0.6	0.6
Zambia	0.5	0.3	0.3	0.5	0.5	0.4	0.4	0.5	0.6	0.6	0.5	0.5
Weighted average	*0.2*	*0.3*	*0.4*	*0.3*	*0.3*	*0.3*	*0.4*	*0.4*	*0.4*	*0.4*	*0.5*	*0.4*

Source: author's estimations based on BACI dataset and COMTRADE (2012).

Notes

1 This research has benefited enormously from useful comments and contributions from the participants of an Expert Group Meeting on 'Export Diversification and Intra-Industry', Lusaka, Zambia, 3–4 May 2012. We are also grateful for comments from Halima Noor Abdi, Patrick Osakwe and James Egbetayo. The views presented in this chapter may not necessarily reflect the position of the United Nations Economic Commission for Africa. Any remaining errors are ours.
2 We are grateful to Patrick Osakwe for bringing these issues to our attention.
3 The study found that the extensive margin accounts for 62 per cent of the greater exports of larger economies based on data from UNCTAD TRAINS collected from national statistical agencies of 76 importing countries covering all 227 exporting countries in 1995.
4 Export sophistication is basically referring to diversification of exports into new products (extensive margin products) and usually with higher value-added.
5 A negative relationship between increased exploitation of natural resources and a decline in manufacturing sector.
6 We thank Patrick Osakwe for raising this issue to our attention.
7 In other words, Country A exports product 'a' to Country B and importing 'a bis' from any other country, including potentially but not necessarily Country B.
8 Trade and Industrial Policy Strategies (TIPS) have also developed a set of analytical templates which includes data on IIT for Southern African Development Community countries. They are available online at: www.tips.org.za.
9 We note that the Grubel–Lloyd index methodology has limitations. An important criticism of the Grubel–Lloyd index is that it is not independent of the trade balance. The upper bound of the index is negatively related to the size of the trade balance, meaning a larger imbalance is associated with lower reported IIT. Aquino (1978) suggested an adjustment, which has fallen out of favour following a critique by Greenaway and Milner (1981) meaning the issue remains empirically unresolved. However, this methodology continues to be the most common used when examining IIT today.
10 The BECs was developed in the late 1960s to summarize data on international trade in goods. The classification by BECs is as follows; BEC 1 – food and beverages, BEC 2 – industrial supplies not elsewhere specified, BEC 3 – fuels and lubricants, BEC 4 – capital goods (except transport equipment), and parts and accessories thereof, BEC 5 – transport equipment and parts and accessories thereof, BEC 6 – consumer goods not elsewhere specified, BEC 7 – goods not elsewhere specified.
11 According to Property Rights Alliance (2011), Africa has the lowest Intellectual Property Right index of all regions of the world.
12 See 'The Africa Report', available online at www.theafricareport.com.
13 Proudly South African, Uganda's Gifted by Nature and Nigeria's Heart of Africa are among the initiatives designed to address this problem.
14 Although outside the scope of this study, this is an interesting preliminary finding worth exploring in future research.
15 'A Scorsese in Lagos: The making of Nigeria's Film Industry', 23 February 2012. Available online at: www.nytimes.com/2012/02/26/magazine/nollywood-movies.html?_r=1&pagewanted=all.
16 The MAcMap-HS6 database offers the option to aggregate protection data using a so-called reference group weight. In this case, the weight used for aggregation does not strictly reflect the trade for the country considered, but rather that of a group of countries (group of reference) to which a country belongs according to its income level. As a consequence, the reference group weight limits possible endogeneity bias between trade and protection. For example, in the case of a prohibited tariff, imports are discouraged. Thus, if the trade weight aggregation method is used, there will be no weight associated to such a tariff line. The reference group weight therefore yields more satisfactory outcomes as it will allow some weight on non-traded tariff lines (ECA, AUC and AfDB, 2012).

17 At the time this research was conducted, 2004 was the most recent data on market access currently available at such a disaggregated level. However, note that a newer version of the MAcMap-HS6 database including data for the year 2007 was released afterwards. Nevertheless, it is important to note that protection structures did not significantly evolve in Africa between 2004 and 2007; changes have occurred more recently, thanks in particular to the COMESA–EAC–SADC tripartite initiative.
18 Laird *et al.* (2006) use a trade weight to aggregate the tariffs while the tariff from the UNECA, AUC, AfDB (2010) are weighted by the reference group weight (as already explained).
19 The authors suggested that the OTRI was developed to overcome two measurement problems – aggregation of different forms of trade policies, and the aggregation across goods with different economic importance – which was problematic for the traditional trade restrictiveness index (TRI). The OTRI tackles different constraints (tariff and non-tariff barriers alike) by bringing all types of trade policy instruments into a common metric by estimating ad-valorem equivalents of non-tariff barriers for each country at the tariff level. Hence, OTRI provides an aggregate percentage of the extent to which trade constraints (all trade policy instruments) limit imports. The OTRI captures ad valorem tariffs, specific duties and non-tariff measures such as price control measures, quantitative restrictions, monopolistic measures and technical regulations (World Bank and IMF 2009).
20 See Coughlin (2010) for some discussion on the measurement problems encountering trade restrictiveness.
21 Average of sum of countries with data available only.
22 Some African economies show extremely high OTRI – Morocco (57 per cent), Algeria (53.9 per cent) and Sudan (52.6 per cent).

References

AfDB (2011) 'The middle of the pyramid: dynamics of the middle class in Africa', AfDB Market Brief, Tunis, Tunisia.

Agbonifoh, A. and J.U. Elimimian (1999) 'Attitudes of developing countries towards country-of-origin products in an era of multiple brands', *Journal of International Consumer Marketing* 11(4): 97–116.

Akamatsu, K. (1962) 'A historical pattern of economic growth in developing countries', *Journal of Developing Economies* 1(1): 3–25.

Amurgo-Pacheco, A. and D. Pierola (2007) 'Patterns of export diversification in developing countries: intensive and extensive margins', mimeo, GIIS, Geneva.

Aquino, A. (1978) 'Intra-industry trade: current perspectives and unresolved issues', *Weltwirtschaftliches Archiv* 114: 275–295.

Armington, P. (1969) 'A theory of demand for products distinguished by place of production', IMF Staff Papers 16, 159–176.

Balancing Act (2012) 'Africa broadcast and film markets: 2nd edition', www.balancingact-africa.com/reports/broadcast/african-broadcast-an-0.

Balassa, B. (1966) 'Tariff reductions and trade in manufacturers among the industrial countries', *American Economic Review* 56(3): 466–473.

Besedes, T. and T.J. Prusa (2007) 'The role of extensive and intensive margins and export growth', NBER Working Paper No. 13628.

Brander, J.A. and P. Krugman (1983) 'A "reciprocal dumping" model of international trade', *Journal of International Economics* 15(3): 313–321.

Brenton, P. and R. Newfarmer (2009) 'Watching more than the discovery channel to diversify exports' in R. Newfarmer, W. Shaw and P. Walkenhorst (eds) *Breaking into New Markets: Emerging Lessons for Export Diversification*, World Bank, Washington DC.

Brenton, P., R. Newfarmer and P. Walkenhorst (2007) 'Export diversification: a policy portfolio approach', Paper presented to the Growth Commission Conference on Development, Yale University.

Brülhart, M. (1994) 'Marginal intra-industry trade: measurement and relevance for the pattern of industrial adjustment', *Weltwirtschaftliches Archiv* 130(3): 600–613.

Brülhart, M. (2008) 'An account of global intra-industry trade, 1962–2006', University of Nottingham Globalisation, Productivity and Technology Research Paper Series, Research Paper 2008/08.

Cadot, O., C. Carrere and S. Strauss-Kahn (2008) 'Export diversification: what's behind the hump?' CEPR Discussion Paper DP6590, Centre for Economic Policy Research, London.

Cattaneo, N. and D. Fryer (2003) 'Intra-versus inter-industry specialization, labour market adjustment and poverty: implications for regional integration in southern Africa', Trade and Industrial Strategies mimeo.

COMTRADE (2012) 'Online database', http://comtrade.un.org.

Coughlin, C.C. (2010) 'Measuring international trade policy: a primer on trade restrictiveness indices', *Federal Reserve Bank of St. Louis Review*, 92(5): 381–393.

de Ferranti, D., G.E. Perry, D. Lederman and W.F. Maloney (2002) *From Natural Resources to the Knowledge Economy: Trade and Job Quality*, World Bank, Washington, DC.

Debaere, P. (2005) 'Monopolistic competition and trade, revisited: testing the model without testing for gravity', *Journal of International Economics* 66(1): 249–266.

Delgado, C.L. (1995) 'Agricultural diversification and export promotion in Sub-Saharan Africa', *Food Policy* 20(3): 225–243.

Dennis, A. and B. Shepherd (2007) 'Trade costs, barriers to entry, and export diversification in developing countries', World Bank Policy Research Working Paper No. 4368, Washington, DC.

Dollar, D. and A. Kraay (2002) 'Trade, growth and poverty', World Bank Policy Research Working Paper No. 2587.

Easterly, W. and A. Reshef (2010) 'African export successes: surprises, stylized facts and explanations', NBER Working Paper 16597.

ECA, AUC and AfDB (2012) 'Assessing regional integration in Africa V: towards an African continental free trade area', United Nations, Addis Ababa.

Eliashberg, J., A. Elberse and M. Leenders (2006) 'The motion picture industry: critical issues in practice, current research, and new research directions', *Marketing Science* 25(6): 638–661.

Ethier, W.J. (1982) 'National and international returns to scale in the modern theory of international trade', *American Economic Review* 72(3): 389–405.

Falvey, R. (1981) 'Commercial policy and intra-industry trade', *Journal of International Economics* 11: 495–511.

Fontagné, L. and M. Freudenberg (1997) 'Intra-industry trade: methodological issues reconsidered,' CEPII Working Papers, #97-01.

Freund, C. and N. Rocha (2010) 'What constrains Africa's exports?', World Bank Policy Research Working Paper 5184.

Gaulier, G. and S. Zignago (2010) 'BACI: international trade database at the product-level: the 1994–2007 version', CEPII Working Paper No. 2010–23.

Greenaway, D. and C. Milner (1981) 'Trade imbalance effects in the measurement of intra- industry trade', *Weltwirtschaftliches Archiv* 117: 756–762.

Grubel, H.G. (1967) 'Intra-industry specialization and the pattern of trade', *Canadian Journal of Economics and Political Science* 33(3): 374–388.

Grubel, H.G. and P.J. Lloyd (1975) *Intra-Industry Trade: The Theory and Measurement of International Trade with Differentiated Products*, Macmillan: London.

Hallak, J.C. (2006) 'Product quality and the direction of trade', *Journal of International Economics* 68(1): 238–265.

Hamilton, C. and P. Kniest (1991) 'Trade liberalisation, structural adjustment and intra-industry trade: a note', *Weltwirtschaftliches Archiv* 127: 356–367.

Hammouda, B., S.N. Karingi, A.E. Njuguna and M. Sadni-Jallab (2006) 'Diversification: towards a new paradigm for Africa's development', Africa Trade Policy Centre Work in Progress No. 35, UNECA, Addis Ababa, Ethiopia.

Harding T. (2009) 'Infrastructure and diversifying through better products' in R. Newfarmer, W. Shaw and P. Walkenhorst (eds) *Breaking into New Markets: Emerging Lessons for Export Diversification*, World Bank, Washington, DC.

Hausmann, R. and D. Rodrik (2003) 'Economic development as self-discover', *Journal of Development Economics* 72: 603–633.

Hausmann, R., J. Hwang and D. Rodrik (2007) 'What you export matters', CEPR Discussion Paper 5444, Centre for Economic Policy and Research, London.

Hirchberg, G.H., I.M. Sheldon and J.R. Dayton (1994) 'The analysis of bilateral intra-industry trade in the food-processing sector', *Applied Economics* 26: 159–167.

Hirschman, A. (1964) 'The paternity of an index', *American Economic Review* 54(4–6): 761–762.

Hummels, D. and P.J. Klenow (2005) 'The variety and quality of a nations exports', *American Economic Review* 95: 704–723.

IISD and IIED (2010) 'The state of sustainability initiatives review 2010: sustainability and transparency', International Institute for Sustainable Development and the International Institute for Environment and Development.

Imbs, J. and R. Wacziarg (2003) 'Stages of diversification', *American Economic Review* 93(1): 63–86.

Interbrand (2011) 'Best global brands 2011', www.interbrand.com/en/best-global-brands/Best-Global-Brands-2011.aspx.

Joffe, A. and Jacklin, N. (2003) 'The film and television industry: promoting the cultural sector through job creation and small enterprise development in the SADC countries', ILO/Seed Working Paper No. 53.

Joffe, A. and M. Newton (2008) 'Creative industries sector report', Research Commissioned by Department of Labour, South Africa.

Karingi, S.N. and M.D. Spence (2011) 'Impact of trade facilitation mechanisms on export competitiveness in Africa', African Trade Policy Centre Work in Progress No. 84, UNECA, Addis Ababa, Ethiopia.

Kee, H.L., A. Nicita and M. Olarreaga (2009) 'Estimating trade restrictiveness indices', *Economic Journal* 119: 172–199.

Klinger, B. and D. Lederman (2006) 'Diversification, innovation and imitation inside the global technological frontier', World Bank Policy Research Working Paper 3872.

Krugman, P.R. (1979) 'Increasing returns, monopolistic competition, and international trade', *Journal of International Economics* 9(4): 469–479.

Krugman, P.R. (1980) 'Scale economies, product differentiation, and the pattern of trade', *American Economic Review* 70(5): 950–959.

Lancaster, K.J. (1980) 'Intra-industry trade under perfect monopolistic competition', *Journal of International Economics* 10: 151–175.

Lewis, W.A. (1954) 'Economic development with unlimited supplies of labour', *Manchester School* 22: 139–191.

Limao, N. and A.J. Venables (2001) 'Infrastructure, geographical disadvantage, transport costs, and trade', *World Bank Economic Review* 15(3): 451–479.

Lin, J.-Y. (2010) 'New structural economics: a framework for rethinking development', World Bank Policy Research Working Paper 5197.

Linder, S.B. (1961) *An Essay on Trade and Transformation*, Almqvist & Wicksell: Stockholm.

McKinsey Global Institute (2010) 'Lions on the move: the progress and potential of African economies', McKinsey & Company.

Okechuku, C. and V. Onyemah (1999) 'Nigerian consumer attitudes toward foreign and domestic products', *Journal of International Business Studies* 30(3): 611–622.

Opoku, R.A. and P.A.K. Akorli (2009) 'The preference gap: Ghanaian consumers' attitudes toward local and imported products', *African Journal of Business Management* 3(8): 350–357.

Pearson, M. (2010) 'Trade facilitation and extensive margin', IFN Working Paper No. 828, www.ifn.se/wfiles/wp/wp828.pdf.

Petersson, L. (2005) 'Export diversification and intra-industry trade in South Africa', *South African Journal of Economics* 73(4): 785–802.

Property Rights Alliance (2011) 'Intellectual property rights index: 2011 report', Property Rights Alliance, Washington, DC.

Rauch, J. (2007) 'Development through synergistic reform', NBER Working Paper No. 13170.

Sangho, Y., P. Labaste and C. Ravry (2010) 'Growing Mali's mango exports: linking farmers to markets through innovations in the value chain', World Bank and JE Austin Associates.

TIPS and AusAid (2006) 'Intra SADC trade performance review 2006', Arcadia, South Africa.

Tybout, J.R. (2000) 'Manufacturing Firms in developing countries: how well do they do, and why?' *Journal of Economic Literature* 38(1): 11–44.

UNCTAD (2001) 'Economic development in Africa: performance, prospects and policy issues', New York, http://unctad.org/en/Docs/pogdsafricad1.en.pdf.

UNCTAD (2011) 'Economic development in Africa report 2010: fostering industrial development in Africa', United Nations, New York and Geneva.

UNECA and AUC (2007) Economic report on Africa 2007: Accelerating Africa's Development through Diversification, UNECA, Addis Ababa, Ethiopia.

UNECA and AUC (2007) 'Economic report on Africa 2007: accelerating Africa's development through diversification', UNECA, Addis Ababa, Ethiopia.

UNECA and AUC (2011) 'Economic report on Africa 2011: governing development in Africa – the role of the state in economic transformation', UNECA, Addis Ababa, Ethiopia.

UNECA, AU and AfDB (2010) 'Assessing regional integration in Africa IV: enhancing intra-African trade', UNECA, Addis Ababa, www.uneca.org/sites/default/files/Publication Files/aria4full.pdf.

UNESCO (2009) 'Analysis of 2007 UIS Statistics on Feature Films', Information Sheet No. 1, www.uis.unesco.org/culture/Documents/Infosheet_No1_cinema_EN.pdf.

Visser, M. (2001) 'The role of intra-industry trade and cross-border supply chains in facilitating regional integration in the SADC markets', DPRU Working Papers No. 01/57, Development Policy Research Unit, University of Cape Town.

wa Gĩthĩnji, M. and O. Adesida (2011) 'Industrialization, exports and the developmental state in Africa: the case for transformation', University of Massachusetts Amherst, Working Paper 2011–18.

World Bank (2003) 'Standards and global trade: a voice for Africa', www.unido.org/fileadmin/import/12960_WorldBank_StandardsGlobalTrade_voiceForAfrica.pdf.

World Bank (2010a) 'The state of tourism in Africa', Joint Publication of Africa House at New York University, the Africa Travel Association and the World Bank, 1(1).
World Bank (2010b) 'Trade in financial services: mobile banking in southern Africa', Mozambique.
World Bank and IMF (2009) 'Global monitoring report 2009: a development emergency', Washington, DC.

8 Capital Flight and Economic Growth in the Franc Zone[1]

Ameth Saloum Ndiaye

Introduction

The implications of capital flight for economic growth have received increasing attention from a number of researchers. In recent years, considerable interest has focused on the extent to which capital flight could have a harmful impact on economic development (UNDP, 2011). According to Ajayi (1995), slower growth and persistent balance of payments deficits in most developing countries have been attributed to capital flight. Indeed, high levels of capital flight pose serious challenges to the mobilization of domestic resources to support investment and economic growth in Africa (Fofack and Ndikumana, 2009, 2010). In addition, the UNDP (2011) regards the extent of capital flight as constituting a major obstacle to the mobilization of domestic resources for development, thereby implying that capital flight aggravates resource constraints and serves to hinder long-term economic growth (Beja, 2007). Accordingly, the extent of capital flight from developing countries acquires significance and poses a serious threat to sustainable economic growth, particularly in Africa (Ayadi, 2008). As Boyce and Ndikumana (2001) observe, many poor countries lose more resources to capital flight than they pay in debt service. This chapter aims to contribute to the debate on this issue by testing the impact of capital flight on economic growth.

The theory of capital flight holds that the phenomenon is caused both by private actors and public authorities (Ndikumana and Boyce, 2003, 2008, 2011b; Ajayi, 2007; Ndiaye, 2009a, 2011). First, according to these writers, capital flight arises when private actors respond to macroeconomic uncertainty, political and institutional uncertainty, an underdeveloped financial system and the prospect of higher returns abroad.[2] In a portfolio choice context (Collier *et al.*, 2004), all of these factors increase the risk of loss of real value of private agents' domestic assets, obliging them to shift the composition of their portfolios toward foreign assets. As private agents transfer their savings abroad, private investment declines. Accordingly, by reducing the amount of private investment, capital flight could reduce economic growth.

Second, capital flight may be caused by public authorities in a context of poor governance and weak institutions (Ajayi, 1992; Awung, 1996; Loungani and Mauro, 2000; Ndikumana and Boyce, 2003; Le and Rishi, 2006; Cerra *et al.*, 2008; Ndiaye, 2009a, 2011). According to these writers, in such a context, corrupt authorities profit from their privileged positions to accumulate personal fortunes abroad (Boyce and Ndikumana, 2001). Those fortunes held abroad come from domestic public resources. Therefore, capital flight attributable to public authorities reduces public resources, which in turn reduces public investment, thereby reducing economic growth.

The motivation for this study relates to the fact that capital flight diverts resources that could have been invested to create wealth in the country of origin. Accordingly, capital flight has a potentially adverse effect on economic growth. The question of the impact of capital flight on economic growth merits particular attention for Franc Zone (FZ) countries for a number of reasons. First, one of the characteristics of the FZ is the existence of a fixed exchange rate between the CFA franc and the euro. This exchange rate fixity implies that FZ countries cannot adjust their exchange rates, making economic growth highly sensitive to real shocks (Savvides, 1996), a situation that encourages capital flight. Moreover, capital flight exerts pressure on the exchange rate by increasing demand for foreign currency to channel wealth abroad (Ndikumana, 2003). Capital flight thus increases the probability of devaluation of the national currency (Ndikumana and Boyce, 2011a), a factor that causes capital flight by encouraging investors to shift the composition of their portfolios toward foreign assets (Cuddington, 1986, 1987). A second characteristic of the FZ is the principle of free movement of capital. Liberalization of the capital account increases the FZ countries' vulnerability to fluctuations in capital flows, in particular by providing legal channels for capital flight (Ariyoshi *et al.*, 2000). The free movement of capital in the FZ therefore facilitates capital flight.

Ultimately, these FZ characteristics – i.e., the fixed exchange rate and liberalization of the capital account – positively influence capital flight in the FZ, which is found to be massive and increasing. Indeed, according to the most recent estimates, capital flight in FZ countries[3] over the period 1970–2010 reached a remarkable US$127.2 billion, representing 123.7 percent of GDP (Boyce and Ndikumana, 2012).[4] At the same time, in terms of comparison, the estimates of Boyce and Ndikumana (2012) show that capital flight in FZ countries is quite substantial compared to capital outflows from other sub-Saharan African countries. According to Boyce and Ndikumana (2012), three FZ countries are also among the ten Sub-Saharan African countries with the largest total capital flight over the period 1970–2010: Côte d'Ivoire ranked third (US$56 billion or 244.4 percent of GDP); Gabon ranked seventh (US$25.5 billion or 192.9 percent of GDP); and Cameroon ranked tenth (US$20 billion or 89 percent of GDP). The eleventh Sub-Saharan African country was the Congo, with US$19.9 billion in flight capital, representing 165.5 percent of GDP.

In the econometric literature, authors are unanimous in recognizing the adverse effects of capital flight on economic growth transmitted through several channels: Lessard and Williamson (1987); Boyce (1992); Ajayi (1995, 1997); Chipalkatti and Rishi (2001); Fedderke and Liu (2002); Greene (2002); Menbere (2003); Červená (2006); Beja (2007); Ayadi (2008); Forgha (2008); Cerra *et al.* (2008); Lan (2009); Gusarova (2009); Ndikumana (2003, 2009); Ndiaye (2009b); Fofack and Ndikumana (2009, 2010); Yalta (2010); Bakare (2011); Ndikumana and

Boyce (2011a). In regard to these studies, this study makes two contributions to the literature. First, it provides the most up-to-date estimates of capital flight in FZ countries available in the literature. Second, it contributes to a better understanding of the role of capital flight in explaining poor performance in terms of economic growth in the zone.

The remainder of this chapter or organized as follows: the second section reviews the literature on the relationship between capital flight and growth, and establishes the conceptual and analytical framework for capital flight. The third section examines the stylized facts on capital flight and economic growth in FZ, and provides an econometric estimate of the effect of capital flight on growth in the FZ. The fourth section concludes the chapter and discusses policy implications.

Capital Flight: Relationship to Growth, Conceptual and Analytic Framework

The Relationship Between Capital Flight and Growth: What Does the Literature Say?

The extent of capital flight from developing countries acquires significance and poses a serious threat to sustainable growth, particularly in Africa (Ayadi, 2008). Boyce and Ndikumana (2001) have observed that many poor countries lose more resources through capital flight than they pay in debt service. The UNDP (2011) regards capital flight, wherever it occurs, as a major obstacle to the mobilization of resources for development, implying that capital flight exacerbates resource constraints and hinders long-term economic growth (Beja, 2007).

In the literature, authors are unanimous in recognizing the damaging effects of capital flight on economic growth, as shown by empirical studies. Bakare (2011) shows that capital flight limits economic growth in Nigeria. Beja (2007) finds that capital flight serves to diminish the quality of long-term economic growth in the Philippines. Červená (2006) finds that capital flight has prejudicial effects on long-term economic growth for African, Latin American, Asian and Eastern European countries. The empirical results of the paper by Lan (2009) support the evidence that capital flight plays a crucial role in influencing the economic growth of Association of Southeast Asian Nations (ASEAN) countries. Forgha (2008) finds that capital flight exerts a negative impact on economic growth in Cameroon. Gusarova (2009) shows that capital flight has an adverse effect on growth in a sample of 139 countries.

The effects of capital flight on economic growth are transmitted through several channels, for example: investment, imports and the tax base, capital inflows, worsening balance of payments, the financial system and corruption.

The Investment Channel

The phenomenon of capital flight arises from the transfer of a portion of private domestic savings abroad. The persistence of this phenomenon leads to a decline in saving. This could result in fewer resources available to finance domestic investment and promote economic growth. Ndikumana (2009) maintains that capital flight reduces domestic investment by diminishing the volume of savings channeled through the domestic financial system, thereby slowing growth.

High levels of capital flight pose serious challenges for the mobilization of domestic resources to support investment and growth in Africa (Fofack and Ndikumana, 2009, 2010), suggesting that capital flight leads to a decline in domestic investment (Lawanson, 2007). In fact, Boyce and Ndikumana (2001) show that capital flight is the cause of low levels of investment in Africa. According to the UNDP (2011), capital flight significantly reduces the volume of resources available for investment in the Millennium Development Goals and productive capacities. By reducing investment, capital flight can adversely affect economic growth. In this regard, Pastor (1990) finds that economic growth is reduced because a portion of investment is diverted and transferred abroad as flight capital. Kosarev and Grigoryev (2000) also regard capital flight as diminishing investment opportunities and prospects for development of the economy.

Empirical literature confirms the evidence that capital flight exerts a negative influence on growth through the investment channel. Fedderke and Liu (2002) maintain that capital flight from South Africa negatively affects the country's economy by reducing private investment. Greene (2002) shows that capital outflows from Asian countries in crisis, during the period before 1997, resulted in low levels of investment in those countries. Using the Generalized Method of Moments (GMM), Fofack and Ndikumana (2009, 2010) show that while capital flight significantly reduces total domestic investment and private investment in sub-Saharan African countries, its impact on public investment is found to be non-significant, suggesting that the adverse effects of capital flight on domestic investment is transmitted through private investment to a greater extent than through public investment. Using the same econometric estimation technique, Ndiaye (2009b) also finds the same result for FZ countries. Using the vector auto regression model approach, Bakare (2011) finds that capital flight crowds out investment and alters capital formation in Nigeria. This result is confirmed by Ayadi (2008) for the same country.[5] In emerging countries, Yalta (2010) finds that capital flight dramatically reduces private investment but has no significant effect on public investment. These low rates of investment are the principal cause of weak economic performance in Africa (Barro and Lee, 1994; Collier and Gunning, 1999).

The Tax Base Channel

Among other negative consequences of capital flight, researchers note the importance of tax base erosion (Pastor, 1990). Ndikumana (2009) maintains that capital flight affects the government budget balance by reducing the tax base through the contraction of economic activity. According to Ajayi (1997), capital flight leads to erosion of the tax base, reducing government revenue and therefore public investment, which may in turn reduce private investment and growth. The tax base is eroded by capital flight because the funds channeled abroad cannot be taxed (Forgha, 2008) since they are beyond the reach of tax authorities in the country of origin (Červená, 2006). Ayadi (2008) views capital flight as a grave danger for any nation because it leads, *inter alia*, to a reduction of the country's tax base. Ndikumana and Boyce (2011a) have demonstrated empirically that the countries with the largest total capital flight tend to have the lowest tax receipts.

The Imports Channel

If the scarce foreign currencies of developing countries, particularly in Africa, are used to finance capital flight, the foreign currencies will not be available to finance imports, which could be crucial for economic growth (Lessard and Williamson, 1987). If flight capital were invested in the production of domestically produced goods or goods for export that could finance imports, the import constraint on economic growth could be removed (Pastor, 1990).

The Capital Inflows Channel

Empirical evidence shows that capital flight significantly increases requirements for foreign borrowing and foreign aid (Boyce, 1992; Chipalkatti and Rishi, 2001; Cerra *et al.*, 2008). According to Ndikumana (2009), capital flight forces the government to increase foreign borrowing, which further increases the burden of external debt and aggravates the budget balance. However, a significant portion of external debt and foreign aid is re-exported in the form of flight capital, as shown by a number of studies (Bauer, 1981; Cuddington, 1987; Duwendag, 1989; Hermes and Lensink, 1992; Boyce, 1992; Henry, 1996; Lensink *et al.*, 2000; Hermes and Lensink, 2001; Chipalkatti and Rishi, 2001; Ndikumana and Boyce, 2003; Quazi, 2004; Salisu, 2005; Beja, 2006; Ljungwall and Wang, 2008; Cerra *et al.*, 2008; Ndikumana and Boyce, 2008, 2011a, 2011b; Ndiaye, 2009a, 2011). One of the functions of external debt and foreign aid is to help finance domestic investment. Therefore, the longer the phenomenon of capital flight persists, the fewer external debt and foreign aid resources are used to finance investment. Accordingly, through the external debt and foreign aid channel, capital flight could lead to reduced domestic investment and therefore slower economic growth.

The Worsening Balance of Payments Channel

According to Ajayi (1995), persistent balance of payments deficits in most developing countries have been attributed to capital flight. Capital flight could contribute negatively to economic growth by exacerbating balance of payments problems (Menbere, 2003).

The Financial System Channel

Capital flight could reduce growth by destabilizing the financial system, since sudden, large outflows of capital could require an adjustment of the interest rate and exchange rate policies (Menbere, 2003). The phenomenon of capital flight arises from the transfer abroad of a portion of private domestic savings. The persistence of this phenomenon could therefore lead to reduced savings. Banks take in fewer resources in the form of savings deposits, which could lead them to reduce credit to the private sector. Consequently, capital flight could reduce the volume of financial intermediation and negatively affect economic growth. According to Ndikumana (2003), capital flight contributes to increasing macroeconomic uncertainty, which depresses the volume of loans and investments and therefore growth.

The Corruption Channel

Capital flight could affect economic growth through corruption. In effect, extensive capital flight is symptomatic of an environment characterized by corruption (Ndikumana and Boyce, 2011a), a circumstance that hinders economic performance by reducing private investment, negatively impacting the quantity and quality of public infrastructures, reducing tax revenue and slowing the accumulation of human capital (Ndikumana, 2006).

Definition of Capital Flight

Following Erbe (1985), World Bank (1985), and Morgan Guaranty Trust Company (1986, 1988), this chapter defines capital flight as normal and abnormal capital outflows. What is of real importance is the fact that for countries facing large current account deficits and external debt payments (and are therefore in need of foreign capital), both normal and abnormal capital outflows increase their difficulties in financing net imports and debt payments (Hermes *et al*., 2002). Accordingly, we regard the phenomenon of capital flight as involving capital outflows associated with residents' concerns for diversifying their portfolios, with domestic commercial banks' acquisitions of foreign assets and with high levels of risk and uncertainty for residents' domestic assets.

However, the fact that capital flight arises from the acts of individuals does not imply that capital flight is a purely private issue. The funds that leave the country through capital flight in the form of private assets could be primarily public funds such as debt, aid and revenue from natural resource exports, as shown by a number of studies (Bauer, 1981; Cuddington, 1987; Duwendag, 1989; Hermes and Lensink, 1992; Boyce, 1992; Henry, 1996; Lensink *et al*., 2000; Hermes and Lensink, 2001; Chipalkatti and Rishi, 2001; Ndikumana and Boyce, 2003; Quazi, 2004; Salisu, 2005; Beja, 2006; Ljungwall and Wang, 2008; Cerra *et al*., 2008; Ndikumana and Boyce, 2008, 2011a, 2011b; Ndiaye, 2009a, 2011). Accordingly, the phenomenon of capital flight also involves capital flows channeled by corrupt officials to conceal public funds in foreign banks. Corrupt officials could in fact profit from their privileged positions to amass personal fortunes abroad (Boyce and Ndikumana, 2001).

Measuring Capital Flight

A number of estimates of the volume of capital flight from FZ countries are available in the literature. Those estimates vary according to the measurement method utilized and the period and sample considered. Ndiaye (2009a, 2009b, 2011), referring to the above definition of capital flight, uses two versions of the residual method, the World Bank version (1985) and the Morgan Guaranty method (1986); both of them adjusted to exchange rate fluctuations, trade mis-invoicing and inflation (Boyce and Ndikumana, 2001).[6]

Adjustment for Exchange Rate Fluctuations

World Bank data on debt are reported in a common currency, the US dollar. However, countries' contract debt are denominated in different currencies.

The World Bank data on debt are converted to dollars using the year-end exchange rate. Exchange rate fluctuations produce changes in the stock of debt and therefore in the measure of capital flight. To correct this unstable aspect of debt, Boyce and Ndikumana (2001) adjust the variation in long-term debt to fluctuations of the dollar exchange rate with other currencies as follows:

$$\Delta DETAJU_t = DET_t - NOUDET_{t-1} \tag{1}$$

where $\Delta DETAJU_t$ is the change in the debt adjusted to fluctuations in the dollar exchange rate with other currencies; DET_t is the stock of debt in year t calculated at the exchange rate in effect at the end of year t; $NOUDET_{t-1}$ is the stock of debt in year $t-1$ calculated at the exchange rate in effect at the end of year t. $NOUDET_{t-1}$ is calculated as follows:

$$\begin{aligned} NOUDET_{i,t-1} = {} & \sum_{j=1}^{7} (\alpha_{ij,t-1} * DETLT_{i,t-1}) / (TC_{jt} / TC_{j,t-1}) + \\ & CRFMI_{i,t-1} / (TC_{DTS,t} / TC_{DTS,t-1}) + AUTRELT_{i,t-1} + \\ & MULTLT_{i,t-1} + DETLTEU_{i,t-1} + DETCT_{i,t-1} \end{aligned} \tag{2}$$

where $DETLT$ is long-term debt; α_{ij} is the proportion of long-term debt held in currency j (j=French franc, German Deutsche Mark, Japanese yen, Swiss franc, Special Drawing Rights (SDR), British pound, euro);[7] TC is the year-end dollar exchange rate with the currency in which the debt is denominated (expressed in units of the currency per dollar); $CRFMI$ is IMF credit denominated in SDR; $AUTRELT$ is long-term debt denominated in other unspecified currencies; $MULTLT$ is long-term debt denominated in multiple currencies; $DETLTEU$ is long-term debt denominated in US dollars; $DETCT$ is short-term debt.

Adjustment for Trade Mis-Invoicing

Following Ajayi (1997) and Boyce and Ndikumana (2001), we calculate trade mis-invoicing between FZ countries and their industrialized trading partners. The total amount of mis-invoiced trade (FALSCOM) is calculated as follows:

$$FALSCOM_{it} = \frac{DEX_{it}}{PMEX_i} + \frac{DIM_{it}}{PMIM_i} \tag{3}$$

where *DEX* is the expert differential between FZ countries and industrialized countries; *DIM* is the import differential between FZ countries and industrialized countries; *PMEX* is the industrialized countries' average share of the FZ countries' exports; *PMIM* is the industrialized countries' average share of FZ countries' imports. *DEX* and *DIM* are calculated as follows:

$$DEX_{it} = IMPI_{it} - (EXPAZF_{it} * CAF_t) \tag{4}$$

$$DIM_{it} = IMPAZF_{it} - (EXPI_{it} * CAF_t) \tag{5}$$

where *IMPI* is the industrialized countries' imports from FZ countries; *IMPAFZ* is FZ countries' imports from industrialized countries; *EXPAFZ* is exports from the CFA countries to industrialized countries; *EXPI* is the industrialized countries' exports to FZ countries; *CAF* is the CIF/FOB factor, representing the cost of freight and insurance.

Inflation Adjustment

Since all the variables are expressed in dollars, we will use the US producer price index to adjust capital flight for inflation. The resultant data are useful in examining the year-by-year change in real capital flight, which is estimated as follows:

$$FCR(BM)_{it} = \frac{(\Delta DETAJU_{it} + INDE_{it}) - (CC_{it} + \Delta RES_{it}) + FALSCOM_{it}}{IPPEU_t} \tag{6}$$

$$FCR(MG)_{it} = FCR(BM)_{it} - \frac{\Delta ABD_{it}}{IPPEU_t} \tag{7}$$

where *FCR*(*BM*) designates real capital flight calculated using the World Bank (1985) residual method adjusted for exchange rate fluctuations, trade mis-invoicing and inflation; *FCR*(*MG*) is real capital flight calculated using the Morgan Guaranty (1986) residual method adjusted for exchange rate fluctuations, trade mis-invoicing and inflation; *ABD* represents domestic bank assets held abroad; *IPPEU* is the US producer price index.

The Relationship Between Capital Flight and Growth: An Empirical Investigation

The sample is composed of all 15 FZ countries: Benin, Burkina Faso, Cameroon, Central African Republic, Chad, Comoros, Republic of Congo, Côte d'Ivoire, Equatorial Guinea, Gabon, Guinea-Bissau, Mali, Niger, Senegal and Togo. The sampling period is 1970–2010 for all countries except: the Comoros (1980–2010);[8] the Republic of Congo (1971–2010); Guinea Bissau (1998–2010), which joined the FZ on May 2, 1997; Equatorial Guinea (1987–2010), which joined the FZ on January 1, 1985;[9] and Mali (1985–2010), which acceded to the treaty establishing the West African Monetary Union on June 1, 1984.

Stylized Facts of Capital Flight and Economic Growth

Table 8.1 presents total and average real capital flight in the FZ over the period 1970–2010 and compares it to GDP and domestic investment. The table shows contrasting capital movements through FZ countries, as also illustrated in Figure 8.1. Capital flight is found to be positive for ten countries: Burkina Faso, Cameroon, Central African Republic, Chad, Congo, Côte d'Ivoire, Equatorial Guinea, Gabon, Guinea Bissau and Togo, implying net capital outflows for those countries over the period. A potential explanation for positive capital flight relates to the fact that those countries are producers of oil and other natural resources and experienced periods of political instability, circumstances that

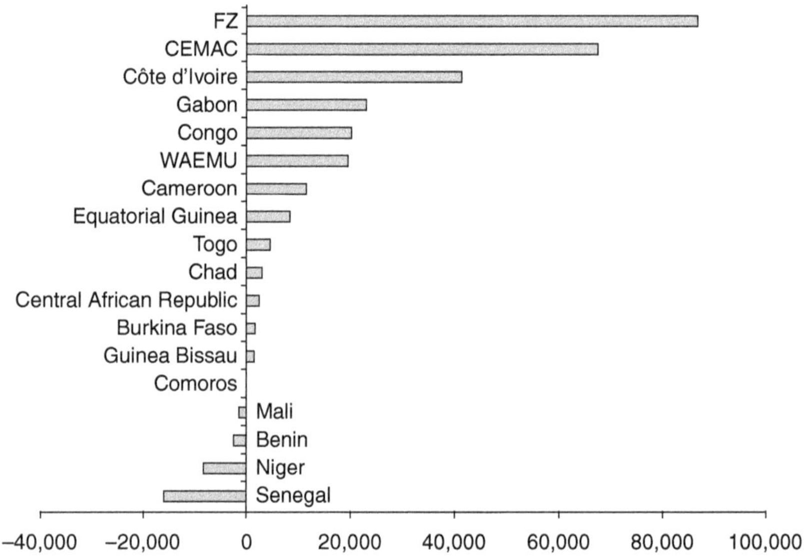

Figure 8.1 Capital Flight by Country, 1970–2010 (US$ million) (World Bank method)

Source: author's calculations using data from: World Bank, *Global Development Finance 2011* (online edition); World Bank, *World Development Indicators 2011* (online edition); World Bank, *Africa Development Indicators 2011* (online edition); IMF, *International Financial Statistics 2011* (online edition); IMF, *Balance of Payments Statistics 2011* (online edition); IMF, *Direction of Trade Statistics 2011* (online edition); IMF, *Selected Issues and Statistical Appendix* (available at www.imf.org).

Notes

The period is 1970–2010 for all countries except the Comoros (1980–2010), the Congo (1971–2010), Equatorial Guinea (1987–2010), Gabon (1970–2010), Guinea Bissau (1998–2010) and Mali (1985–2010). CEMAC: Communauté économique et monétaire de l'Afrique centrale. WAEMU: West African Economic and Monetary Union.

Table 8.1 Real Capital Flight in FZ, 1970–2010[a] (2000 US$ millions, % GDP and % Investment)

Country	*Real Capital Flight, World Bank*[b]				*Real Capital Flight, Morgan Guaranty*[c]			
	Total	*Average*	*% GDP*	*% Investment*	*Total*	*Average*	*% GDP*	*% Investment*
Benin	–2678.2	–65.3	–80.3	–311.3	–3410.8	–83.2	–102.2	–396.4
Burkina Faso	1330.6	32.5	29.3	397.7	465.1	11.3	10.2	356.7
Cameroon	11435.7	278.9	82.2	499.8	10652.7	259.8	76.6	465.6
Central African Republic	2272.7	55.4	215.6	1487.1	2206.7	53.8	209.3	1463.6
Chad	2594.7	63.3	83.8	227.6	2435.1	59.4	78.6	213.6
Comoros	–68.8	–2.2	–27.8	–229.2	–183.6	–6.3	–74.3	–611.7
Congo	20132.6	503.3	397.3	1595.3	19590.6	489.8	386.6	1552.3
Côte d'Ivoire	41170.4	1004.2	352.9	2171.2	40572.3	989.6	347.8	2139.6
Equatorial Guinea	8007.9	333.7	132.2	335.8	7844.2	326.8	129.5	329.0
Gabon	23041.9	562.0	366.5	1259.5	22617.4	551.6	359.7	1236.3
Guinea Bissau	1104.4	85.0	451.9	5140.9	1051.5	80.9	430.2	4894.5
Mali	–1473.4	–56.7	–35.5	–141.4	–2228.2	–85.7	–53.7	–213.8
Niger	–8595.4	–209.6	–307.7	–2123.1	–8839.8	–215.6	–316.4	–2183.5
Senegal	–15867.9	–387.0	–227.7	–727.6	–16742.7	–408.4	–240.2	–767.7
Togo	4436.1	108.2	258.0	1421.8	4089.2	99.7	237.8	1310.6
Franc Zone	*86843.5*	*153.7*	*122.1*	*528.0*	*80119.6*	*141.6*	*112.6*	*487.2*

Sources: author's calculations using data from: World Bank, *Global Development Finance 2011* (online edition); World Bank, *World Development Indicators 2011* (online edition); World Bank, *Africa Development Indicators 2011* (online edition); IMF, *International Financial Statistics 2011* (online edition); IMF, *Balance of Payments Statistics 2011* (online edition); IMF, *Direction of Trade Statistics 2011* (online edition); IMF, *Selected Issues and Statistical Appendix* (available at www.imf.org).

Notes

a The period is 1970–2010 for all countries except the Comoros (1980–2010), the Congo (1971–2010), Equatorial Guinea (1987–2010), Gabon (1970–2010), Guinea Bissau (1998–2010) and Mali (1985–2010).

b Capital flight is measured using the version of the World Bank (1985) residual method adjusted for exchange rate fluctuations, trade mis-invoicing and inflation (Boyce and Ndikumana, 2001).

c Capital flight is measured using the version of the Morgan Guaranty (1986) residual method adjusted for exchange rate fluctuations, trade mis-invoicing and inflation (Boyce and Ndikumana, 2001).

encourage capital flight (Dornbush, 1986; Smit and Mocke, 1991; Nyatepe-Coo, 1994; Lensink *et al.*, 1998, 2000; Hermes and Lensink, 2001; Fedderke and Liu, 2002; Alam and Quazi, 2003; Ndikumana and Boyce, 2003; Quazi, 2004; Fielding, 2004; Collier *et al.*, 2004; Le and Zak, 2006; Davies, 2008). Among those ten countries, four saw massive capital flight, exceeding US$10 billion: Côte d'Ivoire leads with US$41.2 or US$40.6 billion in flight capital (representing 352.9 or 347.8 percent of GDP and 2171.2 or 2139.6 percent of investment, respectively), followed by Gabon with US$23.0 or US$22.6 billion in flight capital (representing 366.5 or 359.7 percent of GDP and 1259.5 or 1256.3 percent of investment, respectively); the Congo, with US$20.1 or US$19.6 billion in flight capital (representing 397.3 or 386.6 percent of GDP and 1595.3 or 1552.3 percent of investment, respectively); and Cameroon, with US$11.4 or US$10.6 billion in flight capital (representing 82.2 or 76.6 percent of GDP and 499.8 or 465.6 percent of investment, respectively). The six remaining countries of the group of ten recorded capital flight ranging from US$1.1 to US$8.0 billion (World Bank method) or US$0.5 to 7.8 billion (Morgan Guaranty method).

Capital flight was found to be negative for five countries in the sample: Benin, Comoros, Mali, Niger and Senegal, suggesting that those countries received net inflows of capital over the period. A potential explanation for negative capital flight could be tied more closely to trade mis-invoicing. Indeed, over the period 1970–2010, our calculations show that with the exception of Mali, those countries recorded negative mis-invoiced trade, implying negative capital flight: –US$13 billion in mis-invoiced trade for Senegal; –US$3.3 billion in mis-invoiced trade for Niger; –US$2.6 billion in mis-invoiced trade for Benin; –US$0.1 billion in mis-invoiced trade for Comoros.

Overall, during the period 1970 to 2010, real capital flight for the 15 FZ countries is found to be positive and massive, at roughly US$86.8 billion or US$80.1 billion, representing US$153.7 million or US$141.6 million per year, 122.1 or 112.6 percent of GDP, and 528.0 or 487.2 percent of domestic investment. Empirical evidence shows that capital flight in FZ comes from economic activities (through trade mis-invoicing by merchandise exporters and importers) as well as individuals (corrupt leaders who channel a portion of external debt and foreign aid abroad as flight capital) (see Ndiaye, 2009a, 2011).

Over the same period (1970–2010), FZ countries recorded low levels of investment at 21.2 percent for total investment, 12.8 percent for private investment and 7.7 percent for public investment. There are also highly volatile total investment, private investment, public investment, economic growth and capital flight, with respective coefficients of variation of 108.8, 100.7, 106.8, 206.4 and 442.3 percent or 486.1 percent. Between 1970 and 1980, capital flight represented US$12.2 billion or US$11.8 billion. Between 1981 and 1990, capital flight increased to US$20.3 billion or US$19.7 billion. This increase can be explained by the eruption of the debt crisis in a number of developing countries. Capital flight declined to US$16.7 billion or US$15.7 billion between 1991 and 2000, then increased to US$37.6 billion or US$32.9 billion between 2001 and 2010

The theory of capital flight suggests that the phenomenon is caused both by private actors and by public authorities (Ndikumana and Boyce, 2003, 2008,

2011b; Ajayi, 2007; Ndiaye, 2009a, 2011). Accordingly, an increase in capital flight could unquestionably lead to reduced public and private investment and therefore a decline in economic growth. The figures in Table 8.1 show that capital flight represents 5.3 or 4.9 times domestic investment in the FZ. It would appear, then, that the volume of capital flight is so large as to exceed domestic investment in the zone. The greater the increase in capital outflows, the fewer the resources available to FZ countries to finance their investment needs and promote their economic growth. Figure 8.2 indicates an inverse relationship between these two variables: over the period 1970–2010, whenever capital flight increases, the rate of economic growth decreases, and vice versa.

The negative relationship between capital flight and annual economic growth is illustrated in Figure 8.3, which reveals that an increase in capital flight is associated with a decline in the rate of economic growth.

The following section examines the effect of capital flight on economic growth from an econometric perspective.

An Econometric Analysis of the Effect of Capital Flight on Growth

The rate of economic growth may be expressed by the following equation:

$$TCPT_{it} = \alpha_1 TCPT_{i,t-1} + \alpha_2 FCRP_{it} + \alpha_3 X_{it} + \alpha_4 Y_{it} + u_i + v_i + \varepsilon_{it} \quad (8)$$

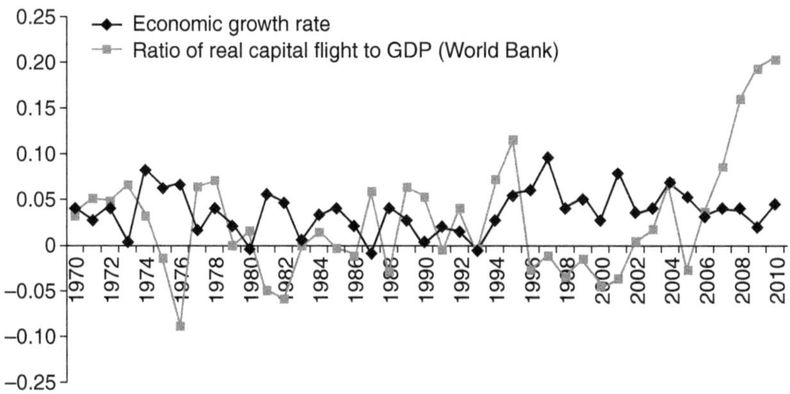

Figure 8.2 Comparison of Economic Growth Rate and Ratio of Capital Flight to GDP in the FZ, 1970–2010

Source: author's calculations using data from: World Bank, *Global Development Finance 2011* (online edition); World Bank, *World Development Indicators 2011* (online edition); World Bank, *Africa Development Indicators 2011* (online edition); IMF, *International Financial Statistics 2011* (online edition); IMF, *Balance of Payments Statistics 2011* (online edition); IMF, *Direction of Trade Statistics 2011* (online edition); IMF, *Selected Issues and Statistical Appendix* (available at www.imf.org).

Notes

The period is 1970–2010 for all countries except the Comoros (1980–2010), the Congo (1971–2010), Equatorial Guinea (1987–2010), Gabon (1970–2010), Guinea-Bissau (1998–2010) and Mali (1985–2010).

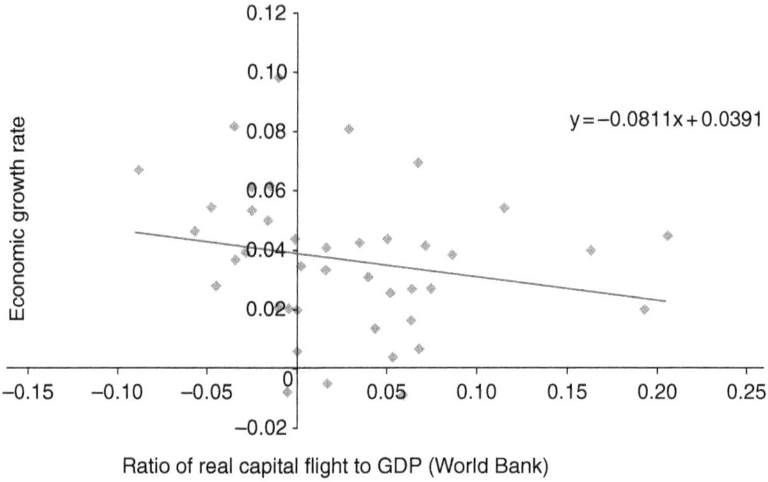

Figure 8.3 Relationship Between Capital Flight and Annual Economic Growth Rate in the FZ, 1970–2010, World Bank Method

Source: author's calculations using data from: World Bank, *Global Development Finance 2011* (online edition); World Bank, *World Development Indicators 2011* (online edition); World Bank, *Africa Development Indicators 2011* (online edition); IMF, *International Financial Statistics 2011* (online edition); IMF, *Balance of Payments Statistics 2011* (online edition); IMF, *Direction of Trade Statistics 2011* (online edition); IMF, *Selected Issues and Statistical Appendix* (available at www.imf.org).

Notes

The period is 1970–2010 for all countries except Comoros (1980–2010), Congo (1971–2010), Equatorial Guinea (1987–2010), Gabon (1970–2010), Guinea-Bissau (1998–2010) and Mali (1985–2010).

where *TCPT* is the rate of real per capita GDP growth; *FCRP* is the ratio of real capital flight to GDP (capital flight is estimated by using equations 6 and 7 above); *X* represents the vector of the macroeconomic control variables including the ratio of domestic investment to GDP, the inflation rate measured by the annual change in the consumer price index (CPI) and the ratio of credit to the private sector to GDP; *Y* designates the vector of institutional control variables including institutional quality measured by constraints on the executive branch, ranging in value from 1 (unlimited executive authority) to 7 (executive parity or subordination) (cf. Polity IV Project Database); u is the specific country effect; v is the specific temporal effect; ε is the error term in the model.

Capital flight may be endogenous in the economic growth model (equation 8). Capital flight may in fact affect growth, but anticipation of weak growth may also affect the volume of capital flight (Morgan Guaranty, 1988; Pastor, 1990; Mikkelsen, 1991; Ajayi, 1992; Muscatelli and Hallet, 1992; Harrigan *et al.*, 2002; Alam and Quazi, 2003; Quazi, 2004; Ljungwall and Wang, 2008; Ndikumana and Boyce, 2008, 2011b). We will therefore use GMM to correct endogeneity problems.

The results, presented in Tables 8.2 (for the World Bank method of measuring capital flight) and 8.3 (for the Morgan Guaranty method of measuring capital flight), confirm the negative coefficient anticipated for capital flight, which is also found to be significant. This result implies that capital flight significantly reduces economic growth in the FZ. Capital flight therefore constitutes a major obstacle to achieving strong, sustainable economic growth in the FZ.

The results also show a negative and statistically significant coefficient for interactions between capital flight and, respectively, investment, credit to the private sector, institutional quality and domestic savings, while the interaction between capital flight and external debt is found to be non-significant. This suggests that by reducing domestic investment, credit to the private sector, institutional quality and domestic savings, capital flight reduces economic performance. Consequently, domestic investment, credit to the private sector, institutional quality and domestic savings play an important role in explaining the influence of capital flight on economic growth in the FZ, and are therefore important channels through which capital flight affects growth.

Note that these results remain invariably true when controlling for other variables and taking into account a given measure of capital flight (adjusted World Bank method or adjusted Morgan Guaranty method).

Conclusion and Policy Implications

This study examined the effect of capital flight on economic growth in the FZ. Over the period 1970–2010, real capital flight for the 15 countries of the FZ was positive and massive at roughly US$86.8 or US$8.1 billion, representing 122.1 or 112.6 percent of GDP and 5.3 times or 4.9 times domestic investment. At the same time, FZ countries recorded weak and highly volatile rates of investment and economic growth. The theory of capital flight holds that the phenomenon is caused both by private actors and public authorities. Accordingly, an increase in capital flight could undoubtedly lead to reduced public and private investment and therefore a decline in economic growth. The results of econometric testing of this hypothesis showed that capital flight significantly reduces economic growth in the FZ. Capital flight is therefore a major obstacle to achieving strong, sustainable economic growth in the FZ. The econometric analysis also reveals that domestic investment, credit to the private sector, institutional quality and domestic savings play an important role in explaining the influence of capital flight on economic growth in the FZ, and are therefore important channels through which capital flight affects growth in the zone.

The key implication of these results is that repatriating flight capital contributes to significantly increasing the volume of investment, credit to the private sector, institutional quality and domestic savings in the FZ, which could aid countries in sustainably stimulating economic growth. The repatriation of flight capital requires minimizing uncertainty as to the macroeconomic and institutional environment in order to reduce the risk of loss of real value of private investors' domestic assets. Moreover, efforts to improve governance and institutional quality and promote a stable political environment are

Table 8.2 Effect of Capital Flight on Economic Growth in FZ, 1970–2010, World Bank Method, GMM

Variables	*(1)*	*(2)*	*(3)*	*(4)*	*(5)*	*(6)*	*(7)*	*(8)*
Ratio of real capital flight to GDP	–0.0372***	–0.108*	–0.00933	–0.0427	–0.0885	–0.0372	–0.157*	–0.0752
	(0.00900)	(0.0603)	(0.0195)	(0.0448)	(0.109)	(0.0830)	(0.0807)	(0.0522)
Dependent variable: 1st lag	0.0400	0.135	0.126	0.329	0.583	0.184	0.270*	0.124
	(0.173)	(0.267)	(0.140)	(0.303)	(0.487)	(0.146)	(0.161)	(0.164)
Ratio of investment to GDP	–	0.231	0.255	0.295	–	–	–	–
		(0.453)	(0.243)	(0.366)				
Inflation	–	–0.0537	–	–0.0959	–	–	–	–
		(0.0425)		(0.193)				
Ratio of credit to the private sector to GDP	–	0.318	–	0.664	0.115	–	–	–
		(0.569)		(0.449)	(0.357)			
Institutional quality	–	0.000305*	–	0.000216	–	4.80e–05	–	–
		(0.000181)		(0.000159)		(0.000181)		
Ratio of external debt to GDP	–	–	–	–	–	–	–0.0188	–
							(0.0176)	
Ratio of domestic savings to GDP	–	–	–	–	–	–	–	0.0232
								(0.0667)
Interaction between capital flight and investment	–	–	–0.654*	–0.542**	–	–	–	–
			(0.334)	(0.221)				
Interaction between capital flight and credit to the private sector	–	–	–	–	–1.764***	–	–	–
					(0.615)			
Interaction between capital flight and institutional quality	–	–	–	–	–	–0.00418*	–	–
						(0.00253)		
Interaction between capital flight and external debt	–	–	–	–	–	–	–0.00497	–
							(0.0396)	
Interaction between capital flight and domestic savings	–	–	–	–	–	–	–	–0.448*
								(0.252)
Constant	0.00663	–0.123	0.0606	0.225	0.0327	0.00460	0.0169	0.000794
	(0.00488)	(0.200)	(0.0490)	(0.145)	(0.0507)	(0.00425)	(0.0115)	(0.00794)
Observations	379	300	433	355	452	513	363	357
Country	15	14	15	14	15	15	15	15
AR(1) test	0.040	0.059	0.076	0.182	0.086	0.025	0.014	0.002
AR(2) test	0.380	0.457	0.267	0.471	0.732	0.326	0.290	0.124
Hansen test	0.459	0.431	0.395	0.480	0.526	0.640	0.533	0.271

Notes

Robust standard errors in parentheses. *** $p<0.01$, ** $p<0.05$, * $p<0.1$.

Table 8.3 Effect of Capital Flight on Economic Growth in FZ, 1970–2010, Morgan Guaranty Method, GMM

Variables	*(1)*	*(2)*	*(3)*	*(4)*	*(5)*	*(6)*	*(7)*	*(8)*
Ratio of real capital flight to GDP	–0.0313*	–0.136**	–0.0326	–0.0432	–0.0684*	–0.0757	–0.159*	–0.0787**
	(0.0166)	(0.0607)	(0.0389)	(0.0483)	(0.0352)	(0.0644)	(0.0813)	(0.0373)
Dependent variable: 1st lag	0.137	0.0676	0.222	0.346	0.175	0.0486	0.287	0.346
	(0.128)	(0.259)	(0.151)	(0.280)	(0.595)	(0.117)	(0.175)	(0.256)
Ratio of investment to GDP	–	0.280	0.0594	0.338	–	–	–	–
		(0.437)	(0.217)	(0.363)				
Inflation	–	–0.0509	–	–0.0839	–	–	–	–
		(0.0404)		(0.185)				
Ratio of credit to the private sector to GDP	–	0.456	–	0.679	0.325	–	–	–
		(0.566)		(0.432)	(0.693)			
Institutional quality	–	0.000287*	–	0.000233	–	0.000181*	–	–
		(0.000163)		(0.000153)		(0.000108)		
Ratio of external debt to GDP	–	–	–	–	–	–	–0.0204	–
							(0.0194)	
Ratio of domestic savings to GDP	–	–	–	–	–	–	–	0.0853
								(0.134)
Interaction between capital flight and investment	–	–	–0.0857	–0.540***	–	–	–	–
			(0.373)	(0.200)				
Interaction between capital flight and credit to the private sector	–	–	–	–	–0.465	–	–	–
					(0.584)			
Interaction between capital flight and institutional quality	–	–	–	–	–	–0.00263**	–	–
						(0.00120)		
Interaction between capital flight and external debt	–	–	–	–	–	–	–0.00637	–
							(0.0432)	
Interaction between capital flight and domestic savings	–	–	–	–	–	–	–	–0.525*
								(0.276)
Constant	0.00332	–0.154	–0.00462	0.230*	0.0590	0.00388	0.0187	0.00841
	(0.00236)	(0.194)	(0.0426)	(0.137)	(0.106)	(0.00574)	(0.0126)	(0.0148)
Observations	235	300	431	355	467	319	362	341
Country	14	14	15	14	15	14	15	14
AR(1) test	0.029	0.067	0.043	0.182	0.032	0.006	0.016	0.009
AR(2) test	0.313	0.560	0.284	0.455	0.861	0.222	0.297	0.064
Hansen test	0.416	0.622	0.586	0.443	0.624	0.618	0.701	0.827

Notes

Robust standard errors in parentheses. *** $p<0.01$, ** $p<0.05$, * $p<0.1$.

Table 8.4 Definition and Sources of Variables

Variables	*Definition*	*Sources*
Dependant variable: per capita economic growth (TCP)	Real per capita GDP growth rate	World Bank, *World Development Indicators 2011* (online edition)
Independent variables		
Impact variable: Capital flight (FCRP)	Ratio of real capital flight to GDP (capital flight is estimated using equations 6 and 7 above)	Author's calculations using data from: World Bank, *Global Development Finance 2011* (online edition); World Bank, *World Development Indicators 2011* (online edition); World Bank, *Africa Development Indicators 2011* (online edition); IMF, *International Financial Statistics 2011* (online edition); IMF, *Balance of Payments Statistics 2011* (online edition); IMF, *Direction of Trade Statistics 2011* (online edition); IMF, *Selected Issues and Statistical Appendix* (available at www.imf.org)
Control variable: investment (INVP)	Ratio of domestic investment to GDP	World Bank, *World Development Indicators 2011* (online edition) and World Bank, *Africa Development Indicators 2011* (online edition)
Control variable: inflation (INF)	Annual change in the consumer price index (CPI)	World Bank, *Africa Development Indicators 2011* (online edition)
Control variable: credit to the private sector (CPP)	Ratio of credit to the private sector to GDP	World Bank, *World Development Indicators 2011* (online edition) and World Bank, *Africa Development Indicators 2011* (online edition)
Control variable: institutional quality (QINS)	Constraints on the executive branch, ranging in value from 1 (unlimited executive authority) to 7 (executive parity or subordination)	Polity IV Project Database

necessary to repatriate flight capital. In this regard, the repatriation of flight capital calls for greater accountability on the part of the FZ country governments, particularly in managing public resources, and ethical responsibility on the part of foreign banks to cooperate in repatriating public funds that were intended to be used to finance social sectors in the FZ, particularly education, health and infrastructures.

Notes

1 The original research paper was presented at the 2012 African Economic Conference, jointly organized by the African Development Bank (AfDB), the United Nations Economic Commission for Africa (ECA) and the United Nations Development Programme (UNDP) in Kigali, Rwanda from October 30 to November 2, 2012. I would like to thank the conference participants for their comments and suggestions. Responsibility for any errors in the chapter is mine alone.

2 The phenomenon of capital flight could arise simply because returns on assets held abroad are higher than on domestically held assets (Pastor, 1990; Ajayi, 1992; Vos, 1992; Boyce, 1992, 1993; Fedderke and Liu, 2002; Hermes *et al.*, 2002; Alam and Quazi, 2003; Ndikumana and Boyce, 2003; Ndiaye, 2009a, 2011).

3 The Boyce and Ndikumana (2012) sample includes only seven FZ countries: Burkina Faso, Cameroon, Central African Republic, Chad, Congo, Côte d'Ivoire and Gabon.

4 Boyce and Ndikumana (2012) used the World Bank residual method adjusted for exchange rate fluctuations, debt amortization, trade mis-invoicing, underreported remittances and inflation. Other recent estimates by the UNDP (2011) place illicit capital flight from 11 FZ countries at roughly US$30.7 billion over the period 1990–2008. The estimation method used by the UNDP (2011) is more restrictive, then, as it considers only illicit capital flight whereas Boyce and Ndikumana (2012) consider a broader set of flows.

5 Other authors have found the effect of capital flight on domestic investment in Nigeria non-significant: Adesoye *et al.* (2012); Adetiloye (2012).

6 In addition to those three adjustments, Boyce and Ndikumana (2001) add a fourth adjustment for imputed interest income. As the authors observe, the adjustment for inflation allows the causes and effects of capital flight to be adequately captured, while the adjustment for imputed interest income facilitates the comparison of capital flight to other aggregates such as external debt, for example. Since our study aims to examine the effects of capital flight on economic growth, we consider only the adjustments for exchange rate fluctuations, trade mis-invoicing and inflation.

7 Euro (beginning in 2001); Deutsche Mark and French franc (through 2000).

8 To estimate capital flight in Comoros, the World Bank method was used for the period 1980–2010. However, the period 1982–2010 was used with the Morgan Guaranty method because data on the foreign assets of Comorian domestic banks are available only for 1982 through 2010.

9 However, the data with which to calculate capital flight are available only for the period 1987–2010.

References

Adesoye, A.B., O.E. Maku and A.A. Atanda (2012) "Capital Flight and Investment Dynamics in Nigeria: A Time Series Analysis (1970–2006)," MPRA Paper No. 35836.

Adetiloye, K.A. (2012) "Capital Flight versus Domestic Investment in Developing Countries: An Empirical Analysis from Nigeria," *International Journal of Economics and Finance*, 4(2), 175–186.

Ajayi, I.S. (1992) "An Economic Analysis of Capital Flight from Nigeria," World Bank, Working Paper 993.

Ajayi, I.S. (1995) "Capital Flight and External Debt in Nigeria," African Economic Research Consortium, Research Paper 35.

Ajayi, I.S. (1997) "An Analysis of External Debt and Capital Flight in the Severely Indebted Low Income Countries in Sub-Saharan Africa," IMF, Working Paper, WP/97/68.

Ajayi, I.S. (2007) "Dynamics of Capital Flight: Causes and Determinants," Paper prepared for the Senior Policy Seminar on "Capital Flight from Sub-Saharan Africa: Implications for Macroeconomic Management and Growth," October 30 to November 2, Pretoria, South Africa.

Alam, I. and R. Quazi (2003) "Determinants of Capital Flight: An Econometric Case Study of Bangladesh," *International Review of Applied Economics*, 17(1), 85–103.

Ariyoshi, A., K. Habermeier, B. Laurens, I. tker-Robe, J.I. Canales-Kriljenko and A. Kirilenko (2000) "Capital Controls: Country Experiences with their Use and Liberalization," IMF, Occasional Paper 190.

Awung, W.J. (1996) "An Economic Analysis of Capital Flight in Cameroon," African Economic Research Consortium, Nairobi.

Ayadi, F.S. (2008) "Econometric Analysis of Capital Flight in Developing Countries: A Study of Nigeria," Paper presented at the eighth Global Conference on Business and Economics, Florence, Italy, October.

Bakare, A.S. (2011) "The Determinants and Roles of Capital Flight in the Growth Process of Nigerian Economy: Vector Autoregressive Model Approach," *British Journal of Management and Economics*, 1(2), 100–113.

Barro, R.J. and J.-W. Lee (1994) "Losers and Winners in Economic Growth," in *Proceedings of the Annual World Bank Conference on Development Economics*, 1993, 267–297.

Bauer, P.T. (1981) *Equality, the Third World and Economic Delusion*, London: Weidenfeld & Nicolson.

Beja, E.L. Jr (2006) "Revisiting the Revolving Door: Capital Flight from Southeast Asia," DESA, Working Paper No. 16 ST/ESA/2006/DWP/16.

Beja, E. Jr (2007) "Capital Flight and Economic Performance," MPRA Paper No. 4885.

Boyce, J.K. (1992) "The Revolving Door? External Debt and Capital Flight: A Philippine Case Study," *World Development*, 20(3), 335–349.

Boyce, J.K. (1993) *The Philippines: The Political Economy of Growth and Impoverishment in the Marcos Era*, London: Macmillan Press.

Boyce, J.K. and L. Ndikumana (2001) "Is Africa a Net Creditor? New Estimates of Capital Flight from Severely Indebted Sub-Saharan African Countries, 1970–1996," *Journal of Development Studies*, 38(2), 27–56.

Boyce, J.K. and L. Ndikumana (2012) "Capital Flight from Sub-Saharan African Countries: Updated Estimates, 1970–2010," PERI Research Report, October.

Cerra, V., M. Rishi and S.C. Saxena (2008) "Robbing the Riches: Capital Flight, Institutions, and Debt," *Journal of Development Studies*, 44(8), 1190–1213.

Červená, M. (2006) "The Measurement of Capital Flight and Its Impact on Long-term Economic Growth: Empirical Evidence from a Cross-section of Countries," Master's Thesis, Bratislava.

Chipalkatti, N. and M. Rishi (2001) "External Debt and Capital Flight in the Indian Economy," *Oxford Development Studies*, 29(1), 31–44.

Collier, P. and J.W. Gunning (1999). "Explaining African Economic Performance," *Journal of Economic Literature*, 37:1, 64–111.

Collier, P., A. Hoeffler and C. Pattillo (2004) *Aid and Capital Flight*, Oxford University: Centre for the Study of African Economies.

Cuddington, J. (1986) "Capital Flight: Estimates, Issues, and Explanations," *Princeton Studies in International Finance*, no. 58, Princeton University.

Cuddington, J. (1987) "Macroeconomic Determinants of Capital Flight: An Econometric Investigation," in D. Lessard and J. Cuddington (eds.) *Capital Flight and Third World Debt*, Washington, DC: Institute for International Economics, 85–96.

Davies, V.A.B. (2008) "Postwar Capital Flight and Inflation," *Journal of Peace Research*, 45(4), 519–537.

Dornbush, R. (1986) *Dollars, Debts and Deficits*, Cambridge, MA: MIT Press.

Duwendag, D. (1989) "Capital Flight from Developing Countries," *Development Co-Operation* (3).

Erbe, S. (1985) "The Flight of Capital from Developing Countries," *Intereconomics*, November/December, 268–275.

Fedderke, J.W. and W. Liu (2002) "Modelling the Determinants of Capital Flows and Capital Flight: With an Application to South African Data from 1960–95," *Economic Modelling*, 19, 419–444.

Fielding, D. (2004) "How does Violent Conflict affect Investment Location Decisions? Evidence from Israel during the Intifada," *Journal of Peace Research*, 41(4), 465–484.

Fofack, H. and L. Ndikumana (2009) "Potential Gains from Capital Flight Repatriation for Sub-Saharan African Countries," World Bank, Policy Research Working Paper 5024.

Fofack, H. and L. Ndikumana (2010) "Capital Flight Repatriation: Investigation of its Potential Gains for Sub-Saharan African Countries," *African Development Review*, 22(1), 4–22.

Forgha, N.G. (2008) "Capital Flight, Measurability and Economic Growth in Cameroon: An Econometric Investigation," *International Review of Business Research Papers* 4(2), 74–90.

Greene, J.E. (2002) "The Output Decline in Asian Crisis Countries: Investment Aspects," IMF, Working Paper, WP/02/25.

Gusarova, V. (2009) "The Impact of Capital Flight on Economic Growth," Master's Thesis, Ukraine.

Harrigan, J., G. Mavrotas and Z. Yusop (2002) "On the Determinants of Capital Flight: A New Approach," *Journal of the Asia Pacific Economy*, 77(2), 203–241.

Henry, L. (1996) "Capital Flight from Beautiful Places: The Case of Three Caribbean Countries," *International Review of Applied Economics*, 10(2), 263–272.

Hermes, N. and R. Lensink (1992) "The Magnitude and Determinants of Capital Flight: The Case for Six Sub-Saharan African Countries", *The Economist*, 140(4), 515–530.

Hermes, N. and R. Lensink (2001) "Capital Flight and the Uncertainty of Government Policies," *Economics Letters*, 71(3), 377–381.

Hermes, N., R. Lensink, and V. Murinde (2002) "Flight Capital and Its Reversal for Development Financing," WIDER, Discussion Paper No. 2002/99.

International Monetary Fund (2011) *Balance of Payments Statistics 2011* (online edition).

International Monetary Fund (2011) *Direction of Trade Statistics 2011* (online edition).

International Monetary Fund (2011) *International Financial Statistics 2011* (online edition).

International Monetary Fund (2011) *World Economic Outlook 2011* (online edition).

Kosarev, A. and L. Grigoryev (2000) "Capital Flight: Scale and Nature," Bureau of Economic Analysis, February.

Lan, S.K. (2009) "Effects of Capital Flight on Economic Growth in Selected ASEAN Economies," PhD Thesis, Malaysia.

Lawanson, A.O. (2007) "An Econometric Analysis of Capital Flight from Nigeria: A Portfolio Approach," African Economic Research Consortium (AERC), Research Paper 166.

Le, Q.V. and M. Rishi (2006) "Corruption and Capital Flight: An Empirical Assessment," *International Economic Journal*, 20(4), 523–540.

Le, Q.V. and P.J. Zak (2006) "Political Risk and Capital Flight," *Journal of International Money and Finance*, 25(2), 308–329.

Lensink, R., N. Hermes and V. Murinde (1998) "The Effect of Financial Liberalization on Capital Flight in African Economies," *World Development*, 26(7), 1349–1368.

Lensink, R., N. Hermes and V. Murinde (2000) "Capital Flight and Political Risk," *Journal of International Money and Finance*, 19, 73–92.

Lessard, D.R. and J. Williamson (Eds.) (1987) *Capital Flight and Third World Debt*, Washington, DC: Institute for International Economics.

Ljungwall, C. and Z. Wang (2008) "Why is Capital Flowing out of China?" *China Economic Review*, 19(3), 359–372.

Loungani, P. and P. Mauro (2000) "Capital Flight from Russia," IMF, Policy Discussion Paper 00/6.

Menbere, W.T. (2003) "Absolute Convergence across Time and Space: New Empirical Evidence for an Old Debate," *Ekonomický Časopis*, 51(10), 1270–1291.

Mikkelsen, J.G. (1991) "An Econometric Investigation of Capital Flight," *Applied Economics*, 23, 73–85.

Morgan Guaranty Trust Company (1986) "LDC Capital Flight," *World Financial Markets*, 2, 13–16.

Morgan Guaranty Trust Company (1988) "LDC Debt Reduction: A Critical Appraisal," *World Financial Markets*, 7, 1–12.

Muscatelli, A. and A.H. Hallett (1992) "How Successfully Do We Measure Capital Flight? Evidence from Five Developing Countries," *Journal of Development Studies*, 28(3), 538–556.

Ndiaye, A.S. (2009a) "Capital Flight and its Determinants in the Franc Zone," *African Journal of Economic Policy*, 16(1), 65–104.

Ndiaye, A.S. (2009b) "Impact de la Capital Flight sur l'Investment Domestique en Franc Zone," in Banque Africaine de Développement and Commission Economique pour l'Afrique des Nations Unies (eds.) *Opportunités and Enjeux du Développement de l'Afrique dans l'Arène Mondiale: Actes de la Conférence Economique Africaine 2007*, Paris: Economica, 344–384.

Ndiaye, A.S. (2011) "Capital Flight and its Determinants in the Franc Zone," African Economic Research Consortium, Research Paper RP 215, January.

Ndikumana, L. (2003) "Capital Flows, Capital Account Regimes, and Foreign Exchange Rate Regimes in Africa," PERI, Working Paper No. 55.

Ndikumana, L. (2006) "Corruption and Pro-Poor Growth Outcomes: Evidence and Lessons for African Countries," PERI, Working Paper No. 120.

Ndikumana, L. (2009) "Capital Flight," in K. Reinert and R. Rajan (eds.) *The Princeton Encyclopedia of the World Economy*, Princeton, NJ: Princeton University Press, 156–158.

Ndikumana, L. and J.K. Boyce (2003) "Public Debts and Private Assets: Explaining Capital Flight from Sub-Saharan African Countries," *World Development*, 31(1), 107–130.

Ndikumana, L. and J.K. Boyce (2008) "New Estimates of Capital Flight from Sub-Saharan African Countries: Linkages with External Borrowing and Policy Options," PERI/UMass, Working Paper No. 166.

Ndikumana, L. and J.K. Boyce (2011a) *Africa's Odious Debt: How Foreign Loans and Capital Flight Bled a Continent*, London: Zed Books.

Ndikumana, L. and J.K. Boyce (2011b) "Capital Flight from Sub-Saharan Africa: Linkages with External Borrowing and Policy Options," *International Review of Applied Economics*, 25(2) 149–170.

Nyatepe-Coo, A.A. (1994) "Capital Flight in Low-Income Sub-Saharan Africa: The Effects of Political Climate and Macroeconomic Policies," *Scandinavian Journal of Development Alternatives*, 13(4), 59–68.

Pastor, M. (1990) "Capital Flight from Latin America," *World Development*, 18(1), 1–18.

Quazi, R. (2004) "Foreign Aid and Capital Flight," *Journal of the Asia Pacific Economy*, 9(3), 370–393.

Salisu, M. (2005) "The Role of Capital Flight and Remittances in Current Account Sustainability in Sub-Saharan Africa," *African Development Review*, 17(3), 382–404.

Savvides, A. (1996) "CFA Franc Zone Membership and Exchange Rate Variability," *Journal of African Economies*, 5(1), 52–68.

Smit, B.W. and B.A. Mocke (1991) "Capital Flight from South Africa: Magnitude and Causes," *South African Journal of Economics*, 59(2), 101–117.

UNDP (2011) "Illicit Financial Flows from the Least Developed Countries: 1990–2008," UNDP, Discussion Paper.

Vos, R. (1992) "Private Foreign Asset Accumulation, Not Just Capital Flight: Evidence from the Philippines," *Journal of Development Studies*, 28(3), 500–537.

World Bank (1985) *World Development Report 1985*, World Bank.

World Bank (2011) *Africa Development Indicators 2011* (online edition).

World Bank (2011) *Global Development Finance 2011* (online edition).

World Bank (2011) *World Development Indicators 2011* (online edition).

Yalta, Y. (2010) "Effect of Capital Flight on Investment: Evidence from Emerging Markets," *Emerging Markets Finance and Trade*, 46(6), 40–54.

Part III
Sectorial Aspects

9 Development of Wind Energy in Africa[1]

Alli D. Mukasa, Emelly Mutambatsere, Yannis Arvanitis and Thouraya Triki

Introduction

With over half a billion people on the continent lacking access to electricity, Africa faces the challenge of generating more power to meet existing and future demand. For many countries, an opportunity exists to do so in a clean and sustainable manner. The continent is well endowed with renewable energy resources which constitute possible solutions to help meet existing power shortages. Indeed, Africa's reserves of renewable energy resources are the highest in the world, and the continent has enough renewable energy potential to meet its future energy needs (World Energy Council, 2010). It is estimated that 18 of the top 35 developing countries ranked highest in renewable energy reserves, normalized by annual domestic energy consumption, are located in Africa (Buys *et al.*, 2007). Similarly, at least eight African countries are among the developing world's most endowed in terms of wind energy potential.

While global wind-based electricity generation is still underdeveloped relative to exploitation of other renewable fuels such as hydro, it has grown at an average annual rate of about 30 per cent between 1996 and 2008; making wind one of the world's fastest-growing energy resources in terms of both coverage and technological innovations. The growth reflects mainly advances in technology and energy security concerns in a decade that saw some of the highest oil prices recorded in history. Climate change considerations have also played a role.

However, despite these positive trends and Africa's potential supply of wind energy, installed capacity of wind-based electricity in Africa, of about 1.1 GW in 2010, does not exceed 0.5 per cent of global capacity. The disparity between potential and extent of exploitation raises questions about constraints to development of wind energy on the continent. The absence of detailed information at the individual project level further restricts developers' and policy makers' understanding of the market.

The goal of this chapter is to improve understanding of how wind energy markets have been developing in Africa. There are two key objectives: provide a mapping of wind energy potential and projects developed on the continent so far; and identify impediments hindering further development of wind energy markets on the continent. We use a sample of 94 wind projects in Africa to perform what we believe is the first continent-wide mapping for the markets.

The chapter is structured as follows: the second section provides an overview of the continent's wind potential and installed capacity. The third section provides a micro picture of the sector by mapping wind energy projects, describing their main characteristics and financing sources, and identifying incentives that have been established to promote the sector. In the fourth section, physical, technical and economic peculiarities that prevent African countries from harnessing their wind energy potential are examined. The final section is a conclusion of the discussions in the chapter and also provides policy recommendations.

Africa's Wind Energy Market: Setting the Stage

To contextualize the development of the wind market in Africa, it is important to set the backdrop against which projects are being developed. This includes mapping of locations with wind resources and the size of potential output, reviewing the electricity generation mix for currently installed capacity, as well as assessing the outlook of the industry. The mapping of potential is important to establish the upper limits of wind energy development on the continent. These limits are most meaningful when set against existing technologies and other important considerations in wind energy development.

While multiple dimensions exist on which wind energy potential could be defined, we adopt for the purposes of this chapter a characterization based on the technical wind energy potential for African countries. This approach takes into consideration the physical upper limit given observed wind speeds, technological efficiency, and other structural and ecological restrictions.[2] We defer to the fourth section of the chapter, below ('Explaining market development trends'), the discussion on soft constraints to wind energy development such as legislative restrictions and limited competition in the energy markets.

Using a technical feasibility method based on technologies available in 2005, Buys *et al.* (2007)[3] find that eight African countries – Somalia, Sudan, Libya, Mauritania, Egypt, Madagascar, Kenya and Chad – have large on-shore wind energy potential. Mauritania's potential, for example, is about four times its annual energy consumption in tons of oil equivalent, while Sudan's is equivalent to 90 per cent of its annual energy needs. Yet, there is variability in terms of geographic location of wind potential across countries. In particular, the study finds that five additional African countries – Mozambique, Tanzania, Angola, South Africa and Namibia – have potentially large off-shore wind energy resources.

A study undertaken by the African Development Bank (AfDB) to create a wind atlas for Africa also revealed significant potential on the continent (AfDB, 2004). This study produced a quantitative map of wind speeds on the continent (Figure 9.1) simulated using the Wind Energy Simulation Toolkit (WEST)[4] model at an altitude of 50 metres and a resolution of 50 km. Results demonstrated that the best wind in Africa is found in the coastal regions of the continent: in the North (Algeria, Egypt, Morocco, Tunisia and Mauritania), the East (Djibouti, Eritrea, Seychelles and Somalia), West (Cape Verde) and South (South Africa and Lesotho). Notably, this study identifies wind potential

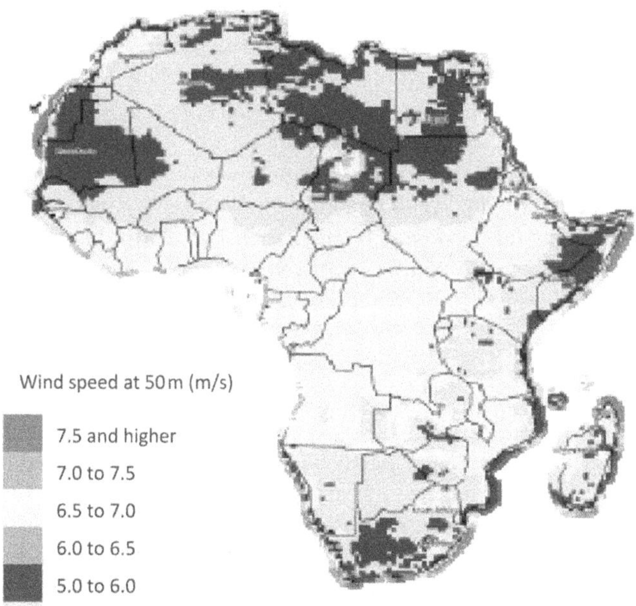

Figure 9.1 Wind Speeds in Africa at an Altitude of 50 m

Source: AfDB, 2004.

in some countries not identified by Buys *et al.* in 2007, highlighting the need for further work to establish accurate data on wind energy resources on the continent.

In general, however, sources show that the highest wind potential exists in coastal areas, which tend also to have both onshore and offshore potential (Figure 9.1). With the exception of countries like Chad and Ethiopia, whose topographies give rise to high speed winds in certain high altitude areas, the rest of mainland (landlocked) Africa's wind intensity is too low to be harnessed for electric power generation.

Despite the high wind energy potential in some African countries, wind-powered electricity generation is still very limited, with an estimated 1.1 GW installed capacity in 2011. Notably, wind-based electricity contributes less than 1 per cent to installed electricity generation capacity on the continent. This share falls below that for Organisation for Economic Co-operation and Development (OECD) countries (3.8 per cent) and for non-OECD emerging markets (1.1 per cent).

Among developing countries, Africa's wind energy potential is comparable to that of Latin America and the Caribbean. While the installed capacity for wind in Africa is expected to increase twelve-fold over the next decade, in line with global trends in renewable energy development and technological innovations, the contribution of wind energy to Africa's electricity generation mix will remain very limited. A similar trend is expected for Latin America whose current capacity falls below that observed in Africa. According to the International Energy Agency's projections (2010) wind energy is expected to contribute only 2 per cent of generated electricity in Africa by 2030 under a business as usual scenario, as compared to other conventional energy sources like coal (37 per cent), gas (32 per cent) and hydro (18 per cent); and relative to a global share of nearly 5 per cent of total electricity generation capacity.

Wind installed capacity in Africa is not only small – both in absolute terms measured by installed capacity, and relative terms as measured by its contribution to the energy mix – but has also been highly concentrated with three countries (Egypt, Morocco and Tunisia) holding about 96 per cent of total installed capacity as at end-2011. Further details about this market feature are provided in the next section.

Mapping Wind Energy Projects in Africa

In this section we first take a historic perspective on wind energy development in Africa to provide stylized facts on the industry and its funding sources, then analyse the market's outlook. Inevitably, there is a strong focus on market leaders including analyses of specific policies, strategies and financing instruments adopted in these countries to develop the market. We use a sample of 94 wind energy projects, compiled from various data sources including the AfDB's project portfolio, Thomson One database, the Wind Power database, the Global Energy Observatory, research papers and various websites as detailed in the references section. Our sample is comprehensive with a near full list of completed projects in Africa between 1980 and 2010;[5] and an extensive, though non-exhaustive, list of ongoing and planned projects.[6]

The Profile of Wind Energy Projects

Based on the individual capacity of projects we identified, Africa's installed wind energy capacity increased twelve-fold between 1995 and 2010 (Figure 9.2), with most of the growth taking place starting early 2000. Notably, between 2000 and 2010, Africa's installed wind capacity grew at a rate of 41 per cent; much faster than the average global growth rate of 27 per cent. Africa's great performance is a reflection of the embryonic nature of the African market characterized by limited initial capacity. Indeed, Africa's growth rate between 2000 and 2010 is very similar to the one reported for other regions during their early stages of market development (i.e. 35 per cent over the period of 1995–2000).

A distribution of projects based on their location and stage of development is provided in Figures 9.3 and 9.4. Of the 94 projects identified, about one-third (30) are completed. Of the completed projects, 93 per cent came on stream after 2000, which is consistent with the nascent nature of this market on the continent. Our database also shows a high concentration of installed wind capacity, with 73 per cent of completed projects located in three North African countries – Egypt, Morocco and Tunisia – which collectively account for 96 per cent of total installed capacity at end-2010. Egypt leads this market, contributing 33 per cent

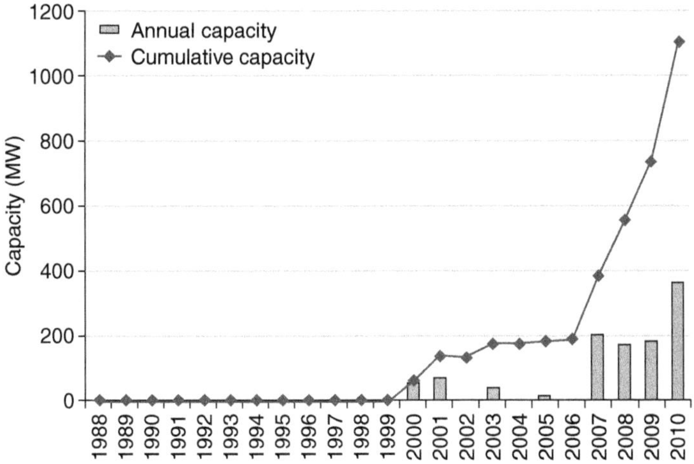

Figure 9.2 Installed Wind Capacity in Africa

Source: authors' analysis.

of total completed projects and 50 per cent of total installed capacity on the continent. Egypt is followed by Morocco which accounts for 30 per cent of total completed projects and 41 per cent of total installed capacity. Tunisia has three completed projects, all located at Sidi Daoud, with a total installed capacity of 54 MW (about 5 per cent of Africa's installed capacity). In Southern Africa,

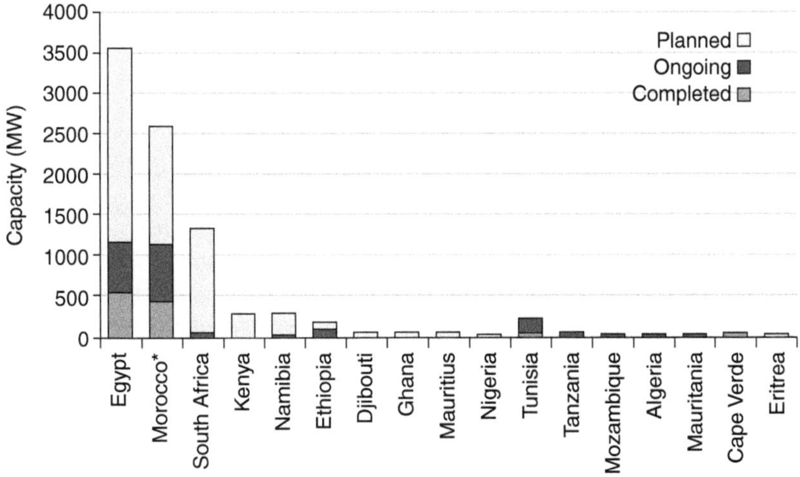

Figure 9.3 Installed Capacity by Country and Stage of Development

Source: authors' analysis.

Note

* Excluding the planned Sahara Wind Project (5000 MW).

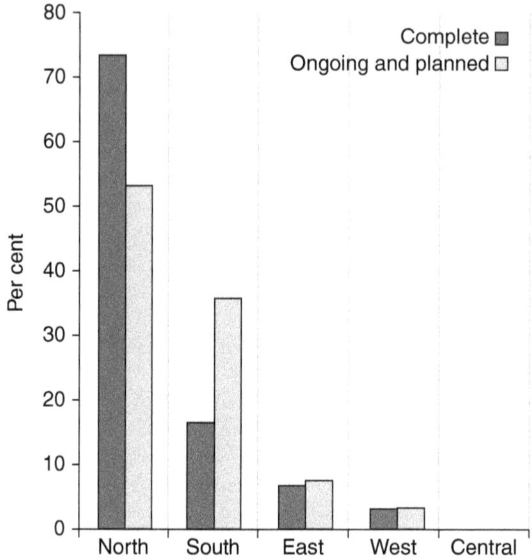

Figure 9.4 Regional Coverage of Projects by Stage of Development (% of projects)

Source: authors' analysis.

Namibia, Mauritius, Mozambique and South Africa already have installed wind energy capacity. So far, South Africa has an installed capacity of only 9 MW. In East Africa, two small projects have been completed; one in Kenya (Ngong Hills) and the second one in Eritrea (Assab Wind Park). No completed wind energy projects were identified in West and Central Africa.

Although North Africa remains the leading region in wind energy markets in Africa, Southern and Eastern African countries are expected to reduce the gap, contributing 36 and 8 per cent respectively of combined ongoing and planned projects. For instance, 35 per cent of all planned projects are located in South Africa followed by Egypt (27 per cent) and Morocco (21 per cent). East Africa is also gaining ground with several projects in the region such as the two ongoing commercial scale projects in Ethiopia and Tanzania (Ashegoba and Njiapanda wind farms, respectively); and some planned projects in Kenya, Djibouti and Ethiopia. The latter include the Lake Turkana wind farm in Kenya, which is the largest wind energy project planned in Sub-Saharan Africa. No ongoing or planned projects were recorded for Central Africa.

Interestingly, concentration is reported for ongoing and planned projects as well with three countries – Egypt, Morocco and South Africa – collectively contributing about 75 per cent of the total number of projects either ongoing or planned (or 83 per cent of total capacity) on the continent. This is due to, among other factors, a stronger political commitment to renewable energy from what are comparatively energy-intensive countries and the high electricity access rates that already exist in these countries (see the fourth section of the chapter).

It is worth noting that the bulk of Africa's completed projects are located either in coastal areas, or sit on islands. The exception is Kenya, which has its largest potential inland around the Lake Turkana highlands whilst having significant coastal potential as well. Both its pilot facility and planned projects are located inland. The wind farms in Algeria, Nigeria and Tanzania are also located inland.

The small size of the African wind market documented earlier reflects not only the limited number of wind farms but also the small-scale nature of the projects. The individual capacity of most projects in Africa, whether completed, ongoing or planned, remains small and broadly ranges between 1 MW and 100 MW (Figure 9.5). Only three completed projects have installed capacity exceeding 100 MW (Zafarana VI and VIII in Egypt and Tangier in Morocco). Notably, most of the larger wind farms have been implemented in phases whereby the individual project sizes generally fall within the above-mentioned range. For example, the Zafarana and Gulf of Zayt wind farms in Egypt consist of eight and seven separate projects respectively, whereas the Touahar wind farm in Morocco is made up of three individual projects. Each individual project in the aforementioned examples may be unique in terms of project sponsors, sources of funding and sometimes the technology used. There is however an increasing trend in the size of projects being implemented. For instance, while only three completed projects have installed capacity exceeding 100 MW, half of ongoing and planned projects have capacity greater than 100 MW. No pilot projects were identified in our sample of ongoing and planned projects, which comprise only commercial-scale wind farms. This suggests either progress towards maturity of the market, or transferability of technologies already tested on the continent.

The 16 ongoing projects we identified are expected to add a cumulative capacity of about 1.5 GW to the current installed wind capacity. The 48 planned projects would add at least another 10 GW inclusive of the Sahara Wind Project, also known as the Moroccan Wind Plan, which is expected to have an installed capacity of 5 GW.

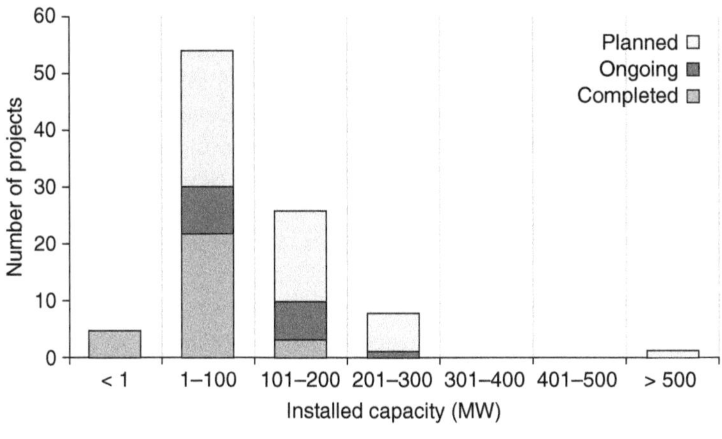

Figure 9.5 Distribution of Projects by Installed Capacity

Source: authors' analysis.

Models of Industry Development

The observed trends emerging from the profiling of projects can be traced back to how the wind energy industry has developed in Africa. Most African countries pursued a phased approach to develop wind energy projects. This often started with pilot and field testing wind projects followed by semi-commercial wind farms, and subsequently by large-scale commercial projects. The phased approach at pilot stage reflects the need to test available technology, insufficient geo-referenced resources and datasets to gauge feasibility and guide investments, and low public sector capacity to oversee the industry's development. Once technologies have been proven feasible in pilot projects, a phased approach towards commercialization is often adopted, mainly reflecting lack of sufficient resources to fund large-scale operations initially.

The first wind farms in Africa were established during the 1980s. In Egypt, a pilot wind farm was developed at Ras Gharib, near the Gulf of Suez, in 1988 which laid the foundation for large-scale projects that were later established. The project was co-sponsored by the then Egyptian Electricity Authority (now Egyptian Electricity Holding Company, or EEHC) and the state-owned General Petroleum Company, partly to meet the energy needs of the General Petroleum Company (USAID, 1986). This was immediately followed by the establishment of the Wind Energy Technology Center at Hurghada, which was established initially as a measurement and turbine testing centre. A small-scale demonstration wind farm was later added at the location. Egypt's first commercial wind project was the first phase of the Zafarana wind farm (30 MW) commissioned in 2001. Seven subsequent phases of Zafarana have since been completed, bringing the farm's capacity to 545 MW as of 2010. There are currently three ongoing developments on the Gulfs of Suez and El Zayt which are expected to add another 200 MW capacity each, and the expansion of the Hurghada wind farm which is expected to have an installed capacity of 1100 MW at completion.

A strong public sector and donor presence can be observed in projects implemented in Egypt. For example, the Ras Gharib pilot project was developed using USAID resources whereas the Hurghada wind farm was funded from Danish and German resources. Zafarana received support from several bilateral investment promotion agencies, mostly the Danish International Development Agency (DANIDA) and Germany's KfW. All completed projects in Egypt (and most ongoing and planned projects) were sponsored by the New and Renewable Energy Authority (NREA), the public entity created in 1986 with a mandate to plan and implement renewable energy programmes. No private developers were active in Egypt on completed projects. The Italian energy generation firm, Italgen, is poised to become the first private developer with its planned 120 MW wind farm along the Gulf of El Zayt. And among NREA's planned projects, one – the Gulf of Suez 200 MW facility – is structured as a public–private partnership (PPP).[7]

Tunisia is following a similar development path, though on a smaller scale and with concessional official development assistance (ODA). The first wind farm at Sidi Daoud was developed in three phases with financial support from

Spain, including (i) concessional lending from the Spanish Development Assistance Financing (FAD) to the Tunisian government, and (ii) commercial debt from the Spanish Export Credit Agency in favour of the Spanish EPC (engineering, procurement and construction) contractor, Gamesa. The state-owned utility Société Tunisienne de l'Electricité et du Gaz (STEG) sponsored these projects. The utility is also sponsoring the planned large-scale operation (190 MW), Centrales Eoliennes de Bizerte 1 and 2, which too is expected to receive Spanish development aid. No significant private operations were identified in the pipeline projects for Tunisia.

In Morocco, the first pilot was a 3.5 MW project near Tetouan (the Al Koudia Al baida project), developed by the public utility Office National de l' Électricité (ONE) with KfW support. But unlike Egypt, Morocco immediately migrated in 2000 to private procurement of wind energy projects: the 50 MW expansion of Al Koudia Al baida was developed by a French consortium Compagnie Eolienne du Détroit (CED) under a 19-year build–own–operate–transfer (BOOT) concession. A third of the completed projects in Morocco were structured as public while the rest were developed as either PPPs or independent power production.

Mauritius followed a path similar to Morocco's; first engaging with public entities for pilot phases before turning to private sponsors. A first attempt was made in the 1980s, but did not yield satisfactory results as cyclone-proof technology was not fully mastered. A 0.2 MW pilot project was later commissioned in 2004 at Rodrigues Island. This project is owned and operated by the state-owned Central Electricity Board. A private French wind energy developer, Aerowatt, is expected to execute the first two commercial operations in the country under BOOT contracts: the 18 MW Eole (Plaine Des Roches) and the 22 MW Britannia wind farms. Similarly, Kenya's only pilot farm at Ngong Hills was developed by its public utility KenGen in 2009. After the successful operation of the pilot project, there are plans to expand this wind farm to a commercial scale. Also in the pipeline is the country's first full-blown commercial operation of 300 MW Lake Turkana wind farm which is also privately sponsored.

Some African countries are moving directly to relatively large-scale projects and with private participation. Cape Verde's first wind farm – also the first commercial operation outside North Africa – was executed as a PPP. However it is interesting to note that the key private shareholders of the project company (Cabeólica SA) – Africa Finance Corporation (AFC), Finnfund and Infraco – are institutions with a development mandate. Similar developments are being observed in Algeria.

In South Africa, the wind energy market remains underdeveloped, with only two completed pilot projects sponsored; one by its public utility Eskom (Klipheuwel wind project), and another through a PPP arrangement with the financial backing of DANIDA (Darling Wind farm). The industry is however poised to grow exponentially, thanks to the private sector-led developments expected following the recent conclusion of a concrete procurement framework for renewable energy Independent Power Producers (IPP) as discussed in the fourth section of the chapter. The first set of grid-connected wind power projects is currently under procurement and is expected to add 634 MW in installed capacity by 2013. New key players will emerge once these developments get under way, the largest being South Africa's Red Cap Investments and the Spanish firm Iberdrola. Namibia is following suit: the quasi-public entity ErongoRED led wind energy development with its pilot farm at Walvis Bay, and a commercial project (Innowind project) is underway with financial support from DANIDA.

Key Players in Wind Markets

Developers, Sponsors and Operators

In order of installed capacity, NREA (Egypt) is the largest owner/operator of wind energy capacity on the continent. It is followed by other North African public utilities, ONE in Morocco and STEG in Tunisia. The profile of private players is heterogeneous in nature, and includes both established international operators, as well as recently established African-based firms, some of which are joint ventures between African and international firms. French, Spanish and Dutch investments are already present on the continent. With the exception of prospective IPP investments by the world's third largest wind energy developer, Iberdrola, foreign direct investment in Africa's wind energy market is driven by relatively small and emerging players.

With regard to African firms, South Africa will soon have the fastest-growing wind energy industry, as indicated by the number of prospective private operators in the market. More than 500 MW is expected to be installed by South African private operators though all operations will be concentrated in South Africa. The emerging South–South cooperation is also noteworthy: some well-established African firms are already seeking investments opportunities elsewhere on the continent, for example Egypt's El Sewedy which has plans to invest in the Ghanaian market.

Developments in the Moroccan market are unique in that they include some operators whose core business lies outside the energy sector, for example, the Chaâbi Group and La Cimenterie de Tetouan self-producers with mostly captive wind energy capacity. Nareva Holding, established in 2005 in Morocco, is set to have the largest market share among private operators.

Wind Turbine Manufacturers

The choice of wind turbine manufacturers on the continent is dominated by global leaders in the industry. Data shows that the world leaders Gamesa and Vestas (fourth and largest wind turbine manufacturers respectively on the world market) dominate in terms of installed capacity and geographic reach.

Production of wind turbine components on the continent has been limited to small-scale system producers mainly in South Africa and Egypt. In South Africa, manufacturers such as Kestrel Renewable Energy, African Wind Power and Palmtree Power produce low capacity turbines (less than 300 kW) that are not adequate for large-scale commercial power production and connection to national grids. At the higher capacity level of localized production in South Africa, Isivunguvungu Wind Energy Converters (I-WEC) produces wind turbine systems with a capacity of up to 2.5 MW. In Egypt, the wind turbine manufacturing industry is dominated by El Sewedy through its two subsidiaries: El Sewedy for Wind Energy Generation (SWEG) with a plant that produces wind turbines of 1.65 MW capacity; and SET SIAG El Sewedy Towers – a joint venture with Germany's SIAG Schaaf Industrie AG that manufactures towers and rotor blades.

The manufacturing landscape is poised to change as more global players increase their presence on the continent. In South Africa, such developments have been encouraged through the Renewable Energy Independent Producers Procurement Programme (REIPPP) that is targeting installation of 1850 MW of onshore wind power with at least 35 per cent local content requirements. Both South Africa and Egypt owe their success in the manufacturing industry to the existence of adequate regulatory and policy frameworks, well-established research and development institutions and a relatively low cost of doing business in the two countries. However, more needs to be done to boost the industry. Policy makers not only need to focus on ways in which international technology providers could be attracted to the continent, but also focus on taking advantage of regional and intra-continental economies of scale and encourage skills and technology transfer through partnerships between local firms and established global manufacturers (IRENA, in press).

Local content in a wind turbine manufacturing industry that is well integrated with the local supply chain creates jobs and enhances capacity for local companies to become more innovative and competitive. Studies have demonstrated that local production of wind energy components could reduce system costs by 25 per cent in the long term (Razavi, 2012).

Financing of Wind Energy Projects in Africa[8]

In this section we discuss trends in project costs and funding sources. Project costs are interesting in understanding industry development because they give an indication of both the resource needs per unit of installed capacity, and signal affordability of wind technologies in Africa as well as the level of maturity of the market. Project costs do not solely depend on installed capacity, but also on the project's location, the requisite off-take infrastructure and general costs of doing business. Therefore, for meaningful conclusions to be drawn from the cost analyses, one needs to look at disaggregated cost data at the individual project level. This information was not available to us on a large enough sample size to conduct this assessment.

From the aggregated cost data[9] some broad observations can be made. Total project costs range from as low as USD 500,000 (the cost of the small pilot at Rodrigues Island in Mauritius), to USD 900 million – the cost of Morocco's largest planned wind farm, the 300 MW Al Koudia Al baida II Wind Farm. As expected, the cost of projects has increased over time. About one-third of the projects, both completed and planned, for which cost statistics were available, are small, costing less than USD 50 million (Figure 9.6).

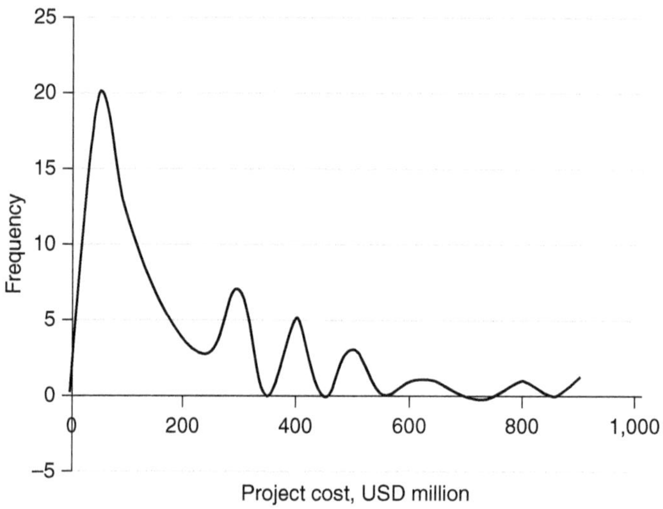

Figure 9.6 Distribution of Total Project Costs

Source: authors' analysis.

On the basis of the restricted sample for which cost data was available, on average, between USD 1.25 and 3 million is spent per MW of installed capacity. A total of 72 per cent of projects fall in this cost range. This is consistent with the expected high upfront costs associated with wind energy technology, and the range of costs observed on global markets of between EUR 1.1 million and EUR 2.25 million per MW (International Energy Agency, 2009). Exceptionally high per unit capital costs are observed in smaller scale operations, for example, the 0.3 MW pilot Inhambane in Mozambique which cost the equivalent of about USD 5 million per MW. We observe a negative correlation of –0.27 between per unit capital cost and installed capacity.

At the aggregate cost level, no clear global trend over time in costs per unit of installed capacity can be deduced from a statistical analysis which does not control for operation size and the costs of ancillary infrastructure such as transmission lines and access roads. Yet, there are few markets where trends can be deduced – Egypt, South Africa and Morocco – where wind farms are located in similar geographic areas, and there is a large enough sample. We find that costs per unit are on a marginally decreasing trend only in Egypt. In South Africa, the cost per unit MW for planned projects appears to be higher than the unit cost for completed pilots; while in Morocco the trend is similar but not strong.

There are several possible explanations: different levels of maturity of the markets especially when comparing Egypt to South Africa, and an economies-of-scale advantage for Egypt (a typical pipeline project in Egypt is about 2.5 times as large as a typical planned project in South Africa). In Egypt, several projects have been planned or implemented in close proximity (for example, the eight and six individual projects at Zafarana and the Gulf of Zayt wind farms respectively); such occurrences significantly reduce the need for new ancillary infrastructure. Meanwhile, South Africa's projects are located in different coastal areas of the country, hence the need to integrate new ancillary infrastructure in the projects. It is also important to note that there could be mispricing in the current bids for IPP-procured wind energy projects (especially in South Africa), given that most projects were at the first bidding stage which focuses on technical aspects, and had not yet competed on price. Unit costs can therefore be expected to stabilize in the medium term.

These cost trends are also closely linked to the profile of project developers in the three countries: government-sponsored projects being least expensive on average, followed by PPPs, then private sponsored projects. This conclusion seems to hold on the full sample as well. This observation is partly a reflection of the terms at which governments mobilize funding for the projects as compared to private sponsors. Whereas governments may have access to cheaper financing through grants and concessional loans from development agencies, private sponsors mobilize financing at commercial terms which are relatively more expensive. In addition, it is likely that private promoters of pipeline projects adopt equipment which is more costly, but more productive in the long term in order to maximize returns over the life of the project. However, the standard deviation of unit costs for government sponsored projects is noteworthy; some projects (mostly the pilot projects) also have higher unit costs.

Further conclusions can also be drawn on the trends in sponsorship of projects. The public sector emerges as the main sponsor of completed wind projects in Africa for the reasons already outlined above. Government sponsorship has been either through domestic utilities or special agencies established to promote clean energy projects like the NREA in Egypt. We find that 78 per cent of all completed projects were government sponsored, relative to 14 per cent private sponsored and 7 per cent public–private sponsored projects. The private sponsored projects include Morocco's industries self-generation projects (for example, the La Farge Wind Farm developed by the cement manufacturer La cimenterie de Tetouan),[10] and the wind energy project sponsored by South Africa's Eskom in Mozambique (Inhambane Wind Project).

The landscape of sponsors is expected to evolve significantly in the coming years. Most countries will seek private (e.g. South Africa) or public–private (e.g. Morocco) sponsorship of wind energy projects. Egypt is expected to increase private sponsorship of projects to about two-thirds of its planned projects portfolio, although at present, NREA is still the primary promoter of pipeline projects. Only 37 per cent of the pipeline projects are expected to be government sponsored, relative to 52 per cent private and 11 per cent public–private sponsored projects.

We also review the mode of procurement, in particular of private sponsored projects, to assess the evolution of roles played by public and private partners in the wind energy industry. Results show that concessions – where the government passes the responsibility and risks of building, operating and maintaining the projects to private operators – are becoming more common. The most common PPP model observed in completed projects is the build–own–operate (BOO) scheme on projects fully owned and managed by the private sponsor. Morocco's auto-producers tip the scale in favour of this model. BOOT contracts are more common in non-captive completed wind projects, as already discussed above. Concession periods generally range between 20 and 30 years. PPPs are attractive from both a resources and risk-allocation perspective, as depicted by the Cabeolica wind farm (Box 9.1).

Box 9.1 Funding Cabeolica Wind Farm, Cape Verde

Project description: Cabeolica Wind Power project was to construct, operate and maintain four wind farms, with a combined capacity of 25.5 MW, on four islands (Santiago, São Vicente, Sal and Boa Vista) of Cape Verde.

Developers: Cabeolica was jointly developed by the Government of Cape Verde, Electra (the state-owned power utility company) and an infrastructure development company, InfraCo. InfraCo, which is privately managed but publicly funded by Development Finance Institutions (DFIs), was heavily involved in upstream activities to design and structure the project. The early stage development risks of the project were borne by the developers which paved the way for other investors to participate in the project.

Project structure: The project was based on a PPP structure involving the Government of Cape Verde, Electra, a private equity fund (FinFund), the AFC and InfraCo. The project was developed using a BOO procurement model implying that the operators would bear the risk of building, operating and maintaining the project.

Financing: The total cost of the project was EUR 64 million of which the sponsors (AFC, InfraCo, FinFund, Electra and the government of Cape Verde) mobilized equity financing worth EUR 19 million. Apart from indirectly providing equity funding to the project through InfraCo, DFIs further contributed all the debt financing. The AfDB and European Investment Bank provided EUR 15 and 30 million respectively in senior loans with a tenor period of 15 years and a grace period of two years.

Risk management: To enhance the bankability of the project, several risk mitigation measures were adopted as demonstrated below:

- The private sponsors of the project were insured against political risk through the World Bank's Multilateral Investment Guarantee Agency (MIGA) facility.
- A 20-year 'take or pay' power purchase agreement was signed between the project company (Cabeolica SA) and the national power utility company (Electra) to purchase all the electricity produced by the project.
- A Support Agreement was signed by the government and Cabeólica SA to guarantee that any payment deficiency on the part of Electra would be covered by the government.

- A turnkey EPC contract and a service agreement, in the form of an Operation and Maintenance (O&M) contract, were signed with a leading company in wind energy technology to reduce the sponsor's exposure to risks during construction and operation of the project.
- Due to the volatility of the local currency, the price for electricity purchased from the project in accordance with the power purchase agreement was expressed in euros.

Source: AfDB (2010b).

About USD 1.8 billion has been invested to develop the 1.1 GW of installed wind generation capacity on the continent. Of the USD 1.8 billion, 59 per cent was contributed by DFIs through non-concessional funding; mostly bilateral development agencies which account for 47 per cent of total financing (Figure 9.7). There is a shift in funding channels used to support wind energy projects in Africa, with ODA[11] funding decreasing progressively while non-concessional contributions from bilateral and multilateral development agencies, and commercial sources, are increasing.

We find limited use of specialized funds, such as the Global Environment Facility (GEF), in financing completed pilot or commercial wind energy projects. This trend is changing as larger pools of funds earmarked for clean technologies become available. For example, six of the pipeline projects located in Egypt, Morocco and South Africa are set to receive a total of about USD 400 million from the Clean Technology Fund (CTF).[12] GEF is supporting the ongoing South Africa Wind Energy Programme (SAWEP), and was present in Eritrea's pilot project at Assab.

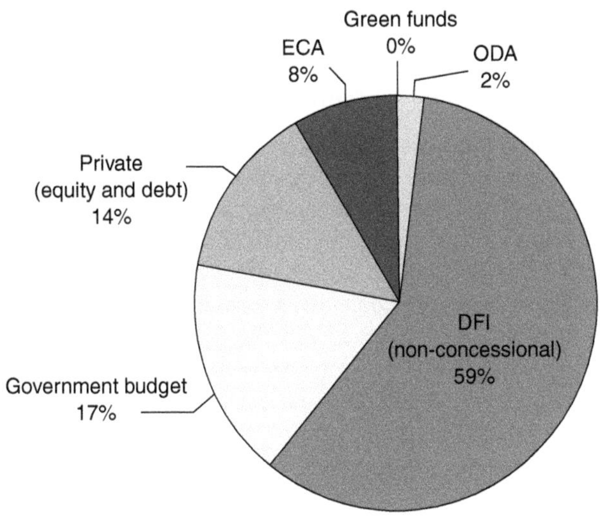

Figure 9.7 Financing of Projects

Source: authors' analysis.

Half of the pipeline projects had equity financing from private investors, relative to less than one-third of completed projects. Data on exact amounts contributed by project financiers was not available for a large enough sample to ascertain larger volumes of private funding towards wind energy projects. However some trends are emerging, for example, the growing presence of international wind energy developers as equity providers in pipeline projects. Among the 32 projects expected to receive private equity financing, 41 per cent will likely be financed by firms with a global footprint. Emerging African firms are expected to finance about 26 per cent of the projects – half through joint ventures with foreign international firms – while equity in 20 per cent of the project is expected to come from auto-producers.

Another hypothesis tested is whether access to carbon finance markets through the Clean Development Mechanism (CDM) has affected technology choices in favour of wind energy developments in Africa. We find that less than one-quarter (23 per cent) of completed projects benefited from CDM. These projects range in capacity from 22 to 120 MW, with an average plant size of 84 MW. Average sales amount to 188,400 tons of CO_2 tons-equivalent per year, equivalent to about USD 2.7 million per year per project, over a modal crediting period of seven years. At these rates, beneficiary projects generate up to 20 per cent of total project costs over the crediting period. CDM funding has been useful in improving the commercial viability of beneficiary projects. For instance, in Zafarana 4, CDM financing helped improve the project's internal rate of return by approximately 2 per cent through an emission reduction purchase agreement spearheaded by KfW covering the 2007–2012 period (Sünnen, 2010). CDM projects include some of the Zafarana wind farm projects in Egypt, as well as some auto-production projects in Morocco. European countries – including Germany, Japan, UK, Denmark, France and Switzerland – are the most active CDM partners for wind projects in Africa. A list of projects, both completed and in the pipeline, that have benefited from CDM financing is presented in the chapter Annex (Table 9.A.2).

Explaining Market Development Trends

The patterns identified in the previous section could possibly be explained by external forces such as conventional foreign direct investment drivers, internal macroeconomic and social considerations, or global considerations such as climate change. In this section, we explore the extent to which these factors have affected the adoption of wind-based electricity generation, starting from the assumption that adequate wind energy potential exists. First, we ran the following hypothesis tests non-parametrically[13] to test the extent to which the wind sector has been influenced by the pursuit of new markets for a growing wind technology manufacturing sector in OECD countries:

i The correlation between the origin of the ODA and of the wind turbines used in pilot projects.

ii The correlation between the origin of ODA in pilot projects and that of private investments in the sector through project sponsorship, development or operation of commercial scale projects.

Results show that the origin of ODA and that of wind turbines adopted in pilot projects is weakly correlated. A weak correlation is also observed between the origin of ODA for pilot and that of wind turbines adopted in commercial operations. There is almost no correlation between the origin of development assistance for pilot projects and the origin of private investment flows into commercial operations. This outcome is consistent with the post-2011 adoption of 'untied aid' frameworks in OECD countries predominant as donors, lenders and investors in this industry.

Other considerations appear to be stronger drivers of the observed trends in developing the wind energy potential in Africa. These include the physical attributes of wind energy, economic, environmental and climate change considerations, as well as aspects related to the regulatory environment in the host country.

Technical Considerations

Wind energy is intermittent, which means that it is not available non-stop due to exogenous factors. The result is irregular electricity output from wind power plants. Nor can wind energy output be stored, in contrast to other renewables such as water which can be stored and dispatched in response to demand. These two features imply that wind energy does not make good base load capacity – the capacity which must be continually available to meet the minimum demand of all users connected to an electricity grid. This capacity dictates volume of new grid connections.

The issue of base load capacity is important in the context of most national grids which are 'demand-driven', thus require stable base load capacity to meet the continuing electricity needs of users connected to the grid. Failure fully to meet these needs at any moment would trigger a system failure. Moreover, integrating large wind-based electricity flows into the grid may require a grid overhaul. This pertains to both grid planning (power plant dispatch systems) and resilience of the network to peaks and troughs in electricity flows from the wind farms. Again, conventional 'demand-driven' grids make this integration particularly complex. Grid integration also requires efficient back-up plants to regulate volatility in electricity flows. Given the state of African national grids, these considerations present a major barrier to the development of wind energy on the continent.

Studies have also shown that on average, wind turbines perform far below their capacity mainly due to the intermittent nature of wind. Typically, a wind turbine will produce electricity at its rated or maximum capacity in wind speeds between 30 and 55 miles per hour. At lower wind speeds, the production falls drastically. Although industry projections estimate capacity factors[14] of 30 to 40 per cent, field experience has shown that it is not uncommon to have annual outputs of just 15 to 30 per cent of the maximum turbine capacity.[15] Compared to capacity factors of other technologies in power generation such as coal (85 per cent), natural gas (87 per cent) and hydro (52 per cent), the average capacity factor of wind energy (34 per cent) further lowers its competitiveness.

But the conversation should not stop there. Science and innovation is moving the frontier of renewable energy technologies, including the field of hybrid and 'smart' grids. In the African context, these cutting-edge technology options are suited mostly for the middle income countries that have reached their energy access goals. It has been shown that the negative effects of intermittency can be managed if many different and complementary energy sources are connected to a fairly large grid which is also robust and 'smart'; i.e. has high self-adjustment capacity. Few examples exist of countries that have advanced their national grids to this level. Europe is leading the way, through its Smart Grid European Technology Platform. To our knowledge, no African country has yet seriously explored the option of smart grids. In South Africa, the conversation around adoption of smart mini grids has started, with the state utility Eskom announcing in March 2012 its plans to start deploying the hybrid smart grid model (Teske *et al.*, 2011).

Power systems based on a conventional grid can also adapt to increasing proportions of renewable energy in the energy mix. At the time of writing (May 2012), Kenya's grid was undergoing fortification in preparation for the 300 MW input from the Lake Turkana wind farm. This process included, among other things, strengthening the Nairobi ring (transmission infrastructure) as well as developing thermal power plants to act as back-up facilities. Associated investment costs figure into the value for money assessment of the wind option, and may reduce its attractiveness.

Another innovation that has been tested in practice to tackle the intermittence of wind power and enhance its adequacy for base load capacity suggests interconnecting wind farms through transmission grids. When farms are interconnected in an array, the probability that all sites experience the same wind regime at the same time reduces and the array consequently behaves like a single farm with steady wind speed and thus steady deliverable wind power (Archer and Jacobson, 2007).

Economic Considerations

There are other reasons why African countries may not opt for the wind energy solution. One relates to the attractiveness of wind-based electricity generation from a commercial viability perspective. This is because value-for-money assessments of project options often do not take into consideration the valuation of negative externalities, nor do they correct for undervaluation of tradable energy resources. Emissions from polluting power generation activities are not always assigned a cost, nor are benefits from renewable energy reflected in prices. In the presence of capital cost disadvantages for emerging technologies such as wind, this implies an implicit bias in financial return comparisons in favour of conventional energy resources.

Indeed, there is substantial competition between wind and other well-established renewable energy sources such as hydro, which have the capital cost advantage and favourable physical attributes such as storability (Figure 9.8).

Competition also arises from fossil fuel resources. About half the wind energy endowed African countries are also rich in conventional thermal resources, i.e. coal, gas and oil. The generation mix in these countries is predominantly thermal. Closely linked to the issue of endowments, are the existing rules regulating pricing of fossil fuels. Under-pricing of fossil fuels especially in net exporting countries is creating an uneven playing field for renewables such as wind energy. Moreover, the higher upfront costs for wind technology, in the absence of favourable tariff regulation, can make capital expenses restrictive. For instance, import duties on renewable energy technologies coupled with subsidies on fossil fuels in Nigeria make renewable energies, in particular wind and solar, uncompetitive (Kennedy-Darling *et al.*, 2008).

The continued growth and sustenance of wind energy, just like several other renewable energies, has come at a significant cost for governments and the public. Many countries, including some African countries, have introduced public policies to make wind energy more affordable for the end user through direct subsidies or other mechanisms such as feed-in-tariffs (FiTs) (see Box 9.2). For instance, the World Nuclear Association estimates that the cost to the German government and consumers to make wind and solar energy accessible and affordable is EUR 5 billion per year in subsidies. Such a cost is obviously beyond what most African countries can afford. Renewable energy subsidies have come under intense pressure especially in light of the economic crisis and public spending cuts forcing several countries including Spain, Germany, Japan, USA and South Africa, among others, to revise such subsidies in order to reduce the fiscal burden on government budgets.

Another important consideration from the commercial perspective relates to the use of wind-based electricity in the generation mix. Wind can best be viewed as a supplementary energy resource, given its unsteady output and the need for back-up capacity.

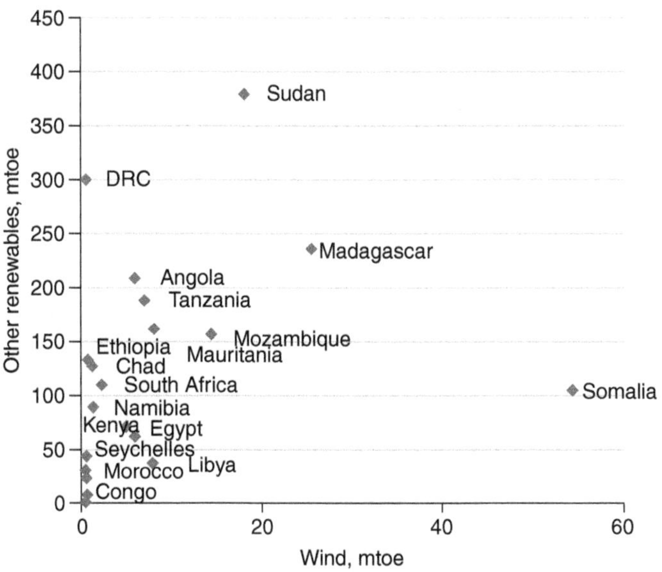

Figure 9.8 Potential from Other Renewable Energy Sources

Source: authors' adaptation using Buys *et al.* 2007 data.[1]

Note

1 Depicts 'high' scenario for renewable energy resources (wind, solar and geothermal). Wind energy potential refers to the sum of onshore and offshore wind potentials.

The main use for wind energy is to replace output from fossil fuels and other storable energy resources. In principle, this serves the dual purpose of lowering operation costs of the electricity grid, and enhancing availability of other sources such as hydro power plants. Because wind power plants, in essence, do not contribute base load capacity, they cannot be the primary basis for electrification programmes targeting to add more users to the grid. Therefore, countries trying to increase access rates are unlikely to choose wind. Indeed, the development of wind energy capacity in Africa has been following electricity consumption trends more than resource endowment levels. Countries with higher access rates are leading the way in wind energy development. This is translated into stronger political commitments from energy-intensive countries to renewable energies. For instance, Egypt has committed to produce 20 per cent of its electricity from renewable sources by 2020, with South Africa and Morocco having announced similar goals.

Climate Change Considerations

From an environmental perspective, wind energy is of interest because it is both renewable and clean. Here we explore the extent of the incentive for African countries to achieve the latter objective. The first test is determining the expected environmental benefits of wind energy. Wind-based power plants produce almost no greenhouse gas emissions directly. However, in evaluating the climate change effects of wind energy, one needs to take a holistic approach that looks at both the direct and indirect effects. We have already discussed the physical features of wind energy and their implications in terms of back-up plants. The variability and intermittency of wind energy implies carbon emissions that are commensurate with the frequency at which back-up power plants are activated to stabilize the grid. Back-up measures require plants which can be dispatched quickly and run on a stable fuel resource. For these reasons, heavy fuel oil and gas make the best back-up energy resources for wind. Accounting for the indirect emissions from these back-up plants, wind-based power generation remains attractive from a 'clean' energy perspective.[16]

The second important question to answer with regard to the potential use of renewable energy to curb carbon emissions is how much African countries value this consideration. This question can be answered by looking first at the marginal contribution of Africa's electricity sector to greenhouse gas emissions. On an aggregate scale, Africa contributed less than 3 per cent of the world's greenhouse gas emissions in 2008.

The electricity sector contributes an even lower proportion of about 1 per cent. The outlook shows a trend that is only slightly different, with Africa's aggregate emissions expected to reach 3.15 per cent of global emission by 2030 under a business as usual scenario (International Energy Agency, 2010). Adopting clean energy solutions is expected to decrease this proportion to 2.74 per cent. In a nutshell, the impact on global scale is small. But African economies are highly heterogeneous when it comes to climate change effects. For instance, South Africa, the largest CO_2 emitter on the continent, is also the twelfth largest contributor on a global scale by measure of stock of annual emissions; tenth largest by measure of emissions per capita (Department of Environmental Affairs Republic of South Africa, 2011). And the bulk of the country's emissions come from the coal-based electricity generation system. Coal-based plants contributed over 90 per cent of the country's electricity output in 2011; and the ongoing addition of two of the world's largest coal power plants will increase this share. In the context of a country like South Africa, renewable energy can make a significant contribution to improving the continent's carbon footprint. But, overall, climate change considerations are generally not as high a priority as access, cost and energy security considerations in determining the adoption of wind energy.

Business Environment Considerations

A legal framework defining investment parameters is a prerequisite to the development of the clean energy sector. To our knowledge, 12 African countries have set up regulations and laws of reasonable scope on renewable energy, such as the 2009 Renewable Energy Development Law No. 13.09 passed in Morocco which set the pace for greater off-grid capacity and allowed a stronger presence of IPPs in the wind and solar energy industries. Morocco has also established a framework to enhance self-production of renewables by energy intensive industries, including increasing the production limit from 10 MW to 50 MW in 2007.

Analysing the array of wind projects in Africa against the regulatory framework in respective countries puts into perspective the importance of establishing clear frameworks to promote the development of renewable energy. We find that about 88 per cent of the completed and pipeline projects are located in countries with a market and existing regulatory frameworks for renewables. Yet, the assessment also shows that regulation is not a condition *sine qua non* for the development of wind farms, as 11 projects have been undertaken in countries without clear renewable energy frameworks. Interestingly, however, out of the 11 projects that were developed in countries without policies, only two projects (Cabeolica and Njiapanda wind farms) received private funding. These projects also had strong DFI support, which possibly explains their success in mobilization of private investors. This suggests that private investors remain reluctant to engage in countries that lack frameworks regulating the industry.

The existence of legal frameworks does not however guarantee sector development. While the presence of legislation is crucial, its quality is decisive. In this respect, Tunisia presents an interesting case. Prior to 2009, wind projects had been developed through the government which used the national power agency (STEG) as the sole entry point into the market. Projects were promoted as PPPs under an existing legal framework that did not allow private sponsors to implement projects on their own. In 2009, a law allowing for captive production or the so-called *auto-production* by private entities was passed. In theory, this law established the framework for project development by the private sector. In spite of this law, projects have not taken off for a core reason: there were few or no private firms that could afford to build wind farms for their own consumption, or had the know how to engage in such investments. At the same time, industry groupings could not get together to build wind farms either as they were faced with a billing issue: creating an ad-hoc company to manage the farm and billing the grouping's members for consumption would violate the National Electricity's company monopoly on power distribution.

Given the cost disadvantage still faced by wind energy relative to conventional energy resources, we take a closer look at the pricing mechanisms adopted to promote private investments in wind energy in Africa. Five countries have adopted the FiT mechanism to promote clean energy. This sets a guaranteed off-take price for power producers selling to utility companies, and is designed to reflect costs and benefits of particular technologies. The main advantage of the FiT mechanism is predictability. However, it eliminates price competition, which is necessary eventually to bring down the cost to utilities of procuring renewables.

Experiences have however shown that alternative pricing methods can work just as well. For example, neither Egypt nor Morocco has adopted the FiT, choosing instead to apply a two-stage process including competitive bidding as a pre-FiT stage, and direct negotiation, respectively. The latter often entails a public transfer to the private developer, in the form of payments in kind or tax relief, to keep the off-take tariff affordable for the utility. South Africa has revised its framework twice since 2009, first lowering the FiT initially announced; then migrating to a new procurement system altogether, whereby developers bid on a technical basis first before bidding on price (Box 9.2).

Box 9.2 FiTs and competitive bidding in South Africa

In 2006, the South African government introduced regulation for a 'licensee to recover the full cost of its licensed activities, including a reasonable margin or return' (art. 16, Electricity Regulation Act 2006). As a follow-up move, the South African Renewable Energy Feed-In-Tariff (REFIT) was introduced in 2009, guaranteeing electricity purchase prices from IPPs. Yet the programme never really became active, as two years later, no purchasing power agreements were negotiated with IPPs: stringent licensing conditions and difficulties in negotiating purchasing power agreements were at the heart of the problem (Edkins, 2012).

In 2011, in an effort to stimulate IPPs, tariff reductions of up to 40 per cent were proposed, though this did not turn out to have any positive effects: the tariffs set were only guidelines and were not framed in the Department of Energy's regulation. This implied that the department was not obliged to comply with them creating difficulties in purchase power agreement negotiations (Bloomberg, 2011). As a consequence, the REFIT programme was abandoned mid-2011 to give way to a competitive bidding process, referred to as 'REBID'. This move was intended to invite investors to submit bids for new capacity generation totalling 3725 MW, of which 1850 MW are from wind and 1450 MW from solar. New projects will benefit from power purchase agreements as determined by the national utility's Multi-year Price Determination plan at prices capped for each technology. For wind projects, the price ceiling was set at USD 115c/Kwh.

The main change from REFIT is that power producers will be required to tender on the pricing for the off-take agreement. In other words, their bids will not only be evaluated based on the technical proposals, but also in terms of the power purchase agreement to be concluded. In addition to pricing, other items included in the bidding process comprise localization, black economic empowerment, community development and job creation amongst others.

This move introduces an important competitiveness element into the pricing for renewable energy, ensuring that the South African government gets a fair deal. Yet, all the above-mentioned changes and the lack of investments in that period highlight the importance of a stable and well-calibrated policy. In light of the insecurity in the renewable energy policy illustrated by the changes which occurred in the past years, project developers took on a 'wait and see' approach which affected their planned investments as well as their ability to secure new financing (Edkins, 2012; Pegels, 2011). To date, it is difficult to assess the new policy in place: reports claim that the first bidding round was a success and that many firms applied for licences. However, concerns have been raised that such a system will incentivize firms to cut costs to make projects work, raising the risks that projects never materialize.

Sources: Bloomberg, 2011; van Dyke and Pollastrini, 2011; Edkins, 2012; Electricity Regulation Act 2006; Pegels 2011.

Conclusion and Policy Implications

Conclusion

The chapter draws several conclusions based on discussions of the structural characteristics, development trends and challenges faced by the wind energy market in Africa. Using a hand-collected comprehensive sample of 94 wind energy projects over the period 1980 and 2010, it is observed that Africa's wind energy capacity increased twelve-fold over the last two decades to stand at 1.1 GW in 2011. While the annual growth rate of Africa's installed capacity was almost twice as much as that reported for global capacity over the period 2000–2010, it remains similar to the growth rate reported for global capacity at the early stages of development for the global market. This growth was achieved mainly through a phased approach, reflecting the countries' lack of familiarity with the technology and insufficient geo-referenced resources at the early stages of market development and limited public resources to undertake large-scale projects in more mature markets. North Africa is currently leading in terms of installed capacity while South Africa is poised to be the fastest-growing market, based on the number of prospective investors in the sector. Interestingly, North African countries followed different paths to develop their markets. While Egypt and Tunisia had a public sector-led model, Morocco relied more on private sector initiatives.

The chapter shows that wind markets in Africa are small both in absolute terms – measured by installed capacity – and in relative terms – measured by their contribution to the energy generation mix. While significant growth in installed capacity is expected, driven by the increasing number of ongoing and planned projects as well as increasing capacity of individual projects, we show that wind energy contribution to energy consumption is expected to remain unchanged. In other words, growth in wind energy production in Africa is not expected to outpace growth in total generation capacity.

Another interesting feature of African markets documented in the chapter is the high level of concentration. Three African countries, Egypt, Morocco and Tunisia, captured 73 per cent of completed projects and 96 per cent of total installed capacity at end-2010. Concentration is also observed for ongoing and planned projects whereby Egypt, Morocco and South Africa collectively account for 83 per cent of total expected capacity. The chapter also shows that public utilities such as NREA (Egypt), ONE (Morocco) and STEG (Tunisia) are the dominant players in the sector while private players remain heterogeneous and include both international companies, mainly from France, Spain and Netherlands, and local players whose core business is sometimes not the energy sector.

Cost and financing data available in our database show that non-concessional resources from DFIs accounted for about 59 per cent of the cost of installed capacity on the continent. The amount spent per MW of installed capacity is consistent with levels observed in global markets. The chapter also shows that concessional funding is being phased out and replaced by non-concessional investments from bilateral and multilateral DFIs, as well as commercial investments. Also, the chapter reports the absence of a correlation between sources of ODA for pilot projects and sources of private investment into commercial operations implemented at later stages, suggesting that ODA is not particularly used to pursue new markets.

The second section of the chapter explains why African countries have been lagging behind despite the continent's important wind potential. It shows that intermittency and output variability are two physically driven states that can make simple economic and financial comparisons between wind projects versus non-renewable energy projects difficult. In addition, pricing that does not take into account all externalities related to renewable energy investments presents an inherent bias against wind projects. Lack of regulatory frameworks and experience in the field constitute additional impediments. Ultimately, this introduces an important dilemma for African countries: whether to invest in what appears in the short term to be reliable and more cost-efficient power generation based on fossil fuels, or to invest in wind energy that is unstable, capital-intensive and requires development of regulations and schemes to cater for what is still a relatively nascent field. Considering the urgency with which African governments must address electricity deficits and Africa's limited global carbon footprint, the former solution will most likely be adopted.

Overall, the analysis provided in the chapter shows that wind-based electricity has limited potential to address the issue of electricity access in Africa on its own. Only countries which could develop large, robust and 'smart' grids, i.e. with high self-adjustment capacity, are poised to capture fully the benefits of wind-based electricity.

Policy Implications

The following policy recommendations emerge from the discussions included in the chapter:

The designation of a national entity dedicated to the promotion of renewable energy should be encouraged. Country experience shows that having national champions helps develop the sector by offering a single focal point for regulation, financing and oversight. In some instances, local agencies could be created but this is not the only route to promote the sector since well-established utilities or divisions within them could play that role ensuring policy continuity. While designating local champions should be the responsibility of local governments, DFIs could assist by making sure government agencies have the right capacity to oversee the industry's development. This calls for DFI's greater involvement in capacity building programmes.

Experience shows that private investors are willing to invest in the sector as long as a clear regulatory framework is in place and wind resources are geo-referenced to gauge feasibility. The public sector therefore has a vital role to play in creating a conducive environment to attract private investors while at the same time investing in upstream operations such as feasibility studies that would pave the way for further sectorial development. DFIs should leverage their global experience to help countries design clear procurement frameworks, adopt best practice in the sector and undertake reforms aimed at facilitating private sector engagement.

Countries with sizeable wind energy markets such as Egypt, Morocco and South Africa, should design and implement robust policies to encourage local manufacturing of wind turbine components. Local manufacturers should be supported by governments and development partners to make them more competitive and able to bid for large-scale projects. It has been shown in the chapter that African manufacturers of wind turbines are still few in number with almost no footprint on the market as all the technology that has been used on the projects is imported. Experience from emerging markets in the industry has shown that government intervention, as policy makers or even financiers, is key for a sustainable manufacturing industry.

Interventions to develop the sector should be adapted to country contexts. Country experiences show that wind energy markets face different constraints and could be developed using different paths. While Tunisia and Egypt had a public sector-led development strategy, Morocco relied more on private procurement of wind energy projects. Kenya adopted the feed-in tariff mechanism, while Egypt and Morocco used a process involving competitive bidding and direct negotiation. For instance, the issue of carbon emissions could be more relevant for South Africa than for Chad. Hence, governments should adopt solutions that best fit their existing challenges instead of seeking to adopt best industry standards. In this context, development partners should avoid the one size fits all approach when designing their interventions and should allow countries to use different approaches depending on their priorities and local constraints.

In order to address the issue of small-scale projects, stakeholders should engage in implementing a regional approach whereby countries with greater potential develop large-scale wind farms to address their needs and possibly the needs of their neighbouring countries. The regional approach could also help solve the intermittency problem in wind electricity generation through the interconnection of wind farms as proposed in the fourth section of the chapter. This calls for greater involvement in regional projects that would enhance interconnections between national grids.

Annex

Table 9.A.1 Sources of Financing for Wind Projects in Africa

Public funding comes in the form of budget contributions and direct or indirect subsidies. Most sustainable of the sources of public funding is taxation buttressed by sustainable tax policies and robust tax administration. Countries have strengthened domestic resource mobilization for infrastructure financing given the subdued flow of aid from traditional development partners in the wake of the global economic crisis and its aftermath. Public sponsorship of wind and solar energy projects is also increasing.	*ODA* towards infrastructure grew to reach its peak of US$3.3 billion per year in 2004 (AfDB, 2009). Since then, commitments have increased; however, actual financial flows have declined as donors continue to adopt austerity measures to curb the effects of the financial crisis which left them with enormous national debts. For renewable energy projects, ODA contributions through 'Climate Funds' have continued on a positive growth trend over the past decade.
Funds dedicated to the development of clean energy are often concessionary, for example, the Global Environment Facility (GEF), Clean Investment Funds (CIF), Africa Green Fund (AGF), Sustainable Energy Fund for Africa (SEFA) and the Renewable Energy and Adaptation to Climate Technologies (REACT), among others. These funds provide grants and contingent financing to offset upfront project preparation costs, with potentially substantial crowding-in effect on private investment. They also provide direct project financing and support for pilot programmes. GEF's US$2 billion portfolio for Africa (1991–2009) includes renewable energy mini-grids for rural electrification in West Africa, covering 18 countries in the region.	*Multilateral development banks* (MDBs) have played a central role in promoting wind and solar energy sectors in Africa. In addition to financing, MDBs also support policy and regulatory reforms in African countries to facilitate adoption of clean energy options. They also provide risk management instruments, financial market development in countries and support activities to create an enabling environment for the preparation and implementation of clean energy projects. MDBs have participated in almost all large-scale wind and solar energy projects in Africa, both completed and ongoing. They also support countries in accessing carbon finance, through instruments such as the Africa Carbon Facility (ACF) launched by the AfDB to promote Africa's carbon markets.
Most of the *private investment* in renewable energy in Africa is concentrated in North Africa and South Africa. Financial instruments such as risk guarantees and credit guarantees, export credit and incentives increase the bankability of projects hence catalysing additional private sector flows. Private sector operations are hugely driven by the expected return on investment and portfolio diversification. From 2005 to 2010, a total of US%4.5 billion was invested in Sub-Saharan Africa by the private sector into renewable energy.	To raise funding on the carbon market, three *carbon finance mechanisms* are commonly employed: auctioning of assigned amount units, auctioning under emission trading systems and offset levies like the CDM. Of the available mechanisms, Africa has mostly benefited from the CDM system. Income from CDM offsets is generally used to recover capital investment costs incurred in the implementation of renewable energy projects. Most carbon offset projects had been registered in Nigeria (four million CERs) and South Africa (three million CERs) by end-2009. In South Africa, the minerals and energy department estimates that the country could generate ZAR 618 million in carbon trade by 2012.
Export credit agencies function to take risks or cover others against political and/or commercial risks resulting from the export of goods or services. ECA support usually takes the form of (i) export credit guarantees or insurance, (ii) investment insurance (political risk insurance only) or (iii) direct loans. Export credit guarantees can insure projects involving trade of green technologies against risks such as non-payment, bank loans or risk insurance to investors in overseas markets.	Clean technology financing can also take the form of *private equity and debt funds*. The private equity fund InfraCo sponsored the Cabeolica wind farm in Cape Verde; while Evolution One is set to support a wind farm and a ten-year roll-out programme for solar water heaters in South Africa.

Source: Mutambatsere and Mukasa (2011).

Table 9.A.2 Projects Benefiting from CDM Financing

Project	*Country*	*CDM Partner*	*Greenhouse Gas Reduction (Metric Tonnes CO_2 Equivalent per Annum)*	*Crediting Period (Years)*	*Capacity (MW)*	*Status*
Zafarana IV	Egypt	Germany (KfW)	171,500	7	47	Completed
Zafarana VI	Egypt	Japan (Japan Bank for International Cooperation, Japan Carbon Finance Ltd)	248,609	7	120	Completed
Zafarana VIII	Egypt	Denmark (Danish Ministry of Climate and Energy, Danish Energy Agency (DEA), Ministry of Foreign Affairs of Denmark (DANIDA))	209,714	7	120	Completed
Cam Sim (Essaouira/Am Ogdoul) Wind Farm	Morocco	France, Switzerland (European Carbon Fund)	156,026	10	60	Completed
Tanger wind farm (Dahr Saadane and Beni Mejmel)	Morocco	UK (Orbeo, Post 2012 Carbon Credit Fund CV)	334,073	10	140	Completed
La Farge Wind Farm	Morocco	France	28,651	7	22	Completed
Zafarana V	Egypt	UK (European Carbon Fund)	170,364	7	85	Completed
Haouma	Morocco	Not available	134,496	7	50	Ongoing
Akhfenir (tan tan)	Morocco	Not available	264,789	7	200	Ongoing
Lake Turkana Wind Farm	Kenya	Not available	736,615	7	300	Planned
Eole (Plaine Des Roches) Wind Farm	Mauritius	Sweden (Swedish Energy Agency)	32,039	7	18	Planned

Source: authors' research.

Notes

1 The authors are grateful for the insights provided by Khalid Benhamou who was an external reviewer of the chapter. The chapter greatly benefited from comments received from colleagues at the AfDB (Tanja Faller, Bertrand Belben and Ignacio Tourino Soto), participants of the Wind Energy Workshop at the 'Tunis-Med Industrie' Conference (2012) and the 2012 African Economic Conference. The authors also acknowledge excellent research assistance from Kolawole Dairo and Ahmed Jeridi and contributions from Linus Mofor. The chapter reflects opinions of the authors and not those of the AfDB Group's management, Board of Directors or the countries they represent.

2 Wind potential could be (i) *theoretic*: the physical upper limit of an energy resource, (ii) *conversion*: theoretic capacity accounting for technology efficiency, (iii) *technical*: conversion capacity accounting for other technological, structural and ecological restrictions (iv) *economic*: technical capacity which is economically feasible (Teske *et al.*, 2011).

3 Buys *et al.* (2007) estimate potential electricity generation from renewable energy resources based on a geo-referenced database of energy indicators from a variety of sources. A key merit of this database is that it adopts a standard unit of measurement – million tons of oil equivalent (mtoe) – which makes estimates ideal for comparison of potential across energy types.

4 The WEST is a dynamic three-dimensional model of wind circulation on a horizontal plane which integrates physical phenomena such as radiation and condensation and parametric analyses of effects such as turbulence and convention (AfDB, 2004).

5 We used data collected in 2011 therefore some new developments in the sector are not captured here. However, since the wind sector in Africa has not changed significantly over the last three years, the analysis remains important for the sector in 2015. The study will be updated in the near future when significant progress in the sector has been recorded.

6 'Ongoing' projects are defined as projects for which construction activities have commenced while 'planned' projects are those in the pre-construction phase.

7 PPPs encompass all forms of engagement involving a private party as part or full owner of the wind project, and including a power purchase agreement with the national utility.

8 For a detailed description of sources available to fund wind energy projects, refer to the Annex.

9 From the list of compiled projects, aggregated data on project cost was available for 65 projects (29 completed, 14 ongoing and 22 planned).

10 This was facilitated by the 2008 electricity self-production law and Morocco's EnergiPro initiative.

11 ODA is defined by the OECD as those flows to countries and territories on the Development Assistance Committee List of ODA Recipients and to multilateral development institutions which are (i) provided by official agencies, including state and local governments, or by their executive agencies and (ii) each transaction of which: (a) is administered with the promotion of the economic development and welfare of developing countries as its main objective; and (b) is *concessional in character* and conveys a grant element of at least 25 per cent.

12 The CTF is a multi-donor pool established to provide grants, highly concessional loans or risk mitigation instruments to projects that improve the environmental footprint of key emerging market economies.

13 Non-parametric tests are based on sample data without imposing assumptions on the statistical form of the full population. This is appropriate given that there are not enough degrees of freedom to support generalizable parametric results.

14 Capacity factor is the actual power output over a period of time, as a fraction of the theoretical output if the plant was operated at rated or maximum capacity. The

capacity factor takes into account, among other aspects, times when wind speeds are not adequate for electricity production, unavailability of the plant during maintenance and equipment failure.

15 According to the United States Energy Information Administration (2010), the average capacity factor for European countries in 2007 was 13 per cent while that of 137 wind projects in the US was 26.9 per cent in 2003.

16 We already mentioned that wind-based electricity generation in the context of conventional electricity grids requires base load capacity supplied by a more stable energy resource. Aside from fossil fuels which are the largest polluters in the electricity generation mix, base load capacity could be provided by nuclear or hydro power plants which are overall less polluting. For African countries, fossil fuels and hydro make up most of the base load capacity, with nuclear-based power generation almost non-existent (the exception is South Africa with installed nuclear electricity generation capacity of 1.8 GW). Base load capacity emissions are often not reflected in indirect emission for wind power plants, but it is important to bear them in mind.

Bibliography

Aboulnasr, S. (2006). 'Financing Large Scale Wind Farms in Developing Countries: Zafarana Wind Farm'. ENC-WEC-renewables.

Affani, F. (2008). 'L'énergie éolienne au Maroc: ressources et projets'. Session de formation des acteurs de l'électrification rurale des pays africains francophones, Centre de Développement des Energies renouvelables (CDER).

African Development Bank (2004). *Strategic Plan for Wind Energy Development in Africa.*

African Development Bank (2009). *African Economic Outlook.*

African Development Bank (2010a). 'Infrastructure Deficit and Opportunities in Africa'. *Africa Economic Brief*, 1(2), 7 September.

African Development Bank (2010b). 'Project Appraisal Report for a EUR 15 Million Senior Loan to Finance the Cabeolica Wind Project'. May.

African Development Bank (2011a). *Climate Finance Newsletter*, 1(2), January.

African Development Bank (2011b). Infrastructure Database.

Archer, C. L. and M. Z. Jacobson (2007). 'Supplying Baseload Power and Reducing Transmission Requirements by Interconnecting Wind Farms'. *Journal of Applied Meteorology and Climatology*, 46, 1701–1717.

Bloomberg (2011). 'South Africa Decides to Give Wind and PV a Tender Embrace'. *Research Note – Clean Energy*, 13 September.

Buys, P., U. Deichmann, C. Meisner, T. Ton That and D. Wheeler (2007). 'Country Stakes in Climate Change Negotiations: Two Dimensions of Vulnerability'. Policy Research Working Paper 4300 WPS4300, World Bank, August.

De Jager, D. and M. Rathmann (2008). 'Policy Instrument Design to Reduce Financing Costs in Renewable Energy Technology Projects'. IEA Implementing Agreement on Renewable Energy Technology Deployment, October.

Department of Environmental Affairs Republic of South Africa (2011). South Africa's Second National Communication under the United Nations Framework Convention on Climate Change, Pretoria, November.

Edkins, M. T. (2012). 'Local, National and Regional Policy, Barriers and Incentives: Renewing Wind Policy Risk in South Africa'. World Wind Energy Conference, Bonn, Germany.

European Wind Energy Association (2009). 'The Economics of Wind Energy'.

Georgy, R. Y. and A. D. Soliman (2007). 'Mediterranean and National Strategies for Sustainable Development Priority Field of Action 2: Energy and Climate Change Energy Efficiency and Renewable Energy'. Egypt – National study, Plan Bleu Regional Activity Centre.

Global Environment Facility (2009). 'Annual Report'.

Helimax Energie Inc. (2012). Map of Wind Energy.

International Energy Agency (2009). *World Energy Outlook 2009*. Paris: IEA.

International Energy Agency (2010). *World Energy Outlook 2010*. Paris: IEA.

International Renewable Energy Agency (IRENA) (in press). Strategic Framework for Localisation of Value Addition in the Renewable Energy Equipment Manufacture and Deployment Chain in Africa.

Jerome, A. (2008). 'Private Sector Participation in Infrastructure in Africa'. NEPAD.

Karekezi, S. (1994). 'Renewable Energy Technologies as an Option for a Low Carbon Energy Future for Developing Countries: Case Examples from Eastern and Southern Africa'. African Energy Policy Research Network.

Kennedy-Darling, J., N. Hoyt, K. Murao and A. Ross (2008). *The Energy Crisis of Nigeria: An Overview and Implications for the Future*. Chicago, IL: University of Chicago.

Mutambatsere, E. and A. D. Mukasa (2011). 'Pre-requisites to Private Sector Development in Africa: Infrastructure'. African Development Bank.

Organisation for Economic Co-operation and Development (2005). 'Wind Power Integration into Electricity Systems'. International Energy Technology Collaboration and Climate Change Mitigation, COM/ENV/EPOC/IEA/SLT(2005)5.

Painuly, J. P. (2001). 'Barriers to Renewable Energy Penetration: A Framework for Analysis'. *Renewable Energy*, 24(1), 73–89.

Pegels, A. (2011). 'Pitfalls of Policy Implementation: The Case of the South African Feed-In Tariff'. German Development Institute.

Razavi, H. (2012). 'Clean Energy Development in Egypt'. African Development Bank, Tunis, Tunisia.

Renewable Policy Network for the 21st Century, www.ren21.net.

Renewable Policy Network for the 21st Century (REN 21) (2010). 'Renewables Global Status Report 2010'.

South African Electricity Regulation Act (2006). www.info.gov.za/view/DownloadFileAction?id=67855.

Sünnen, R. (2010). 'Clean Development Mechanism in Egypt: Project Example Zafarana'. Power point presentation, www.clima-pro.de/uploads/media/CDM-Projektbeispiel_AEgypten_-_Windpark_Zafarana_-_Rainer_Suennen.pdf.

Teske, S., A. Zervos, C. Lins, M. Steele, F. Musana, R. Teule and F. Adam (2011). 'A Sustainable Energy Outlook for South Africa'. Advance Energy [R]evolution. European Renewable Energy Council and Greenpeace.

Thomson One database. www.thomsonone.com.

UK Energy Research Centre (2006). 'The Costs and Impacts of Intermittency: An Assessment of the Evidence on the Costs and Impacts of Intermittent Generation on the British Electricity Network'. London.

United Nations Environment Programme (2004a). 'Financial Risk Management Instruments for Renewable Energy Projects'. First Edition.

United Nations Environment Programme (2004b). 'Making it Happen: Renewable Energy Finance and the Role of Export Credit Agencies'. Executive Briefing.

United Nations Framework Convention on Climate Change (2009). 'Copenhagen Accord'. FCCC/CP/2009/L.7.

United States Agency for International Development (1986). 'Statement of Work for the Field Test, Wind Farm at Ras Ghareb'. A report prepared by Maridian Corporation.

United States Energy Information Administration (2010). 'Annual Energy Outlook 2011'. DOE/EIA-0383(2010).

United States Energy Information Administration Database (2011).

Van Dyke, J. and B. Pollastrini (2011). 'South Africa: REFIT – Gone with the Wind?' mondaq, 6 December.

WindPower website (2011). www.thewindpower.net.

World Bank (2006). 'Technical and Economic Assessment of Off-Grid, Mini-Grid and Grid Electrification Technologies'. Washington, DC.

World Bank (2011). 'Private Participation in Infrastructure Database'. http://ppi.worldbank.org.

World Energy Council (2010). '2010 Survey of Energy Resources'.

10 Impact of Improved Agricultural Technology Adoption on Sustainable Rice Productivity and Rural Farmers' Welfare in Nigeria

Bola Amoke Awotide, Taiwo Timothy Awoyemi, B.T. Omonona and Aliou Diagne

Introduction

Agriculture holds the key to broad-based economic growth, poverty reduction and food security in Sub-Saharan Africa (SSA). This is due to the importance of the sector for SSA economies, the extent of rural poverty and the dependence of 50 million small farms on agricultural incomes (Schaffnit-Chatterjee, 2014). Thus, one of the overarching goals of Nigerian agricultural development goals is increasing agricultural productivity for accelerated economic growth and development. As stated in Diagne *et al.* (2009), productivity increases in agriculture can reduce poverty by increasing farmers' income, reducing food prices and thereby enhancing increments in consumption. Based on this assertion, the Department for International Development (2003) estimated that a 1 per cent increase in agricultural productivity reduces the percentage of poor people living on less than US$1 a day by between 0.6 and 2 per cent, and they also concluded that there is no any other economic activity capable of providing such enormous benefit for the poor.

Observably, it is becoming increasingly difficult to meet the food needs of the ever increasing world population through land area expansion or relying on irrigation (Datt and Ravallion, 1996; Hossain, 1989). Therefore, the quest to generate an increase in agricultural productivity has necessitated the development and dissemination of cost-effective, yield increasing improved agricultural technologies such as fertilizer, improved seed of many staple food crops and improved land management practices. The fact remains that much of the needed increase in productivity could be achieved through the adoption of these yield enhancing improved agricultural technologies. In addition, the potential benefit to be derived from the increased productivity is not limited to the farmers alone, but the entire farming community stands to benefit. Such activities according to Mwabu *et al.* (2006) can increase the value of locally produced crops, generate local employment, stimulate local cash flow and, through processing, marketing and related activities, can bring about improvement in socio-economic status and the quality of life. One of the major findings in the literature in relation to improved agricultural technology adoption is the fact that it contributed immensely to the green revolution in Asia.

From the 1960s to 1980s, the "green revolution" in Asia and Latin America helped to double food production and saved hundreds of millions of lives. For instance, Larson *et al.* (2004) concludes that the green revolution was instrumental in increasing production of food grains and other crops in India. Therefore, it could also lead to a significant increase in agricultural productivity in Africa and stimulate the transition from low productivity subsistence agriculture to a high productivity agro-industrial economy (World Bank, 2008). Against this background, several efforts in the form of programmes, policies and strategies have been adopted at various points in time, particularly in developing countries in order to achieve a sustainable increase in agricultural productivity. In particular, much of the attention has been devoted to the attainment of an increase in rice (*Oryza sativa*) productivity. This is because rice has become a national commodity in most developing countries, particularly in SSA. Rice is very importance in Nigerian diets and the majority of the population live on rice and their primary food security is entirely dependent on the volume of rice produced. Also in the producing areas, for instance, it provides employment for more than 80 per cent of the inhabitants as a result of the activities that take place along the distribution chains from cultivation to consumption (Ogundele and Okoruwa, 2006).

Notably, among all the several efforts, the development and dissemination of improved rice seed varieties appears to the most remarkable. This is due to the strong belief that seed is one of the most fundamental components of rural farming households' livelihoods. The quality of the seed planted has a very significant effect on the quality and the quantity of the output to be realized. According to FAO (2009), the potential benefits from increasing the use of quality seeds of a diverse range of crop varieties by farmers are widely acknowledged as it increases food security through improved crop productivity. Furthermore, the traits of the seed planted in terms of its genetic potential, purity and germination, resistance to disease, its adaptation to local agro-ecological situations among many others, set a limit to the gains in productivity to be attained from the use of expensive inputs like fertilizer, pesticide, herbicide and management techniques (Adekoya and Babaleye, 2009). Additionally, the improved rice varieties enable farmers to crop several times within a planting period because of a relatively short growing period; the genetic potential of these seeds also ensures bumper harvests, disease and pest resistance, and drought tolerance; the improved varieties can compete favourably with weeds (Somado *et al.*, 2008). Therefore, with the help of international donors, several improved rice varieties have been developed such that in Nigeria, for example, more than 60 improved rice varieties have been developed and disseminated to the farmers through different programmes and projects.

Despite all the aforementioned efforts, several research findings revealed that the adoption of improved seed is not yet universal. Over 90 per cent of the crops in developing countries are still planted with farmers' varieties and farm-saved seed (Neate and Guei, 2010). Dixon *et al.* (2006), reported that despite the release of nearly 1700 improved wheat varieties in developing countries during the period 1988–2002, only a relatively small number has been adopted on a substantial scale by farmers. Similarly, Christensen and Cook (2003) also discovered that despite a good history of development of varieties of millet, sorghum, maize, rice and cowpea, most Malian farmers still retained their own seed or exchanged with nearby farmers; few used improved high yielding varieties. In the same vein, Longley and Sperling (2002) discovered that studies of seed security in most disaster situations increasingly indicated that good quality seed was locally available in many emergencies and that often the problem was that some farmers lacked access to quality seed. Furthermore, as noted by Seck (2008) one of the biggest constraints to the successive adoption of improved varieties is the availability of improved seed.

Access to seed is a necessary condition for the adoption of improved varieties (Dontsop-Nguezet *et al*., 2011) and the adoption of improved varieties is an important component of agricultural productivity, food security and sustainable economic growth (Faltermeier and Abdulai, 2009). Therefore, the persistence of lack of access to seed and its attendant low adoption of improved rice varieties in developing countries, particularly in Nigeria, can jeopardize all the efforts to achieve increase rice productivity and attainment of self-sufficiency; which is important in order to reduce the excessive reliance on rice importation and eliminate or reduce the effects of global price shocks such the 2008 global food crisis which led to a global doubling of prices of major staple food crops such as rice, maize and wheat on the economy.

This study was conducted to assess the determinants of adoption of improved rice varieties in Nigeria and also provide a consistent estimate of the impact of adoption on rice productivity and welfare of the farming households using LATE estimation techniques to deal with the problem of non-compliance. This is because the impact on the lives of resource poor farmers is believed to be the most functional benefit of agricultural technologies, policies and programmes and also the preoccupation of the stakeholders (Collinson and Tollens, 1994). However, the mixed results of development assistance has generated a lot of questions of whether and by how much development assistance contributes to economic growth and poverty reduction in recipient countries (Rajan and Subramanian, 2005; Easterly, 2001). Increasingly, therefore, the development community, including donors and governments, are looking for more hard evidence on the impacts of public programmes, such as the improved agricultural technologies, aimed at reducing poverty of poor households. Hence, considerable attention and resources have been devoted to poverty impact assessment in recent years.

The rest of the chapter is organized as follows: the next section presents the literature review. The analytical framework and estimation techniques are presented in the third section. The fourth section presents the data and descriptive statistics, followed in the fifth section containing the results and discussion. The finally section summarizes the main findings, concludes the chapter and presents some policy recommendations

Literature Review

Assessing the impact of a treatment on a population of a selected group of people or households is not a new area in the literature, as considerable research has been done in that regard from both econometric and statistical perspectives. Precisely, the econometric literature goes back to early work by Ashenfelter (1978) and subsequent work by Ashenfelter and Card (1985), Heckman and Robb (1985), Lalonde (1986), Fraker and Maynard (1987), Card and Sullivan (1988) and Manski (1990). The focus in the econometric literature is traditionally on endogeneity or self-selection issues and motivated primarily by applications to the evaluation of labour market programmes in observational settings. According to Imbens and Wooldridge (2008) individuals who choose to enrol in a training programme are by definition different from those who choose not to enrol. These differences, if they influence the response, may invalidate causal comparisons of outcomes by treatment status, possibly even after adjusting for observed covariates.

Observably, different methods have been developed and used in the literature to assess the impact of programmes, policies and adoption of improved agricultural technologies on poverty reduction or welfare with mixed results and conclusions. For example, Mendola (2007) adopted the Propensity Score Matching (PSM) methods to assess the impact of agricultural technology adoption on poverty in Bangladesh and observes that the adoption of high yielding improved varieties has a positive effect on household wellbeing in Bangladesh. In the same vein, Kijima *et al.* (2008) conducted a study on the impact of New Rice for Africa (NERICA) in Uganda and found that NERICA adoption reduces poverty without deteriorating the income distribution. Diagne (2006) also assessed the impact of NERICA adoption on rice yield in Côte d'Ivoire. The results show a positive and significant increase in yield, particularly on the female farmers. Other studies that also show a positive impact of NERICA adoption include Winter *et al.* (1998), De Janvry and Sadoulet (1992) and Dontsop-Nguezet *et al.* (2011). In contrast however, a study conducted by Hossain *et al.* (2003) in Bangladesh reveals that the adoption of improved varieties of rice has a positive impact on the richer households, but has a negative effect on the poor. Furthermore, another study conducted by Bourdillon *et al.* (2002) reveals that the adoption of improved varieties of maize leads to a moderate increase in income of the adopters.

Dontsop-Nguezet *et al.* (2011) examined the impact of NERICA adoption on farmers' welfare in Nigeria. The result of the study among many other interesting findings shows that adoption of NERICA varieties has a positive and significant impact on farm household income and welfare (measured by the per capita expenditure) and poverty reduction in rural Nigeria. However, a close examination of all the above studies showed that the majority of the studies focused on NERICA varieties alone; however, NERICA is just one of the numerous improved rice varieties that have been developed and disseminated to farmers. Particularly in Nigeria, over 60 improved rice varieties have been released. Therefore, any specific observed impact of NERICA adoption cannot be generalized to the entire improved rice varieties adoption in Nigeria. More so, NERICA was only disseminated in some selected states, which means that not all rice farmers in Nigeria were aware of the existence of NERICA. In addition only the upland NERICA varieties have been released so far and this could also further limit its adoption only to the upland rice farmers and places where its awareness has been created. Therefore, a gap exists in the literature that this study intends to fill.

Analytical Framework and Estimation Technique

Determinants of Improved Agricultural Technology Adoption

In this study, a farmer was defined as an adopter if he or she was found to have been growing any improved rice variety for at least five years. Thus, a farmer could be classified as an adopter and still grow some traditional varieties. The adoption variable was therefore defined as 1 if a farmer is an adopter of an improved rice variety and 0 otherwise. Although this issue of whether or not to treat adoption as a dichotomous choice had been raised by Feder *et al.* (1985), data limitation hinders researchers studying adoption to think otherwise. This study adopted logistic regression to assess the factors that determine the farmers' adoption status. The response variable is binary, taking values of 1 if he or she has been planting any improved rice variety for the past five years, and 0 otherwise. The independent variables are essentially the farmers' socio-economic and demographic characteristics.

The justification for using logit is based on its simplicity of calculation and the fact that its probability lies between 0 and 1. The probability approaches 0 at a slower rate as the value of the explanatory variable gets smaller and smaller, and also approaches 1 at a slower and slower rate as the value of the explanatory variable gets larger and larger (Gujarati, 1995). Hosmer and Lemeshew (1989) pointed out that the logistic distribution has some advantages over the others in the analysis of dichotomous outcome variable, in that it is extremely flexible and an easy to use model from a mathematical point of view and provides a meaningful interpretation. The binary logistic model does not make the assumption of linearity between dependent and independent variables and does not assume homoscedasticity (CIMMYT Economics Program, 1993). Another advantage of using the logit model is that it does not require normally distributed variables and, above all, the logit model is relatively easy to compute and interpret. Hence, the logistic model is selected for this study. The probability that a farmer will adopt at least one improved rice variety was postulated as a function of some socio-economic, demographic characteristic and institutional factors. Therefore, the cumulative logistic probability model is econometrically specified as follows:

$$P_i = F(Z_i) = F(\gamma + \sum \lambda_i X_i) = \frac{1}{1+e^{-Z_i}} \tag{1}$$

where P_i is the probability that a farmer will adopt at least one improved rice variety or not given X_i; e denotes the base of natural logarithms, which is approximately equal to 2.718; X_i represents the ith explanatory variables; and γ and λ are parameters to be estimated. Hosmer and Lemeshew (1989) pointed out that the logit model could be written in terms of the odds and log of odds, which enables one to understand the interpretation of the coefficients. The odds ratio implies the ratio of the probability (P_i) that a farmer adopts to the probability ($1-P_i$) that the farmer is a non-adopter.

$$(1-P_i) = \frac{1}{1+e^{Z_i}} \tag{2}$$

Therefore

$$\frac{P_i}{1-P_i} = \frac{1+e^{z_i}}{1+e^{-z_i}} = e^{z_i} \tag{3}$$

The natural log of equation (3), will give:

$$Z_i = \ln\left(\frac{P_i}{1-P}\right) = \gamma + \lambda_1 X_1 + \lambda_2 X_2 + \ldots + \lambda_m X_m \tag{4}$$

If the disturbance term (U_i) is taken into account, the logit model becomes:

$$Z_i = \gamma + \sum_{i=1}^{m} \lambda_i X_i + U_i \tag{5}$$

Equation (3) was estimated by the maximum likelihood method. This procedure does not require assumptions of normality or homoscedasticity of errors in predictor variables. This analysis was carried using STATA version 11.0.

Econometric Framework for Impact Assessment

Inverse Propensity Score Weighting Techniques

Following the impact assessment literature, this study adopted the Rubin Causal Model popularly referred to as the potential outcome framework, developed by Rubin (1974). This framework has been adopted by many researchers such as Imbens and Wooldridge (2009), Heckman (2010), and is currently the standard method for impact evaluation in the absence of randomization (Imbens and

Table 10.1 Description of Variables Used in the Logit Model

Variable	*Definition*
Age	Age of household head in years
Gender	Gender of household head,1 male and 0 otherwise
Household size	Number of persons per households
Educational background	Number of years of formal education of household head
Contact with extension agents	1 if farmer has contact with extension agent and 0 otherwise
Main occupation	1 if main occupation is farming and 0 otherwise
Log of income from other crops	Income from other crop production in Naira
Ownership of farm land	1 if farmer owns land and 0 otherwise
Access to mobile phone	1 if farmer owns a mobile phone, 0 otherwise
Years of experience in rice production	Number of years of experience in rice production
Access to radio	1 if farmer owns a radio, 0 otherwise
Vocational training	1 if farmer attends vocational training, 0 otherwise
Distance to seed source	Distance to the nearest seed source (km)
Access to seed	1 if a farmer has access to seed, 0 otherwise
Livestock	1 if farmer owns livestock, 0 otherwise

Wooldridge, 2009). Under this econometric framework, each farming household has *ex-ante* two potential outcomes: an outcome when the household is an adopter, denoted by h_1 and an outcome when it is a non-adopter denoted by h_0. Supposing, we use s as the binary outcome variable to represent the household adoption status, with $s=1$ meaning adoption and $s=0$ meaning non-adoption, then the *observed* outcome h of any rice farming household can be presented as a function of the two potential outcomes: $h=sh_1+(1-s)h_0$. Therefore, for any rice farming household, the causal effect of the adoption on its observed outcome h is simply the difference between its two potential outcomes: h_1-h_0. However, the two potential outcomes are mutually exclusive for any household. This implies that only one of the two can be observed *ex post*, thus making it impossible to measure the individual effect of adoption of improved rice varieties on any given rice farming household. The only possible parameter that can be estimated is the mean effect of adoption on a population of rice farming households: $E(h_1-h_0)$, where E is the mathematical expectation operator. Such a population parameter is referred to as the Average Treatment Effect (ATE) in the literature. It is also possible to estimate the mean effect of the adoption of improved rice varieties on the sub-population of adopters: $E(h_1-h_0|s=1)$, which is called the ATE on the Treated and is usually denoted by ATE1 (or ATT). The ATE on the *Untreated*: $E(h_1-h_0|s=0)$ denoted by ATE0 is also another population parameter that can be defined and estimated.

Several methods have been proposed in the statistics and econometric literature to remove the effects of observable and unobservable biases and deal with the problem of non-compliance or endogenous treatment variable. These methods can be classified under two broad categories based on the types of assumptions they require to arrive at consistent estimators of causal effects (see Imbens, 2004). First, there are the methods designed to remove the bias due extensively to the observable characteristic of the farmers only. These according to Rubin (1974) and Rosenbaum and Rubin (1983) are based on the "ignorability" or conditional independence assumption. These methods suggests that there is a set of observed covariates z which, when controlled for, makes the treatment status s become independent of the two potential outcomes h_1 and y_0. The estimators using the conditional independence assumption are either a pure parametric regression-based method, where the covariates are possibly interacted with the treatment status variable to account for heterogeneous responses, or they are based on a two-stage estimation procedure where the conditional probability of treatment $P(d=1|\,x)\equiv P(x)$ (called the *propensity score*), is estimated in the first stage and ATE, ATE1 and ATE0 are estimated in the second stage by parametric regression-based methods or by non-parametric methods; the latter include various matching method estimators such as those used by Mendola (2007). Following Diagne (2006), we adopted the conditional independence-based estimators of ATE, ATE1 and ATE0 known as the Inverse Propensity Score Weighing estimators (IPSW), given by the following formulae (see Imbens, 2004; Lee, 2005; Diagne, 2006; Diagne *et al.*, 2009; Dontsop-Nguezet *et al.* 2011; Awotide *et al.*, 2011):

$$A\hat{T}E = \frac{1}{n}\sum_{i=1}^{n}\frac{\left(s_i - \hat{p}(z_i)\right)h_i}{\hat{p}(z_i)\left(1-\hat{p}(z_i)\right)} \tag{6}$$

$$A\hat{T}E1 = \frac{1}{n_1}\sum_{i=1}^{n}\frac{\left(s_i - \hat{p}(z_i)\right)h_i}{\left(1-\hat{p}(z_i)\right)} \tag{7}$$

$$A\hat{T}E0 = \frac{1}{1-n_1}\sum_{i=1}^{n}\frac{\left(s_i - \hat{p}(z_i)\right)h_i}{\hat{p}(z_i)} \tag{8}$$

where n is the sample size,

$$n_1 = \sum_{i=1}^{n} s_i$$

is the number of treated (i.e. the number of improved rice variety adopters) and $\hat{p}(z_i)$ is a consistent estimate of the propensity score evaluated at z. The probit specification was used to estimate the propensity score.

Local Average Treatment Effect (LATE) Estimation Techniques

Another approach to impact evaluation is the instrumental *variable* (IV)-based methods (Heckman and Vytlacil, 2005; Imbens 2004; Abadie, 2003; Imbens and Angrist, 1994) which are methods designed to eliminate the biases due to observable and unobservable characteristics and also to deal with the problem of endogenous treatment. The IV-based methods according to Diagne *et al.* (2009) assume the existence of at least one variable r called the *instrument* that is capable of explaining the treatment status, but is redundant in explaining the outcomes h_1 and h_0, once the effects of the covariates z are controlled for. Different IV-based estimators are have been used in the literature, each method, however, differs based on the functional form assumptions and assumptions regarding the instrument and the unobserved heterogeneities. In this chapter, we use two different IV-based estimators to estimate the LATE of adoption of improved rice varieties on rice productivity and total household expenditure. The first one is the simple non-parametric Wald estimator proposed by Imbens and Angrist (1994) and which requires only the observed outcomes variable h, the treatment status variable s and an instrument r. The second IV-based estimator is Abadie's (2003) generalization of the LATE estimator of Imbens and Angrist (1994) to cases where the instrument z is not totally independent of the potential outcomes h_1 and h_0; but will become so conditional on some vector of covariates z that determine the observed outcome h (Diagne *et al.*, 2009).

From the observation of Imbens and Angrist (1994)'s LATE estimator and that of Abadie (2003), we noted that the binary variable denoting the farmers' access to improved rice varieties status is a "natural" instrument for our treatment variable (adoption). This is because no farmer would have been able to adopt any of the improved rice varieties if they had had no access to the seed. In addition, it is also plausible to infer that access to seed can only affect the overall household welfare outcome indicators, such as increase in yield and consumption expenditure, if the farmers adopted the improved rice varieties. This implies that merely having access to seed of any improved rice variety without adopting it does not in any way affect the welfare outcome indicators of the farmers. This shows that the two most vital necessary conditions for the farmers' access to the seed of any improved rice variety status variable to be an effective instrument for the adoption status variable, are met.

If we let r be a binary outcome variable taking the value 1 when a farmer has access to the improved variety and the value 0 otherwise and let s_1 and s_0 be the binary variables designating the two potential adoption outcomes of the farmer with and without access to the seed respectively. Obviously, no farmer would have been able to plant (adopt) any improved variety without having access to the seed, so $s_0=0$ for all the rice farmers and the *observed* adoption outcome will be $s=rs_1$.

Thus, the sub-population of potential adopters and the actual adopters are described by the condition $s_1=1$ and $s=1$, respectively (which is equivalent to the condition $r=1$ and $s_1=1$). Now, if we assume that r is independent of the potential outcomes s_1, h_1 and h_0 (an assumption equivalent to assuming that access to seed is random in the population), then the mean impact of improved variety adoption on sustainable rice productivity and welfare of the sub-population of potential adopters of the improved rice varieties (i.e. the LATE) is as given by Imbens and Angrist (1994), Imbens and Rubin (1997) and Lee (2005):

$$E\left(h_1 - h_0 \mid s_1 = 1\right) = \frac{E\left(h \mid r=1\right) - E\left(h \mid r=0\right)}{E\left(s \mid r=1\right) - E\left(s \mid r=0\right)} \tag{9}$$

Estimation of the right hand side of (9) can be carried out using the sample analogue:

$$\left(\frac{\sum_{i=1}^{n} h_i r_i}{\sum_{i=1}^{n} r_i} - \frac{\sum_{i=1}^{n} h_i (1-r_i)}{\sum_{i=1}^{n} (1-r_i)} \right) \times \left(\frac{\sum_{i=1}^{n} s_i r_i}{\sum_{i=1}^{n} r_i} - \frac{\sum_{i=1}^{n} s_i (1-r_i)}{\sum_{i=1}^{n} (1-r_i)} \right)^{-1} \tag{10}$$

Equation (10) is the well-known *Wald* estimator.

Local Average Response Function (LARF)

One of the numerous assumptions is that farmers' access to the seed of an improved variety is random; however, this is an unrealistic assumption. Following Diagne and Demont (2007), Dontsop-Nguezet *et al.* (2011) and Awotide *et al.* (2011) among many others, this study went further to adopt Abadie's LATE estimator which requires only the conditional independence assumption. Under this assumption, the instrument r is independent of the potential outcomes s_1, h_1 and h_0 conditional on a vector of covariates z determining the observed outcome h. With these assumptions, the following results can be shown to hold for the conditional mean outcome response function for potential adopters $f(z, s) \equiv E(h \mid z, s; s_1 = 1)$ and any function g of (h, z, s) (see Abadie, 2003; Lee, 2005):

$$f(z,1) - f(z,0) = (h_1 - h_0 \mid z, s_1 = 1) \tag{11}$$

$$E\left(g(h,s,z)\middle|s_1 = 1\right) = \frac{1}{P(s_1 = 1)} E\left(k \cdot g(h,s,z)\right) \tag{12}$$

where

$$k = 1 - \frac{r}{p(r = 1|z)}(1 - s)$$

is a weight function that takes the value 1 for a potential adopter and a negative value otherwise. The function $f(z, s)$ is called a *LARF* by Abadie (2003). Estimation proceeds by a parameterization of the LARF:

$$f(\theta; z, s) = E(h|z, s; s_1 = 1) \tag{13}$$

Then, using equation (7) with $g(h, s, z) = (h - f(\theta; z, s))^2$, the parameter θ is estimated by a weighted least squares scheme that minimizes the sample analogue of $E\{\kappa(h - f(\theta;\ z,s))2\}$. The conditional probability $P(r = 1|z)$ appearing in the weight κ is estimated by a probit model in a first stage. Abadie (2003) proves that the resulting estimator of θ is consistent and asymptotically normal. Once, θ is estimated, equation (11) was used to recover the conditional mean treatment effect $E(h_1 - h_0|z, s_1 = 1)$ as a function of x. The LATE is then obtained by averaging across x using equation (12). For example, with a simple linear function $f(\theta, s, z) = \alpha_0 + \alpha s + \beta z$ where $\theta = (\alpha_0, \alpha, \beta)$ then $E(h_1 - h_0|z, s_1 = 1)$. In this case, there is no need for averaging to obtain the LATE, which is here equal to α. Hence, a simple linear functional form for the LARF with no interaction between s and z implies a constant treatment effect across the sub-population of potential adopters. In the estimation below, we postulated an exponential conditional mean response function with and without interaction to guarantee both the positivity of predicted outcomes (rice productivity and welfare) and heterogeneity of the treatment effect across the sub-population of the potential improved rice varieties adopters. Because access to seed is a necessary condition for adoption, it can be shown that the LATE for the sub-population of potential adopters (i.e. those with $s_1 = 1$) is the same as the LATE for the subpopulation of *actual* adopters (i.e. those with $d = rs_1 = 1$).

Data and Descriptive Statistics

This study focused on rice farming households randomly selected from the three major rice growing systems in Nigeria. The data were collected using multistage random sampling techniques. In the first stage, three major rice growing systems were selected. This led to the selection of upland, lowland and irrigated rice ecologies. Each of the rice ecologies has a 30, 47 and 17 per cent share of the national rice area, respectively. The second stage involved the random selection of one state from each of the rice producing ecologies. Hence, Kano, Osun state and Niger were selected to represent irrigated, upland and lowland rice ecologies respectively. In the third stage, two Agricultural Development Programme (ADP) zones that were basically rural were purposively selected from the ADP zones in each state. The fourth stage involved the random selection of five Local Government Areas (LGAs) from each of the zones. The random selection of three villages from each of the LGAs constituted the fifth stage. While the last stage involved the selection of rice farming households from each of the villages. The number of rice farming households selected from each village was proportionate to size. This generated a total of 500 rice farming households. Data were collected on socio-economic/demographic characteristics, access to seed, household endowments, household expenditure, agricultural income and non-agricultural income etc. After thorough data cleaning 481, representing 92.6 per cent, were finally utilized for the analysis.

The socio-economic/demographic characteristics of the farmers by adoption status are presented in Table 10.2. The result showed that the majority (92 per cent) of the respondents were male and 89 per cent of the adopters and 93 per cent of the non-adopters were male. Average age of the respondents was 46 years. The mean age of the adopters (49 years) was not significantly different from the non-adopters (46 years). In terms of educational background of the household heads, 53 per cent of the total respondents had no formal education. The proportion with no formal education is significantly different between the adopters and non-adopters. About 33 and 58 per cent of the adopters and non-adopters, respectively, had no formal education. The proportion with primary education in the total population was 25 per cent, while 36 and 22 per cent of adopters and non-adopters, respectively, had at least primary education. About 28 per cent of the farmers that adopted had vocational training, while only 7 per cent among the adopters attended vocational training. The majority of the adopters (85 per cent) had experience in upland farming, while only 18 per cent of the non-adopters had experience in upland rice framing. The majority of the non-adopters had experience in lowland farming.

Overall, the majority of respondents had farming as their major occupation, and are also mainly natives of the study area and had spent an average of 42 years in the study area. The analysis further revealed that not many of the respondents had contact with extension agents either from an ADP or the National Cereal Research Institute (NCRI). The household size was also large, with about ten persons per household. This could have both positive and negative effect on households' welfare. The positive effect could arise if the large household size is used as a source of family labour, thereby reducing the cost of labour and cutting down production expenditure. However, a large household size could also worsen the poverty situation of a farming household particularly if it is composed of a large number of dependants, which means the family has more mouths to feed.

Table 10.2 Socio-Economic Characteristics of Respondents by Adoption Status

Variable	*Pooled Data (N = 481)*	*Adopters (N = 101)*	*Non-Adopters (N = 380)*	*Mean Difference*
Gender				
% male	92.00	89.00	93.00	4.00
% female	8.00	11.00	7.00	4.00
Educational background				
% with no formal education	53.00	33.00	58.00	25.48***
% with primary education	25.00	36.00	22.00	13.80***
% with secondary education	20.00	31.00	17.00	14.11***
% with tertiary education	3.00	1.00	4.00	2.4
% with experience in upland rice farming	29.00	85.00	14.00	71.50***
% with experience in lowland rice farming	54.00	3.00	68.00	65.00***
% with experience in irrigated rice farming	16.00	8.00	19.00	10.76***
% of farmers that are native	80.00	78.00	81.00	23.08
% that attended vocational training	12.00	28.00	7.00	20.35
% that have farming as main occupation	84.00	51.00	92.00	39.73***
% that have access to seed	19.00	70.00	5.00	65.29***
% that have contact with ADP	13.00	8.00	14.00	6.00
% that have contact with NCRI	9.00	1.00	11.00	9.50***
Average age of household heads	46.00	49.00	46.00	3.74***
Average household size	10.00	10.00	10.00	0.59
Average years of residence in the village	41.00	42.00	41.00	1.65

Source: Field Survey, 2009.

Notes
The T-test was used to test for difference in socio-economic/demographic characteristics between adopters and non-adopters.
* significant at 10 per cent; ** significant at 5 per cent and *** significant 1 per cent.

Results and Discussion

Households Endowments by Adoption Status

A household's endowment is usually used as a measure of wealth of the farming household and can reveal a lot about the living conditions of the farming households. A well-endowed household could better adopt an improved agricultural technology than otherwise. A comparison of household assets was made between adopters and non-adopters of improved rice varieties. This was done with a view to examine if adopting improved varieties has any effect on households' assets (the result of this analysis in tabular form is available on request). Generally in the population only very few (7 per cent) are owners of their farmland. Very few (3 per cent) and only 8 per cent among the adopters and non-adopters own their farm land, respectively. This suggests that access to farmland could still be a constraint to rice production and adoption of high yielding improved varieties in the study area. Rearing of animals could be an additional source of income, particularly during the off-season and can be used to augment households' income. Farmers who have an additional source of income could afford to adopt improved rice varieties consequently; the analysis revealed that about 30 per cent of the adopters had livestock, while only 15 per cent of the non-adopters had livestock.

Households' assets such as radio, television, mobile phone, electricity and access to media are vital in the dissemination of information about the improved varieties which can influence adoption. Only 39 and 50 per cent of the non-adopters and adopters have a mobile phone, respectively. A larger percentage of the non-adopters (57 per cent) had access to media compared with 51 per cent among the adopters. This implies that some of the non-adopters could be aware of the improved rice varieties through the media and yet did not adopt. In terms of access to electricity, only 47 per cent of the non-adopters and 67 per cent of the adopters had access to electricity. Therefore, access to electricity could be one of the constraints militating against adoption: although farmers could have radio or television, without an adequate supply of electricity at the right time, they might be missing out on some important information aired when there is no light.

In addition, households' endowments such as: house, number of rooms in the house, good sanitation, access to portable water, good roofing sheet could all combine to improve the wellbeing of all the farming households' members and also encourage adoption of improved rice varieties. However, not many of the respondents were endowed in most of these assets. For instance, only 20 and 28 per cent of the adopters and non-adopters had access to portable water. In the same vein, only 22 and 47 per cent of adopters and non-adopters had good sanitation facilities. Although many of the respondents (over 60 per cent) lived in their own houses, however, the adopters seemed to be better-off in terms of the use of good roofing sheets as a larger percentage (66 per cent) of them use roofing sheets as opposed to the use of a thatched roof, while only 39 per cent of the non-adopters use roofing sheets. Overall, the adopters can be said to be better endowed than the non-adopters. Therefore, adoption of improved rice varieties could improve farming households' living conditions through the increase in yield which can further translate into an increase in income.

Determinants of Improved Rice Varieties Adoption

The factors that influenced adoption of improved rice varieties were examined using the binary logistic regression method. Farmers that had planted, at least once, improved rice varieties over a period of five years were classified as adopters and those that had engaged in the cultivation of traditional rice varieties or had adopted briefly and discontinued adoption were classified as non-adopters. The results from the logit model used to examine the factors affecting the adoption of improved rice varieties in Nigeria using maximum likelihood estimation are presented in Table 10.3. An additional insight was also provided by analysing the marginal effects, which were calculated as the partial derivatives of the non-linear probability function, evaluated at each variable sample mean (Greene, 1990). The log-likelihood of –43.55, the Pseudo R^2 of 0.67 and the LR (Chi^2) of 176.00 (significant at the 1 per cent level), implies that the overall model fitted and the explanatory variables used in the model were collectively able to explain the farmers' decision regarding the adoption of improved rice varieties in Nigeria. The decision to adopt improved rice varieties in Nigeria was discovered to be influenced by many socio-economic/demographic and institutional variables.

Among the variables, number of years of residence in the village, access to media, access to a mobile phone, vocational training, livestock, access to seed and income from other crop production, significantly increased the probability of adoption. Number of years of residence in the village positively increases the probability of adoption. This could be attributed to the fact that the longer a farmer stays in a locality, the more stable and familiar with he or she becomes with the environment and this could influence adoption. Information about the improved variety increases awareness: a farmer cannot adopt a technology without being aware of it (Diagne and Demont, 2007). Access to media creates awareness and hence increases the probability of adoption. Communication about availability, source, price can be passed from one farmer to the other through the use of a mobile phone and this can positively influence adoption.

Vocational training as well as main occupation had a positive and significant influence on the decision to adopt improved rice variety. This is because vocational training improves the level of a farmer's knowledge and having agriculture as the main occupation will also enable the farmers to seek productivity improved information and be more devoted to farming. Livestock is a means of income diversification, and can be a source of additional income and can also be an insurance against risk and uncertainty. Possession of livestock could therefore increase the probability of adoption through its influence on income. Even though a farmer is aware of a technology, access to seed is also paramount in the adoption process. As noted by Dontsop–Nguezet *et al.* (2011) access to seed is a necessary condition for the adoption of a technology. Diversification into other

Table 10.3 Determinants of Improved Rice Varieties Adoption

Variables	*Coefficient*	*Std Error*	*Z-Value*	*P*>|*Z*|	*Marginal Effect*
Age	0.025	0.034	0.75	0.453	0.002
Residence in the village (years)	0.076**	0.034	2.25	0.024	0.004
Household size	0.021	0.097	0.22	0.825	0.001
Main occupation	–3.659***	1.114	–3.29	0.001	–0.138
Education (years)	0.052	0.076	0.68	0.496	0.003
Media	1.942**	0.749	2.59	0.010	0.012
Farming experience	–5.036***	1.717	–2.93	0.003	–0.408
Ownership of farm land	–2.510*	1.433	–1.75	0.080	–0.007
Mobile phone	4.336**	2.086	2.08	0.038	0.022
Gender	–0.344	1.698	–0.20	0.839	–0.003
Vocational training	3.941***	1.233	3.20	0.001	0.188
Livestock	2.124**	0.962	2.21	0.027	0.032
Access to seed	4.421***	0.860	5.14	0.000	0.188
Contact with extension agents	3.144	1.464	2.15	0.032	0.105
Distance to seed source	–0.038	0.047	0.83	0.409	–0.002
Income from other crop	0.746*	0.442	1.69	0.091	0.005
Constant	–35.124	2831.48	–0.01	0.990	–
Number	481.00				
LR $Chi^2(18)$	176.30				
Prob.>Chi^2	0.000				
Log-likelihood	–43.53				
Pseudo R^2	0.6695				

Notes:
* significant at 10%
** significant at 5%
*** significant at 1%

crops can also generate an increase in income and reduces the propensity of a farming household to fall below the poverty line. Thus, income from other crops can positively influence adoption.

However, contrary to a priori expectation, having agriculture as the main occupation had a negative and significant effect on the adoption of improved rice varieties in the study area. This could be due to the fact that full-time farmers are always missing out on information because of their long stay on the farm. Most of them occasionally do not attend training sessions and also do not avail themselves of the opportunity to meet with extension agents through which information about improved seeds could be obtained. Farming experience was also negative and significant. This implies that the propensity to adopt decreases as experience in farming, measured by the number of years put into farming activities, increases. This could be due to the fact that farmers become adapted to certain ways of doing things and the tendency to adopt a new innovation is always difficult. The farmers that farm on rented land also tend to have the higher probability of adopting an improved variety. This could be attributed to the desire to achieve a higher output per hectare.

Impact of Adoption on Rice Productivity and Total Household Expenditure

Descriptive Analysis of the Impact of Adoption

This section presents the descriptive analysis of the impact of improved rice varieties adoption on income from rice production, income from other crops, total agricultural expenditure, per capita consumption expenditure, average farm size and the incidence of poverty among the farmers (the tabular presentation of these results is available on request). The average area cultivated by all the farmers was 3.23 ha, while the difference test showed that the area cultivated by the non-adopters (3.39 ha) was significantly higher than that of the adopters (2.64 ha). However, despite the higher area cultivated by the non-adopters, they seem not to be better-off in terms of household income. For instance, the adopters had a significantly higher income from both the production of rice and other crops than the non-adopter; consequently the adopters were also able to spend more (₦95151.92) on agricultural production than the non-adopters (₦72215.08).

In terms of the welfare impact of improved rice varieties adoption, a comparison was made between the consumption expenditure of adopters and non-adopters. The per capita expenditure is a clear reflection of the actual household consumption and therefore provides information on the food security status of households. The result revealed that the consumption expenditure of the adopters (₦9877.71) was higher than that of the non-adopters (₦9588.92). This implies that the adopters had better welfare than the non-adopters. The analysis of the incidence of poverty showed that about 50 per cent of the farmers were poor. The incidence of poverty was, however, higher among the non-adopters (51 per cent) than the adopters (46 per cent). These results are consistent with other related studies on the impact of agricultural technologies on poverty (Mendola,

2007; Diagne *et al.*, 2009; Javier and Awudu, 2010). From all the analysis above it appears the adopters were better off than the non-adopters. However, these comparisons did not account for the effects of other characteristics of the farmers that could influence these outcomes. Hence, these observed differences cannot be attributed entirely to the adoption of improved varieties due to the problems of selection bias and non-compliance and, thus, cannot be given any causal interpretation (Heckman and Vytlacil, 2005; Imbens and Angrist, 1994). This, therefore, necessitated the adoption of other statistical methods to assess the impact of adoption on rice productivity and welfare.

Impact of Improved Rice Varieties Adoption on Rice Productivity

Due to the problem of selection bias and particularly non-compliance which is also referred to as endogeneity, this study used a combination of methods to assess the impact. Specifically, the impact of improved varieties adoption on rice productivity and welfare was estimated using the LATE model. Meanwhile, for the purpose of comparison, models based on other techniques such as the ATE using IPSW techniques was estimated. The LATE estimate was carried out for each of the two outcomes of interest (rice productivity and welfare) using the two different estimation methods proposed by Imbens and Angrist (1994) and Abadie (2003). The LARF estimation that is required in Abadie's method used as explanatory variables, in addition to the improved varieties adoption status, a set of other household characteristics to account for heterogeneity in the impact. In order to avoid having some of the predicted outcome to be negative, the LARF was also estimated using the weighted least squares procedure.

The result of the impact of improved rice varieties adoption is presented in Table 10.4. The result of the mean difference showed that there was a significant difference of 165.94 kg/ha in rice productivity between the adopters and non-adopters. This signifies that the adopters had a yield of about 165.94 kg/ha higher than the non-adopters. The ATE in the entire population was 249.45 kg/ha, the ATE on the sub-population of adopters was 267.12 kg/ha. This implies that the adopters had an increase of 267.12 kg/ha in rice productivity. Specifically, the LATE estimates suggested that the adoption of improved rice varieties significantly increased rice productivity by 358.89 kg/ha. This could be interpreted as the change in rice productivity that is attributed to a change in improved agricultural technology status. The result revealed further that the impact was much higher among the female headed households (445.46 kg/ha) than the male headed households (154.90 kg/ha). Furthermore, the impact was also higher among the poor farming households (648 kg/ha) than the non-poor farming households (442.78 kg/ha). This implies that adoption of improved rice varieties is pro-poor in nature.

Impact of Improved Rice Varieties Adoption on Total Household Expenditure

The empirical results of the impact of improved rice varieties adoption on welfare, proxied by total household expenditure is presented in Table 10.5. It

Table 10.4 Impact of Improved Rice Varieties Adoption on Rice Productivity

Estimation	*Parameter*	*Robust Std Error*	*Z-Value*
Estimation by Mean Difference			
Observed difference	165.94*	35.68	1.66
Adopters	170.96***	63.76	8.81
Non-adopters	154.36***	66.22	10.15
Inverse Propensity Score Weighting Estimation			
ATE	249.45**	125.00	2.00
ATE1	267.12**	135.79	1.97
ATE0	220.93**	107.79	2.05
Local Average Treatment Effect Estimation			
LATE by Wald estimators	200.67	125.99	0.05
LATE by LARF	358.89***	147.22	3.22
Impact by Gender			
Male	154.90	210.25	0.06
Female	445.46***	255.07	3.67
Impact by Poverty Status			
Poor	648.78***	189.00	2.64
Non-poor	442.78***	223.89	2.99

Source: Field Survey, 2009.

Notes
Significance level *$p<0.10$, **$p<0.05$, *** $p<0.01$.

showed that the adoption of improved rice varieties exerted a positive and significant impact on household expenditure in Nigeria. The LATE estimate showed that improved technology adoption significantly increased the total household expenditure by ₦32890.82. This represented the average change in total household expenditure brought about by the adoption of improved rice varieties. Furthermore, the result also showed that the female headed households had a higher impact than the male headed households. Comparison by poverty status further revealed that the impact was pro-poor in nature as it had a significantly higher impact on the poor farming households (₦22573.30) than the non-poor (₦14589.58). The ATE estimates also showed a positive impact just like the LATE estimates. However, the ATE estimates of the impact of improved rice varieties adoption on rice productivity and welfare do not have a causal interpretation due to the problem of non-compliance. Hence, only the results of the LATE estimates can be interpreted as the impact of improved varieties adoption on productivity and welfare.

Summary, Conclusion and Policy Recommendations

This study assessed the impact of improved rice varieties on rice productivity and welfare among the rice farming households in Nigeria using different estimation techniques. Among the many findings, the result of the logistic regression showed that access to seed is an important variable determining improved rice varieties

Table 10.5 Impact of Improved Rice Varieties Adoption on Total Household Expenditure

Estimation	*Parameter*	*Robust Std Error*	*Z-Value*
Observed difference	₦17936.83***	4080.77	4.40
Adopters	₦95151.93***	3112.59	5.60
Non-adopters	₦77215.08***	2639.04	9.26
ATE	₦3414*	117.96	1.67
ATE1	₦8809***	104.47	3.05
ATE0	₦6428.54**	129.90	1.99
LATE by Wald estimators	₦26280.16**	1020.16	2.24
LATE by LARF	₦32890.82***	3701.00	8.90
Impact by gender			
Male	₦18200.00***	3872.06	4.70
Female	₦24842.91***	4330.00	7.00
Impact by poverty status			
Poor	₦14589.58***	1462.34	4.50
Non-poor	₦22573.30***	6657.26	3.39

Source: Field Survey, 2009.

Notes
Significance level $*p<0.10$, $**p<0.05$, $***p<0.01$.

adoption in Nigeria. Specifically, the LATE method was utilized in order to deal with the problem of non-compliance and, hence, provide a consistent estimate of the impact of improved rice varieties adoption on productivity and welfare. Generally, the adoption of improved rice varieties positively and significantly impacted rice productivity and total household expenditure. The impact on all the outcomes of interest was also higher among the female headed households than the male headed households. The results also showed that, overall, the adoption of improved rice varieties was also pro-poor in nature, as it had a higher positive impact on the poor households than the non-poor households in all the outcomes of interest considered in this study. In conclusion, improved agricultural technology adoption can lead to the much desired increase in productivity which can generate national and household food security and can also be away out of the menace of rural poverty in Nigeria. Based on the above findings, this study therefore recommends that efforts should be geared towards making adequate seed available to rural farmers in order to encourage its adoption. All necessary efforts, such as creation of awareness about the potential benefits inherent in the adoption of improved rice seed, an increase in farmers' education and more publicity about the varieties released through the media, should be intensified. All efforts and strategies to eradicate poverty and improve rural farming households' welfare in Nigeria should incorporate agricultural technologies adoption as part of the components.

References

Abadie, Alberto, (2003) "Semi-parametric Instrumental Variable Estimation of Treatment Response Models". *Journal of Econometrics* 113(2): 231–263.

Adekoya, E.A. and T. Babaleye (2009) "Consistency in Technology Adoption among farmers in Northern Nigeria". *Journal of Food, Agriculture and Environment* 7(3/4): 457–460.

Ashenfelter, O. (1978) "Estimating the Effect of Training Programs on Earnings". *Review of Economics and Statistics* 60: 47–57.

Ashenfelter, O. and D. Card (1985) "Using the Longitudinal Structure of Earnings to Estimate the Effect of Training Programs". *Review of Economics and Statistics* 67: 648–660.

Awotide, B.A., A. Diagne, T.T. Awoyemi and V.E.T Ojehomon (2011) "Impact of Access to Subsidized Certified Improved Rice Seed on Income: Evidence from Rice Farming Households in Nigeria". *OIDA International Journal of Sustainable Development* 2(12): 43–60.

Bourdillon, M., P. Hebinck, J. Hoddinott, B. Kinsey, J. Marondo, N. Mudege and T. Owens (2002) "Assessing the Impact of HYV Maize in Resettlement Areas of Zimbabwe". International Food Policy Research Institute, Washington, DC, Discussion Paper 161.

Burtless, Gary (1985) "Are Targeted Wage Subsidies Harmful? Evidence from a Wage Voucher Experiment". *Industrial and Labour Relations Review* 39: 105–115.

Card, D. and D. Sullivan (1988) "Measuring the Effect of Subsidized Training Programs on Movements In and Out of Employment". *Econometrica* 56(3): 497–530.

Christensen, P. and A.D. Cook (2003) "Mali Seed Sector Development Plan. Initiative to End Hunger in Africa: Agricultural Policy Development Program". Prepared for US Agency for International Development, Mali Mission, Department of State, Washington DC, PCE-1-00-9-00033-00 (Order No. 5).

CIMMYT Economics Program (1993) "The Adoption of Improved Agricultural Technology: A Guide for Survey Design". Mexico, DF.

Collinson, M.P. and E. Tollens (1994) "The Impact of International Agricultural Research Centres: Measurement, Quantification and Interpretation". *Experimental Agriculture* 30(4): 395–419.

Datt, G. and M. Ravallion (1996) "How Important to India's Poor is the Sectoral Composition of Growth?" *World Bank Economic Review* 10(1): 1–26.

De Janvry, A. and E. Sadoulet (1992) "Agricultural Trade Liberalization and Low Income Countries: A General Equilibrium Multimarket Approach". *American Journal of Agricultural Economics* 74(2): 268–280.

Department for International Development (2003) "Agriculture and Poverty, Reduction: Unlocking the Potential". ADFID policy paper. Available at www.eldis.org/vfile/upload/1/document/0708/DOC14385.pdf

Diagne, A. (2006) "Diffusion and Adoption of NERICA Rice Varieties in Côte d'Ivoire". *Developing Economies* 44(2): 208–231.

Diagne, A. and M. Demont (2007) "Taking a New Look at Empirical Model of Adoption: Average Treatment Effect Estimation of Adoption Rates and their Determinants". *Agricultural Economics* 37(2007): 201–210.

Diagne, A., S.A. Adekambi, F.P. Simtowe and G. Biaou (2009) "The Impact of Agricultural Technology Adoption on Poverty: The Case of Nerica Rice Varieties in Benin". A shorter version of the paper is being presented as contributed paper at the 27th Conference of the International Association of Agricultural Economists, Beijing, China, 16–22 August 2009.

Dixon, J., L. Nalley, P. Kosina, R. La Rovere, J. Hellin and P. Aquino (2006) "Adoption and Economic Impact of Improved Wheat Varieties in the Developing World". *Journal of Agricultural Sciences* 144: 289–502.

Dontsop-Nguezet, P.M, A. Diagne, V.O. Okoruwa and V.E.T. Ojehomon (2011) "Impact of Improved Rice Technology Adoption (NERICA Varieties) on Income and Poverty among Rice Farming Households in Nigeria: A Local Average Treatment Effect (LATE) Approach". *Quarterly Journal of International Agriculture* 50(3): 267–291.

Easterly, William R. (2001) "The Lost Decades: Developing Countries' Stagnation in Spite of Policy Reform 1980–1998". *Journal of Economic Growth* 6(2): 135–157.

Faltermeier, L. and A. Abdulai (2009) "The Adoption of Water Intensification Technologies and Farm Income: A Propensity Score Analysis for Rice Farmers in Northern Ghana". *Agricultural Economics* 40: 365–379.

Feder, G., R.E. Just and D. Zilberman (1985) "Adoption of Agricultural Innovation in Developing Countries: A Survey". *Economic Development and Cultural Change* 33: 255–298.

Food and Agricultural Organization (FAO) of the United Nations (2009) "Seed Security for Food Security in the Light of Climate Change and Soaring Food Prices: Challenges and Opportunities". Committee on Agriculture, Twenty-first Session, Rome, 22–25 April.

Fraker, T. and R. Maynard (1987) "The Adequacy of Comparison Group Designs for Evaluations of Employment-Related Programs". *Journal of Human Resources* 22(2): 194–227.

Greene, W.H. (1990) *Econometric Analysis*. New York: Macmillan

Gujarati, N.D. (1995) *Basic Econometrics*, 3rd edn. McGraw-Hill, Singapore.

Heckman, J.J. (2010) "Building Bridges between Structural and Program Evaluation Approaches to Evaluating Policy". *Journal of Economic Literature* 48(2): 356–398.

Heckman, J.J. and R. Robb (1985) "Alternative Methods for Evaluating the Impact of Interventions". In J.J. Heckman and B.S. Singer (eds), *Longitudinal Analysis of Labour Market Data*. Cambridge University Press, Cambridge.

Heckman, J.J. and E.J. Vytlacil (2005) "Structural Equations, Treatment Effects and Econometric Policy Evaluation". *Econometrica* 73(3): 669–738.

Hosmer, D.W. and S. Lemeshew (1989) *Applied Logistic Regression*. Wiley-Inter Science Publication, New York.

Hossain, M. (1989) *Green Revolution in Bangladesh: Impact on Growth and Distribution of Income*. Dhaka, Bangladesh: University Press Ltd

Hossain, M., D. Lewis, M.L. Bose and A. Chowdhury (2003) "Rice Research, Technological Progress, and Impacts on the Poor: The Bangladesh Case". International Food Policy Research Institute (IFPRI), Discussion paper 110.

Imbens, G.M. and J.M. Wooldridge (2008) "Recent Development in the Econometrics of Programme Evaluation". NBER Working Paper 14251. Available at www.nber.org/paper/w14251.

Imbens, G.W. (2004) "Nonparametric Estimation of Average Treatment Effects under Exogeneity: A Review". *Review of Economics and Statistics* 86: 4–29.

Imbens, G.W. and J. Angrist (1994) "Identification and Estimation of Local Average Treatment Effects". *Econometrica* 61(2): 467–476.

Imbens, G.W. and D.B. Rubin (1997) "Estimating Outcome Distributions for Compliers in Instrumental Variable Models". *Review of Economic Studies* 64(4): 555–574.

Imbens, G.W. and J.M. Wooldridge (2009) "Recent Developments in the Econometrics of Program Evaluation". *Journal of Economic Literature* 47(1): 5–86.

Javier, B. and A. Awudu (2010) "The Impact of Improved Maize Varieties on Poverty in Mexico: A Propensity Score-Matching Approach". *World Development* 38(7): 1024–1035.

Kijima, Y., O. Keijiro and D. Sserunkuuma (2008) "Assessing the Impact of NERICA on Income and Poverty in Central and Western Uganda". *Agricultural Economics* 38(3): 327–337.

Lalonde, R.J. (1986) "Evaluating the Econometric Evaluations of Training Programs with Experimental Data". *American Economic Review* 76: 604–620.

Larson, D.W., E. Jones, R.S. Pannu and R.S. Sheokand (2004) "Instability in Indian Agriculture: A Challenge to the Green Revolution Technology". *Food Policy* 29(3): 257–273.

Lee, M.-J. (2005) *Micro-Econometrics for Policy, Program and Treatment Effects: Advanced Texts in Econometrics*. Oxford University Press, Oxford.

Longley, C. and L. Sperling (eds) (2002). "Beyond Seeds and Tools: Effective Support to Farmers in Emergencies". Special issue of *Disasters* 26(4): 283–287.

Manski, C. (1990) "Nonparametric Bounds on Treatment Effects". *American Economic Review Papers and Proceedings* 80: 319–323.

Mendola, M. (2007) "Agricultural Technology Adoption and Poverty Reduction: A Propensity Score Matching Analysis for Rural Bangladesh". *Food Policy* 32(2007): 372–393.

Mwabu, Germano, Wilfred Mwangi and Hezron Nyangito (2006) "Does Adoption of Improved Maize Varieties Reduce Poverty? Evidence from Kenya." Poster paper prepared for presentation at the International Association of Agricultural Economists Conference, Gold Coast, Australia, 12–18 August.

Neate, P.J.H. and R.G. Guei (2010) "Promoting the Growth and Development of Smallholder Seed Enterprises for Food Security Crops: Best Practices and Options for Decision Making". Food and Agricultural Organization (FAO) of the United Nations. Available at www.fao.org/docrep/013/i1839e/i1839e00.pdf.

Ogundele, O.O. and V.O. Okoruwa (2006) "Technical Efficiency Differentials in Rice Production Technologies in Nigeria". AERC Research Paper 154, African Economic Research Consortium, Nairobi, Kenya.

Rajan, R. and A. Subramanian (2005) "Aid and Growth: What Does the Cross-Country Evidence Really Show?" IMF Working Paper WP/05/127.

Rosenbaum, P. and D.B. Rubin (1983) "The Central Role of the Propensity Score in Observational Studies for Causal Effects". *Biometrika* 70(1): 41–55.

Rubin, D. (1974) "Estimating Causal Effects of Treatments in Randomized and Non-Randomized Studies". *Journal of Educational Psychology* 66: 688–701.

Schaffnit-Chatterjee, C. (2014) "Agricultural Value Chains in Sub-Saharan Africa: Emerging Markets". Deutsche Bank Research, 60262 Frankfurt am Main, Germany.

Seck, P.A. (2008) "Can Rice Crisis be Turned into Opportunity for Africa?" West African Rice Development Association (WARDA), Cotonou, Côte d'Ivoire, 15 May.

Somado, A., R.G. Guei and S.O. Keya (eds) (2008) "NERICA: The New Rice for Africa: A Compendium". Africa Rice Center.

Sperling, L. (1997) "The Effect of the Rwanda War on Crop Production and Varietal Diversity: A Comparison of Two Crops". Network Paper No. 75. AgREN, ODI, London.

Splawa-Neyman, J. (1923) "On the Application of Probability Theory to Agricultural Experiments: Essay on Principles". Section 9 (with discussion). Translated and edited by D.M. Dabrowska and T.P. Speed (1990) *Statistical Sciences* 5(4): 465–472.

Winter P., A. De Janvry, E. Saudolet and K. Stamoulis (1998) "The Role of Agriculture in Economic Development: Visible and Invisible Surplus Transfers". *Journal of Development Studies* 345: 71–97.

Woodbury, Stephen and Robert Spiegelman (1987) "Bonuses to Workers and Employers to Reduce Unemployment". *American Economic Review* 77: 513–530.

World Bank (2008) "World Development Report: Agriculture for Development". World Bank, Washington, DC.

Index

Page numbers in *italics* denote tables, those in **bold** denote figures.

For Product Safety Concerns and Information please contact our EU
representative GPSR@taylorandfrancis.com
Taylor & Francis Verlag GmbH, Kaufingerstraße 24, 80331 München, Germany

www.ingramcontent.com/pod-product-compliance
Ingram Content Group UK Ltd.
Pitfield, Milton Keynes, MK11 3LW, UK
UKHW022117190926
475702UK00013B/1500
* 9 7 8 0 8 1 5 3 5 8 1 1 4 *